The Perpetual Truth

~ The Basis of Shi'aism ~

The Perpetual Truth

~ *The Basis of Shi'aism* ~

Compiled By

Dr. S. Manzoor Rizvi

First Edition
2009

Published
By
MESSAGE OF PEACE INC.
(*Pyame Aman*)
PO Box 390
Bloomfield NJ 07003
USA

The Perpetual Truth

The Basis of Shi'aism

ISBN 978-0-9822146-2-6

MESSAGE OF PEACE INC.
(Pyame Aman)
PO Box 390
Bloomfield NJ 07003 USA

Typeset and Formatted by S. Nazim Zaidi
Printed in China
By
NORDICA

First Edition February 2009

From the Desk of the Publisher

For centuries, the Shi'as have been defensive about their faith and ideals where the bottom line is that we have nothing to be apprehensive about, suspicious or self-conscious. The fact is that the Shi'as since day one, have adhered to the Truth, Qur'an and the Sunna of the last Prophet and his beloved Family. As Allah's Prophets and Imams were never aggressive while their Shi'as were subdued following their example of civility and humility.

If there are certain factions who claim to be Muslims and label not only the Jews and Christians but also Shi'as as unbelievers, and hence have the license to kill the later, then they need to justify their own deeds. We have no ill feelings for our Sunni brothers. We have nothing but love and respect for them. Despite some differences in religious practices we have been standing shoulder to shoulder with them in practicing Sha'riah and in defending Islam.

Besides the fact that through such actions by twisting the actual meaning of the Qur'an and ahadith with their own demented views for their own personal gains and agenda, the ball is now in their court. They alone are responsible for their terrorism, tyranny and massacres which now must be confronted and addressed. The Shi'as do not have to prove that they are the sincere believers. No, that time is long gone. Now these fanatics and terrorists not only have to prove that they are on the right path and that any one and every one who does not adhere to their twisted logic and frenzied way of thinking is not a believer. The reality is that they can not prove otherwise hence they utilize the tool of fear, terror, hate and aggression. That is the only substance they have with their so-called religion that clearly goes against all that is good and decent in Islam, and all of humanity.

As a result, Message of Peace Inc. has decided to publish this vital book so that our children understand and realize the beauty that Shi'aism possesses and not the filth that others create and market. This book is to supply our youths with the correct knowledge and accurate facts so that they are able to comprehend the Perpetual Truth of Shi'as and their ideals.

The Publisher
Pyame Aman

Acknowledgment

The compilation of this book has been a long and arduous endeavor. We have been able to borrow from so many books, articles, journals and letters by some great authors. It is high time they should be acknowledged and appreciated for their hard work.

My special thanks to Dr Abul Qasim of Allahabad, India, for the introductory article validating the authenticity of Shi'a Islam.

Very–very special thanks to Mr. Nazim Zaidi who has taken the time and energy to painstakingly edit and re-edit the manuscript again and again. Without his assistance and effective suggestions, this project would not have been completed.

I am also obliged and grateful to Mr. Nadeem Bilgrami for all of his consistent support and encouragement.

Thanks to Hasan Rizvi, my eldest son who helped me in so many ways, in particular with the typing of the original handwritten notes, providing the various references along with his lively comments. Thanks to my family in particular my wife for their support and patience during this endeavor.

I am thankful and indebted to Allah (SWT) for enabling us to complete this needed task and providing us the tools and resources. I have always had a desire to complete a book that provides the basic answers to frequently asked questions about our faith. It certainly won't stop the hate mongers, the slander and the evil but at least it will provide our youths with the basis of our faith.

May Allah (SWT) bless all the contributors, big and small, during the preparation of this book, and accept this humble service.

Wassalaam,

Dr. S. Manzoor Rizvi

The printing of this book was made possible by the generous contributions from Mr. Nadeem Bilgrami, Dr. Iqbal Jafri, and Dr. S. Manzoor Rizvi.

TABLE OF CONTENTS

INTRODUCTION

It was the Muharrum procession of 2005 in Manhattan, New York City. A few followers of Al-Qaeda viz., Wahhabis barged themselves in the peaceful procession and distributed some nasty flyers that are appended at the end of the book. These flyers calling Shi'as Kafir were full of age-old false accusations and old craps -- Shi'as are Kafir because they curse Sahaba, they are Kafir because they believe in Taqiyah, and they are Kafir because they believe in Mut'a among others. These accusations date back to 1,400 years and these have been refuted time and again by Shi'as and Sunnies both. Every sensible and wise person knows that these accusations are total lies and a number of books have been written to refute these nonsense topics. Obviously, these books are written for those who are learned and enlightened readers and not for illiterate thugs.

An attempt has been made in this volume to collect and compile material on these topics in a book form for the seekers of the truth and those who want to quench their thirst of knowledge. Now read the following:

My son has a good Sunni (Arab) friend. One day he went to his home. They had their dinner with the family. Then he departed after thanking the family and the friend for the nice dinner. While still in the hallway he overheard the conversation between mother and his son (friend of my son). The mother said to her son, "What a nice and polite friend you have." The son (friend of my son) replied, "Yes he is very nice but unfortunately he is Shi'a." Alas! What a discredit.

This is not the story of an individual. The entire Shi'a community all over the world is taunted for being Shi'a. They are oppressed, tormented, terrorized, and killed just because they are Shi'as. Be it Afghanistan, Egypt or Saudi Arabia, the Shi'as are plundered and taken, if at all, as a second grade citizen. Even in countries where Shi'as are in majority they are oppressed and marginalized. In Bahrain, Beirut, and Iraq, Shi'as have no standing and are belittled and are punished.

Introduction

This brings us to the question, why is it so? We the Shi'as believe in one God, one Qur'an, all prophets, Prophet Muhammad to be the last prophet, believe in Qiyamah, Salat, Saum, Zakat, Hajj, and Jihad. We believe in the Islamic system of jurisprudence and total surrender to the Will of God. We believe in every word of Qur'an. We are a nation of peace and believe to live and let others live. We believe in what Imam Ali has said that everyone is our brother—Muslims as a coreligionist and non-Muslims as the creator of the same God. We are open-minded people and listen to all. Even if we have difference of opinion we do not label any one as Kafir and do not issue Fatwa to kill anyone who does not believe in us. This is in our blood. We have lived like this for the last 1,400 years.

On the other hand, Wahhabis are strange creed. They have their own limited interpretation of Islam. Islam which is for the universe has been limited to a sphere by them. They have become the creed of petro-dollar. If no one believes in their limited vision of Islam he or she is condemned as worthy of being killed and his property confiscated. Their *madrassahs* have become the factory for producing mass murderers which are produced in scores every year.

Our new generation living in the Europe and the United States of America highly resent this Wahhabi's attitude. They have lot of problems going to colleges with their colleagues of Wahhabi's mentality. They want to stop these arrogance and atrocities. It is getting difficult to control them but they can never be given permission to fight. We are a nation of peace and a law-abiding section of the society. We can not allow an innocent person to be killed irrespective of the fact that he is the known killer of our brother in faith. We can not take the law in our hands, we will handover the killer of our brother to the proper authorities. Most certainly, we do not believe in suicide bombing and innocent mass killing. For us mosques, imambargahs, churches, and synagogue are places of worship and not battlefields.

Now the question arises as to why Shi'as are condemned. Before detailing the reasons we want to make it clear that we have no dispute with our Sunni brothers. We love them and they love us. They take part in our activities and we in theirs. They love our leaders and adore the Prophet and his progeny as much as we do. We respect their beliefs and they ours. We are brothers and will remain so. Our differences are of Fiqh and we live like brothers in spite of these differences in some aspects of Fiqh. It is the Wahhabis/the Al-Qaeda and followers of Osama who are the main culprits of stoking the fire of differences and thus causing the deterioration of the Islamic umma. Here are the five probable reasons for condemning the Shi'a community by Wahhabis.

The *first* reason for condemning Shi'as is our stand for the righteousness. The Qur'an teaches us to be upright and truthful and so we do. We do not bow down to lie, be it in front of king or idol. We always say a spade a spade and we clearly distinguish between the light and darkness. This has caused Shi'a community great harm in the past: Abudhar Ghaffari was thrown out in the desert; Meesum Tammar lost his tongue; Malik-e-Ashtar was murdered; Hujr-Ibn-Adi was cut into pieces; Shaheed Awwal and Shaheed Sani were killed in Iraq and Shaheed Salis in India; Baqar-us-Sadr and his sister were murdered in cold blood; and Baqar-al-Hakim was blown up recently in a bomb blast. This lesson of truth was given by the Qur'an and taught and practiced by the Prophet and our Imams. We have been living like this for the last 1,400 years and it is difficult to change it now. The so-called Muslim rulers of today want to suppress Shi'as against their will but it is not possible. Imam Ali has said that non-Muslim governments may run but not a tyrant government. This is the reason why Shi'as live in much more peace and security in India, Europe, and the U.S.A. than in the so-called tyrant Muslim states.

The *second* reason for condemning Shi'as is their belief in *Nahi Anul Munkir* and *Amr-bil-Ma'roof.* This is again based on the Qur'an and on the teaching of the Prophet and his progeny. Shi'as do not tolerate injustice for a minute. Shi'as say bad things bad and try their best to stay away from them. They love goodness and try to achieve it. The Qur'an has done Tabarra (curse) on bad things and they do it too. The Qur'an appreciates goodness and Shi'as believe in Tawalla (praise). They pay salutation—God's blessings on the Prophet and his progeny. They curse the enemies of Allah, enemies of the Prophet and his progeny based on the recommendations of Allah and the Prophet.

They are not against any particular person or persons but they are against his or her bad deeds and nobody can compel them to appreciate the bad deeds. If every one speaks against a bad deed and appreciates good deeds then this world would be an altogether different place to live.

The *third* reason for condemning Shi'as is difference in opinion about the companions of the Prophet. Shi'as respect, love, and adore companions of the Prophet. They know and realize their lofty position in the eyes of the Prophet and Allah. They know and deeply appreciate their sacrifices, sometimes the ultimate sacrifice of their lives for the sake of Islam. However, the difference lies in the definition of the companion. We believe that a companion is one who believes in the Prophet and loves him and his progeny, has good deeds and lived pious and died as pious irrespective of his seeing the Prophet or meeting the Prophet. Our brothers, on the other hand, take anyone as a companion who saw or met the Prophet irrespective of his beliefs or actions later in his life. Their dictum is to follow every one of them and get a ticket to heaven. We surely differ with this line of action and this has created a lot of animosity. Fortunately or unfortunately, we have no intention of changing our position simply because we find ourselves on solid grounds.

The *fourth* reason is our Azadari or the mourning of Imam Husayn. Mourning of Imam Husayn is our identity as it regenerates amongst us a power of struggle against all and every type of injustices and evils. It makes us search our soul and helps strengthen our belief in Allah, in His Power and Authority. It reminds us of the sacrifice of a great man for the sake of Allah. It gives us strength to sacrifice for others and for Allah. It makes us highly sensitive to the injustice being perpetrated any where in this world. We may not be able to do any thing but we feel it. The tragedy of Karbala teaches us difficulties, however insurmountable these may be, but the victory at the end belongs to the righteous people. This is our Jihad. This is our holy war. This is a Jihad in which we do not hurt anyone. This is the most peaceful struggle going on for the last 1,400 year. How long it will go; till there is any trace of injustice in this world. Why it scares some, because it reminds them of theirs as well as their forefathers' injustices. They are afraid that people will get to know the real culprits and the world would awake one day.

The *fifth* and the last reason is the perception of the personality of the Prophet. For us, the Prophet was the Prophet from the day he was born till the day he died. He was the Prophet for us night or day, whether he is sleeping or awake. We believe in what he told us and we took what he gave us. We stop where he stopped. We believe that he was a born and divine Prophet. Others take him as a part-time Prophet. For them the prophethood was bestowed on him after he reached forty and he was a Prophet when he was delivering the Message of Allah and at other times he was like an elder brother who acted as a postman and after delivering his message his work was over. This made their life easy. They wanted to take whatever they wanted and rejected whatever they did not like. They never believed wholeheartedly in his prohethood and they insisted not being under any command. They are still doing whatever they want to but feel they would have been better off if the Prophet had not come. They hated the Prophet, his progeny, and his companions. They were called Nasibis and Kharjis during the time of the Prophet and are now representing Talibans and the likes. They were complaining during the time of the Prophet in various ways and forms. They hated Imam Ali as their forefathers were killed by Imam Ali. They felt that they were transferred by force into the fold of Islam. As they can not say openly any thing about the Prophet and Imam Ali so they take their revenge from us. We believe in the Prophet and his progeny wholeheartedly and this makes them jealous and develops a bitter animosity against us.

We have a message for them. We were not afraid of them yesterday and we are not afraid of them today. We were here yesterday and we would be here tomorrow. We had the Prophet and our Imams yesterday and we have our Imams today on our head and will remain so till the Day of Resurrection.

Dr. S. Manzoor Rizvi

New Jersey, U.S.A.
February 2009.

PART ONE: THE TRUTH

Salutation

Indeed Allah and His angles send blessings on the Prophet. O! Believers, you also should ask and send blessings and peace on him.

The Holy Qur'an (33:56)

It is incumbent upon all brothers in faith to say salutations wherever they read the names of the Holy Prophet and/or his progeny in this text.

Chapter: 1

VALIDITY AND AUTHENTICITY OF SHI'A ISLAM

BY

DR. SYED ABUL QASIM

The truth and validity of a religion rests on the rationale of its ideology, sound doctrine, logical principles, legal consistency, best value system, and the perfect knowledge and purity of its prophets and preachers. On all these counts, if evaluated objectively, Islam will be adjudged as the most sound of all religions provided it is properly displayed and properly understood.

The misfortune with Islam has been that the original Islam was hijacked before it could touch its native homeland. The original Islam takes root in the climate of Divine Justice and Divine Justice manifests itself in human infallibility. The quality of infallibility in human being has been the subject of debate, as the word 'human' is closely associated with error. To err is human has been accepted as a universal fact. However error is the product of three things: (1) lack of knowledge, (2) lack of power, and (3) lack of moral purity. If these imperfections are removed, error can creep neither into human words nor into human actions.

These constituents of infallibility namely the perfection in knowledge, power and purity are not found in the common man as his entire life is a series of movements from ignorance to knowledge, from powerlessness to power and from impurity to purity. But the system of Divine Guidance necessitates that the Guide be free from errors or sins or fallibility otherwise he will lose the ability and the right to guide. He would be one of the common men prone to errors. This divides the entire mankind into two categories, one set of men born as the uncommon men to guide, to teach, to inform and to lead, whereas the other set of men born as common men to follow the guidance, to learn, to be informed and to be led. The prophets, the messengers and the Imāms appointed by God belong to the category of the uncommon men who are taught, trained and sent by God for the guidance of humanity. Their identity is their knowledge right from their birth, their powers and the purity of their conduct.

The essential doctrine of infallibility is inseparable from the doctrine of revelation. If the book is revealed, it has to be error-free and if the guide is the revealed man, he too has to be error-free. The common man's knowledge and power and conduct are evolved from his childhood onwards. He is the product of experience and learning through a series of trial and error. The Guides sent by God are evolved only in their bodies from their births to infancy to childhood till their death or martyrdom, but spiritually they are matured right from their births. This maturity is the product of revelation and not of evolution in the popular sense.

The most notable fact of the Shi'a Islam is that it never departed from this doctrine. The whole axis of the Divine Guidance in Shi'a Islam, right from Adam, the first Prophet, down to the last Prophet and right from the first Imām after the Prophet down to the last Imām is an unbroken chain of the infallible Guides.

The word Shi'a literally means group. The Qur'an has hinted at the fact that to be the Shi'a of an authentic prophet is the virtue of a prophet (as in the case of Ibrahim whom Qur'an praises as one of the Shi'as of Noah). It is also a virtue to be the friend of a prophet (as in the case of Moses whose follower has been called his Shi'a in the holy Qur'an). The word 'Shi'a is symbolic of the religion of Ibrahim which is distinguished from other religion in being "Hanif" (one which never deviates from the axis of truth and righteousness, and always cuts off from falsehood and non-truth). Therefore just as Islam is the most rational and logical of all other religions, the Shi'a faith, is the most intact and protected from deviations and distortions of all other sects of Islam.

The religion of Ibrahim consisted of three distinguished features.

ICONOCLASTIC

He had the knowledge and conviction of a perfect monotheist and had the bravery and courage to be an iconoclast, the idol-breaker.

SACRIFICE

He was tested of the power of his patience in sacrificing all his property for the sake of the beautiful names recited by the angel sent by God for his trial. He was ready to sacrifice his own life when he was thrown into the huge fire prepared by Nimrod. He sacrificed the life of his own beloved son getting the hint of God's Will in his dream.

INFALLIBLE PROGENY

On his asking the God about the continuity of Imāmate in his progeny, he was told that it will go among his progeny only to him who is infallible to the extent that no injustice of any nature may ever touch his words and deed. Though his property, his life and his son all were saved by the Will of God but we came to learn of the distinguished merits in a prophet, which entitle him to be made the Imām of Mankind. We learned from the appointment of Ibrahim as Imām that an Imām has three basic qualities. He has the bravery of breaking the false icons of his time, he has the immense patience to sacrifice any beloved thing he has with him, and he has a progeny of the infallible children in his posterity, so infallible that no injustice of any kind can ever touch them.

A number of prophets were born in the progeny of Ibrahim. Both of his sons namely Ismā'īl and Ishāq were prophets and all the prophets of the Banī Israel were from the progeny of Ishāq, two of them namely Moses and Jesus were the Major Prophets. In the progeny of his elder son Ismā'īl, there was to be the last but the greatest of all prophets namely Muhammad in whom the whole revealed treasure was to be concluded and preserved. The basic quality of all these prophets was their infallibility, a quality, which can not be acquired by human efforts. It is the quality imparted specially to those who are meant to serve as the Guides to draw mankind from darkness and lead them into light. They are made infallible only by God. He equips them with uncommon knowledge both in degree and kind. He purifies them to an extent, which stands beyond human comprehension and gives them the power of miracles as a proof of their claim to have come from God to teach and not to learn, to guide and not to be guided by men.

THE DELICATE POSITION OF THE LAST PROPHET

Every prophet, among other official duties had two main obligations. First he had to attest the validity of the previous prophet, and secondly he had to give them the good tiding of the coming of the next prophet after him.

The last Prophet had no prophet to come after him so who will attest to his prophet-hood and preserve his teachings. If his teachings get lost or distorted, the entire treasure of the revealed wisdom and knowledge would be lost. And all labor and sacrifices made by the prophets from Adam down to the last Prophet would be wasted and ruined. So it was highly delicate situation for the last Prophet to ensure that the religion of Islam is well established and no difference finds its way into its original content and form.

This situation was made more delicate by the fact that the majority of his companions were his enemies before the conquest of Mecca, and had proclaimed Islam after the conquest under compulsion and they were determined to avenge themselves. They had no better way to avenge themselves than by infiltrating among the Muslims and waiting for the Prophet to die. These pseudo Muslims being in majority were determined to destroy his mission and change the interpretation of the Qur'an to create all kinds of doubts and differences among the Muslims and capture the ruling power to push their motives forward with ease and confidence.

This delicate situation of the last Prophet could be safely tackled only by clearly focusing both the pro-Islamic and anti-Islamic forces going to emerge after him. The Prophet left nothing in doubt and pinpointed both these forces.

He left nothing to doubt as to who would succeed him. He made people realize that only an infallible may succeed an infallible, only light can replace a light, only knowledge and purity can take the place of knowledge and purity. As Ali had all these attributes, he made him openly his successor in an open place before the maximum crowd he could gather. He addressed this vital issue for a long duration on the field of Ghadeer. He raised Ali above his shoulders to leave no doubt in any mind that his mission was protected in the guidance and guardianship commanded by Ali exactly on the same line as it used to be commanded by himself in his lifetime.

At the same time he left no doubt as to who was the mastermind of the hostile forces secretly plotting against his mission. He openly turned him out of his last meeting when he asked to get him a piece of paper and a pen to let him write the prescription of guidance. As Umar countered this command with his own impudent command, saying,"No! Don't do so as the Prophet is in delirium and talking nonsense. As for guidance, Qur'an is sufficient for us!" The Prophet ordered him and his coteries to get out of his room as Umar had stopped the people to take Prophet's holy progeny together with the Qur'an to be guided safely and rightly.

This well known event which, in the eyes of Ibne Abbās, was the saddest of the events in the life of the Prophet, made it brilliantly clear that the original Islam was safe nowhere except with Ali and the infallible line of his children. And the worst plight of the originality of Islam was bound to emerge at the hands of the opposition. The true and false Islam got polarized. On the one pole was the true Islam residing with Ali and the chain of his infallible children as named and pinpointed by the Prophet. On the other pole was the false Islam of the group endeavoring in opposition to Ali.

Following are the reasons which will further illustrate why it was dangerous for the Muslims to follow the dictates of this group saddled to dislodge the originality of the Prophet's mission.

The followers of the above group were against the group adhered to Ali as enjoined by the Prophet. This group is well known as the Shi'as of Ali. Even in the dictionaries of Arabic, Persian, Urdu and other languages, the popular meaning of the word Shi'a is given as the follower of Ali. This is how "Shi'a" has become a symbol of the original Islam saved from deviations, distortions, misinterpretations and misrepresentation. Shi'aism alone covers the implication of the *Dīn-e-Hanīf* of Ibrahim, the *Dīn* divinely protected from the virus of *Shirk* and unauthentic leadership.

REASONS WHY SHI'AS DISCREDIT COMPANIONS TO BE THE GENUINE GUIDES OF ISLAM

Following are the historical evidence in support of the fact that the so called leading companions who are popularly projected as the rightly guided companions had dubious characters.

1. Companions were not infallible. Ten companions including the so called 'rightly guided ones' took wine in a secret meeting. (Ibne Hajar in his *Fathul Bārī*, v.X, p.30; Bukhārī in *Sahīh* commenting on the verse concerning wine in Ch.Vth in the Qur'an; Imām Ahmad Bin Hanbal, in his *Musnad*, v. XXX, p.181; Ibne Kathīr in his *Tafsīr*, v. X1, p. 93; Suyutī in his *Dur al-Manthūr*, v, p.321; Tabarī in his *Tafsīr*, v. VII, p.24; Ibne Hajar Asqalānī in his *Isābā*, v. IV p.22; *Fathul Bārī*, v.X p.30; and Baihaqī in his *Sunan*, pp.286 and 290, have recorded this fact with detailed explanation.)

2. Some companions broke pledge made at Uhad, Hunain, and Hudaibiyah and they broke their pledge made on the Day of Ghadeer in an organized manner (as recorded in the famous books of Islamic history).

3. Some companions concocted ahadīth to misguide people. The hadīth "My companions are like stars, all of them are just and true, follow any of them you will be guided," is concocted and contrary to Qur'an. (Qazi Ayaz in his *Shah-e-Shifa* and Baihaqi in his *Kitāb* have proved that this is a forged hadīth).

4. Some companions doubted the status of Muhammad as a true Prophet.

5. Some companions had among them majority of the hypocrites who were impatiently waiting for the departure of the Prophet to unfold their secret plans to eliminate Islam and the Divine Protectors of Islam. In fact they were the real dangers under their cover of Islam.

6. Some companions fled the battle field leaving behind the Prophet when the life of the holy Prophet was most endangered. They turned their backs even when the Prophet would call them to return (as in the battle of Uhad).

7. The appointments of the companions as caliphs were not made on any standard doctrine or uniform and consistent

principle of selection. Their selection was made on arbitrary rules varying from caliph to caliph as suited the case of a particular caliph.

The First Caliph: He was elected by a group of vested companions in a rather maneuvered hurry keeping uninformed the pious and righteous companions in a secluded meeting hall far away from the Prophet's mosque. It was conducted while the Prophet's body was waiting to be shrouded and buried. Only few companions were present on this crucial occasion while the majority was either threatened if they said that the Prophet had died or engaged in the business of making the Caliph of their own choice fitting most to their stratagem. This selection was called by Umar himself the mastermind of this stratagem as *Falta* (the decision taken in hurry).

The Second Caliph: He was nominated by the first Caliph. The right of nomination was available to him while the Prophet was deprived of this right when it was highly needed that he nominated his successor as directed by Allah to save the Muslim nation from being torn into sectarian segments. In fact the responsible Prophet did nominate his successor as ordained by Allah in the broad daylight and in an overflowing crowd of Muslims represented by all Muslim states and regions in the presence of all companions of the Prophet, wives of the Prophet and the household of the Prophet. It took him three days to make sure that no shadow of doubt was left to the nomination of Imam Ali. The nomination of the second Caliph by the first Caliph was an open defiance of the Qur'an, the Prophet and of Allah together.

The Third Caliph: He was appointed by a new mode of selection. An advisory committee of six-member comprised of Usman, his brother in law, his votaries and Ali. The term and condition of selection was such that Ali was bound to be dropped and Usman was bound to be selected. Ali outrightly rejected the condition which called upon him to follow the tradition of the two previous caliphs together with the tradition of the Prophet. Ali argued that doing so would amount to adding something not approved by the holy Qur'an and the tradition of the Prophet. As a result, Ali was dropped. Usman forthwith accepted the condition and was seconded by his votaries and as was preplanned, he was selected as the third Caliph.

8. There are inconsistencies and contradictions in jurisprudence (religious laws) in the Islam of the companions. The Islam which was supposed to have been based on a single constitution free from inconsistency and mutual contradiction, divided into four schools of Jurisprudence. The school of Abu Hanīfa was different from that of Imām Shāfa'ī, which was different from Imām Malikī which in turn was different from Imām Ahmad Bin Hanbal.

9. There is a daring misinterpretation of the Qur'anic verse in justification and glorification of the ruling authority. The companions' main objective was to displace the Divine Authority and replace it with the authority evolved by human discretion best suited to make access to the ruling power.

This took them to misinterpret the Qur'anic term *Ulil Amr* in the Verse: *"Obey Allah and Obey the Prophet and the Ulil Amr from among you."* (4:59)

Ulil Amr was interpreted as the ruler and "from among you" was interpreted as the one made from among you either by vote or by nomination or by dynastic inheritance. The ruler, howsoever made, was meant to be obeyed as religiously as Allah and His Apostle were to be obeyed. The verse quoted above clearly asserts that the *Ulil Amr* sought to be obeyed with Allah and His Apostle must be free from sin and error otherwise his obedience will run contrary to Allah the Glorified and the Prophet who is infallible.

10. Some of the companions conspired to eliminate the true Ahlul Bayt either by taking their life or by concealment of their facts. The history of Islam is troubled with the conflict between the will of "Islam" and the will of the hypocrites under the cover

of their companionship to the Prophet. This conflict told so badly that the very face of real Islam was defaced beyond recognition.

The caliphs who are passed as the "Rightly Guided Caliphs" were in fact not always guided and it is they who lay the foundation stone of sectarian divisions and emotional fragmentation in Muslim community. They made way for Islam to be gradually transformed into imperialism so much so that imperial glory became synonymous with the glory of Islam. Every act howsoever un-Islamic and unjust was lawful if it helped to expand the territory of the kingdom and enlarge the glory of the royal splendor.

This caliphate, suffering gaps of few years in between the two dynasties, finally exhausted, deflated and ended in the early 20th century in Turkey. Now there is no caliph left in the world, what is left is only the pockets of Muslim states and the kings and princes with their pleasurable lives fully known to the world at large, yet living under the slavish fear of the political superpowers.

In contrast to the Islam passed out to Muslims by the companions, the Shi'a Islam passed out to them by the Prophet and the infallible Imams, is far more rational, consistent and in perfect conformity to the holy Qur'an, the tradition of the Prophet, universal logic, common sense, and wisdom.

MERITS OF CREDIBILITY OF SHI'A ISLAM

INFALLIBILITY OF THE IMĀMS

Divine Guidance, in principle, and of necessity, calls for an essential merit in the Divine Guides that they be infallible and sin-free, otherwise their words and deeds both will lose credibility. So from Adam down to the last Prophet the principle of infallibility has been sustained. Even the slighted lapse (*Tark-e-Aula*, not amounting to sin) was never compromised by Allah as in the case of Adam, Yūnus , Yusuf etc. and they were forthwith exhorted, and they begged of His forgiveness. All prophets were infallible, their ranks of infallibility, of course, was graded which reached to its utmost perfection in the last Prophet.

The rank and position of Imām is not granted by Allah unless a man is thoroughly tested as to how much patience and perseverance he has to be able to handle the office of an Imām. Prophet Ibrahim was accorded the rank of *Imāmate* after having been thoroughly tested by Allah. As Imām has to lead the mankind of his time to the Day of Resurrection, his knowledge and conduct both have to be utterly sound and perfect because even a trivial amiss in knowledge or moral fortitude may land the leader and his follower to a wrong destiny.

The Prophet therefore left nothing to doubt as to who will lead the Muslim Nation after him. He also told their numbers, their names and their attributes. He referred to the Qur'an when he told that the there were twelve *Naqīb'* of Moses, twelve *Hawārīs* of Jesus and there will likewise be his twelve successors each following the other without any gap in between them. When their enemies would kill them either by sword or poison and the last will survive, Allah will protect him by keeping behind the veil so no one can see him until it is the time to make him come out of the Veil and fulfill the mission of Allah to establish justice and order on earth. He will crack down upon all the false leaders and the followers of the false caliphs and remove the trace of all *Shirk* and injustice and rectify the earth of all the tyrants and mischief makers in the name of Islam or any other religion.

RATIONAL CONSISTENCY IN BASIC PRINCIPLES OF SHI'A ISLAM

The five cardinal principles of the Shi'a Islam are: (1) *Tawheed* (absolute Oneness of Allah); (2) *Adl* (Divine Justice); (3) Prophethood (The infallible agency with which Allah communicates to mankind); (4) *Imāmate* (The extension of the Divine mission through the infallible Guides to protect and keep intact the originality of Islam); and (5) *Qiyāmah* (The Day of Resurrection and Judgment). *Tauhīd* is connected with Justice, Divine Justice is manifested in Prophethood, the Prophethood is connected with *Imāmate* and the *Imāmate* is connected with *Qiyāmah* (as Allah says in the Qur'an: *"We will call all the mankind on the Day of Resurrection along with their Imāms."*(17: 71)

All these principles make enough sense without leaving any doubt that TRUTH abides in this Islam, and hold abundant logic to satisfy human reason. The rational potential of these principles establish the superiority and uniqueness of this religion over all other religions and over all variants of Islam.

RATIONAL CONSISTENCY IN SHI'A JURISPRUDENCE

Shi'a jurisprudence has been hailed by Muslim scholar as being free from inconsistency and contradictions as has been noted in the four schools of Jurisprudence, each being widely different from the other.

Shi'a Islam has a transparent historical perspective right from the day the universe was created down to the day universe will be folded back to the first state it was begun from.

Shi'a Islam has the most brilliant track record of the luminous lives of its Imāms pouring enough light on grand human virtues like the purity of words and conduct, charity, valor, knowledge, patience, forgiveness, devotion to the Will of God, compassion to mankind etc., etc.

The Qur'an together with Ahlul Bayt serves as the abundant Light Post to guide the ship of humanity safely and confidently to the shore of real salvation and eternal bliss. Any Islam other than Shi'a Islam is wrought with doubts, conjectures, speculation, and fatal risks.

Chapter: 2

MEANING AND ORIGIN OF SHI'AISM

BY

Allama Sayyid Saeed Akhtar Rizvi

MEANING OF SHI'A

The word "Shi'a" is from Arabic word *at-tashayyu* which means "to follow". According to major dictionaries like *al-Qāmūs* and *Lisānu'l-Arab*, the friends and followers of a person are known as his Shi'a. This word is equally used for singular and plural as well as for masculine and feminine gender. In the Qur'an it has been used for the followers of the prophets of Allah:

(a) In the story of Prophet Mūsa, it says: "*This was from his followers (shi'a) and that from his enemies (aduww). And he who was of his shi'a asked him for help against him who was his aduww;*" (28:15)

(b) In the story of Prophet Nūh, it says: "*And, verily, of his Shi'a is Ibrāhīm.*" (37:83)

Arabic dictionaries, after giving the literal meaning of Shi'a, usually add that "this name is generally used for those who love and follow Ali and the people of his house, and that it has become their proper name."[1] Sheikh al-Mufīd (d. 413 A.H./1022 C.E.) has explained that when the word "Shi'a" is used with the definite article "al" (al-shi'a – the Shi'a) then it only means "the group which follows Imām Ali with love and the belief that he was the Imām after the Prophet without any gap."[2]

In short, Shi'as got this name because they follow Imām Ali and his sinless progeny, and reject the claims of others to the office of Imāmate (leadership after the Prophet). As you will read below, it was the Prophet himself who gave this name to the followers of Imām Ali.

---

[1] *Al-Qumus*, vol. 2; at-Tarihi, *Majma'u 'l-Bahrayn*, vol. 2, p. 539; Ibn al-Athir al-Juzuri, *an-Nihayah*, vol. 2, p. 267.
[2] Al-Mufid, Shaykh, *Awa'ilu 'l-Maqalat* (Qum: 2nd edition. 1370 A.H.) pp. 2-3.

ORIGIN OF SHI'AISM

The origin of Shi'aism is the same as that of Islam. The main difference between the Sunnis and the Shi'as is about the successorship of the Prophet of Islam. The Sunnis believe that Abū Bakr was the first successor; the Shi'as believe that Imām Ali was the first rightful successor. When a non-biased scholar studies the declarations of the Prophet as recorded by the Sunni scholars in their commentaries of the Qur'an, traditions of the Prophet, biographies and history, he has to admit that it was the Prophet himself who was the originator of Shi'aism.

The first open declaration of prophethood was the very occasion when the first declaration of the caliphate of Imām Ali was made. The occasion is known as "the Feast of the Clan." The relevant paragraphs are quoted here from the *Tā'rīkh* of at-Tabarī:

> Imām Ali said, "When the verse *And warn thy clan of near kindred* (26:24) was revealed to the Messenger of God, he called me and said to prepare food and invite the descendants of Abdul-Muttalib, so that he could talk to them. They were about forty persons, among them his uncles Abū Tālib, Hamzah, Abbās and Abū Lahab. Then the Messenger of God delivered a lecture saying:
>
> 'O Sons of Abdul-Muttalib! I know no man in all Arabia who brought to his people anything better than that which I have brought to you. I have brought to you the good of this world and the hereafter. And Allah has commanded me to call you to it. Who, therefore, among you will help me in this matter, on the condition that he would be my brother, my heir *(wasī)* and my successor *(khalifah)* among you?'"
>
> Imām Ali continues the narration: "Nobody came forward; so I said (though I was the youngest in age): 'O Prophet of Allah! I shall be your helper in this (task),' so the Prophet put his hand on my neck and said: 'Verily, he is my brother, my heir and my khalifah among you. Listen to him and obey him."

The assembly stood up laughing and telling Abū Tālib that Muhammad has ordered him to listen to his son and obey him.[3]

This was the beginning.

In the last months of his life, the Prophet declared at a place called Ghadeer Khum that Imām Ali was his successor and leader of the Muslims. This event has been recorded by numerous Sunni scholars. Imām Ahmad bin Shu'ayb an-Nasa'ī (d. 303 A.H./915-6 C.E.) has narrated this event through several chains of narrators in his *al-Khās'is*, one of which is as follows:

> Abu't-Tufayl said that Zayd bin Arqam said, "When the Prophet returned from the last pilgrimage, and stayed at Ghadeer Khum and said, 'It is as though I have been called (back by God, meaning that death is soon approaching) and I have accepted that call. And I am leaving among you two precious things, one of them is greater than the other: the Book of Allah and my descendents, my family-members. So look out how you deal with them after me because they will not

---

[3] At-Tabarī. Muhammad bin Jarīr, *Tā'rīkh.* vol. 3 (Laden EJ Brill. 1882-1885) pp. 1171-1173. It is interesting to note that in the Cairo 1939 edition of at-Tabarī's *Tā'rīkh* which claims to have been checked with the Laden edition, the important words *"wasiyyi wa khalifati"* (my heir and my successor) have been changed to *"kadha wa kadha"* (so and so)! How sad it is to see the academic world sacrificing its integrity on the altar of political expediency. It should be mentioned here that this tradition with the crucial words has been narrated by at least thirty Sunni scholars, historians, traditionalists and commentators of the Qur'an. Imām Ahmad bin Hanbal has narrated this hadīth in his *Musnad* (vol. 1. p. 111) with following asnad: (a) Aswad bin 'Amir, from (b) Shark, from (c) al-A mash, from (d) al-Minhāl, from (e) Iad bin 'Abdullah al-Asadī, and from (f) Ali. Now (a), (c) and (e) are among the narrators of both al-Bukhārī and al-Muslim, while (b) is among the narrators of al-Muslim and (d) among those of al-Bukhārī. Also, Ahmad b. Shu'ayb an-Nasa'ī, whose *Sunan* is one of the six authentic sources of Sunni hadīth, has narrated this hadīth from Ibn Abbād in his *al-Khasā'is*, p. 6. For other references of this hadīth, see *al-Murāji'āt* of Abdu 'l-Husayn Sharafu 'd-Dīn, letters 20 to 23. Its English translation entitled as *The Right Path* by M. Amir Haider Khān was original printed by P.E.I Trust, Karachi and has since been reprinted several times in Iran, UK, and USA.

separate from each other until they come to me at the fountain (of Kawthar on the Day of Judgment). I am the master *(wali)* of every believer.' Saying this, he took the hand of Imām Ali and said, 'whosever's master I am, this [Imām Ali] is also his master. O Allah, love the person who loves Ali, and be enemy of one who has enmity towards him.'"

Abū't-Tufayl says, "I asked Zayd, 'Did you hear it from the Messenger of Allah?' He said, 'There was no one in the oasis but saw him with his eyes and heard him with his ears.'"[4] This tradition is known as "the tradition of two precious things."

In the same book, Imām an-Nasa'ī quotes another hadīth from Zayd bin Arqam which contains these words of the Prophet: "Don't I have more authority on every believer than his own self? " They replied, "Surely, we bear witness that you have more authority upon every believer than his own self." The Prophet then said, "So, verily, he whose master *(mawlā)* I am, also this is his master *(mawlā)*." Saying this he lifted Imām Ali's hand.[5] This tradition is known as "the tradition of mastership."

Both the above traditions have been jointly and severally narrated by hundreds of traditionalists. Nawwāb Siddīq Hasan Khan of Bhopal says : "Hakim Abū Sa'īd says that the traditions of 'two precious things' and 'mastership' are *mutawātir* (*mutawātir* means a hadīth narrated by so many people that no doubt can be entertained about its authenticity) because a great number of companions of the Prophet have narrated them. So much so that Muhammad bin Jarīr has written these two traditions by seventy-five different chains of narrators *(asnād)*."[6]

Al-Amīnī has classified the narrators of the tradition of mastership and has found that among them there are hundred and twenty companions of the Prophet *(sahabah)* and eighty-four disciples of the companions *(tabi'īn)*. The number of the scholars of hadīth who have narrated this hadīth reaches three hundred and sixty. Two hundred and sixty books (several of them in many

---

[4] An-Nasa'i, *al-Khas'is*, p. 15.
[5] Ibid. p. 16.
[6] *Minhaju 'l-Wusul*, p. 13.

volumes) have been compiled by Shi'a and Sunni scholars on this tradition only.[7]

ORIGIN OF THE NAME

When we see that between these two events, the Prophet repeatedly referred to the followers of Imām Ali as "Shi'a," we have to admit that not only the faith of Shi'aism, but the name also was originated by the Prophet himself. The following ahadīth are quoted from Sunni sources:

(1). Ibn Asākir narrates from Jabīr bin Abdullah that he said, "We were with the Prophet when Ali came (to us). The Prophet said, 'I swear by Him in whose hand is my soul, verily, this (Imām Ali) and his Shi'a are successful on the Day of Resurrection.' Then the following verse was revealed: *Verily those who believe and do good deeds, it is they who are best of creatures.* (96:7)"[8]

(2). At-Tabarānī says that the Prophet said to Imām Ali, "O Ali, verily you will come before Allah, you and your Shi'a, well-pleased (with Allah) and well-pleasing (to Him)."[9]

There are so many ahadīth from so many narrators that Sunni scholars could not reject them. So they tried to fit these ahadīth in their own group. For example, after quoting these traditions, Ibn Hajar al-Makkī writes, "And the Shi'as of Ahlul-Bayt are Ahlus-Sunna wa l-Jama'a (i.e., the Sunnis), because it is they who love the Ahlul-Bayt as was ordered by Allah and His Messenger. So far as others are concerned, they are in fact enemies (of the Ahlul-Bayt)." This claim was repeated by Shah Abdul-Azīz Dehlawī in his *Tuhfah-e Ithna-ashariyyah*, where he says: "It should be known that the first Shi'as (who are the Sunnis and the Tafdiliyyah) in old

---

[7] See al-Amīnī, *al Ghadīr*, vol. which deals exclusively with this subject.

[8] As-Suyutī, Jalālud 'd-Dīn (d. 910/1504-5) in his commentary *ad-Durru 'l-Manthūr*, vol. 6, p. 376. He narrates similar ahādīth from Ibn Abbās and Ali also in the same place. Al-Khuwarizmī (d. 569/1173-4) in *al-Manāqib*. Other ahādīth of the Prophet declaring that the Shi'a of Ali will succeed in the hereafter are narrated by Abdullah, Abū Rafi, Jabir bin Abdullah, Ibn Abbās and Ali by Sunni authorities including at-Tabar ān ī in his *al-Mu'jamu 'l-Kab īr*, Ahmad bin Hanbal in his *al-Man āqib*, Ibn Mardawayh al-Kanj ī ash-Shafi' ī in his *Kafayatu't-T ālib* and many others.

[9] Ibn Ath īr in *an-Nihayah;* Ibn Hajar al-Makk ī in *as-Saw ā'iqu 'l-Muhriqah* (Cairo, n.d.) p. 92. He narrates many ah ād īth to this effect.

days were known as Shi'as. When the Ghul āt and the Rawafid
Zaydiyyah and Isma'iliyyah took the name for themselves.....the
Sunnis and the Tafdiliyyah did not like this name for themselves
and so they took the name Ahlu s-Sunna wa l-Jama'a."[10]

Such claims should not be dignified by a reply. But seeing
that an abridged Arabic translation of *Tuhfa* has recently been
published in Egypt, I quote here the comment of another Sunni
scholar, Ubaydullah Amritsarī. After quoting the above claim in
his book *Arjahul'-Matalib,* Amritsarī says, "To say that Sunnis in
the beginning were known as Shi'as is just a claim for which no
proof can be found. Had the Sunnis been called Shi'as, then at
least some of the Sunni elders should have been known by this
name before the advent of Zaydiyyah (in 120 AH).....Moreover,
had the Sunnis been known by this name, the Zaydiyyah and
Isma'iliyyah would never have tolerated this name for themselves
(because of the enmity) and would have selected some other name
for themselves."[11]

THE FIRST SHI'AS

During the lifetime of the Prophet of Islam, the word Shi'a
was used as a name first of all for the four highly respected
companions of the Prophet: Salmān al-Fārsī, Abū Dharr Jundab
bin Junādah al-Ghifarī, Miqdād bin Aswad al-Kindī and Ammār
bin Yāsir. *Kashfu 'z-Zunun* (vol. III) quotes from *Kitābu z'-Zinah* of
Abū Hātim Sālah (sic) bin Muhammad Sajastanī (d. 205 AH):

"In the days of the holy Prophet the word Shi'a was
mentioned with reference to four persons: Salmān
al-Fārsī, Abū Dharr al-Ghifarī (sic), Miqdād bin
Aswad al-Kindī and 'Ammār bin Yāsir."[12]

These were the first Shi'as and this was the beginning of Shi'a
faith under the kind guidance of the Prophet of Islam himself.

---

[10] Ad-Dehlawī, *Tuhfa-e Ithna-Ithna-'ashariyya* Lucknow: Nawalkishore Press, (n.d.)
p. 11.
[11] Ubaydullah Amritsarī, *Arjahu 'l-Matalib* (Lahore: 2nd edition) p. 608 which is
wrongly printed as 164.
[12] As quoted by Hasan al-Amīn in *Islamic Shi'ite Encyclopaedia,* vol. 1 (Beirut.
1968) p. 12-13.

Chapter: 3

DIFFERENCE BETWEEN SHI'A AND SUNNI MUSLIMS

By

Allama Syed Muhammad Musawi

Islam is one religion sent from Allah to all human beings as the last and final massage. It was never divided into different sects like Hanafī, Shāfi'ī, Mālikī, Hanbalī, Wahābī, Sūfī etc, but only because of people's interference in the religion which is the word of Allah. All previous religions suffered from the same problem of division up to the extent of loosing their real messages. Islam being the last and final message from Allah, was preserved by Allah, so, real Islam was kept and still remains and will remain intact, in spite of many divisions existing and even governing many Muslim countries.

The real Islam is the Prophetic Islam which was preached and practiced by the Prophet and his noble progeny, Ahlul Bayt, and not any other Islamic sect, though Islamic sects have many Islamic practices, but the complete real Islam is none but the Islam of the Prophet and Ahlul Bayt which existed originally from the beginning of Islam before any Islamic sect came into existence, and continued till now through Ahlul-Bayt.

DIFFERENCE STARTED

The leadership of Islam after the Prophet was the main subject on which the division started. The question is: Who appoints the successor of the Prophet to lead the umma? Is it Allah who appoints or anybody from the people? Those who believed in Allah as the source and authority to appoint the divine leaders are the followers of Ahlul-Bayt, while Sunnis believed that Islamic leadership can come through group of individuals as what happened in Saqifah, or one individual, as when Abū Bakr appointed Umar as a Caliph after him, or just six individuals from the whole umma as Umar appointed six to select one of them, or to be killed if they were unable to select one. Majority of Sunnis believe that any person can be a Caliph as far as he is able to get the power by any way even by killing the previous Caliph and sitting in his place.

DIVINE LEADERSHIP (IMAMATE)

There are plenty of very authentic evidences from the Qur'an and authentic Sunna that the Prophet did not leave the umma without leadership after him. He said many times in accordance to Allah's orders that the leader after him would be Imam Ali followed by the infallible Imams from Ahlul Bayt. These evidences are mentioned even in famous Sunni books where they narrated the prophetic hadīth stating that the Caliph after him would be twelve, all of them from Quraysh or the Imams after him would be twelve, all of them from Quraysh[1]. They also admitted Hadīth Al-Thaqalain stating that he is leaving behind two greatest things, that you will never go astray as far as you keep following both of them; the book of Allah, and my Ahlul Bayt.[2]

It is the belief and practice of the followers of Ahlul Bayt who are known as Shi'a Muslims to follow the Qur'an and Ahlul Bayt, who teach the real Sunna and know the real *tafsīr* of Qur'an. They are in fact following Allah's orders by following the legitimate Islamic leadership, and getting themselves saved from going astray.

SAQIFAH FOLLOWERS

Other Muslims who call themselves Sunni Muslims do not believe in the immediate leadership of Ahlul Bayt after the Prophet and claim that the Prophet has left the Umma without any specific system for leadership, though many of them claim it as Shoora (election). Shoora in fact is applicable in managing worldly affairs, but never in religious affairs, as no Prophet came through election, so how Prophet's successor can come through election? It is only Allah who knows who is the best to lead mankind, and He appoints him.

---

[1] *Sahīh Al-Bukhārī* vol. 9 p. 541 and *Sahīh Muslim* vol. 3 p. 1452.
[2] *Sahīh Muslim* vol. 4, p. 1874; *Sunan Al-Tirmithi* vol. 5, p. 662; *al-Mustadrak* by Al-Haakim Vol. 3, p. 109; *Musnad* Ahmad Bin Hanbal vol. 3, p. 14, *Tafseer Ibn Katheer* vol. 4, 114; and *Tafseer Al-Durr Al-Manthur* by Soyooti vol. 5, p. 702 and many others.

Shoora was an excuse to justify bypassing the Qur'anic and Prophetic orders stating the leadership of Imam Ali. Those who claimed Shoora were trying to legitimize the incident of Saqifah which brought Abu Bakr's government, but such claim can not justify why Abu Bakr himself appointed Umar as a Caliph after him and did not leave the Muslims to elect a Caliph by Shoora as it was claimed by Sunnis as if it was done by the Prophet. Why they accept Abu Bakr appointing Umar after him and do not accept the Prophet appointing Imam Ali after him, knowing that the Prophet's statements are from Allah, while Abu Bakr's statements were from him.

In Saqifah few people from Quraysh led by Umar and Abu Bakr along with few from Ansār, gathered and argued and even quarreled, and then Umar proposed the name of Abu Bakr to be the Caliph, in the absence of Imam Ali, who was busy in the preparation of the funeral of the Prophet. Ahlul Bayt and leading Sahāba like Imam Ali, Salmān Al-Fārisī, Ammār Bin Yāsir, Abū Thar Al-Ghifarī, Al-Miqd ād Bin Aswad, Al-Abb ās Bin Abdul-Muttalib, uncle of the Prophet, and others refused the outcome of Saqifah which was against the orders of the Prophet who told the Umma on many occasions that Imam Ali was the leader after him. Those who accepted Saqifah are called now Sunni Muslims, where those who followed the divine leadership of Ahlul Bayt are called Shi'a Muslims.

PROPHETIC STATEMENTS

The Prophetic statements and ahādīth support the fact of the leadership of Imam Ali and Ahlul Bayt after the Prophet. Many of these ahādīth are narrated in main Sunni references, so must be accepted by all Muslims. Here are just a few examples:-

1. The Prophetic hadīth stating: "O Ali you are the leader who will lead my umma to the right path when they differ after me."[3]

2. The Prophetic hadīth: "O Ali, your status from me is as the status of Har ūn from M ūsa, but there will be no prophet after me." The Qur'an also states that Hārūn was always the Caliph

---

[3] *Al-Mustadrak Alal Sahīhain* by Al-Hākim Al-Nīsabūrī vol. 3 page 122; *Kanz Al-Ummāl* vol. 6 page 156; *Tārīkh Dimāshq, Biography of Imam Ali,* vol. 2, and p. 488.

and deputy of Mūsa till the end of Hārūn's life. This hadīth was narrated in many Sunni sources.[4] This hadīth is well known in the Islamic books as Hadīth Al-Manzilah. (The Hadīth of the Status).

3. The Prophetic hadīth: "This, Ali, is my brother, my trustee, and my Caliph (deputy) on you, so listen to him and obey him."[5] This hadith is well known as Hadīth Al-Dār. (The Hadīth of the House).

4. Hadīth Al-Ghadeer: When the Prophet said in front of thousands of Sahāba after asking them whether they accept him as a master on them more than themselves on themselves, and their reply was 'Yes', then he announced that: "For whomsoever I am the master (leader), Ali is his master (leader), O Allah, support him who follows Ali and be enemy of him who becomes enemy of Ali."[6]

5. The Prophetic Hadīth stating: "O Ali you are from me and I am from you."--- *Sahīh Al-Bukhārī*, vol. 5, p. 278, as well as the Prophetic Hadīth stating: "Ali is from me and I am from him, and he is the leader of every believer after me."[7]

6. The Prophetic Hadīth: "Whosoever believed in me and had faith that I brought the truth, must follow Ali Ibn Tālib, because following Ali is following me, and following me is following Allah."[8]

---

[4] *Sahīh Al-Bukhārī*, vol. 5, p. 280; *Sahīh Muslim*, vol. 4, p. 1870; *Sunan Al-Tirmithī*, vol. 5, p. 638; *Musnad Ahmad Bin Hanbal*, vol. 1, p. 170; *Al-Mustadrak* by Al-Hākim, vol. 3. p. 109; *Sunan Ibn Mājah*, vol. 1, p. 42 and many others.

[5] *Musnad Ahmad Bin Hanbal*,vol. 1, p. 111; *Tafsīr Ibn Kathīr*, vol. 3, p. 352; *Tārīkh Dimashq* by Ibn Asākir Imam Ali biography, vol. 1, p. 99; *Shawāhid Al-Tanzīl* by Al-Hasakānī, vol. 1, p. 371; *Al-Khasā'is* by Al-Nisā'ī, p. 24; *Al-K āmil Fil Tār īkh* by Ibn Al-Ath īr, vol. 2 p. 41; and many others.

[6] *Sunan Ibn Mājah*, vol. 1, p. 43; *Sunan Al-Tirmithī*, vol. 5, p. 633; *Musnad Ahmad Bin Hanbal*, vol. 1, p. 84; *Al-Mustadrak by Al-Hākim*, vol. 3, p. 109; *Al-Bidāyah Wal-Nihāyah* by Ibn Kathīr vol. 5, p. 209; *Tafir Al-Durr Al-Manthūr* by Suyūtī, vol. 2, p. 519; *Shawāhid Al-Tanzīl* by Al-Hasakānī, vol. 1, p. 157; *Tārīkh Al-Khulafā*, by Suyūtī p. 200, *Al-Khasā'is* by Al-Nisā'ī, p. 28; and many others.

[7] *Sunan Al-Tirmithī*, vol. 5, p. 632; *Al-Mustadrak* by Al-Hākim, vol. 3. p. 110; *Al-Manāqib* by Ibn Al-Maghāzilī Al-Shāfi'ī, p. 152; *Al-Khasā'is* by Al-Nisā'ī, p. 25; and many others.

[8] *Muntakhab Kanz al-Ummāl* by Munad Ahmad, vol. 5, p. 32; *Tārīkh Dimashq* by Ibn As ākir, *Biography of Imam Ali*, vol. 2, p. 91.

Part One: The Truth

WHERE IS THE REAL SUNNA?

All Muslims claim following the Prophetic Sunna, but the majority of such claims are clearly baseless with the vast differences and contradictions between many Islamic sects in faith and practice, keeping in mind that the Prophet's Sunna can not contradict itself. The differences are based on different ahādīth stating different statements in the same matter and situation. These are the fabricated ahādīth which were made to meet worldly benefits of certain people or governments or groups etc. The fabricating of ahādīth started during the time of the Prophet and was so much that he declared on the pulpit that: "Lying on me has become so much, beware, whosoever lies on me deliberately should be sure of his place in the fire."

No doubt, hadīth fabricating was much more after the departure of the Prophet since many governors like Mu'awiya and Hajjaj and many others were paying money to fabricators like Abu Hurairah and many others. Hundreds of thousands of fabricated ahādīth were mentioned in the books and on pulpits to please the governors or to oppose their opponents. Sunni *Ulama* admit this unfortunate fact.

The big question for all Muslims who really want to follow the Prophet is, from where can they get the real Sunna and be away from the fabricated ahādīth? The most authentic source for getting the real Sunna are Ahlul Bayt, not only because they were living with the Prophet most of the time, but also because their highest degree in truthfulness and nobleness, beside the Prophetic statements that "I am the city of knowledge and Ali is it's gate, so, whosoever wants the city must come through it's gate."[9]

Following the Qur'an and Ahlul Bayt means making the Prophetic Sunna from Ahlul-Bayt and leaving anything away from them. If all Muslims follow the real Sunna, there will be no disputes or differences among them, because of the fact that one Prophet's Sunna is just one Sunna which leads all into the one Islam. The followers of Ahlul Bayt take the real Sunna from the

---

9 *Al-Mustadrak* by Al-Hākim, vol. 3, p. 126; *Shawāhid Al-Tanzīl* by Al-Hasakānī, vol. 1, p. 81; Hadīth no. 118, *Al-Jāmi' Al-Saghīr* by Suyūtī, vol. 1, p. 108; and many others.

most authentic sources who are Ahlul Bayt and the authentic Sahaba, while the followers of other Islamic sects take their religion from sources which are never strong and authentic as Ahlul Bayt. So, the main two differences between Shi'a Muslims and Sunni Muslims lie in the answer to the following two questions:

(1) Is Islamic leadership comes from Allah, or from anybody else? Shi'as believe it comes from Allah.

(2) From where to get the real Sunna? Shi'as take it from the most authentic sources who are Ahlul Bayt and authentic Sahaba.

Chapter: 4

COMPULSION OR FREEDOM OF MAN'S ACTION

By

Allama Sayyid Saeed Akhtar Rizvi[1]

THE DIFFERENCES

The most vital difference amongst the Muslim sects is the question of compulsion or freedom of man in his actions. There are four groups:

1. The *Mu'tazilah* say that man is completely free to do whatever he wishes; and that God has no power over his actions at all. This group is also known as *Qādariyyah*.

2. The *Mujabbirah* (also known *Jabriyyah*) say that "man has no power over any of his action. He is a tool in the hands of Allah like pen in our hand." This view is known as *jabr--compulsion*.

3. The *Ashā'irah* say that man has no power of will of his own in his action; but he still "earns" or "acquires" the action. The term they use to describe their belief is *kasb* which literally means to earn, to acquire. What they actually mean is a riddle.

4. The Shi'a Ithna-'Asharis says that man is neither completely independent of Allah nor compelled by Allah, but the actual position is between these two extremes. The Shi'as' belief is known as *al-amr bayna' l-amrayn*. This will be explained later on.

It will be seen that the theories of *Mu'atazilah*, the *Mujabbirah* and the Shi'as are easily understood for what they stand. But the *Ashā'irah's* theory of *kasb* is as incomprehensible as the Christians' belief of three-in-one god. It is clear that they have used the term *kasb* as a mask to hide their actual belief which is completely identical to the *Mujabbirah's* belief of compulsion. Allama Shiblī Nu'mānī, a famous Sunni scholar of India, says, "Those who were

---

[1] Reproduced from the Bi-Monthly Magazine, *The Light*, Dar Es Salaam, Tanzania.

-25-

bold enough; openly adopted the belief in compulsion came to be known as *Jabriyyah*. Those who were hesitant to use the word *Jabr*, used the guise of *kasb* and *irradah*. This guise was invented by Abu'l-Hasan al-Ash'arī."[2] I, therefore, will treat both the Jabriyyah and the Ashā'irah as one. And as the present day's Sunnis are all Asha'irah and as the topic under discussion is of vital importance, I propose to deal with it in some detail.

THE SUNNIS' BELIEF

The position of the Sunnis in this respect has been explained by Imam Abū Hāmid al- Ghazālī as follows: "No act of any individual, even though it is earned *(kasb)* by him, is independent of the will of Allah for its existence; and therefore does not occur in either the physical or the extra-terrestrial world the wink of an eye, the wind of a thought, or the most sudden glance, except by the decree of Allah, of His power, desire and will. This includes evil and good, benefit and harm, success and failure, sin and righteousness, obedience and disobedience, polytheism and true belief."[3]

It will not be out of place to mention that this belief was invented by, and under the influence of, Banū Umayyah to provide a respectable mask to their debauchery and tyranny. As, Allama Shiblī Nu'mānī has admitted in his book *Ilmu'l-Kalam*: "Although all the causes were present which were responsible for the differences in faith, yet the political differences started the ball rolling. The reign of Banu Umayyah was full of cruelty and bloodshed; and in reaction to that there was a spirit of revolt among the common people by saying that 'whatever happens takes place according to the will of Almighty, and as such, people should not raise their voice at all.' Everything was destined beforehand; and whatever happens, good or bad, happens according to the will of Allah; and we should bow down to that."[4]

I think this disclosure--the idea of *jabr* (and its disguised version known as *Kasb*) was nothing but a weapon of tyrant rulers

---

[2] Shiblī Nu'mānī, *Ilmu'l-Kalām*, p. 28.
[3] Al-Ghazālī, Ihya' Ulumi'd-Dīn (*Kitāb Qawā'idu'l-'Aqā'b*), vol. I, p. 193; also see al-Ash'ari, *Kitābu l- Luma*, p. 53, 239.
[4] Shiblī, Op. Cit., p.25.

to subdue the oppressed masses--is more than enough to discredit this belief.

THE SHI'A BELIEF

al-Amr Bayna'l-Amrayn: The Shi'a Ithna-'Asharis, on the other hand, say that we know the difference between falling down from a rooftop and coming down by ladders. The second act is done by our own power, will, and intention; while the falling down is not so. And we know that our actions are not like falling down from the rooftop; instead they are like coming down the ladder with our own will and power. Therefore, what we do are our own actions and should not be attributed solely to Allah.

Again, we see that there are some of our actions for which we are either praised or blamed, while for other happenings we are neither praised nor condemned. It clearly shows that the first category is within our power and will. For example, we may be advised to treat an ailment in this or that way, but we cannot be advised to recover from the illness. It means that getting treatment is within our power, but getting well is not within the sphere of our activities.

Therefore, we say that there are many things and aspects of life which are within our power and will, while some others are not within our power. Those things, for which we can be advised, praised or blamed, are within our power and will. And the commandments of religion (the *shari'ah*) come under this category, because we are praised when we obey those commands and blamed when we disobey them. Therefore, it is absolutely wrong to say that our sins and righteousness, our obedience and disobedience, our true beliefs and wrong beliefs are by decree of Allah and His desire and will.

Shaykh as- Sadūq says, "Allah possesses foreknowledge of human actions, but does not compel them to act in any particular manner."[5] But neither does this mean that man is completely independent of Allah. In fact, the power and will to act as we like is given to us by Allah. Thus Imam Ja'far as-Sadiq said, "There is no compulsion (by Allah), nor is there absolute delegation of

---

[5] As -Sadūq, *al-I'tiqādāt*, chp. 4, p.58.

power (from Allah to man); but the real position is between these two extremes--*al-amr bayna'-amraym."*[6]

The following example clearly portrays this "middle position." Suppose a man's hand is totally paralyzed to an extent that he can not move even a finger. A doctor has fitted an electrical device on his hand which, on being switched on, enables the man to use his hand freely in a normal way. The device is activated by a remote control which the doctor keeps in his own custody, when the doctor switches the device on, the man uses his hand in any way he intends, but when the device is off, he cannot do anything. Now if the device is on, and the patient does not work, can that work be attributed independently to him? No because the power comes from that device which is fully controlled by the doctor. Then can it be attributed to the doctor? No, because the man had done it by his own free will and choice. This is exactly the position of our activities. We are not under compulsion because the will and choice is ours; nor are we completely independent, because the power to do whatever we intended to do comes from God.[7]

And at what point does our ability to do things start? Imam Muse al-Kāzim said," A man acquires that ability when four conditions are fulfilled: (1) When there is nothing to hinder his plans; (2) his health; (3) the faculties (needed for the work) are up to the required standard; and (4) Allah provides him the occasion of that work. When all these conditions are fulfilled, a man becomes capable of acting according to his own free will."

When asked for an example, the Imam said, "Let us suppose that there is a man, without any hindrance, of good health and proper strength; yet he cannot commit adultery unless he finds a woman. When he gets a woman (and the fourth condition is fulfilled), then it is up to him to choose one of the two alternatives: either he controls his evil emotions and saves himself as (Prophet) Yusuf did, or he commits adultery. And if he commits the sin, it does not mean that he was forced by Allah to do so."[8]

---

[6] Ibid, chp. 5, p.58.

[7] Al-Khū'ī, *al Bayān fī Tafsīr -il-Qur'an*, p.102. This example has been slightly modified by us.

[8] as-Sadūq, Op. Cit., chp.9, p. 60.

Predestination and the Day of Judgment: According to our point of view, if anyone believes in predestination, then he can not at the same time believe in the Day of Judgment (*Qiyāmah*). If Allah decrees every act which is done by us, then why should He inflict punishment upon us for those sins, evils and transgressions, for polytheism, disbelief and immoralities which He Himself predestined for us? It will be gross injustice.

Here is a talk of Imam Musa al- Kāzim in his childhood with Imam Abū Hanīfah, the founder of the Hanafī school of Sunni laws:

Abū Hanīfah once went to meet Imam Ja'far as-Sadiq. The Imam was inside his house and Abū Hanīfah was waiting for him to come out. In the meantime, a small child came out and Abū Hanīfah, just to pass some time, asked him, "O child, from whom is the action of man?" The child at once said, "O Abū Hanīfah, there are only three imaginable sources: either the man himself is the originator of his action; or God is the doer of that action; or both together are the originators of that action. Now if God is the doer of the action of man, then why does He inflict punishment on man for the sins? Is it not injustice (*zulm*)? And Allah says, 'Verily Allah is not unjust to His creatures.' And if both man and God are partners in that crime, then is it not gross injustice that the powerful partner (i.e., God) punishes the weaker partner (i.e., man) for an action which both of them performed together? And as these two alternatives are proved to be illogical and impossible, the third theory is proved to be correct that man does his action by his own power and will."[9]

Abū Hanīfah kissed the forehead of the child. That child was Musa, later known as al-Kāzim, the seventh Imam of the Shi'as.

ABŪ HANĪFAH AND BAHLUL

Imam Abū Hanīfah, of course, believed that man does nothing by his own will and power. In spite of the clever and logical discourse of Imam Musa al- Kāzim, mentioned above, he

---

[9]At-Tabrasī, *al-Ihtijāj*, vol. 2, pp. 387-388; al-Majlisī, *Bihāru-l-Anwār*, vol.5, pp.4, 27.

did not change his belief. Once his theory led to a tragic-comic event.

Bahlul means wise and chief. It was the name of a famous companion of Imam Ja'far as-Sādiq who lived up to the last days of Imam Ali an-Naqi and saw Imam Hasan al-Askarī also. As a twist of fate, he is commonly referred to as Bahlul *Majnūn* (Bahlul, the lunatic). This is so because he pretended to be insane in order to save himself from the responsibilities of judgeship offered to him by the Caliph Harūn ar- Rashīd. But wise as he was, he took advantage of his supposed lunacy and always censured great people of his time (including the kings) for their short comings.

Once he heard Imam Abū Hanīfah (who lived in Kūfa) telling his disciples that, "I have heard three things from Imam Ja'far as-Sādiq which I think are wrong." The disciples asked what those things were. Imam Abū Hanīfah said:

"First of all, Imam Ja'far as-Sādiq says that Allah cannot be seen. But it is wrong. If a thing does exist, then it must be seen. Secondly, he says that Satan will be punished in Hell. But it is absurd. Because Satan was created from fire; how can fire do any harm to a thing or person made of fire? Thirdly, he says that a man's action is done by his will and power, and that he is responsible for it. But it is wrong because all the actions of man are done by Allah's will and power, and Allah is, actually, responsible for it."

The disciples' applaud had just begun when Bahlul took a lump of clay and sent it hurdling towards Abū Hanīfah. It hit him on the forehead. He cried in anguish and pain. The disciples caught Bahlul and Abū Hanīfah took him to the judge. The judge heard the complaint and asked Bahlul whether the allegation was true.

Bahlul: "O Judge! Imam Abū Hanīfah alleges that he is suffering from a searing pain in his head because of the clay which hit him. But I think he is lying. I can not believe him until I see the pain."

Abū Hanīfah: "You really are crazy! How can I show you the pain? Has any body ever seen a pain?"

Bahlul: "But, O Judge, he was just teaching his disciples that if a thing does exist, then it must be seen. As he cannot show the pain, I submit that according to his own belief, he is not suffering from any pain at all."

Abū Hanīfah: "Oh! My head is splitting because of the pain."

Bahlul: "O Judge, there is another matter which I just remember. He was also telling his disciples that as Satan is made of fire, the fire of Hell can not do him any harm. Now man is made of clay, as the Qur'an says, and it was a lump of clay which hit him. I wonder how he can claim that a lump of clay did harm to a man made of clay."

Abū Hanīfah: "O Judge! Bahlul wants to go scot-free by his verbosity. Please, take my revenge from him."

Bahlul: "O Judge, I think Imam Abū Hanīfah has very wrongfully brought me to this court. He was just teaching his disciples that all the actions of man are done by Allah, and Allah is responsible for those actions. Now, why did he bring me here? If he really is suffering from the effect of that lump of clay, he should file suit against Allah who did hit him with that clay. Why a poor harmless person like me should be brought to the court. What all I am supposed to do was in fact done by Allah?"

The Judge acquitted Bahlul.

MAN'S WILL IN REGARD TO BELIEF AND DISBELIEF

It has been mentioned earlier that God does nothing without a purpose. So we may ask: what is the purpose of creating man?

God created man so that he may acquire those virtues which may bring him nearer to God. Man comes in this world like a blank paper. During his span of life various designs appear on that paper as the effect of his thoughts and deeds. Virtues which he acquires are like beautiful designs, and vices are like monstrous drawings. God says, *"Blessed be He... Who created death and life that He may try you-which of you is best in deeds."* (67: 1-2)

God gave wisdom, will and power to man so that he may acquire the virtues. He has shown the right path and has warned him against going astray. But He has not compelled him to do good deeds nor to commit vices. He has given him power to do as he wishes in this life. The Qur'an says, *"I swear by... the soul and*

Him who made it perfect, then He inspired it (the knowledge of) right and wrong for it. He who purifies it (i.e., the soul) will indeed be successful; and he who corrupts it will indeed fail." (91:7-10)

Tawfiq and Khidlan: As the purpose of our creation is to acquire virtues by obeying God and as we have been given freedom of choice, God does not compel us to select a certain path. Still, in His infinite mercy, He helps a man who sincerely wants to obey Him; but that help does not amount to any compulsion from God.

Let us take the example of a mason who is asked to repair a roof. He agrees to do the work, and starts work, and starts preparation. But then he finds some difficulty in obtaining a ladder of proper height. You know that he is going to do the job anyway; but you also know that he will face difficulty because of the shortness of the ladder. So you loan him your own ladder which is of proper height, and thus you made his work easier for him. But remember that the help was given to him when the mason had the firm intention of doing the job, when he had made all his preparations. So this help did not compel him to start his work, nor did it create the intention or will or power to repair roof. The power, the intention, the will, all was there beforehand. What you did was just to help him in carrying out his intention.

Such help from God, given to those persons who sincerely want to obey His commands, is called *tawfiq*. *Tawfiq* means helping someone to succeed.

Now let us look at the other side. Suppose the mason did not want to repair that roof and refused outright to accept the job; or even after agreeing to do the work, he started delaying tactics and putting lame excuses. You knew that he had no intention of doing the job. Therefore, there was no sense in providing him with the ladder and you did not offer it to him. Can it be said that by withholding the ladder from him, you compelled him not to do the job (or was postponing it without any genuine cause). Your ladder had nothing to do with his decision.

That withholding of the help from those persons, who choose to disobey the commands of God by their own free will and power, is called *khidlan*. *Khidlan* means abandonment. You will find many verses in the Qur'an which refer to these two aspects of God's act: helping and withholding the help. Take for example: *"Whomsoever Allah wills to guide, He opens his heart to Islam; and whomsoever He wishes to leave straying, He makes his heart narrow and constricted, as if he was climbing into the heights--thus does Allah heap the punishment on those who do not believe."* (6:125)

Mark that God does not mislead the unbelievers--He just leaves them straying. It means that they had gone astray and then God left them to wander. This meaning becomes clearer when you see the last phrase "thus does Allah heap the punishment on those who do not believe." It clearly shows that they were left in their wandering as a sort of punishment for their disbelief. They had chosen, on their own accord, not to believe in God; and then, as a result of that disbelief, God left them straying. Another verse says: *"By it (i.e., the Qur'an) He leaves many straying, and many He leads into the right path. But leaves not straying except those who transgress divine commandments."* (2:26) Here also only those have been left straying who had already transgressed the laws by their own choice. It is clear that they were left in their wandering because they had gone astray themselves by their own wrong choice.

Knowledge of God and Action of Man: God knows everything. He knew before that, for example, Bakr would be an unbeliever. Now, if Bakr accepts Islam, it would mean that the knowledge of God was wrong; and since God's knowledge can never be wrong, therefore, it is necessary for Bakr to remain an unbeliever. Now the question is: Does it not mean that Bakr had to remain an unbeliever because of the knowledge of God?

Answer: It is one thing to know what is going to happen; and quite another to cause that thing to happen. Suppose there is a doctor who, after examining a patient, declares that the patient can not survive more than half an hour and the patient dies within half an hour. Can it be said that the doctor caused the death of that patient because he knew that the patient was going to die? Can a claim be lodged against him that he killed the patient? No. Instead this incident will be quoted to show how experienced that doctor is because he foresaw what was going to happen to the patient after half an hour.

Let us look at this example again. The doctor knew that the patient was going to die, because he was in such a condition that he could not survive more than half an hour. So, that knowledge was derived from the condition of the patient; not that the patient died because of the knowledge of the doctor. The knowledge was the result of the condition of the patient; the condition of the patient was not the result of the knowledge of the doctor.

This simple difference was overlooked by the majority of the Muslims who thought that as God knew everything which was to happen, so it must happen accordingly. They failed to realize that Bakr was to die as an unbeliever, because he was going to die in the condition of disbelief by his own will; that the knowledge of God was based upon that independent will of Bakr; not that Bakr died an unbeliever because of the knowledge of God.

Of course, there is a difference between the knowledge of a doctor and the knowledge of God. The knowledge of doctor is imperfect and incomplete. Therefore, his forecast can be wrong at certain times. But the knowledge of God is perfect and complete in every respect forever. Therefore, His knowledge cannot be wrong at any time. Still it does not mean that His knowledge causes the sin or polytheism or hypocrisy or faith and virtue of His creatures.

LUTF- THE GRACE OF GOD

If a person can do something good to someone without harming any other person and still he does not do so, then his reluctance from helping the others is against virtue, it is evil. Therefore, if God can do anything beneficial for His creatures and then suppose that He does not do so, it will be against the virtue of God, and not commendable. It is for this reason we believe that "it is morally incumbent upon Allah to do every act of *lutf* (grace) in dealing with mankind."[10]

What is the meaning of *lutf* which has been roughly translated above as "grace"? *Lutf* is the action on part of God which would help to bring His creatures nearer to His devotion and obedience, and facilitate moral correction. It must be

---

[10]al-Hillī, *al Babu-l-Hādī Ashar*, p. 99.

mentioned here that, "Allah has ordered us to be just, but He Himself treats us with some thing better than justice, namely *tafaddul*--grace."(*Tafaddul* has same meaning as *lutf*.) The belief that *lutf* is morally incumbent upon God is the distinctive belief of the Shi'a Ithna-'Asharis. The Sunnis do not believe that *lutf* is incumbent upon God. They say that even justice (*adl*) is not incumbent upon God, let alone *lutf*. According to the examples given by them, if God sends good and virtuous persons to Hell and sends Satan to paradise, it will be quite right. There would be nothing wrong (this is Sunnis belief).

Both *Tawfiq* and *lutf* as mentioned above are primarily meant to help the individual or the groups in obeying the commandments of God. However, sometimes such help is offered to an obstinate person not because he is expected to take its advantage and perform his duties, but just to close the door of argument, to refute all his excuses, so that he may not claim that had he been given a bit of encouragement, he would have been an obedient servant of God. This type of help is known as *itmāmu-l-hujjat*.

Some Examples of Lutf: Now we know that God created us to acquire virtues in this life so that we may be nearer to God in the hereafter. The question is: How are we to know what is virtue and what is evil? Human intellect does appreciate inherent virtue or evil of many of our actions, but can we expect everybody to act according to the perfect reason? Certainly not. Many times desire or anger suppresses the force of wisdom; many times an immediate benefit (obtainable by evil means) seems more impressive than the fear of condemnation by society or losing the grace of God in the life after death.

If God had left mankind without any effective device to check their evil thoughts and desires, it would have been tantamount to defeating His own purpose. Therefore, He laid down some rules and sent the prophets and Imams to bring those rules to His creatures, and to explain and protect those laws from corruption. And He did not leave us at that, he also appointed a day when all will be gathered to give account of their beliefs and actions. And, He, in His mercy and justice, sent us the news that there will be a Day of Reckoning, a Day of Judgment, a Day of Reward and

Punishments. This information helps the creatures in obeying those laws which were brought by the Prophets.

Thus sending the *shari'ah* is a *lutf* which helps the mankind to achieve the purpose of life. Also, sending the Prophets and the Imams, and appointing a Day of Judgment are *lutf* for the same reason. And because these acts are *lutf*, they are incumbent upon God.

The rules of the *shari'ah* are called *taklīf*. *Taklīf* literally means to put in hardship. As any law, though it may be the simplest one, appears to human nature as a 'hardship,' the *shari'ah* is called *taklif*. (By the way, lawlessness in the end brings real hardship and calamities, while the law brings peace and happiness.) Though the rules of the *shari'ah* are called 'hardship,' in reality they are well below our strength and ability. God says, *"On our soul does Allah place a burden but less than its capacity."* (2:286). Imam Ja'far as-Sādiq said, "Allah did not give orders to His servants but that they were less than their strength... Because He told them to pray five times a day, fast one month in a year, pay zakāt five dirhams in two hundred and to go to hajj once in a life; but the people have strength to do more than this minimum."[11]

Significantly, the word used in the above verse is not *tāqat* - strength and ability, but *wu'* which carries the idea of "ease" and "comfort" and here means "less than its strength or capacity." This is one aspect of God's infinite mercy as He says, *"Allah intends every facility for you and He does not want to put you in difficulties."*(2:185)

---

[11] as-Sadūq, *Risālatu-l-I'tiqādāt*, chp.3, p.57.

Chapter: 5

BELIEF IN TWO RESURRECTIONS

By

Allama Sayyid Saeed Akhtar Rizvi[1]

The Holy Qur'an speaks of two resurrections, the first one being selective and partial, and the second one total, all-inclusive and final. The Muslims know the second one as *Qiyāmah*, and it is a fundamental Islamic belief, without which no one can be called a Muslim.

The first one is called in Shi'a theology as Raj'at i.e., Return. It is this selective resurrection to which the Qur'an refers when it says: "*And on the day when We will gather from every people a party from among those who rejected our signs, then they shall be formed into groups.*" (28: 83)

Note that it speaks of gathering only a party or group from among people. But on the Day of *Qiyāmah* the whole mankind will be gathered, and no one will be left behind, as the Qur'an says: "*And the day when we will cause the mountains to pass away, and you will see the earth a leveled plain, and we will gather them (and) then leave not any one of them behind.*" (18: 47) Also the Qur'an declares: "*This is a day on which the people shall be gathered together and this is a day that shall be witnessed.*"(11: 103)

Clearly the day when only some groups will be resurrected and gathered is other than the Day of Judgment when the whole mankind shall be gathered and no one will be left behind.

Raj'at is one of the *Dharuriyāt-e-madhhab*, (i.e., commonly accepted belief) of the Shi'a Ithna' Asharī faith. One who does not believe in it is not a true follower of the faith. In short, it means that after the re-appearance of Imam Mahdī from Occultation (*Ghaybat*), some extremely pious and some extremely evil persons both from this umma and previous ones will be resurrected by

---

[1] Reproduced from the bi-monthly Islamic magazine, *The Light*, (October 1999), Bilāl Muslim Mission of Tanzania, Dar Es Salaam, Tanzania.

Allah, in order that the good ones should rejoice on seeing the true Kingdom of God and the evil ones should be distressed by it.

The principle of Raj'at is established from the Qur'an; but the details are not fully known. It is not only Raj'at; Allah had kept secret many details of the stages through which man has to pass from his death to his final destination of Paradise or Hell. The belief, in principle, is described by ash-Shaykh at-Tusi in his *Usūlul-Aqā'id* in these words: "Our Prophet and our Ma'sūm (sinless) Imams will return in the days of (Imām) al-Mahdī, together with a group from the previous nations and the present one (it will happen) in order to establish their kingdom and right. It has been described by *Mutawātir* traditions and Qur'anic verses; for example: *'And on the day when We will gather from every people a party...'* Therefore, belief in "Return" is *wājib* (obligatory)."

It is certain that this return will take place after the appearance of those signs of *Qiyāmah* about which Allah says in the Qur'an: *"On the day when some of the signs of your Lord shall come, its faith shall not profit a soul which had not believed before or had not earned good through its faith."*(6:158) When those signs will appear, the opportunity for the unbelievers will be lost forever; even if they professed Islam (after seeing those signs) it will not be accepted from them; nor will any good deed done by them after that be credited to their account. In modern language, we may say that their accounts will be closed and no newly claim of faith or fresh attempt to rectify their previously-done sins will be accepted. In this period the eleven previous Imams will rule on the earth, and the enemies of Allah will be made to suffer for what they had done. The believers will rejoice in the Kingdom of God and their enemies will be punished. This reward and punishment will be a sort of fore-taste of the reward and punishment of the *Ākhirat* (Day of Resurrection).

The Return is "The day of the known time" up to which the Satan has been given respite. When Allah ordered Satan to get out of heaven and cursed him, the Satan had asked for respite up to the day of resurrection; that is, during Imām al-Mahdī's era when "Return" will take place and people's accounts will be finally closed. Allah says describing the above-mentioned episode of Satan: *"He (Allah) said: 'Then get out of it, for surely you are driven away; and surely My curse is on you to the Day of Judgment.' He (Satan) said: 'My Lord! Then respite me to the day that they shall be raised.' He (Allah) said: 'Surely you are among the respited ones, till the period of the time known.'"* (38: 77-81)

At the end of the period of Raj'at, all of them, without any exception, will die. Then the whole mankind, without any exception, will be resurrected, for the Day of Judgment.

There is another verse in the Qur'an which points to the Return: *"They shall say: Our Lord! Twice didst thou cause us to die, and twice hast thou made us alive, so we do confess our sins; is there then a way to get out?"* (40:11)

Muslim scholars have tried to explain the meaning of this verse: what is actually meant by giving them death twice and making them alive twice? But no explanation fits the verse perfectly. The real "trouble" is that the word *al-ihyā* (to be made alive) presupposes a preceding death; therefore it cannot be logically applied to this worldly life of ours, because before it we were not "dead," we were "non-existent." The verse in actuality refers to (1) death after this worldly life, (2) being made alive in the Return, (3) death after the life or Return, and (4) being made alive on the Day of Judgment.

Objection: Allah says in the Qur'an: *"And it is forbidden to a town which We destroyed that they shall not return."* (21: 95) It shows that there will be no return after death.

Reply: We should not look at the verse in isolation. It is connected with preceding verses It begins:*"...to us shall all come back. Therefore whoever shall do of good deeds and he is a believer, there shall be no denying of his exertion, and surely We will write (it) down for him. And it is forbidden to a town which we destroyed that they shall not return."* (21: 93-95)

It shows the contrast between believing good-doers and others at the time of death when all go back to Allah. The one who does good deeds, provided he is a believer, his efforts shall be appreciated. Next is the verse under discussion which according to the context must refer to those who do good deeds but are not believers. It alludes to their despair and earnest desire to be returned to this world so that they could rectify their errors. The verse says that they shall not be returned, because their examination time is finished. Its meaning may easily be understood with help of the following verses which say: *"Until when death overtakes one of them, he says: send me back, my Lord, send me back; perhaps I may do good in that which I have left. By no means! It is a (mere) word that he speaks; and before them is a barzakh (barrier) until the day they are raised."* (23: 99-100)

So the verse quoted in the question speaks about this very thing which is described in verses 23: 99-100.

But the Return which we believe in, shall take place when the accounts of deeds and belief will be closed, and any soul who had not believed before or had not done good before will not get any benefit from his fresh protestation of faith or fresh attempts to rectify his error.

Allah in the Qur'an has described three different episodes of resurrection, in which men and animals were raised after their death. The first is the story of Uzayr (Ezra) when he and his donkey were made alive after remaining dead for a hundred years when their bones too had disintegrated. Allah says: *"Or like him who passed by a town, and it had fallen down upon its roofs; he said: how will Allah give it life after its death? So Allah caused him to die for a hundred years, and then raised him to life. He said: How long have you dead? A day or less than a day, he replied. He (Allah) said: Nay! You were dead for a hundred years; then look at your food and drink- years have not passed over it; and look at your donkey, and that We may make you a sign to men; and look at the bones, how We assemble them together, them clothe with flesh; so when it became clear to him, he said: I know that Allah has power over all things."* (2: 259)

The second is the episode of Prophet Ibrahim when on his prayer Allah showed him how He would give life to the dead--by making four birds alive after they had been cut into pieces. Allah says: *"And (remember) when Ibrahim said: My Lord! Show me how Thou givest life to the dead. He said: What! And do you not believe? He said: Certainly but that my heart be at ease. He said: Then take four of the birds, then cut them (into pieces), then place on every mountain a part of them, then call them they will come to you flying; and know that Allah is Mighty, Wise."* (2: 260)

The third event is of thousands of people who had fled for fear of death. Allah says: *"Did you not see those who went forth from their homes, and they were (in) thousands, for fear of death. Allah said to them, Die. Then He gave them life; most surely Allah is Gracious to people, but most people thank (Him) not."* (2: 243)

The Qur'an is not a story book. The past events and historical facts mentioned in it have been revealed for our guidance. By recording these events Allah has shown us that it is not only possible for dead men to be given new life in this world, but it has already taken place repeatedly.

CONCLUSIONS

1. Raj'at means that there will be a resurrection of some selected persons before the total all-inclusive resurrection of the Day of Judgment.

2. Raj'at is a Qur'anic reality. It is not only possible according to reason, but has also got precedents in previous nations.

3. It will happen after the reappearance of Imām al-Mahdī, when some special signs of *Qiyāmah* will appear and the accounts of deeds and belief will be closed. In other words, there will be no chance then for the unbelievers and wrong-doers to rectify their errors.

4. *Mutawātir* ahādīth of the Imams of Ahlul Bayt prove that in Raj'at our Prophet and the previous eleven Imams will come back. So will some extremely good believers and some extremely bad persons from this and the previous nations.

5. It will be done to enable the Prophet and the Imams to rule on the earth; to let good believers rejoice and bad people feel despair in the Kingdom of God. It will be a fore-taste of the reward and punish which they will be given in *Ākhirat*.

Chapter: 6

DISCRETION OF KNOWLEDGE BY ALLAH: BADA'

By

Allama Sayyid Saeed Akhtar Rizvi[1]

An unknown author writes that one of the several proofs of Shi'as' being *kāfir* is that they believe that Allah is subject to Bada'. That is to say that the knowledge to Allah changes from time to time, because Allah is not fully aware of the causes and their consequences. It is the manifestation of the author's ignorance. First let me make clear what Bada' means.

Every sane person knows that the knowledge of Allah can never be wrong. In other words, there can never be any change in the knowledge of Allah. In contrast to it is the knowledge given by Allah to the angels and the prophets. Their knowledge, though the most complete and perfect of all creatures, is still incomplete when compared to the knowledge of Allah. Allah in His mercy constantly replenishes, perfects, and completes their knowledge.

Also, we know that Allah often puts his servants to test and trial. Again, it appears from many stories in the Qur'an that sometimes Allah, in His mercy and wisdom, reveals only a part of His future plan to the angels or the prophet concerned. They are informed of His plan to a certain stage, and the knowledge of the later stages is not revealed to them in advance. Before going ahead, let me give here two examples from the Qur'an.

THE SACRIFICE OF PROPHET ISMĀ'ĪL

Prophet Ibrahim was shown in a dream that he was sacrificing his only son for the pleasure of God. As it was a dream, he must have seen how he was killing Isma'il. He must have seen himself binding the hands and feet of the child, blind-folding himself and them putting the knife on the child's throat and pressing it down. Naturally, he could not have seen who or what was actually being

---

1 Reproduced from his book *Wahhābis Fitna Exposed*, A Pyame Aman Publication, Message of Peace Inc., Bloomfield, New Jersey: U.S.A., 1999.

killed as his eyes were covered. By seeing the dream he believed that he was required to kill his son, Ismā'īl in that way. Therefore, he steeled his heart to sacrifice his only child.

The child heard it and prepared himself to be sacrificed in obedience to the command of God. The father and the son both were willing to sacrifice every thing in the name of Allah. Prophet Ibrahim did as he had dreamed himself doing: he bound the hands and feet of the child and put him in the required position and, blindfolding himself, put the knife and cut the throat. After removing the blindfold from his eyes, he saw Ismā'īl smiling and a lamb slaughtered in his place.

Prophet Ibrahim thought that he had failed in his test. But he had clearly done what he had seen himself doing in the dream. Of course, Allah had not informed him of the events of the last stage. For if Ibrahim had known that Ismā'īl would be saved, or if Ismā'īl had known that he would be saved, there would have been no meaning in that test; there would not have been any chance of showing their willingness to sacrifice everything in the name of Allah. So God showed to Ibrahim in his dream the events to a certain stage but kept him unaware of the final stage; not informing him how the whole episode was going to end. As they did not know the result, Ibrahim and Ismā'īl were able to show how willing they were to obey the command of God even to the extent of sacrificing their lives and the lives of their dear ones in His name. If they had known the result from the beginning, the test would have been meaningless.

TAWRAH GIVEN TO PROPHET MUSA

Another example concerns Prophet Musa and the revelation of the Tawrah. Prophet Musa was ordered to go to Mount Sinai, fast there for thirty days in preparation for receiving the tablets of the Tawrah. On the thirtieth day he cleansed his teeth and went to Mount Sinai. There he was asked by God as to why did he cleanse his teeth. He explained that as he was coming to holy place, he thought it proper to make himself neat and clean. God told him that the smell of the mouth of a fasting person was sweeter before God than the smell of musk and ambergris. And then he was told to return to his staying place, and fast for ten days more and then come to Mount Sinai without cleansing his teeth. Thus it was on the fortieth day that he was given the stone tablets of the Tawarah.

Allah knew before hand that Musa would come after cleansing his teeth, and would be asked to fast for ten days more. But neither Musa nor the Israelites had been told about it; nor was Musa told before hand that he was not to cleanse his teeth on the thirtieth day.

When Allah refers to His knowledge, He describes the whole period of forty nights together: *"When we made appointment with Musa for forty nights. Then you* (the Israelites) *took the* (image of) *calf* (for your God) *after he lift you and thus you transgressed."* (Qur'an, 2: 51)

And where Allah refers to the knowledge of Musa, He mentions thirty days and ten days separately: *"And We made an appointment with Musa for thirty nights; and We completed with ten* (more)*; thus was completed the term of his Lord forty nights."* (Qur'an, 7: 142)

The reason of not giving advance information is clear from the behavior of the Israelites who because of his ten days delay, discarded the worship of the only and true Allah and started worshiping the image of a calf. The story is given beautifully in these verses of the Qur'an: *"Said God to Musa, 'Verily we have tested thy people in thy absence, and the Samiri had led them astray.' So returned Musa unto his people angered and sorrowful. Said he, 'O my People, did not your Lord promise you a good promise? Did then the promise seen long to you, or did you want the wrath from your Lord should light upon you, that you violated the promise with me?' Said they, 'We violated not thy promise of our own accord....' Then he* (Samiri) *brought forth for them a calf, a mere body with a lowing sound. Then they said, 'This is your god and the god of Musa, but he* (Musa) *has forgotten.'"* (Qur'an, 20: 85-88)

Just imagine a whole community of several thousand companions of an *ulu-l-azm* Prophet, in the presence of his successor and vicegerent Hārūn, leaving the path of true religion and starting idol worship, just because Musa was delayed for a few days! This test of faith could not stay for forty days; or if he had been told before hand not to cleanse his teeth on the thirtieth day.

This is the meaning of Bada'. It has not been mentioned any where that "the knowledge of Allah changes because Allah is not fully aware of the causes and their consequences?"

The name Bada' and its meaning, both are derived from the Qur'an. Allah says: "*And became plain to them from Allah what they had never thought.* (Qur'an, 39: 47) This is the meaning of Bada'; and the term is applied when Allah makes something happen to the creatures which they had not expected. The change occurs in the creatures' knowledge, not that of Allah.

The writer has quoted a hadīth from *Al-Kāfi*, from Imām Razā that "Allah did not ever send a Prophet but that he should proclaim wine as forbidden, and that he should as well recognize that Allah is subject to Bada' (the proposition that if a new circumstance should intervene it may cause Allah to alter His determination.)"[2]

What the hadīth in *Al-Kāfi* says is simply this: "Never had Allah sent any prophet except with the prohibition of intoxicant and with the affirmation to Allah of Bada'." The unknown author has given a totally wrong meaning of Bada' in brackets and has put it within the quotation marks to deceive the readers, who might think that the said meaning was a part of the hadīth. It is for people like him that Allah says in the Qur'an: "*Most surely there is a party among them who distort the Book with their tongue that you may consider it to be a part of the Book while it is not a part of the Book ... and they tell a lie against Allah whilst they know.*" (Qur'an, 3: 78)

If this unknown writer had really seen *Al-Kāfi*, he would have read the following ahād īth which are recorded before the had īth he has quoted.

"Ab ū Abdill āh said: 'No Bada ' occurs to Allah because of ignorance.'"

"Ab ū Abdill āh said: 'Verily, Bada ' does not occur to Allah because of ignorance.'"

"Mans ūr ibn H āzim says: I asked Ab ū Abdillāh: 'Can any thing happen today which was not in the knowledge of Allah yesterday?' He said: 'No. Whoever says it, may Allah humiliate

[2]Al-Kulaynī, *Al-Kāfi*, Al-Maktabah Al-Islamiyah, Tehran, 1388, vol. 1, p. 115.

him.' I said: 'Tell me, is it not that what has already happened and what is to happen up to the Day of Resurrection, is all in the knowledge of Allah?' He said: 'Certainly, even before He created the creatures.'"[3]

Incidentally, this is the belief of many of the Sunnis too, although they do not call it Bada'. It means that they too accept the meaning although they differ from us in the name. For example, look at the following quotations from three Sunni *tafāsīr*:

(1) Imām Fakhruddīn ar-Rāzī writes under the verse, "*Allah erases out whatever He pleases and writes (whatever He pleases): and with Him is the mother of the book.*" (Qur'an, 13: 39) "There are two sayings about this verse. First, that it is general (encompassing) all things, as the apparent wording demands. They say that Allah erases the sustenance and increases it; and likewise is the case of death and *sa'adah* (felicity) and *shaqāwah* (infelicity) and *Imān* and *Kufr*. This is (also) the belief of (the companion) Amr ibn Mas'ūd: and (the companion) Jabir has narrated it from the Messenger of Allah.

"Second, that it is restricted to some things, and there are many aspects of it: (1) Erasing and writing refers to abrogation of a previous order and bringing another order in its place.... (8) It concerns sustenance, and misfortunes and calamities, that Allah writes it in the book and then removes it through invocation and *sadaqah* (alms), and this contains exhortation to attach oneself exclusively to Allah Ta'ala... (10) He erases whatever He pleases from His orders without informing anyone about it, because He has the absolute authority to order as He pleases: and He has the independent authority to bring into being and to destroy, to give life and death, to make rich or poor, inasmuch as no one of His creatures is appraised of His *ghayb*."[4]

(2) Allama Az-Zamakhsharī writes under the verse, "*and no one whose life is lengthened has his life lengthened, nor is anything diminished of his life, but it is in a book: surely this is easy to Allah.*" (Qur'an, 35: 11) "It means, we do not increase a man's life or decrease it, but it is written in a book. That is, it is written in the

---

[3] Ibid.

[4] Imām Ar-Rāzī, *Tafsir Mafātihu 'l-ghayb*.

Lawh (Tablet) that: If that man performed hajj or participated in jihād then his life will be forty years; and if he did both, then his life will be sixty years. Now if he combined both and reached the age of sixty then his life was lengthened; and if he did only one (i.e., either hajj or jihād) and did not go beyond forty years, then it means that the life was shortened from the final limit of sixty. And it is this reality which the Messenger of Allah had pointed to in his saying: 'Verily *sadaqah* and good behavior towards relatives keep the homes populated and increase the lives.'"[5]

(3) Mufassir al-Qadī al-Baydawī writes under the same verse: "It is said that increase and decrease in a person's life occurs because of various causes which have been written in the Tablet. For example, it may be written in it that if Amr did hajj then his life will be sixty years; otherwise it will end at forty years."[6]

This unknown writer does not know his own religion or the writings of his own Ulama. Leave aside the writing, he cannot even pronounce correctly the names of the books of the Sunni scholars, and he has taken upon himself to write about the Shi'as. If this unknown author really desires to see what his co-religionists (Ahlul hadīth al-Hashawiyyah) believe about the knowledge and decision of Allah, he should read the report by Abul Fath Muhammad ibn Abdul-Karīm ash-Shahristānī (467-548 A.H.), quoted on pp. 30-31. It states: "And a group of Ashabul-hadīth al-Hashawiyah has explicitly declared their belief of Tashbih (i.e., Allah is like His creatures)... so much so that they have said that once Allah's both eyes were ailing, so the angels went to see Him; and that He wept (grieving) on Noah's flood until his eyes were inflamed."[7]

Why did Allah weep on Noah's flood? Was He not aware of the consequences when He had sent the flood? Should not this unknown writer offer his sympathies to his god as the angels had supposedly done?

---

[5] az-Zamakhsharī, *Tafsīr Al-Kashshāf*.

[6] al-Bayadāwī, *Tafsīr*.

[7] ash-Shahristānī, *Al-Milal wa 'n-Nihal* printed on the margin of *Kitābu'l-fasl* of ibn Hazm, p. 141.

Chapter: 7

SHI'AS AND THE QUR'AN

By

Imām Muhammad Jawad Chirri [1]

The late Egyptian Muslim scholar Muhammad Abū Zahrā said in his book *Al-Imām Al-Sādiq* that Muhammad Ibn Ya'qūb Al-Kulaynī, (a hadīth recorder who died in 329 A.H.), recorded in his book *Usūl Al-Kāfī* that the Imām Ja'far Al-Sādiq said that the Qur'an which was revealed to the Prophet Muhammad contained seven thousand verse, while the verses which we read in the Qur'an are only 6,262. The rest is treasured by the members of the House of the Prophet.

Sheikh Abū Zahrā issued a harsh judgment against the hadīth recorder Al-Kulaynī while Sheikh Al-Kulaynī is unable to defend himself because he met his Lord centuries ago. In spite of Sheikh Abū Zahra's harsh judgment against Al-Kulaynī, he did not try to accuse all the Shi'as with what he accused Al-Kulaynī. Al-Kulaynī's report concerning the incompleteness of the Qur'an is unacceptable to the Imamate Shiites (who are the overwhelming majority of the Shiites). They say that the Qur'an is complete without addition, deletion, or change.

Professor Muhammad Abū Zahrā in his book *Imām Al-Sādiq* said that Al-Safī, (a prominent Shiite scholar), said in his commentary on the Qur'an: "According to Sheikh Abū Ali Al-Tabarsī, another prominent Shiite scholar, 'there are no words added to the Qur'an. Any claim of added words is unanimously denied by the Shi'as. As to the deletion, some Shi'as and some Sunnis said that there is change or deletion. Our scholars deny that.'"

Sayed Al-Murtadha, another prominent Shi'a scholar, said: "....our certainty of the completeness of the Qur'an is like our certainty of the existence of countries or major events which are

---

[1] Reproduced from his book *The Shiites under Attack* (Chapter 1, *Do the Shiite Muslims Say That the Qur'an Is Incomplete*), Islamic Center of America in Chicago, 1986.

self-evident. Motives and reasons for recording and guarding the Holy Qur'an are numerous. Because the Qur'an is a miracle of the Prophethood and the source of Islamic knowledge and religious rule, their concern with the Qur'an made the Muslim scholars highly efficient concerning its grammar, its reading, and its verses."

With this unequalled concern, there is no possibility the Qur'an was changed or deleted in some parts. The mercenary writers (who only try to divide Muslims as a service to the hypocrite Muslim governments) should be informed of the following:

1. Al-Kulaynī is not an Imām of the Shi'as. He is only a hadīth recorder who reported what was conveyed to him through one or more sources. He did not say that he heard from Al-Imām Al-Sādiq. He only said that a hadīth came to him through some reporters. He did not live during the days of the Imām Al-Sādiq. As a matter of fact, he was born over a century after Al-Sādiq. He did not see any of the Imāms or the members of the House of the Prophet.

2. The reporters of the incompleteness of the Qur'an from the Sunnite are numerous. Al-Kulaynī was not the only scholar who reported the incompleteness of the Qur'an. There are many hadīth recorders, in the books of Sunni scholars, who reported that the Caliph Umar, Ayeshah, and a number of the companions of the Prophet said that the Qur'an is incomplete.

THE AUTHENTIC OF AL-BUKHARI

Al-Bukhārī recorded in his *Sahīh* (Authentic), Part Eight, and pages 209-210, that Ibn Abbas reported that Umar Ibn Al-Khattāb said in a discourse which he delivered during the last year of his caliphate:

"Certainly Allah sent Muhammad with the truth and revealed to him the Book. One of the revelations which came to him was the verse of stoning. We read it and understood it.

"The Messenger of God stoned and we stoned after him. I am concerned that if time goes on, someone may say 'By God, we do not find the verse of stoning in the Book of God'; thus, the

Muslims will deviate by neglecting a commandment the Almighty revealed.

"Stoning is in the Book of God. It is the right punishment for a person, who commits adultery if the required witnesses are available, or there was pregnancy without marriage or adultery is admitted."

Again, we used to read in what we found in the Book of God: "Do not deny the fatherhood of your fathers in contempt because it is disbelief on your part to be ashamed of the fatherhood of your fathers."

Similar reports were recorded by Imām Ahmad in part one of his *Musnad* (in the *Musnad* of Umar under the caption of the hadīth Al-Saqīfah, pages 47 and 55). Ibn Hishām recorded similar reports in his *Sīrah of the Prophet*, part 2, page 658, (second printing, 1955).

THE AUTHENTIC OF MUSLIM

Muslim in the seventh part of his *Sahīh* (commentary of Al-Nawawī) in the book of *Al-Zakāt* about the virtue of being satisfied with whatever God gives and about urging people to have that virtue, pages 139-140, reported that Abu Al-Aswad reported that his father said:

"Abū Musa al-Asharī invited the Qur'an readers of Basra. Three hundred readers responded to his invitation. He told them: 'You are the readers and the choice of the people of Basra. Recite the Qur'an and do not neglect it. Otherwise, a long time may elapse and your hearts will be hardened as the hearts of those who came before you were hardened.' We used to read a chapter from the Qur'an similar to Bara-ah in length and seriousness, but I forgot it. I can remember only these words from that chapter: 'Should a son of Adam own two valleys full of wealth, he would seek a third valley, and nothing would fill Ibn Adam's abdomen but the soil.' We used to read a chapter similar to the Musabbihāt and I forgot it. I only remember these words out of it: 'Oh you who believe, why you say what you do not do? Thus, a testimony will be written on your necks and you will be questioned about it on the Day of Judgment.'" These words which Abū Musa mentioned are obviously not from the Qur'an, nor are they similar to any of the words of God in the Qur'an. It is amazing that Abū Musa claims that two suras from the Qur'an are missing, one of them similar to Bara-ah (the chapter of Bara-ah contains 130 verses).

AYESHAH

Muslim also reported in the book Al-Ridhaa (book of nursing), part 10, page 29, that Ayeshah said the following:

"There was in what was revealed in the Qur'an that ten times of nursing known with certainty makes the nursing woman a mother of a nursed child. This number of nursings would make the woman 'harām' (forbidden) to the child. Then this verse was replaced by 'five known nursings' to make the woman forbidden to the child. The Prophet died while these words were recorded and read in the Qur'an."

UMAR SAID CHAPTER 33 IS INCOMPLETE

Al-Muttaqi Ali Ibn Husam Alddeen in his book *(Mukhtasar Kanz Al-ummāl*, printed on the margin of Imām Ahmad's Musnad, part two, page two), in his hadīth about chapter 33, said that Ibn Murdawayh reported that Huthaifah said: "Umar said to me 'How many verses are contained in the chapter of Al-Ahzāb?' I said '72 or 73 verses.' He said it was almost as long as the chapter of the Cow, which contains 286 verses, and in it there was the verse of stoning."

MUSTADRAK AL-SAHIHAIN

Al-Hakim al-Nisābūri in his book *Al-Mustadrak* in the book of commentary on the Qur'an, part two, page 224, reported that Ubay Ibn Ka'ab (whom the Prophet called the leader of Al-Ansār), said that the Messenger of God said to him: "Certainly the Almighty commanded me to read the Qur'an in front of you, and he read 'The unbelievers from the people of the Book and the pagans will not change their way until they see the evidence. Those who disbelieve among the people of the scripture and idolaters could not change until the clear proof came unto them. A Messenger from Allah, reading purified page...' " And of the very excellent part of it: "Should Ibn Adam ask for a valley full of wealth and I grant it to him, he would ask for another valley. And if I grant him that, he would ask for another valley. And if I grant him that, he would ask for a third valley. Nothing would fill the abdomen of Ibn Adam except the soil. God accepts the repentance of anyone who repents. The religion in the eyes of God is the Hanafiyah (Islam) rather than Yahudiya (Judaism) or Nasrāniya (Christianity). Whoever does good, his goodness will not be denied."

Al-Hakim said: "This is an authentic hadīth but the two sheikhs (Al-Bukhārī and Muslim) did not record it. Al-Thahabi also considered it authentic in his commentary (on Al-Mustadrak)."

Al-Hakim reported also that Obay Ibn Ka'ab used to read: "Those who disbelieved had set up in their heart the zealotry of the age of ignorance; and if you had a similar zealotry, the Sacred Mosque would have been corrupted, and God brought down His peace of reassurance upon His Messenger."

When this reading was conveyed to Umar, he became very angry with Obay. He sent for him while he was treating his she-camel with tar. He also invited other companions, including Zaid Ibn Thābit. Obay came to him. Omar asked: "Who among you would read the chapter of Al-Fatah (victory)? Zaid Ibn Thābit read the chapter the way we read it now. Omar spoke to Obay angrily. Obay said 'Shall I speak?' Omar said 'Speak out.' Obay said 'You know that I used to enter the house of the Prophet, and he used to teach me the reading of the Qur'an while you and others were by the door. If you want me to teach people the way the Prophet taught me, I will teach them; otherwise, I will not teach them one letter ever.' Umar said to him: 'Continue teaching people how to read.'"

Al-Hakim said this is authentic according to the standards of the two sheikhs (Al-Bukhārī and Muslim). However, they did not report it. Al-Thahabi also considered it authentic in his *Commentary on Al-Mustadrak*, part two, and pages 225-226.

If we take the report of Ibn Mardawayh which Huthaifah attributed to Umar in which he said that the chapter of Al-Ahzab, which contained 72 verses, was as long as the chapter of the Cow (which contained 287) and take the report of Abū Musa which says that a chapter equal in length to the chapter of Bara-ah (which contains 130 verses) was deleted from the Qur'an, then the deletion in the Qur'an according to these reports would be about 345 verses.

If this is true, what would be the difference between the deletion according to these reports and the report which is attributed to Al-Kulaynī that claims a deletion of 600 verses?

Furthermore, suppose that Al-Kulaynī had recorded in his book *Al-Kāfī* that some of the Qur'anic verses were deleted. Why should all the Shi'as be accused of the belief in the incompleteness of the Qur'an? Kulaynī is not an Imām of the Shi'as, and the Shi'as are not his followers. Al-Kulaynī was no more than a hadīth recorder. If a scholar like him makes a mistake, why should we attribute that mistake to the millions of Shi'as who are not even his followers?

If such an accusation is permissible, why should we not accuse all the Sunnis of the belief in the incompleteness of the Qur'an because they all are followers of Umar who was quoted by Al-Bukhārī, Muslim, Imām Ahmad, and Ibn Mardawayh to have said that the Qur'an was incomplete, and that more than 200 Qur'anic verses were deleted?

Why should the Caliph Umar, Ayeshah, Abū Musa, and Obay Ibn Ka'ab not be accused of the same thing because all of them stated the incompleteness of the Qur'an?

Accusing Muslims of Kufr or deviation is abhorable to God. We have been commanded by the Qur'an and the Prophet to consider anyone who declares that there is no God but Allah and that Muhammad is the Messenger of God to be a Muslim. Al-Bukhārī reported that Abdullāh Ibn Umar reported that the Messenger of God said: "When a person calls his Muslim brother a Kāfir, one of the two would carry the sin."

We believe that the Qur'an as it is now is the entire Qur'an without addition, subtraction, or change. It is the Qur'an in which no falsehood from the era of pre-revelation or post revelation entered it. It is a revelation from the Mighty, the Praised.

Allah promised that He will protect the Qur'an. He said *"Certainly We revealed the Reminder (the Qur'an), and certainly We shall preserve it."* (15:9)

It is the Qur'an through which the Messenger and the Members of his House commanded us to test the authenticity of every hadīth, and accept the hadīth which agrees with the Qur'an and reject the hadīth that disagrees with it.

We believe that whoever says that the Qur'an is incomplete, or was added to, or changed, is completely wrong. What was reported on this subject from Caliph Umar, Abū Musa, Obay Ibn Ka'ab, Al-Bukhārī, Imām Ahmad, Muslim, Al-Hakim, and Al-Kulaynī is completely rejected and absolutely unacceptable.

We certainly reject all of these reports, but we will not pass any judgment on any of the above mentioned reporters. Passing judgment belongs only to Allah.

It is hoped that what was offered on this subject is sufficient for those who try to find the truth, that the Shi'a Muslims are true believers deserving respect from their Sunni brothers. It is unbecoming of those who seek the truth to accuse others of a sin of which they are entirely not innocent, especially when the accusers have committed worse than that of which they accuse others.

CONCLUSION

Finally, I would like to say that Al-Kulaynī's report concerning the incompleteness of the Qur'an does not indicate that he believed in what he recorded. Al-Bukhārī, Muslim, Imām Ahmad, and Al-Hakim have reported that Umar, Ayeshah, and a number of companions stated that the Qur'an is incomplete. Yet we do not say that these hadīth recorders believed in what they recorded. I am inclined to believe that Al-Kulaynī did not subscribe to what he reported because he mentioned in his book *Al-Kāfī* that all ahādīth should be tested by the Book of God (the Qur'an). Whatever agrees with the Qur'an should be accepted, and whatever disagrees with the Qur'an should be rejected.

Al-Kulaynī mentioned in his introduction to his book: "Brother, may God lead you to the right road. You ought to know that it is impossible for anyone to distinguish the truth from the untruth when Muslim scholars disagree upon statements attributed to the Imāms. There is only one way to separate the true from the untrue reports, through the standard which was declared by the Imām: 'Test the various reports by the Book of God; what ever agrees with it take it, whatever disagrees with it reject it. Take what is agreed upon (by scholars). Certainly the universally accepted should not be doubted.'" These words indicate the Al-Kulaynī believed that the Book of God is the Qur'an which we read; otherwise, how can we test the various reports through the Book of God?

At the same time, these words indicate that the reports which indicated the incompleteness of the Qur'an should be rejected because they are in disagreement with the Book of God, which declares: "*Certainly We (the Almighty) have revealed the Reminder (the Qur'an), and We shall preserve it.*"

The Imām said: "Take the agreed upon, for the agreed upon by the Islamic scholars should not be doubted." And we know that the Book of God is the one on which all the Islamic scholars agree.

Chapter: 8

KALIMA IN THE QUR'AN

By

Dr. S. Manzoor Rizvi

In the Qur'an there is no Ayat defining and specifying that this is the Kalima which each Muslim is obliged to profess. The Qur'an underlines the fundamental beliefs without which no one can be called a Muslim. These fundamental beliefs of Islam are:

1. *Tauhīd* (Absolute Oneness of Allah)
2. *Nabuwat* (Prophethood or the infallible medium through which God communicates with mankind)
3. *Qiyāmah* (the Day of Resurrection, Judgment and accountability of actions)

The Prophet called upon the people of Mecca to (say) *'Qūlū Lā Ilāha Illallāh, Tuflihū'* 'say no God but (one) Allah, and you will reap benefits'. As such the basic *Kalima* (words carrying the cardinal articles of belief) is *'Lā Ilāha Illallāh, Muhammadu-r-rasūl ullah'* (There is no gods but God and Muhammad is His Messenger). This minimum expression is the core of the entire corpus of Islam, and commonly shared, believed and observed by all the sects of Islam.

The five *Kalimas* of the Sunnis including this core *Kalima* are prescribed of their own accord without having any support from the Qur'an or Sunna.

The Shi'as, too, believe the basic Kalima to be *'Lā Ilāha Illallāh, Muhammadu-r-rasūl ullah'*, The addition of *'Aliyun Wali-ullah'* is an inseparable supplement inherent in *'Muhammadu-r-rasūl ullah'* As Muhammad was the last prophet, it was the highest responsibility of his office to make sure that after him no deviations, distortions, and misrepresentation of Islamic facts as revealed to the Prophet and articulated by him to the community-in-faith, may take place. History has the irrefutable evidence that after the departure of a prophet, the people would seek to alter the text of the revealed book and indulge in misinterpreting the laws as would fit to their desires and selfish needs. But the next prophet would come and reorient the distorted matters to their correct and original place. As Muhammad was the last prophet, and no next prophet was expected to come and rectify God's religion, he had the utmost obligation to leave behind him an error-proof chain of infallible, knowledgeable, and morally sound and wise men to guard Islam from any unlawful innovation and alteration carrying divisions in the community of Islam and damaging its solidarity. So he left nothing to doubt that after him the charge of leading Islam will be undertaken by Imam Ali, just as the Prophet had handled its leadership till the last sermon of his prophetic-career. As Imam Ali shared Prophet's knowledge, wisdom, purity, and piety and the excellence of virtues, his vice regency (*Wilayah*) was publicly announced by the Prophet after his return from his pilgrimage, on 18th Zul-Hijjah 10 A.H. on the plain of 'Ghadeer' in the broad day-light. So Imam Ali's *Wilayah* is an inherent component of the office of the prophethood of the last Prophet.

Believing in Muhammad as the messenger of Allah implies to be faithful to his last most important message namely the continuation of Divine Guidance through the chain of the infallible Imams, the first of whom is Imam Ali. So *'Aliyun wali-ullah'* is not an addition but a continuation of the belief that 'Muhammad is the Messenger of Allah, which is the inseparable part of the basic *Kalima*. So Shi'a's basic *Kalima* is the same and the addition of *'Aliyun-Wali-ullah'* only reminds that they did not change the verdict and command of the Prophet either by vote or by any other mode of alteration adopted against the Qur'an and Sunna.

Chapter: 9

SHI'A- SUNNI DIFFERENCES IN OFFERING PRAYERS

Dr. S. Manzoor Rizvi[1]
AND
Maulana Syed Rizwan Rizvi

There are some other points relating to theology whereon the Shi'as differ from the Sunnis who raise objection to the beliefs of Shi'as with regard to those points in the Shi'a theology; but if any one makes a thorough research, it will confirm that the Shi'as have strong grounds therefore. Some of these points are purely academic and relate to the grammar of the Arabic language, such as the pronunciation of the Arabic words occurring in Qur'an, but the argument put forth by the Shi'a scholars even in this particular regard is not without basis; it has support of several Sunni scholars, including the Hanbalīs, Mālikīs and the Shāfi'īs. These are discussed below briefly for the benefit of our readers.

THE ABLUTION

Take the case of ablution first; the belief of the Shi'a in this regard is that washing of feet is not necessary, because it has not been ordained by Allah in the Qur'an. They argue that the word 'wash' occurring in the verse of the Qur'an relating to ablution is restricted to the faces and hands and the word of 'Masah' (wipe or rub with fingers) applies to both, the head and the feet.

Imām Rāzī, a great Sunni 'Ālim says: "Let the word be pronounced any way it would remain in the objective case and covered by the order of Masah and not by wash."[2] Sheikh Muhaiyuddīn Ibne 'Arabī, another great Sunni scholar has endorsed the views of Imām Rāzī. This amply proves Shi'a's view point regarding 'Masah' of the feet.[3]

---

[1] Excerpted from the title *Shiaism Explained* (various chapters), No Author, Peermahomed Ebrahim Trust, Karachi: Pakistan, 1972

[2] *Tafsīr Kabīr*, vol 3, p.368.

[3] *Futūhāte Makkiyah*, vol.1 p.448.

FURTHER PROOF

Nawāb Siddique Hasan Khan, a great scholar of Ahle Hadīth while explaining the verse of the Qur'an relating to ablution has reported Qartabī saying on the authority of Hazrat Ibne Abbās, a companion of the Prophet who has said that ablution consists of two washings and two Masahs. He has also said that Akrame used to perform ablution with two washings and two Mashas saying that there was no divine order for the washing of feet in ablution, also adding that the revelation in this regard consisted of Masah only. A'mirush Shabaī also said that the angel Gabriel had come down with the commandment of Allah for Masah of the feet. What Qatada has said in this regard is also note-worthy. He has mentioned two washing and two Masahas as ordained by Allah.[4] The Prophet also performed Masah of his feet, with fingers while performing Wudū (ablution).[5] Imām Ali used to perform ablution with Masah of his feet. Imām Muhammad Bāqir, Ibne Omar, Alqama, Hasan Basrī, Jābir and Ibne Zaid, etc. also performed Masah of their feet in ablution.[6]

Hāfiz Ibne Hajar Asqalani in his explanatory notes on *Sahīh Bukhārī* entitled *Fathul Bārī* (part I, p. 187) has agreed that Imām Ali, Ibne Abbās and Anas were against the washing of feet in ablution, but he has simultaneously put forth an excuse that all these three personalities had gone back on it and turned to their original practice in this regard. But it appears to be lame rather strange excuse, because it amounts to the claim that Imām Ali and two well-known Ashāb, Ibne Abbās and Anas after

---

[4] *Tafsīr Fathul Bayān* by Allama Siddique Hasan Khan of Bhopal, part 1. p. 693. In this connection *Tafsīr Tarjumānul Qur'an* by the same author, vol. 3, page 842 may also be referred to.

[5] *Isāba Fī Tamyizis Sahāba* by Hāfiz Hajar Asqalani, vol. 1 p. 192; *Tafsīr Ibne Jurair Tabri*, vol. x, p. 75; *Sharhe Ma'ānī ul-Āsar Thānwī*, vol. 1, p. 21; *Nailul Autār Sharkānī*, vol 1. p. 164; *Kanz ul-Ummāl* by Allma Ali Muttaqi bin Hisamuddin. Vol.v; *musnad of Tamim bin Zaid Mazani*, p. 102 (Hadīth No. 2193); *Kanz ul-Ummāl* (musnad Hazarat Ali , p. 147 (Hadīth No 2403).

[6] *Sharhe Ma'ānī ul-Āsar Thānwī*, vol. 1, p. 21. Also see *Musnad Ahmed Hanbal*, vol.1, p 116, *Taijumānul Qur'an* by Siddique Hassan of Bhopal, vol. III, p. 842, and *Tafsīr Kabīr* of Fakhurddīn Rāzī, vol. III p. 363. For any further proof with regard to the fact that only masah of the feet in the performance of ablution has been ordained by Allah, *Umdatut Tafsīr Ma'ālimāt Tanzīl* on the margin of *Tafsīr Khāzin*, part II, p. 16 may be referred to.

performing ablution according to the practice of the Prophet and with him side by side had (God forbid) first gone back on their original practice and proclaimed to be against it, (God forbid) and then (God forbid) turned to the original practice again which is not only contradictory in itself but contrary to all the historical records available on the subject some of which have already been referred to by us.

The last excuse wherein those who are against Masah of the feet in ablution take shelter in the claim that washing of feet therein has been the practice of the Prophet and therefore, they follow it as Sunna. This last excuse is also strange as any thing else, because the Prophet could never act against the clear commandment of Allah in this regard, it being against the sacred status of his prophethood. This is a clear proof of the fact that washing of feet while performing ablution is not a tradition of the Prophet in support of which we have already quoted several authorities on history as well as the traditions of the Prophet.

In the end it must be remembered that if the ablution is not performed according to the word of Allah, the prayers shall go null and void.

PRAYERS

BEGINNING AND END

It is a well known fact that the Prophet used to begin all his prayers with *al-Hamd*, the word with which Surah Fātiha starts and he also used to end it with *takbīr* (Praises of Allah with words 'God is Great').[7]

It must be remembered that *Bismilla hir-Rahmā nir-Rahīm* (In the name of Allah, the beneficent, the Merciful) is the first verse of Surah Fātīha (*al-Hamd*) and is, therefore, a part and parcel thereof.[8] Imām Jalāluddīn Suyūtī, a Sunni Scholar, has reworded a

---

[7] *Sahīh Bukhārī*, printed in Egypt, vol: I, chp. on prayers, p. 100; *Sahīh Muslim* with Urdu translation and notes by Nowi (Arabic); published Saudia Press, Karachi, vol. II, pps. 74 and 75; *Mishkāt* with translation (Urdu), Saeedi Press, Karachi, vol. I, p. 183.

[8] *Sharhe Ma'ānī ul-Āsār Thānwī*, vol. I, pages 117-18; *Sunan Kubra Baihaqī*, printed at Hyderabad (Deccan), vol. II, pages, 44 and 45.

tradition reported by Dar Qutni, Hakim and Baihaqī on the authority of Abu Huraira to the effect that the Prophet used to recite *Bismillah* in prayer audibly.[9] Imām Ali believed in reciting *Bismillah* audibly in all his prayers.[10]

All the Ale Muhammad were unanimous on reciting *Bismillah* in prayers audibly.[11]

Āmīn: To say Āmīn (Amen) in prayers is an innovation according to a unanimous accord of all the Ale Muhammad (Imām Shaudani in his *Nadīmal Autār*, together with marginal notes (Awnul Bārī) thereon.

Qunūt: It has to be remembered that the Shi'as recite Qunūt in prayers taking it to be Sunna (practice of the Prophet and not as *farz* (ordained by Allah in the Qur'an). All authentic records are unanimous on the fact that the Prophet used to recite Qunūt in his prayers. Some of these records are:

(1) *Sahīh Muslim,* Nawal Kishore vol. I, p 237, also translation of *Sahīh Muslim* by Alama Waheed-uz-zama, Siddqui Press, Lahore, p. 754-55. (2) *Faqhae Omar* by Shah Waliullah Muhaddith of Delhi, p 68. (3) *Sunane Nisā'ī* Translated by Allama Waheed-uz-zaman, Maktabe Ayubia, Karachi vol. I, p 270 Ch: Al-*Qunnot Fī Salātil Maghrib*, reported by Bara bin Aszib (a companion of the prophet). (4) *Mishkat* (translation, Saeedi Press, Karachi vol. I, Babul Qunnot, pp. 290-91).

RAISING OF HANDS

The Holy Prophet used to raise his hands with each and every Takbīr (Allaho-Akbar) in all his prayers. (*Sahīh Muslim* translation read with marginal note by Nayi Maktabe Saudia, Karachi, vol. II, page 10; *Sunane Abū Dāwūd* (Arabic) printed in Egypt; ch: 1 (Raf-ul-

---

[9] *Durre Manthūr,* vol. I, p. 8.

[10] *Tafsīr Kabīr Fakhruddīn Rāzī,* vol. I, p. 159, also *Sunane Kubra Baihaqi,* vol. II, p. 48.

[11] *Nadīmal Autār* by Imam Shaukānī, together with the marginal notes (*Awnul Bārī,* vol. II, p.91). For further clarification regarding recitation of Bismillah audibly in prayers the following record may also be referred to, if necessary (1) *Dar Qutni,* Faruqi Press, Delhi, pp. 114 and 116; (2) *Izālatul Khifa* by Shah Waliullah Muhaddith of Delhi, Saeedi Press, Karachi, p, 162; (3) *Kanz ul-Ummāl,* Dāeratul Maarif Press, Hyderabad (Deccan), vol. IV p. 96; and also Hadīth No. 2004, p. 209 and Hadīth No. 4480, p. 210.

Yadain), page 269; and *Hujjatul Bāligha* (Arabic) by Shah Walliullah Muhaddith of Delhi, printed at Boolaque Press, Egypt, Page 10).

COMBINING PRAYERS

Without any cause like traveling or rain, the Prophet used to say his two prayers together i.e., *Dhuhr* and *Asr*; *Maghrib* and *Ishā*. For a proof of the above the following records unanimously acknowledged by all the Sunnis may be referred to. These are:

(1) Translation of *Sahīh Bukhārī*, Saeedi Press Karachi, vol. I. (2) *Kitābul Mawāqītus Salāt*, Ch: 5 Hadīth No. 532, page 272. (3) Translation of *Sahīh Muslim* together with *Sarhe Navi*, Maktabe Saudia, Karachi vol. page 258 or Al Muslim Translation of *Sahīh Muslim*, Siddiqui Press Lahore, pp. 754-55. (4) *Sunane* Abū Dāwūd (Arabic), Saada Press, Egypt, p.8 Ahadīth Nos. 1210 and 1211. (5) *Sharhe Ma'āniul Āsār Thānwī*, Islamia, Press, Lahore, vol. I, page 95. (6) *Moatta Imām Mālik* (Arabic), Nur Muhammad Asahhul Matabe, Karachi, page 126. (7) Allama Wahid-uz-zman of Hyderabad (Daccan), a great scholar of Ahle Hadīth says as follows: "Saying two prayers together without any excuse, journey or rains is allowed, but it is better to say them separately."[12] .

Some people criticize the Shi'as for combining the five prayers, offering them at only three times. They combine the *Dhuhr* and *'Asr* prayers and the *Maghrib* and *Ishā'* prayers, whereas the Prophet and Muslims offer them at their five specified times.[13]

The Answer: According to the opinion of the majority of scholars, it has been established that the Prophet combined the *Dhuhr* and *'Asr* prayers without fear (of war) or traveling. The author of *Jāmi'ul-Usūl*, vol. 6 p. 459 quoting from the *Sahīh* of Muslim says, "The Prophet offered the *Dhuhr* and *'Asr* prayers at one time without being in a state of fear or while traveling." He added that az-Zubeir said, "I asked Sa'īd, 'Why did the Prophet do that?' He answered, 'I asked ibn Abbās about this and he

---

[12] *Hadyatul Mehdi*, vol. I, p. 109.

[13] This and the subsequent three paragraphs excerpted from Abū Tālib At-Tabrīzī, *Spurious Arguments about the Shi'a*, Ansariyan Publications, Qum, Iran, 2001.

answered: 'The Prophet did not want to cause difficulty for the umma.'" In another quotation, he added, "without fear and there was no rain."

It has been established from the tradition of the infallible Imāms that when the sun passes the zenith, it is the time for the two prayers but this (the first prayer) is before that (the second prayer). Similarly, when the evening comes, it is time for the two prayers but *Maghrib* is before *Ishā'*.

Allah has permitted the joining of the prayers and His Messenger did so without any purpose other than of making it easy for his umma. Why should Muslims have to make it difficult upon them just to make the separation of the prayers obligatory and sometimes miss the *'Asr* and the *Ishā'* which has happened not only to ordinary people but to some of the Sunni scholars as well?

RECENT FATWA OF COMBINING PRAYERS

In October 2008, Turkish Muslims have been allowed through a fatwa to pray only three times a day in view of their modern day heavy commitment with work or personal issues. Taking cognizance of the Sunni Sharī'ah law which allows for the possibility of offering prayers three times a day in case of sickness or travel the fatwa extends this option without mentioning practice of the Prophet of saying two prayers together. The Turkish fatwa echoes a similar fatwa that has already taken place in Egypt. They are reverting to an age-old practice of combining the *Dhuhr* and *'Asr*; *Maghrib* and *Ishā'* prayers. (See Appendix 3)

SAJDAGAH FOR PROSTRATION

Imām Bukhārī has recorded: Abdul Walīd, Shuaba, Sulaymān Shaibānī and Abdullāh bin Shaddād have narrated on the authority of Hazrat Maimūna that the Prophet used to put his forehead on *Khumra* (tablet made of clay) while in the state of prostration.[14] Khumra is the one on which the Shi'as now put their foreheads in prayers while in the state of prostration."[15]

---

[14] For further proof refer to *Sunane Kubra Baihaqī*, p. 421.

[15] *Majma' Bihārul Anwār* by Allama Muhammad Tahir, Nawal Kishore Press, vol. I, p. 377. Maulana Ahmed Raza Khan, the chief of the Barelvi group of Sunnis

Part One: The Truth

KEEPING HANDS STRAIGHT

The famous scholar Allama Muhammad Ismail alias Shaheed of Deeoband, author of the book. *Taqwiyatul Īmān*, and in his other book, *Tanwīrul Ainain*, (Arabic) says as follows:

"But as far as keeping hands straight in prayers is concerned as has been narrated (as a tradition) by some Tābe'īn (immediate successors of the companions of the Prophet such as Hasan Basrī. Ibrahim, Ibne Mussayyab and Ibne Sirīn) and also reported by Ibn Shaiba, it is apparent that these personalities if at all heard any thing else (such as folding the hands in prayers), they did not accept that as a directive tradition of the Prophet but only a habit of praying later adopted by the Sahaba and the Tābe'īn for their convenience. They therefore, followed their previous practice under the tradition of the Prophet."

Therefore, they did not adopt the new practice but kept on practicing the previous form thereof that is, praying with straight hands. (Translation of Arabic from *Tanwīrul Ainain*, Din Muhammadi Press, Lahore, p. 30). *Rawdatun Nādia*, p. 65 may also be referred to in this regard, if necessary.

Maulana Muhammad Ismail of Deeoband has also said in his above mentioned book (*Tanwīrul Ainain*, p. 21) to the effect that it is generally said that insofar as the religious order with regard to keeping the hands straight is concerned it is still in force as it was in the life of the Prophet and in the immediately succeeding period thereafter, and the religious scholars remained unanimous thereon till late. Further Maulana Ismail of Deoband has said that as this practice resembled the one followed by the Shi'as others might have given it up and it were only the Shi'as then who continued to follow the original practice.

Note: It is to be remembered that the Mālikīs who follow the fiqh of Imām Mālik follow the original practice of praying with straight hands and are in agreement with the Shi'as therein,

---

has mentioned Allama Muhammad Tāhir as "a great scholar and Muhaddith." (*Hayātul Mawāt*, p. 85, by Maulana Ahmad Raza Khan, Nuri Kutib Khana, Bazaar Data Sahib, Lahore).

whereas various groups among the Sunnis are divided amongst themselves and keep their hands folded in prayers in different place and forms, that is, praying with folded hands is not sufficient for them but it varies in form from group to group among the Sunnis, whereas the Shi'as and the Mālikīs are united in praying with straight hands and only in one form. Allama Aini says in commentary on *Kanz-ud-Daqāiq*, p, 25: "Said Imām Mālik that the confirmed order in this regard is that the hand must be kept straight but folding of the hands is also allowed."

Mufti Abdul Hai Fārūqī Firangi Mehalli has accepted the existence of tradition regarding keeping the hands straight while saying prayers. According to what he has offered is an interpretation in this regard to the effect that this order applies only to keeping the hands straight for a while before starting the prayers. (Fatwa Abdul Hai, Yūsufī)

It is a queer explanation in view of the unanimous explanation of Imām Mālik and his follower as well as that of Hasan Basrī, Ibrahim Ibne Musayyab and Ibne Sirīn as already quoted from *Tanwīrul Ainain*. Besides, when folding of hands in this regard has been proved, to be a new practice requiring a religious evidence according to what Allama Ismail Dehlive Deobandi said as already quoted, this interpretation or explanation provided by the said Maulana Firangi Mehalli does not stand any where but loses the ground.

While writing a marginal note on *Mowatta*, Imām Mālik (called *Kashful Mughatta*), Maulana Ashfāqur Rehmān of Kandhla has said that according to what Imām Mālik said that he (Imām Mālik) was not even aware of (the report) about the hands in the obligatory prayers and that he thought it to be a detestable practice. But he allowed it in *Nawafil* (extra prayers) which are spread over long periods. Perhaps to have the convenience to save the strength for standing for longer periods in *Nawafil* he allowed it. (*Kashful Mughatta* explanatory notes on *Mowatta*, Imām Mālik, p. 142.)

In case any further proof with regard to the original practice followed by the Shi'as in respect of keeping the hands straight down in all prayers is required, if at all required, the following documents which are unanimously acknowledged by the Sunni scholars and regarded to be the most authentic may be referred to:

(1) *Sharhe Sahīh Muslim* by Novi, vol. 1, p. 173.

(2) *Kibrīte Ahmar* (marginal notes on Al Yuwagest ul Jawahir), p. 51.

(3) *Nail ul Autar* by Imām Shaukani, together with the marginal notes therein called *Aunul Bari*, vol. II, p. 72.

(4) *Taiseerul Wusool Ila jameul usool*, p. 327.

(5) *Jameul Fawaed Min jameul Usool* by Ibne Ather, p.73-74

FASTING

Another difference between Shi'as and Sunnis which is markedly witnessed during Ramadan is in (Iftār) breaking of fast. Sunnis break their fast immediately after sunset whereas Shi'as wait for start of the night which comes eight to nine minutes later. Yet another difference is that Shi'as break their fast after offering *Maghrib* prayers and Sunni brothers first break their fast and then offer *Maghrib* prayers. For our Sunni brothers the fast becomes *Makruh* if it is not terminated by eating or drinking at the sunset. Shi'as do not have to break their fast by eating or drinking. Once the night starts the fasting is over and they can eat or drink after finishing their single or both prayers i.e., *Maghrib* and *Isha*. Let us look at the Qur'anic verse in this respect.

The Qur'an says: *"Eat and drink until the white streak of dawn becomes distinguishable from darkness. Complete your fast till the night appears..."*(2:187) Our brothers of Ahle Sunnat break their fasts right at sunset, while it's still bright outside, contrary to the verse of the Quran which clearly states that, *"...and complete your fasts when its night time..."*(2:187) The Quran did not use the word evening to distinguish the fact that there is a fine line between night and evening time. If the sun's disc disappears from the horizon it doesn't necessarily mean that its night time yet, and this is where the Quran is drawing our attentions. Just the same way after sunrise it takes about eight minutes for the first rays of sun to reach the earth; it takes time for its rays to disappear as well.

The word night stands for that part of the natural day when the sun is beneath the horizon, or the time from sunset to sunrise, especially, the time between dusk and dawn, when there is no light of the sun, but only moonlight, starlight, or artificial light.

It is Mustahab that a person breaks his fast after offering *Maghrib* and *'Ishā'* prayers. However, if he feels terribly inclined to eat, so much that he can not concentrate on the prayers, or if someone is waiting for him, it is better that he should break his fast first and offer the prayers later. However, as far as possible, he should try to offer the prayers during the prime time (Fadīlat).[16]

Another interesting point which is made apparent from this verse is the difference between the two mornings, known as *Sādiq* and *Kāzib*. Therefore, at the end of the night the first whiteness, very insignificant, appears on the sky vertically is resembled to the tail of a cat, which is known as the false morning (Subhe Kāzib). But after a short while the whiteness is spread horizontally on the sky, resembling the white thread which is extending alongside the darkness of night, this is the true morning (Subhe Sādiq). This is the official start of the day, time for Fadīlat al-fajr[17], and also the time for *Imsāk* (Seher). As a recommended precaution one should stop eating a few minutes before Subhe Sādiq.

In *Sahīh Bukhārī* narrated by Anas: Zaid bin Thābit said: "We took the Seher (the meal taken before dawn while fasting is observed) with the Prophet and then stood up for the (morning) prayer." I asked him how long the interval between the two (Seher and prayer) was? He replied: The interval between the two was just sufficient to recite fifty to sixty *Āyāt*.[18]

TARĀWĪH

There is no proof to the effect that the Prophet ever said any prayer by the name of Tarāwīh (extra prayer in the month of Ramadan) at night except Tahajjud. This is what has been recorded by Bukhārī, on the authority of Ayeshah.

Bukhārī says: "It has been narrated by Abū Salma bin Abdur Rehman that once he asked Ayeshah as to how did the Prophet

---

[16] *Islamic Laws*, Ayatullāh Sistānī, p. 319
[17] *Tafsīr Namūnah*, vol. 1, pp. 654-655.
[18] *Sahīh Bukhārī*, vol. 1, Book 10, (Times of Prayers).

pass his nights during the month of Ramadan in as much as the prayers are concerned." To this Ayeshah replied that he, the Prophet never said more than eleven *Rak'āt* (units) of his prayer (Tahajjud) at night, may it be Ramadan or not (Urdu translation with original text of *Sahīh Bukhārī*, Nur Muhammad Asahhul Mata'bea, part 8, vol. I, *Kitābus-Sawm* (Namāze Tarāwīh), Tradition No. 1857, p. 448). A similar narration is contained in the translation (with original text) of *Sahīh Muslim*, published by Maktaba Saudia, Karachi, vol. II, p. 227.

Allama Waheed-uz-zaman of Hyderabad, a well-known scholar of Ahle Hadīth, after giving details of the prayer called Tahajjud, says in his famous book entitled *Hadiyyatul Mehdi* (vol. I, p. 109) to the following effect: "Like Tahajjud, Tarāwīh in Ramadān is believed by Ahle Hadīth to be sunna, but that too, is Tahajjud." It is better known to him as to why Allama Waheed-uz-zman has confined Tarāwīh to the month of Ramadan when he has admitted in his statement quoted above that Tarāwīh is Tahajjud and that it is nothing but Tahajjud. A natural question arises here as to when Tarāwīh is Tahajjud and why it is restricted to Ramadān? Being Tahajjud, as admitted by Allama Waheed-uz-zaman himself, it could be said at any night, without restriction, as sunna. This is already roved by a quotation from *Sahīh Bukhārī*. It appears that the Ahle Hadīth are in the habit of naming Tahajjud as Tarāwīh during Ramadān and after the month of Ramadān is over they rename it Tahajjud. Otherwise, we are at a loss to understand the above statement of the Allama which on the face of its words is Latin and Greek to us.

TAHAJJUD IN CONGREGATION

As it is known to each and every Muslim, Tahajjud or any *Nawafil* prayers are never said in congregation. That is why to one who ordered it to be a compulsory feature in the month of Ramadān himself called it a "Good new thing," a good innovation for the Muslims as is evident by what is contained in *Sahīh Bukhārī* in this regard. (*Sahīh Bukhārī*, ch. 8, also *Mishakāt*, (Urdu Translation), vol. I, Hadīth No. 1216. p 239.) For details also see: (1) *Al-Fārūq* by Shamsul Ulama Shiblī Numānī, (Printed at Mansur, Press, Lahore) Part 2, p. 663. (2) Urdu Translation of *Tārīkhul Khulafā' Suyūtī*, p 73-74. (3) *Hayātul Haiwān Muhammad*

Rasūlullāh by Muhammad Raza of Egypt, p.129. (4) *Tārīkh Abul Fida*, Printed in Egypt, vol. I, p. 174. (5) *Intiqād ur-Rajīh* by Sidique Hasan of Bhopal, p 62-63.

ĀZĀN AND TAKBĪRĀT IN FUNERAL PRAYERS

The Arabic sentences framed for the Āzān (call for prayers) still stand as a bone of contention between the two sects of the Muslims, that is, the Shi'as and the Sunnis. The following records we believe will remove the doubt from the minds of those readers of this book who still think that the Shi'as are responsible for adding or deleting some words and sentences in the earliest set up of the Āzān as well as fixing the number of the *takbīr* (Greatness of Allah) in the funeral prayers.

Hayya 'Ala Khairil Amal: These words, which denote that the caller is calling the Muslims to join the congregation for prayers, are not new but they were included in the Āzān in the lifetime of the Prophet and deleted from it thereafter. Leaving the question aside as to who deleted them and substituted them by the words *Assalātu Khairun Minan Nawm* (Prayers are better than sleep) only in the morning prayers the fact remains that it is the Shi'as who still follow the original practice in the matter and are correct. The following records collected and compiled by the reputed Sunni scholars will bear a testimony to it: (1) *Nadīmul Autār*, Imām Shaukānī, vol. I, p.39. (2) *Sahīh Muslim* (with translation), vol. II, p. 10. (3) *Kanz ul-Ummāl*, vol, IV Hadīth No. 5489, p. 266. (4) *Al-Fārūq*, part II, p.663. (5) *Rawdatul Ahbāb*, by Muhaddith Jamāluddīn, p. 307. (6) Urdu translation of *Izālatul Khifa* by Shah Waliullah Muhaddith of Delhi, p. 158. (7) *Tehqīq-e-Ajīb* by Muftī Abdul Hayī Fārūqī Firangi Mehali, p. 5. (8) *Mowatta*, Imām Mālik (Arabic), Chapter on Āzān, p. 57. As far the adding of *Ash-Hadu-Anna Amīr al Mominīn waliullāh*, it is said by Shi'as as Sunnat and is not *Wājib*.

Takbīrāt in Funeral Prayers: For coming to a correct conclusion regarding the original number of Takbīrāt in the funeral prayers and as to when and by whom these were restricted to only four instead of five as believed by the Shi'as, the following works by three outstanding Sunni scholars may be referred to: (1) *Al-Fārūq* by Shiblī Numani printed at Mansur Press, Lahore, p. 663; (2) *Tārīkhul*

Khulfa Suyūtī (Urdu), Siddique Press, Lahore, pp. 73-74; and (3) *Tārīkh Abdul Fida* (Arabic), printed in Egypt, vol. I, p. 174.

COMPARISON (*QIYĀS*) PROHIBITED

To make *qiyās* or comparison of any kind in religious matters is prohibited by all the Imāms in the lineage of the descendants of the Prophet whose orders are obeyed to the letter by all the Shi'as, although they are made target of several objections therefor. That *Qiyās* has no religious sanction. Allama Waheeduzzaman, a great scholar of Ahle Hadīth says about it in the relevant chapter of his translation of *Sahīh Muslim*. He says; "A religious order is only the one which is proved by any tradition of the Prophet and no *Qiyās* on ones part is allowed in this regard, particularly when it stands contrary to the clear orders of the Prophet in any case, notwithstanding the concurrence of the whole (Muslim) world thereon."[19]

The Decision of Ahlul Bayt: The Ahlul Bayt, as has also been admitted by several Sunni scholars, were not in favor of any *Qiyās* in the religious matters. Sheikh Muhammad Mo'īn of Lahore has said in plain words in his book entitled *Dirāsatul Labīb* that the twelve Imāms of the lineage of descendants of the Prophet did not believe in *Qiyās* with regard to any religious matter. Preceding that the above named author has narrated an incident to the effect that Imām Ja'far Sādiq once addressed a well- known (Muslim) personality saying; "I hear that you are in the habit of making your own *Qiyās* in the religious matter. Don't do it (in future.) Verily the one who made a *Qiyās* for the first time was *Iblīs* (Satan)."[20]

---

[19]*Sahīh Muslim*, Urdu translation by Allama Waheed-uz-zaman together with explanatory notes by Novi, vol II, p. 277.
[20] *Dirāsatul Labīb*, by Sheikh Muhammad Mo'īn of Lahore, published by Sindhi Adabi Board, Karachi, P. 45.

PART TWO: THE BASIS

Chapter: 10

THE PURITY OF PROPHETS

By

Various Authors[1]

The Merciful and Wise God inspired the prophets, so that through their leadership and guidance human society might recognize the right way as opposed to the precipitous way, and might be able to stride up to the highest peaks of true pride, perfection and laudable virtues, and stay on that way.

With the same intention, the Merciful and Wise God also made His prophets and messengers immune from every kind of sin and error, and in one word, made "faultless" (*ma'sūm*), so that they might be able to lead mankind towards real elevation in all directions, and towards obedience and submission to the commands of God without any error or mistake.

PROPHETS MUST BE MA'SUM

It is obvious that the very same reason which prompted the need for prophethood and the sending of prophets also requires that the prophets be immaculate and immune from all kinds of sin, impurity, error, and fault. Since the aim and purpose of sending prophets is to lead society towards guidance and instruction, this aim is to be secured through the faultlessness of the prophets and messengers, for it is clear that to do things which are repulsive or indecent, to sin, and also to be a source of error and fault is a reason for people to be averse to and diverted from these things, and thus the aim, which was the guidance and instruction of society, would be lost.

Of course, we know that no wise person does things against his aim, and that he takes regard for what is effectual in attaining and reaching his aim. For example, someone who wants a number of distinguished individuals to take part in a celebration in his

---

[1] Reproduced from the book, *Roots of Religion*, No Author, Noor-e-Islam Imambarah, Faizabad: India, 1986.

honor knows that no one without an invitation can honorably attend. He will never send an invitation to someone who is averse to him, rather he will try to send his invitations in such a way that they will all be accepted, and, if he doesn't do this, his work will not have been prudent and wise, and it will be regarded as having been unseemly and unbecoming.

The Merciful and Wise God also takes account of what basically interferes with the guidance and education of society, and does not want people to depend on and follow the will of capricious and impure men, and so to end up far from, and be deprived of their true development. Therefore He has sent immaculate prophets so that the guidance and instruction of society might be in the best possible way.

And now we shall read in more detail why the prophets must be without fault.

THE PRINCIPLE OF INSTRUCTION

The purpose of sending prophets was to educate humanity, and we know that in teaching the teacher's behavior is a more effective instrument than his speaking verbal instruction.

The habits and deeds of the teacher can bring about a radical transformation in man, because, on the basis of the principle of imitation, one of the indisputable principles of the working of the mind, man gradually adopts the manner and conduct of his teacher, and becomes of the same color, so that it is as if he is the clear, limpid surface of a pool which reflects the image of the sky above him.

Speech alone can not play the part of instruction, rather it serves instruction, and this is the idea of the prophetic mission, that prophets must possess praiseworthy habits and qualities and must be untainted with sin and error so that they can effectively attract the people of this world towards the sacred aim.

It is clear that one who has soiled his hands with sin, even though in secret and without anyone being aware so that he himself remains pure in the eyes of his fellow men, will never have that unwavering strength of mind to bring about a radical transformation in the area of the human spirit. One who taints his lips with wine can never dissuade others from drinking it, and raise the voice of truth and mobilize his iron will in combating this act.

The intense discomfort and disquietude of the prophets, and especially the noble prophet of Islam, about the sins and indecencies of people is itself the best witness to the fact that they were disgusted with every evil and were never soiled by it.

The great secret of the progress of the prophets was their coordination of word and deed, and it is this coordination which enabled them to transform the fundamentals of human thought and lead societies toward perfection.

CONFIDENCE AND ACCEPTANCE

The greater the degrees of faith and confidence that people have in a speaker, the more their agreement with him increases, and vice versa. For this reason, the prophets, who divulged the Divine commands and restrained people from sin and immorality, must, according to this assertion, be endowed with the greatest, most admirable qualities, and be free from every kind of sin and indecency, even error and mistake, so that people's confidence and faith in them may be greater and they may accept their guidance and what they say, and so that people may strive more assiduously in carrying out the plans and putting into practice the reformative instructions of the prophets, and understand from the depths of their hearts their leadership. Thus the aim of the prophetic mission, that is to say the leading of the human race to development on all sides, will be accomplished; the aim of the prophetic mission will not be obtained under any other circumstances, and that would be very far from the wisdom of God.

This purity and worthiness of the prophets was so extraordinary that people became devoted to them to such a degree that their followers felt great love towards them and gave up their lives in following and obeying them, without heed for the consequences. However, the question as to how one man can be completely free from sin and error is a matter to which we shall now turn our attention.

HOW CAN A MAN BE MA'SUM?

REAL LOVE OF GOD

The holy prophets were deeply devoted to the Merciful Lord and God, and why should they not have been? They, who with their seeing and hearing and profound insight knew God better than anyone, who understood His greatness and splendor and majesty to be above all things, who deem Him alone worthy of love, devotion and obedience, who had nothing except His pleasure in view, who gave their hearts to none but He, who did everything with devotion to Him, and who knew Who they were worshiping.

It was for this very reason that the prophets welcomed difficulties and formidable situations, and also paid attention to God with smiling, open faces even when they were in the most critical circumstances. And so, when, in their beloved, true way, they met with difficulties, they became overflowing with joy.

History has recorded the endeavors of these heavenly, torch-bearing men of guidance, as also the condemnable behavior of people towards them. Could steadfastness in these difficulties have had another motivation apart from love of God and the performance of His command? Surely, it could not be.

How can it be imagined that those who are completely engrossed in their beloved way, and who utter nothing except according to His wish, and in whose heart, soul, spirit and thoughts not one corner is empty of remembrance of Him, can disobey His commands? Or can give themselves up to sin? Rather, they followed the path of obedience to Him and were devoted to Him.

Someone asked the Prophet of Islam why he applied himself to worship to such an extent with suffering and hardship since he was purified and had no sin. His answer was that why should he not be a grateful and thankful slave of God.[2]

Imam Ali made reference to the great qualities of the Prophet of Islam when he said that God had so deeply affected the Prophet

---

[2] *Nūr ath-Thaqalayn*, vol. 3, p. 367.

with the messenger-ship and leadership that he was a witness for creation, the bearer of good news, and a warning, in his childhood he was better than everyone, in his maturity more preferred, and his nature was, of all the pure ones, the purest. His bounty and his generosity were more freely shown than that of any other benefactor.[3] "He is the leader of the pious and the eyes of those who are led."[4] Thus we see that the perfect knowledge of the prophets and the deep and true love which they had for God resulted in faultlessness and absolute purity, so that, in addition to precluding sin from their will and thinking, they withheld themselves from sin.

DEEP AND PERFECT INSIGHT OF PROPHETS

Perceptiveness is not the same in everyone. Someone who is ignorant and illiterate will never think like a doctor does about microbes and the contamination of vessels by them. A doctor who has spent years investigating microbes, has watched their multiplication under a microscope, and has witnessed the fate of those who were infected by them can never neglect microbes and their dangers. Thus we see that the ignorant person proceeds to drink water contaminated with microbes and has no worry, whereas the doctor would never be prepared to drink such water and would never even entertain the idea.

The only motive for refraining from drinking is the knowledge and information which this doctor has concerning the bad effects of microbes. So, for example, the illiterate, ignorant person would also keep himself from eating something filthy, for in this case, he is aware of the impurity and harmful effect of it. But a one-year-old child into whose reach that filthy thing fell would probably put it into his mouth.

Another point is that there are some people who attach little importance to incremental harm, although they fear sudden, unexpected dangers and avoid them. For example, someone may be rather lazy about extracting a decayed tooth and may procrastinate about resorting to a dentist, till such time as his other teeth become affected, and a great deal more discomfort

---

3 *Tarīkh Tabarī*, vol. 5, p. 2269-71.
4 *Nahj al-Balāghah*, Sermon 115.

comes his way. The toll for this is that he may be affected by very serious ailments. However, the very same person, as soon as the pain of appendicitis appears and there is a possibility of real danger, will entrust himself to the hands of a surgeon with all haste.

If a knowledgeable doctor becomes addicted to alcohol, it can only be because he is not fully informed of the damage of alcohol to the spirit and the soul, and because its accumulative harm becomes obscured through his appetites and his desire to gratify himself. Ordinary people take a superficial view of evil, and do not take sufficient note of its physical and spiritual, bodily and psyche effects.

However, the prophets, who, with the help of a higher power, have supremacy in their vision and knowledge over the rest of mankind, who have a profound and perfect insight into all the effects of evil, and who, by a secret witnessing, see even those effects of evil which will materialize in the next world, will never come under the influence of their own bodily desires and soil their hands with the contamination of sin; even the thought of it will never enter their hearts. The prophets saw the effects of sin in the intermediary and next worlds, and gave an account of them to people, and many traditions have been recorded from the great Prophet of Islam on this subject, and we shall give a sample of them now.

"Imam Ali said: 'I and Fatima az-Zahrā went to the Prophet; we saw that he was weeping excessively. I said 'For the sake of my father and mother, why are you weeping?' He said 'The night they took me on *mi'rāj*, I saw a group of women from my people in severe torment. One woman I saw hung up by her hair, and the brain in her head was boiling from the intensity of the heat. Another was strung up by her tongue, and they were pouring caustic water into her throat.....Another was eating the flesh of her boy and fire was burning under her feet. Another one had her hands and feet bound, and the snakes and scorpions of Hell were crawling over her. Another one, the flesh of her body was being cut up with flaming scissors.......Another one had grown the face of a dog and fire was entering her from underneath and coming out of her mouth, and the angels of punishment were striking her with fiery clubs on her head and her body.' Fatima az-Zehra, the daughter of the Prophet, said 'These women, what had they done that Allah was punishing them in this way?'

"The Prophet said, 'The one who was hung up by her hair had not, in this world, concealed her hair from stranger, and the one who was strung up by her tongue had tormented her husband.....and the one who was eating flesh of her own body had beautified herself for strangers, and the one whose hands and feet were bound and over whom snakes and scorpions crawled had given no importance to *wudū* and the purity of her clothes, nor to *ghusl* after sexual impurity and *ghusl* after menstruation, and had counted her prayers as nothing....but the one whose flesh was cut by scissors was a woman who had given herself to the will of unfamiliar and strange men.....and the one who had grown the face of a dog and whom fire entered from underneath and came out of her mouth had been a singer.' Then the great Prophet of Islam said, 'Woe to that woman who made her husband angry and how good it is for the case of that woman whose husband is happy because of her.'"[5]

The Prophet also said: "I came across a group who had been strung up on fiery hooks. I asked Jibrā'īl who they were and he said, 'They are people whom Allah had made unmindful of what is *halāl* and *harām*, but they had run after what is *harām*.' And I also came across a group, the flesh of whose bodies was being sown with a thread of fire. I asked who they were, and Jibrā'īl said, 'They are individuals who had illegal relationships with unmarried girls.'"[6] And he also said that someone who profited through usury, Allah fills his stomach with the fire of Hell to the extent of the usury by which he profited.[7]

In short, remembrance of judgment and the witnessing of the effects of sin in the next world was the best way to keep the prophets from sin and indecency. Allah has said in the Qur'an: *"And commemorate Our servants, Abraham, Isaac and Jacob, possessors of Power and vision. Verily We chose them for a special* (purpose)

---

[5] Majlisī, *Bihār al-Anwār*; vol. 18, p. 351.

[6] Ibid, p. 333.

[7] *Thawāb al-A'māl wa 'Aqāb al-A'māl*, p. 336.

proclaiming the message of the hereafter. They were in Our Sight, truly of the company of the Elect and the Good." (8:45-47)

INFALLIBILITY OF PROPHETS

NECESSITY FOR MIRACLES

After man has realized that he needs the guidance of prophets in order to reach an all-embracing happiness, and that he can only construct the glorious edifice of perfection through their instructions, he naturally feels affection for those teachers who work for his benefit ad sacrifice their sinless souls for his advantage. Thus belief comes to reach such a degree that people do not spare themselves any hardship in order to advance the aims of the prophets, and they prefer the demands of the prophets to the demands of their on souls. But this deep-rooted and comprehensive influence and importance of the prophets, and the love and belief of people in them cause some ambitious persons to take advantage of them, seeking to become influential and obtain their desires by claiming prophet-hood.

So, if someone claims prophethood and people gather round him one can not believe in him without some investigation. It may be possible that he falsely proclaims prophethood, as many people have done up to the present day and thus collects a following. In order to find out if someone is a genuine prophet, this latter must bring some evidence with him so that people can be sure of him and accept his claim. Thus the real prophets can be distinguished from the false. This evidence that distinguishes the true prophets from the false is known as miracles, and God gave miracles to His prophets and messengers so that people could be saved from mistakes and the dangers of those who seek to deceive them, and so that the face of truth may never be hidden from people. So far we have seen that messengers must bring miracles so that people can know that they bear a message from God, and that what they say is true, and so that they may be completely obedient to them and follow their teachings with faith and conviction.

WHAT ARE MIRACLES?

Miracles (*mu'jizah*) are what the prophets did according to the Will of God in order to affirm the prophethood they claimed, and which others are unable to copy. Miracles are only a proof of prophethood

A group of those who sought excuses for their lack of faith demanded various things as miracles, not through a desire to have the prophethood confirmed, but in order to loose the prophets. They even asked for things that were logically impossible. However, because the prophets brought enough miracles they did not accede to these demands and told these people that the position of a prophet is to guide, to bring good tidings and to warn. This is why miracles are according to the Will of God and in situations where they are necessary, as is mentioned in the Qur'an with reference to such people.

The Qur'an says: "*The signs are only with Allah, and I am only a warner, plain and simple.*" (29:50) "*But no apostle was given a miracle unless God dispensed.*" (40:78)

Chapter: 11

FAITH OF PROPHET'S ANCESTORS

By

Allama Sayyid Saeed Akhtar Rizvi[1]

It is the accepted belief of the Shi'a Ithna-asharīs, Hanafīs and Shafi'īs that the ancestors of the Prophet from Abdullāh to Quaidar bin Ismā'īl, and from there right up to Adam, were true believers. They believed in the One and Only God, and faithfully followed the Divine religion of their times. From Quaidar to Abdullah, all of them followed the *shari'ah* of Prophet Ibrahim which was the religion prescribed for them by God.

The famous Sunni scholar, Allama Jalāluddīn Suyūtī, has written nine books on this subject, and has proved beyond doubt that all the ancestors of the Prophet were true believers. Sheikh Abdul-Haqq Dehalawī has written: "All the ancestors of the Prophet from Adam up to Abdullah were pure and clean from the uncleanliness of disbelief and paganism. It was not possible for Allah to put that 'Holy Light' (of the Prophet) into dark and dirty places, i.e., the loin of a pagan man or the womb of a pagan woman. Also how could it be possible for Allah to punish the ancestors of the Prophet on the Day of Judgment and thus humiliate him in the eyes of the world?"

The Prophet himself said: "I was always being transferred from the loins of the clean ones to the wombs of the clean ones."

Allama Majlisī has written that it is the unanimous belief of the Shi'a scholars that the father, mother and all the ancestors of the Prophet followed the true religion, and his light never entered into the loin of any pagan man or the womb of any pagan woman. Also, the accepted traditions say that all his ancestors were *Siddiqīn* (True Ones) — either they were Prophets or the successors of the Prophets.

---

[1] Reproduced from the Bi-monthly Islamic Magazine *The Light*, October 1990, published by Bilāl Muslim Mission of Tanzania, Dares Salaam, Tanzania.

And after Ismā'īl, all his ancestors were successors of Prophet Ismā'īl. Other traditions specify that Abdul-Muttalib was a *Hujjat* (Proof) of Allah and Abū Tālib was his successor.

Imām Ali said: "By Allah, neither my father ever worshipped the idols, nor my grandfather Abdul-Muttalib, nor his father Hāshim, nor his father Abd Munāf. They prayed facing towards Ka'bah and followed the religion of Prophet Ibrahim."

If you look at the short life-sketches of some of the ancestors of the Prophet, you will find that many of the traditions established by them are now included into the tenets of Islam. Qusyi started the night-stay at Mash'arul-Harām in Hajj; and Allah would not confirm a rite established by a pagan?

Also, read again the events of the discovery of *Zamzam*, and appearance of the foundation in the desert. Read again the events of *Aamul-Fīl*, and see the firm conviction that Allah would surely save His House. That statement, repeated several times, shows that Abdul-Muttalib knew beforehand what was going to happen. Why was he so sure? There can be only one explanation—He was informed by Allah.

And this, in its turn, proves the earlier statement that he was a *Hujjat* of Allah.

In all these events and narrations, he is always seen praying to Allah; and there is no hint from any quarter that he ever prayed to the idols of Quraysh (Hubul, Lat or Uzza). When he finds *Zamzam*, he exclaims *Allahu Akbar* when he emphasizes anything, he swears by the name of Allah; when he states his claim, he says that it was given to him by Allah. What further proof is needed to show that it was a family of True Believers?

The Prophet said: "Jibrā'īl (Gabriel) told me, 'I hunted the east and west of the earth, but I did not find anyone superior to Muhammad; and I hunted the east and west of the earth, but I did not find the children of any father better than the children of Hāshim.'"

Also, the Prophet said; "Verily, Allah chose Kanana from the children of Ismā'īl; and selected Quraysh from Kanana; and chose the children of Hāshim from the Quarysh and selected me from the children of Hāshim."

Abdul-Muttalib was born in Medina at his maternal grandfather's house; and he was only a few months old when Hāshim died. After Hāshim, his brother Muttalib succeeded him in all the privileges mentioned earlier. After some time Muttalib went to Medina and brought his nephew riding behind him on his camel, some people said: "This is the slave of Muttalib." Muttalib said: "No he is my nephew and son of my deceased brother, Hāshim." But the name struck; and nowadays few people know about the real name of Abdul-Muttalib was 'Shaibatul-Hamd'.

Muttalib loved Abdul-Muttalib and looked after him very well. But Abdus-Shams and Nawfil were inimical towards him. At the death of Muttalib, Abdul-Muttalib succeeded him in the two privileges held by him: i.e. *Sequaya* and *Rifada*.

ABDULLAH

When at the time of digging the Zamzam, Abdul-Muttalib encountered the enmity of Quraysh, he was very much worried, because he had only one son to help him. So he prayed to Allah, and made a *Nazr* that if Allah gives him ten sons, who would be his helpers against his enemies, he would sacrifice one of them to please Allah. His prayer was granted, and Allah gave him twelve sons, out of which five are famous in Islamic history — Abdullah, Abū Tālib, Hamza, Abbās and Abū Lahab. Other seven were Hārith (already mentioned), Zubayr, Ghaydaque, Muqawwim. Dharar, Qutham, Hijl (or Mughira). Also he had six daughters; Atika, Amima, Baydha, Barra, Safiyya and Arwi.

When ten sons were born, Abdul-Muttalib decided to sacrifice one of them according to his Nazr. Lot was cast and the name of Abdullah came out. Abdullah was the dearest to him; but he did not flinch from the decision of the fate. He took Abdullah's hands and started towards the place where sacrifices were done. His daughters started crying and begged him to sacrifice ten camels in place of Abdullah. At first Abdul-Muttalib refused. But when the pressure of the whole family (and in fact, the whole tribe) mounted, he agreed to cast the lot between Abdullah and ten camels. Again the name of Abdullah came out. On the suggestion of the people, number of the camels was increased to twenty; again the same result. Repeatedly, the number was increased to thirty, forty, fifty, sixty, seventy, eighty, and ninety. But the result was always the same. At last the lot was cast between 100 camels and Abdullah. Now the lot came out for the camels. The family was jubilant; but Abdul Muttalib was not satisfied. He said: "Ten times the name of Abdullah has come out. It is not fair to ignore those lots just for one lot." Three times more repeated the lot between Abdullah and camels and every time the lot came out for 100 camels. Then Abdul-Muttalib sacrificed the camels and the life of Abdullah was saved.

It was for this reason that the Prophet used to say: "I am the son of two sacrifices," referring to the sacrifices of Prophet Ismael and Abdullah.

The name of the mother of Abdullah was Fatima, daughter of Amr bin Aa'edh, bin Amr bin Makhzūm. She was the mother of Abū Tālib, Abdullah, Zubayr, Baidha, Amima, Barra and Aatika.

One year before the year of elephant, Abdullah was married to Amina daughter of Wahāb bin Abd Munāf bin Zuhra bin Kilāb. In that very sitting, Abdul-Muttalib married Hala daughter of Wuhayb, i.e., the cousin of Amina. Hala gave birth to Hamza; and Thawbiyya, the slave-girl of Abu Lahab, breast-fed him.

Abdullah is said to be 17 (or 24 or 27) years old at the time of the marriage. Abdullah went with the trade-caravan to Syria; and in the return-journey, fell ill and stayed at Yathrib (Madina). When Abdul-Muttalib sent Hārith to look after him and bring him back, he had already expired. Abdullah was buried in Yathrib. His grave is now walled up and nobody is allowed to visit it. Abdullah had left some camels, goats and a slave girl, Umme-Ayman. The Prophet got all this as his inheritance.

Chapter: 12

FAITH OF ABŪ TĀLIB

By

Allama Sayyid Saeed Akhtar Rizvi[1]

Because of the prestige of Abū Tālib, Quraysh did not dare to hurt the Prophet. But they were making him suffer with as much affliction as was possible, no less was the heartache caused to him by the suffering of the helpless Muslims. He himself said: "No prophet had to suffer as many afflictions as I had". And all along, Islam was gaining adherents not only from Quraysh, but also from the neighboring tribes. The oligarchy of Mecca was now desperately trying to stem out the movement.

The forbearance of the Prophet was making the Quraysh wonder as to why a man should put himself in such a precarious position. Their outlook was materialistic; their ideals were wealth, beauty and power. They, naturally, ascribed the same motives to the Prophet. Utba bin Rabia, the father-in-law of Abū Sufyān, was sent to him to convey the message of Quraysh: "Muhammad! If you want power and prestige, we will make you the overlord of Mecca; or do you want marriage in a big family? You may have the hand of the fairest maiden in the land. Do you want hoards of silver and gold? We can provide you with all these things and even more. But you should forsake these nefarious preaching which imply that our forefathers who were worshipping these deities of ours were fools."

Quraysh were almost certain that Muhammad would respond favorable to this offer. But the Prophet recited Sura 41 in his replay which, *inter alia*, contained the following warning: *"but if they turn away, say thee: I have warned you of a stunning punishment like that which overtook the Aad and the Thamūd!"* Utba was overwhelmed with this

---

[1] Reproduced from the Bi-monthly Islamic Magazine *The Light*, (*Hazrat Abū Tālib and the Holy Prophet*) October 1990, published by Bilāl Muslim Mission of Tanzania, Dares Salaam, Tanzania.

.

ringing warning. He did not accept Islam, but advised Quraysh to leave Muhammad alone, and see how he fares with other tribes. Quraysh said that he also was bewitched by Muhammad.

Then a deputation was sent to Abū Tālib. They demanded that Abū Tālib should either persuade his nephew to desist from his Mission or hand him over to suffer the extreme penalty, or be prepared to fight the whole tribe. Finding the odds too heavy against him, Abū Tālib said to the Prophet: "O my son, do not put such a burden on my shoulders which I am unable to bear." The Prophet's reply to his uncle gives an indication of his indomitable will, his profound trust in God and confidence in his Mission. Said he: "O my uncle, if they placed the sun on my right hand and the moon on my left, to persuade me to renounce my work, verily I would not desist there from until God made manifest His cause or I perished in the attempt." Saying this, he was overwhelmed with grief. Abū Tālib was moved by this reply and said: "By Allah, the Quraysh can never reach thee in spite of their great number until I am buried to the earth. Therefore, pronounce what order thou hast; nobody can do any harm to you; be happy with this (promise) and keep thy eyes cool (i.e. be consoled). "

In their final attempt, they took a young man, Ammara bin Walid, to Abū Tālib and offered to exchange him with Muhammad. They told him: "This young man is a well-known poet of the tribe, and also he is very handsome and wise. You better exchange Muhammad with him. You may make him your son: he would be a good helper to you. And give us your Muhammad we will kill him. Thus, you will not suffer any loss, because you will have Ammara in place of Muhammad, and by removal of Muhammad all this strife and friction in the tribe will come to and end." Abū Tālib was extremely furious on hearing this proposal. His voice was raised in wrath. He said: "What a worst bargain have you proposed; why, you want me to give you my son, so that you may kill him; and take your son and look after him? Go away, this bargain is nothing if not foolishness."

BAN ON CLANS OF HASHIM AND MUTTĀLIB

Frustrated, the idolaters decided to ostracize the whole clans of Hāshim and Muttālib; and thus destroy them completely. An agreement was signed to boycott these two clans. The agreement said that they would neither take the daughters of these two clans nor will they give them nor buy anything from them. Not only that, they would not have any contact with them nor would they allow any food or drink to reach them. "This boycott would continue till these clans agree to handover Muhammad to Quraysh." It was written by Mansur bin Irima, and was hung in the Ka'bah.

Abū Tālib had no alternative but to take these two clans (who have always stood together) into Sha'yb Abī Tālib. It was a place in the mount Hajun which belonged to Abū Tālib. There were 40 adults in the clans. For three long years they were beleaguered: it had begun in Muharram, 7th year of Be'sat and continued up to the beginning of 10th year. They were made to undergo the most acute hardships and deprivations; so much so that, at times, they had nothing but leaves of trees to sustain them. Only twice a year they dared to come out, in Rajab and Dhul-Hijja, when every type of violence was taboo according to the Arabian custom. If any relative sent them any food, and the news leaked out, that relative was publicly insulted and put to shame. The Qurayshites used to express their pleasure on hearing the cries of hungry children.

In all these years of sufferings, Abū Tālib had only one worry: how to keep the Prophet out of the harm's way. Historians unanimously say that it was the habit of Abū Tālib to awaken the Prophet after all people had gone to sleep and take him to another place and order one of his own children or brothers to sleep in the bed of the Prophet. This was done so that if any enemy had seen where Muhammad was sleeping and if an attack was made on him at night, his own child or brother would be killed but the Prophet would be saved.

All of them suffered these hardships and did their utmost to save the life of the Prophet. History is unable to produce another example of such devotion and loyalty. And imagine that this continued not for one or two days or weeks, but for three long years. One day the Prophet told Abū Tālib: "I have been informed by Allah that the agreement of the Quraysh has been eaten away by the termites and no writing has been left therein except the name of Allah." And Abū Tālib never had any doubt about any saying of the Prophet.

Thus he came out of his place at once and went to Masjid-ul-Harām where Quraysh had gathered. As the luck would have it, the subject of discussion was the same boycott. Hishām, son of Amr, Zubair and a few others who were related to Khadija and the clans of Hāshim and Muttālib, and who lived near the Sha'yb of Abū Tālib and thus used to hear the cries of the children day and night had decided to persuade the Quraysh to abrogate the agreement. The arguments were very heated and had reached a climax, when they saw Abū Tālib approaching. Abū Jahl and others who opposed the idea of abrogating the boycott, said: "Abū Tālib is coming; it seems that now he is tired and wants to hand over Muhammad to us. Thus, the boycott would end to the satisfaction of us all. Keep silent and hear what he wants to say. But Abū Tālib had gone there to challenge them, not to surrender. He stood before the gathering and said: "My son says that the agreement which you had written had been eaten away by the termites, and nothing remains therein except the name of Allah. Now look at that paper. If the news given by my son is correct then you must end your injustice and high-handedness; and if the news is wrong then we will accept that you were right and we were wrong." The agreement was brought out and opened. There was nothing left of it except the name of Allah in one place.

Now, the voice of Abū Tālib thundered and he condemned them for their tyranny. Those who wanted that boycott ended, said that now there was no agreement at all to be adhered to. Abū Jahl and others tried to outwit them but they failed and the boycott ended with total moral victory of Islam over infidels.

THE YEAR OF SORROW

But the difficulties and deprivations of these three years took their toll. Within nine months, Abū Tālib died and three days after him Khadija also left this world. With the disappearance of their protecting influence, the Meccans had a free hand and redoubled their persecution. These two deaths, at a time when the Prophet was in dire need of both, left a very deep impression on him. He was so grieved that he named that year as 'Āmul-Huzn' (The year of Sorrow). How valuable was their support, may be judged from the fact that Allah counted them as two of His Highest Graces upon the Prophet. He says in Sura 93: *"Did He not find thee an orphan and gave thee shelter; and He found thee lost (in thy tribe) and guided (them towards thee); and He found thee in need and made thee independent."*

All the commentators of the Qur'an say that the first Ayat means "Did not Allah find thee an orphan and gave the shelter with Abū Tālib?" and the last Ayat means "He found thee poor and made the rich through Khadīja. If we remove (in imagination) the prestigious influence of Abū Tālib from the early history of Islam, we cannot see how the life of the Prophet could be saved, and if we take out (in imagination) the wealth of Khadīja, we cannot think how the poor Muslims could be sustained, and how the expenses of the two *Hijars* of Ethiopia (Abyssinia) could be met.

It is not the place to fully explain the share of Abū Tālib in the foundation of Islam. Therefore, the best tribute would be to quote some of his poetry lines, overflowing with love of, and devotion to, the Prophet. Abū Tālib said:

"Did not you know that we found Muhammad the Messenger of Allah, the same as was Musa? It is written in the scriptures." Compare it with the Ayat of the Qur'an: *"Verily, We have sent to you a Messenger to be a witness concerning you, as We sent a Messenger to Pharaoh."*

Somewhere also he says: "And strengthened him the Lord of the world with His help; and he proclaimed the religion which is true, not false. Do not they know that our son is not doubted by us and that we do not care about the false saying (of his enemies)?"

Once Abū Tālib asked Imam Ali: "What is this religion which you are following?" Imam Ali said; "I believe in Allah and His Messenger, and I pray with him." Abū Tālib said: "Surely Muhammad will not call us but to a good thing. Never leave Muhammad. Follow him faithfully."

Once he saw the Prophet praying, with Khadīja and Imam Ali behind him. Ja'far was with Abū Tālib. Abū Tālib told Ja'far to go ahead and join in the prayer. When Hamza accepted Islam in the sixth year of Be'sat, Abū Tālib was overjoyed, and said: "Be patient, O Abū Yāla (Hamza) on the religion of Ahmad. And proclaim the religion with courage, May Allah help you.

"I was glad when you said that you were Momeen (Believer). Therefore, help the Messenger of Allah the way of Allah.

"And announce to the Quraysh your decision; and tell them that Ahmad was not a sorcerer."

It was the policy of Abū Tālib to keep the Quraysh in suspense about his true belief, because, if he had announced that he had accepted the religion of Muhammad, his position as the respected leader of Quraysh would have been undermined. And then he could not extend his protection to the Prophet. Thus, while always declaring his firm belief that Muhammad can not tell but truth and exhorting his children and brother to follow the religion of Muhammad, he assiduously refrained from declaring in so many words that he was a Muslim. Thus he maintained his position with the hierarchy of Quraysh and protected the Prophet by his influence. Even on his death-bed, while there was still chance that he might survive; he very diplomatically announced his faith in such a way that the Quraysh could not understand what he meant. When they asked him on which religion he was, he replied: "On the religion of my forefathers."

As it has already been explained that Abdul-Muttālib and all their ancestors were on Divine religion, one cannot but admire the prudence and wisdom of Abū Tālib in that difficult situation. In the last moments of his life, the Prophet advised him to recite *Kalima* loudly (as is the custom of the Muslims). Abbas, who had not yet accepted Islam saw the lips of Abū Tālib, and then said to the Prophet: "O my nephew, Abū Tālib is saying what you wanted him to say."

Allama Ibn Abi'l-Hadīd Mu'tazilī has truly said: "If it had not been for Abū Tālib and his son (i.e. Imām Ali), the religion of Islam could not take any shape nor could it stand on its legs. Thus Abū Tālib in Mecca gave shelter and protection; and Imam Ali in Medina rubbed shoulders with death." Abū Tālib died at the age of 85 years, in the middle of Shawwal or Dhul-qa'da, 10th year of Be'sat. Imam Ja'far Sādiq said: "The ancestors of the Prophet would be in the Paradise and Abdul-Muttalib would enter Paradise having upon him the light of the prophets and dignity of the kings; and Abū Tālib would be in the same group."

Chapter: 13

MEMBERS OF THE FAMILY OF THE PROPHET

By

Abū Tālib At-Turābī[1]

Some people criticize the Shi'as for limiting the Prophet's family to Imām Ali, Fatima az-Zahrā and their sons Hasan and Husayn and excluding the Prophet's wives and uncles.

The Answer: The Prophet's sayings prove that his family members are only those four persons. Such sayings, narrated by some of the Companions are mentioned in many Suuni books.

At-Tirmidhī mentioned in his book *as-Sahīh*, (vol. 13 p. 200, Egyptian edition), a tradition narrated by Umar bin Abū Salma where he said that the Qur'anic verse, *"Allah only desires to keep away the uncleanness from you, O people of the House, and to purify you with a thorough purification. (33:33),"* was revealed in Umm Salma's house. Then the Prophet called for Fatima az-Zahrā, Hasan, Husayn and Imām Ali to come behind him. He then covered them with a garment and said: "O Allah, these are my family. Keep away uncleanness from them and purify them thoroughly." Umm Salma said, "Am I with them?" The Prophet answered, "You have your standing and you will be to a good end." But she was not allowed to come under the garment. The author mentioned other relations that are narrated by Umm Salma, Ma'qil bin Yasār, Abul-Hamra' and Anas bin Mālik.

Following are some sources of the Prophet's saying regarding the above-mentioned Qur'anic verse of Purification concerning Imām Ali, Fatima az-Zahrā, Hasan and Husayn, that are recorded in Sunni books quoted from our book *Jami' Barāhīn Usūl ul-I'tiqādāt:*

> 1. Narrated by Umar bin Atiyah, from Abū Sa'īd Al-Khudrī from Umm Salma *(The History of Baghdad)*, vol. 9, p. 126.

---

[1] Reproduced from Author's book, *Spurious Arguments about the Shi'a*, published by Ansariyan Publications, Qum: Iran, 2001.

2. Al-Husayn bin al-Hasan from Abū Sa'īd al-Khudrī from Umm Salma (The Prophet's wife) *(The History of Baghdad)*, vol. 9, p. 126.

3. Hishām bin Salīm, from Wahhāb bin Abdullāh, from Umm Salma *(Al-Mu'jam ul-Kabīr)*, p. 134.

4. Abdul-Malik bin Sulayman from Ata' from Umm Salma *(Al-Mu'jam ul-Kabīr)*, p. 134.

5. Sharik bin Namr, Ata', Umm Salma *(Ma'alimut Tanzīl)*, p. 213.

6. Muhammad bin Sawqa from someone from Umm Salma *(Akhlaq un-Nabī)*, p. 116.

7. Abdullah bin Abu Riyah, from someone, from Umm Salma (Ath-Tha'labi's *Tafsīr*) Manuscript.

8. Abdullāh bin Abū Riyah, Hakim bin Sa'd, Umm Salma (Ibn Kathīr's *Tafsīr*), vol. 3, p. 483.

9. Atiyah from his father from Umm Salma (Ibn Kathīr's *Tafsīr*), vol. 3, p. 483.

10. Atiyah, from Shahr bin Hawshab, from Umm Salma (Ibn Kathir's *Tafsīr*), vol. 3, p. 483.

11. Sufyān bin Zayd, Shahr bin Hawshab, Umm Salma (At-Tirmidhī's *Sahīh*), vol. 13, p. 248.

12. Zubayd, Shahr bin Hawshab, Umm Salma *(Mawzihul-Awhām)*, vol. 2, p. 281.

13. Abdul-Hamīd bin Bihrām, Shahr bin Hawshab, Umm Salma (Ahmad's *Musnad*), vol. 6, p. 298.

14. Dāwūd bin Abū Auf, Shahr bin Hawshab, Umm Salma *(Al-Qawlul-Fasl)*, vol. 2, p. 177.

15. Ajlah, Shahr bin Hawshab, Umm Salma (Ahmad's *Musnad*), vol. 2, p. 173.

16. Athal, Shahr bin Hawshab, Umm Salma (Al-Bukhārī's *History*), vol. 1, p. 70.

17. Shu'ayb bin al-Mini', Shahr bin Hawshab, Umm Salma (Al-Bukhārī's *History*), vol. 1 p. 70.

18. Ja'far bin Abdur-Rahman, al-Hakam bin Sa'id, Umm Salma (Al-Bukhārī's *History*), vol. 1, p. 70.

19. Muhammad bin Shirīn, Abu Hurayra, Umm Salma *(Tafsīr Jāmi'ul-Bayān)*, vol. 22, p. 7.

20. Awām bin Hawshab, from his cousin, from 'Aa'isha *(Al-Qawlul-Fasl)*, vol. 2, p. 215.

21. Mus'ab bin Shayba, Safiyyah, 'Aa'isha (*as-Sunanul-Kubra*), vol. 2, p. 149.

22. Awza'i, Abū Ammār, Wathīla bin al-Asqa' (*Mustadrak*), vol. 2, p. 152.

23. Abdur-Rahmān bin Amr, Shaddad bin Abdullah, Wathīla bin al-Asqa' (*Siyer A'lamin-Nubala'*), vol. 3, p. 212.

24. Al-A'mash, Atyah, Abū Sa'īd al-Khudrī, (*Jāmi'ul-Bayān*), vol. 22, p. 6.

25. Abul-Hijāf, Atiyah, Abū Sa'īd al-Khudrī (*Al-Mu'jam us Saghīr*), vol. 1, p. 134.

26. Imrān bin Muslim, Atiyah, Abū Sa'īd al-Khudrī (*The History of Baghdad*), vol. 10.

27. Ibn Umar al-Kirmānī, Atiyah, Abū Sa'īd al-Khudrī (*Tabaqatul-Muhadditheen*), p. 149.

28. Abdur-Rahmān bin Abū Bakr, Isma'il, from his father Abdullah bin Ja'far (*Al-Qawlul-Fasl*), p. 185.

29. Abdur-Rahmān bin Abū Bakr, Ibn Abbās (*Arjahul-Matālib*), p. 54.

30. Hammād bin Salma, Ali bin Zayd, Anas bin Malik (Ahmad's *Musnad*), vol. 3, p. 259.

31. Abdur-Rahmān bin Abū Bakr, Hāmid, Anas bin Malik (*Al-Mustadrak*), vol. 3, p. 159.

32. Abād bin Abū Yahya, Abū Dāwūd (p. 6), Abul-Hamra' (An-Najārī's *Kuna*) p. 25.

33. Yūnus bin Abū 'Ishāq, Abū Dāwūd, Abul-Hamra' *Muntakhab Theyl al-Mutheyl*), p. 83.

34. Mansūr bin Abul-Aswad, Abū Dāwūd, Abul-Hamra' (*Al-mu'jam ul-Kabīr*), p. 134.

35. Abū 'Ishāq as-Subey'ī, Abū Dāwūd, Abul-Hamra' (*History of Islam*), vol. 2, p. 97.

36. Umayr Abū Arfaja, Atiyah (*Usdul-Ghaba*), vol. 3, p. 413.

37. Al-Aufī, Amr bin Atiyah and al-Husayn bin al-Hasan, from Atiyah (*The History of Baghdad*), vol. 9, p. 126.

38. Bukayr bin Mismār, Aamir bin Sa'd, Sa'd (*Jāmi'ul-Bayān*), vol. 22, p. 8.

39. Abū Balah Amr bin Maymun (*Al-Mustadrak*), vol. 3, p. 132.

40. Yahya bin Ubayd, Attar bin Abū Riyah, Umar bin Abū Salma (at-Tirmidhī's *Sahīh*), vol. 13, p. 200.

41. Yahya bin Ubayd, Sahl bin Sa'd *(Al-Isti'āb)*, vol. 2, p. 460.
42. Abū Hurayra, Sahl bin Sa'd *(Al- Isti'āb)*, vol. 2 ,p. 56.
43. Bureyda al-Aslami, Sahl bin Sa'd *(Al- Isti'āb)*, vol. 2, p. 56.
44. Abdullāh bin Umar, Sahl bin Sa'd *(Al- Isti'āb)*, vol. 2, p. 56.
45. Imrān bin al-Husayn, Sahl bin Sa'd *(Al- Isti'āb)*, vol. 2, p. 56.
46. Salma bin al-Aqua', Sahl bin Sa'd *(Al- Isti'āb)*, vol. 2, p. 56.
47. Ma'qil bin Yassar (At-Tirmidhī's *Sahīh*), vol. 13, p. 248.

Finally, the tradition concerning the Qur'anic verse of purification and its being specifically about them, in the words of al Haddah al Hadhramī is one of the correct, famous, widespread, and well known traditions upon which all the umma has agreed and seventeen of great muhadith have confirmed that it was true.

THE INFALLIBILITY OF THE TWELVE IMĀMS

Some people criticize the Shi'as for believing that the Imāms of the honorable Prophet's family were infallible.

The Answer: The Shi'as believe that the Imām, who has been appointed by Allah, must be infallible. Allah says: *Surely, I will make you an Imām of men. Ibrahim said, 'and of my offspring?' My covenant does not include the unjust, said He.* (2:124). *And whoever goes beyond the limits of Allah, he indeed does injustice to his own soul.* (65:1) *And whoever exceeds the limits of Allah those are they that are the unjust.* (2:229).

Infallibility was a condition for the divine Imāmate and it was limited, after Prophet Muhammad, to the twelve Imāms for no one else was infallible other than them according to consensus. In addition to this, the Qur'anic verse; *Allah only desires to keep away uncleanness from you, O People of the House, and to purify you with a thorough purification.* (33:33), confirms that Imām Ali, Imām Hasan and Imām Husayn were infallible. In Shi'a fiqh all prophets were also infallible.

Chapter: 14

AHĀDITH OF PROPHET TO FOLLOW AHLUL BAYT

By

Dr. Muhammad Ali Tejani al Samavi[1]

TWO WEIGHTY THINGS

The messenger of Allah said, "O People, I leave amongst you two things which, if you follow, you will never go astray. They are the Book of Allah (Qur'an) and my Ahlul Bayt (family)." He also said: "The messenger of my God is about to come to me and I shall answer. I am leaving with you the two weighty things: The first is the Book of Allah, in which you find guidance and enlightenment, and the second is the people of my household. I remind you, by Allah, of the people of my household..." [2]

If we examine with some care this honorable tradition, which has been cited by the *Sahih* of the Ahle Sunna al-Jamā'ah, we will find that the Shiites alone followed the two weighty things: The Book of Allah and honorable members of the Prophet's Household. On the other hand, the Ahle Sunna al-Jamā'ah followed the saying of Umar, "The Book of Allah is sufficient for us", but I wish they had followed the Book of Allah without interpreting it in their own ways. If Umar himself did not understand the meaning of *al-Kalalah* and did not know the Qur'anic verse regarding the Tayammum and other rules, so how about those who came later and followed him without the ability to interpret the Qur'anic texts?

Naturally they will answer me with their own quoted saying, and that is: "I have left with you the Book of Allah and my tradition (Sunna)." [3]

---

[1] Reproduced from his book, *Then I was Guided*, Message of Peace (Pyame Aman Inc.), Bloomfield, New Jersey: U.S.A., 1991.
[2] *Sahīh Muslim*, Chapter on the Virtues of Ali, vol. 5 p 122; *Sahīh*, vol.5, p. 328; *Mustadrak al-Hākim*, vol. 3, p. 148; *Musnad Imām Ahmed ibn Hanbal*, vol. 3, p. 17.
[3] The saying is cited in al-*Nisā'ī*, al-*Tirmidhī*, Ibn Majah, and Abū Dāwūd.

This tradition, if it were correct--and it is correct in its general meaning--would correspond to the tradition of the two weighty things, because when the Prophet talked about his Household (Ahlul Bayt) he meant that they should be consulted for two reasons. Firstly, to teach the tradition (Sunna), or to transmit to people the correct tradition because they are cleared from telling any lies, and because Allah made them infallible in the purification verse.

Secondly, it is to explain and interpret the meanings and aims of the tradition, because the Book of Allah is not enough for guidance. There are many parties who claim to follow the Qur'an but in actual fact they have gone astray, and the Messenger of Allah said, "How many are the readers of the Qur'an whom the Qur'an curses!" The Book of Allah is silent and could be interpreted in various ways, and it contains what is vague and what is similar, and to understand it we have to refer to those who are well endowed with knowledge as regards the Qur'an, and to Ahlul Bayt, as regards to the Prophet's traditions. The Shiites referred everything to the infallible Imāms of Ahlul Bayt (the Prophet's Household), and they did not interpret anything unless it had a supporting text.

If we ask our religious leaders, "Which Sunna do you follow?" they answer categorically, "The Sunna of the Messenger of Allah!" But the historical facts are incompatible with that, for they claim that the Messenger of Allah said, "Take my Sunna and the Sunna of the Rightly Guided Caliphs after me. Hold firmly to it." But the Sunna they follow is often the Sunna of the Rightly Guided Caliphs, and even the Messenger's Sunna which they claim to follow is in fact transmitted by those people. However, we read in our *Shahis* that the Messenger of Allah prevented them from writing his Sunna so that it was not confused with the Qur'an. Abū Bakr and Umar did the same thing during their caliphate, we therefore have no proof for the saying, "I left you my Sunna."[4]

The examples that I have cited in this study--besides many that I have not mentioned--are enough to refute this saying, because there are elements in the Sunna of Abū Bakr, Umar and

---

[4] The term "my Sunna" doesn't appear in any of the six Sahihs. It appears in *al-Muwatta* by Malik ibn Anas, some of the subsequent writers, such as al-Tabarī and Ibn Hishām referred to the sayings as translated by Malik.

Usman which contradict and negate the Prophet's Sunna, as is so apparent.

THE FIRST INCIDENT

The first incident that took place immediately after the death of the Messenger of Allah, which the Sunnis as well as the historians recorded, was the argument between Fatima az-Zehra and Abū Bakr regarding the alleged saying, "We, the prophets, do not leave an inheritance, all that we leave behind should go to charity." Fatima az-Zehra denied and refuted this saying, with the support of the Book of Allah, and protested against Abū Bakr's allegation and said that her father, the Messenger of Allah, could not contradict the Book of Allah which was revealed to him, for Allah said: *"Allah enjoins you concerning your children. The male shall have the equal of the portion of two females..." (Qur'an 4:11.)* This Qur'anic verse is general and is applicable to prophets and non-prophets alike.

She also protested with the following words of the most High: *"And Sulaymān was Dāwūd's heir, "*(Qur'an 27:16) and both of them were prophets. Also in the Qur'an: *"....Grant me from Thy-self an heir, who should inherit from me and inherit from the children of Ya'qūb, and make him, my Lord, one with whom You are well-pleased."* (Qur'an 19:5, 6)

THE SECOND INCIDENT

The second incident that involved Abū Bakr during the early days of his caliphate, which the Sunni historians recorded, was his disagreement with the nearest of all people to him, Umar ibn al-Khattab. The incident evolves around Abū Bakr's decision to fight those who refused to pay *Zakāt* (alms) and kill them, but Umar protested and advised him not to fight them because he had heard the Messenger of Allah saying: "I have been ordered to fight the people until they say, 'There is no other god but Allah and Muhammad is the Messenger of Allah.' And he who says it can keep his wealth to himself and I have no right to his (blood), and he is accountable to Allah."

This is a text cited by Muslim in his *Sahīh*: "The Messenger of Allah gave the flag to Imām Ali on the Day of Khayber, and Imām Ali said, 'O Messenger of Allah, what am I fighting them for?'"

The Messenger of Allah replied, "Fight them until they testify that there is no other god but Allah and that Muhammad is the Messenger of Allah, and if they do that then they will prevent you from killing them and taking their wealth, except by justice, and they will be accountable to Allah."[5] But Abū Bakr was not satisfied with this tradition and said, "By Allah, I will fight those who differentiate between the prayers and Zakāt because Zakāt is justly charged on wealth." And also said, "By Allah if they refuse me a rope which they used to give to the Messenger of Allah, I will fight them for it." After that Umar ibn al-Khattāb was satisfied and said, "As soon as I saw Abū Bakr determined I felt very pleased."

I do not know how Allah could please somebody who is preventing the tradition of the Prophet. This interpretation was used to justify their fight against Muslims although Allah had prohibited making war against them, and Allah said in His Glorious Book: *"O you who believe! When you go to war in Allah's way, make investigation, and do not say to any one who offers you peace, 'You are not a believer.' Do you seek the goods of this world's life? But with Allah there are abundant gains, you too were such before, then Allah conferred a benefit on you; therefore make investigation, surely Allah is aware of what you do."* (Qur'an 4:94)

Those who refused to give Abū Bakr their Zakāt did not deny its necessity, but they only delayed it to investigate the matter. The Shiites say that these people were surprised by the succession of Abū Bakr, and some of them had been present with the Messenger of Allah at the Farewell Pilgrimage and had heard the text in which he mentioned Imām Ali ibn Abī Tālib. Therefore they decided to wait for a while until they obtained a clarification as to what had happened, but Abū Bakr wanted to silence them lest they spoke the truth. Because I do not reason with nor protest against what the Shiites say, I will leave this issue to somebody who is interested in it.

However, I should not forget to note here that the Messenger of Allah had an encounter with Tha'alabah who asked him repeatedly to pray for him to be rich and he promised Allah to

---

[5] *Sahūh Muslim*, vol. 8, p. 151.

give alms. The Messenger of Allah prayed for him and Tha'alabah became so rich that his sheep and camels filled al-Medina, and he started to neglect his duties and stopped attending the Friday prayers. When the Messenger of Allah sent some officials to collect the Zakāt, he refused to give them anything saying that it was a Jizyah (head tax on free non-Muslims under Muslim rule) or similar to it, but the Messenger of Allah did not fight him nor did he order his killing, and Allah revealed the following verse about him: "*And there are those of them who made a covenant with Allah. If He gives us out of His Grace, we will certainly give alms and we will certainly be of the good. But when He gave them out of His Grace, they became niggardly of it and they turned back and they withdrew.*" (Qur'an 9:75, 76)

After the revelation of the above Qur'anic verse Tha'alabah came to the Messenger of Allah crying and asked him to accept his Zakāt, but the Messenger of Allah refused to accept it, according to the story. If Abū Bakr and Umar were following the tradition of the Messenger why did they allow the killing of all these innocent Muslims just because they refused to pay the Zakāt?

As for those apologists who were trying to correct Abū Bakr's mistake when he interpreted the Zakāt as a just tax on wealth, there is no excuse for them nor for Abū Bakr after considering the story of Tha'alabah who withheld the Zakāt and thought of it as *Jizyah*. Who knows, perhaps Abū Bakr persuaded his friend Umar to kill those who refused to pay the Zakāt because otherwise their call would have spread throughout the Islamic world to revive al-Ghadeer's text in which Ali was confirmed as successor (to the Messenger of Allah). Thus Umar ibn al-Khattab wanted to fight them, and it was he who threatened to kill and burn those who remained in Fatima az-Zehra's house in order to extract the acclamation from them for his friend.

THE THIRD INCIDENT

The third incident which took place during the early days of Abū Bakr's caliphate in which he found himself in disagreement with Umar, and for which certain Qur'anic and Prophetic texts were interpreted, was that of Khālid ibn al-Walīd who killed Malik ibn Nuwayrah and took his wife and married her on the same day. Umar said to Khālid, "O enemy of Allah, you killed a Muslim man, then you took his wife....by Allah, I will stone you."[6] But Abū Bakr defended Khālid, and said, "O Umar, forgive him, he made a mistake, but do not rebuke him."

This is another scandal that history has recorded for a prominent Companion, and when we talk about him, we talk with respect and reverence; we even gave him the title, "The ever drawn sword of Allah." What can I say about a Companion who did all that, and killed Malik ibn Nuwayrah, the honorable Companion, leader of Bani Tamin and Bani Yarbu, famous for his courage and generosity, and furthermore the historians tell us that Khālid killed Malik and his followers put down their arms and stood together to pray. They were tied by ropes and with them was Leyla bint al-Minhal, wife of Malik, who was considered to be one of the most beautiful Arab ladies of her time, and Khālid was captured by her beauty. Malik said, "O Khālid, send us to Abū Bakr and he will be our judge." And Abdullah ibn Umar together with Abū Qutadah al-Ansari intervened and urged Khālid to send them to Abū Bakr, but he refused and said, "Allah will never forgive me if I do not kill him." Malik then turned to his wife Leyla and said, "This is the one who will kill me." After that Khālid ordered his execution and took his wife Leyla and married her that very night.[7]

What can I say about those Companions who trespassed on that Allah deemed to be forbidden; they killed Muslims because of personal whims and permitted themselves to have women that Allah had forbidden us to have. In Islam, a widow cannot be wed by another man before a definite period of time had elapsed, and this period of time has been specified by Allah in His Glorious Book. But Khālid followed his whims and debased himself, for what would this period of time ('Iddah) mean to him after he had already killed her husband and his followers despite the fact that they were Muslims. Abdullah ibn Umar and Abū Qutadah have testified to this, and the latter became so angry about Khālid's

---

[6] *Tārīkh Tabari*, vol. 3, p. 280; *Tārīkh al-Fide*, vol. 1, p 158; *Tārīkh al-Ya'qubi*, vol. 2, p. 110; *Al-Isabah fi Marifat al-Sahabah*, vol. 3, p.336.

[7] *Tārīkh al Fida*, vol. 1, p 158; *Tārīkh al-Yaqubi*, vol. 2, p 110; *Tārīkh Ibn al-Shihnah*, vol. 2, p.114 (on the margin of *al-Kamil*, vol. 11, p 114); *Wafayat al-Aayan*, vol. 6, p.14.

behavior that he returned to al-Medina and swore that he would never serve in an army led by Khālid ibn al-Walīd.[8]

As we are talking about this famous incident, it is worth looking at what Haykal said in his book *al-Siddiq Abū Bakr* in a chapter entitled *The opinion of Umar and his reasoning on the subject matter*, that Umar, who was an ideal example of firm justice, saw that Khālid had dealt unjustly with another Muslim man and took his widow before the end of her *'Iddah*, therefore he should not stay in command of the army. So that no such incident would be repeated again and spoil the affairs of the Muslims and give them a bad name amongst the Arabs, he said, "It is not right to leave him unpunished after his affair with Leyla."

Let us suppose that it was right that he passed a judgment on Malik but got it wrong, which was something Umar would not permit, what he had done with his widow alone would have meant that he had to be brought to justice. Furthermore, being the "sword of Allah" and the commander of the victorious army, did not give him the right to do what he had done, otherwise people like Khālid would abuse the law. Worse still, they would be bad examples for all Muslims on how to respect the Book of Allah. Thus Umar kept the pressure on Abū Bakr until he recalled Khālid and rebuked him.[9]

May we ask Mr. Haykel and other scholars like him: Who would compromise in order to preserve the honor of the Companions? Why did Abū Bakr not bring Khālid to justice? And if Umar was an ideal example of firm justice, as Haykel puts it, why did he only remove him from the command of the army, and not bring him to justice so that he would not be a bad example for all Muslims of how to respect the Book of Allah, as he said? And did they respect the Book of Allah and discharge the laws of Allah? Nay! It was politics! It does wonders; it changes the truth and throws the Qur'anic texts over the wall.

Some of our scholars tell us in their books that the Messenger of Allah once became very angry when Usāmah tried to mediate

---

[8] *Tārikh Tabarī*, vol. 3, p. 280; *Tārīkh Al Fida*, vol. 3, p 336; *Tārīkh al-Ya'qūbī*, vol. 2, p 110.

[9] *Al-Siddīq Abū Bakr* by Haykal, p. 151.

on behalf of an honorable woman accused of stealing, and the Messenger said, "Woe unto you! Do you mediate about one of the laws of Allah? By Allah if it was Fatima the daughter of Muhammad, I would cut her hand, He destroyed those before you because they would let the thief go if he was an honorable person, but would bring him to justice if he was a weak one." How could they be silent about the killing of the innocent Muslims, and the marriage of their widows on the same night despite the tragic loss of their husbands? I wish they had remained silent! But they try to justify Khālid's misdeed by inventing various virtues for him, they even called him "The ever drawn sword of Allah." I remember being surprised by a friend of mine, who used to like joking and changing the meaning of the words, when I mentioned the virtues of Khālid ibn al-Walīd during my days of ignorance and called him "The ever drawn sword of Allah." He replied, "He is the crippled sword of the devil!"

I was surprised then, but after my research, Allah has opened my eyes and helped me to know the true value of those who seized the caliphate, changed the laws of Allah and violated the boundaries of Allah.

There is a famous story about Khālid which happened during the lifetime of the Prophet who sent him on a mission to Bani Judhaymah to call them to Islam, but did not order him to fight them. But they did not declare their Islam very well, instead they said, "We are turning to.....we are turning to (Islam)." As a result Khālid started to kill them and took prisoners from them, and pushed them towards his friends whom he ordered to kill those prisoners. But some of his friends refused to do what they were told because they realized that these people had been truly converted to Islam, and they went back and told the Prophet what had happened.

The Prophet said, "O Allah, I am innocent of Khālid's deed." He said it twice,[10] and then sent Imām Ali ibn Abi Talib to Bani Judhaymah with money to pay compensation for their dead and for the loss of their wealth, even down to a dog. The Messenger of Allah stood up and faced the *Qiblah* (the direction of al-Ka'bah)

---

[10] *Sahīh Bukhārī*, vol. 4, p. 171.

and raised his hands to the sky then said, "O Allah, I am innocent of Khalid's deed," three times."[11]

May we ask where the alleged fairness of the Companion, which these people claim to have had, is? If Khālid ibn al-Walīd who is considered to be one of our greatest military leaders was the sword of Allah, does that mean that Allah drew His sword to kill the innocent Muslims and to violate the integrity of people? There is a clear contradiction here, because Allah forbids the killing of human beings and prohibits the committing of vile deeds, but Khālid seems to have drawn the sword of injustice to kill innocent Muslims and to confiscate their wealth and to take their women.

There is a blatant lie and a clear deception. Praise and thanks be upon You, our God....Blessed be You the Most High....Praise be upon You, You did not create the skies and the earth and what is in between them unjustly. There are the doubts of those who blaspheme. Woe to those who committed blasphemy, for Hell is awaiting them. How did Abū Bakr, who was the Caliph of the Muslims, allow himself to listen to all these crimes and be silent about them? Moreover he asked Umar to stop attacking Khālid and was very angry at Abū Qutadah because he protested strongly about Khālid's action. Was he convinced that Khālid had passed a judgment but got it wrong? What excuse could be given to those corrupt criminals who violated human integrity and claimed to have passed judgment? I do not think that Abū Bakr was trying to pass judgment on Khālid who Umar ibn al-Khattab called "The enemy of Allah." Umar thought that Khālid should be killed because he had killed an innocent Muslim, or be subjected to a hell of stones because he had committed adultery with Leyla, the widow of Malik. But nothing like that happened to Khālid; rather he defeated Umar because he had the full support of Abū Bakr who knew the whole truth about Khālid more than anybody else.

Historians have recorded that after this terrible misdeed, Abū Bakr sent Khālid on a mission to al-Yamamah, from which he came out victorious and subsequently married a girl from there in

---

11 *Sirat Ibn Hishām*, vol. 4, p. 53; *Tabaqāt Ibn S'ad, Usd al-Ghābah*, vol. 3, p. 102.

the same way as he had Leyla, before the blood of those innocent Muslims and the blood of the followers of Musaylama had dried. Later, Abū Bakr rebuked him about what he had done and used stronger words than those he used during the affair of Leyla.[12] Undoubtedly, this girl's husband was killed by Khālid who took her for himself, in the same way as he had Leyla, the widow of Malik. It must have been so; otherwise Abū Bakr would not have rebuked him using stronger words than the previous event. The historians mention the text of the letter which Abū Bakr sent to Khālid ibn al-Walīd in which he said, "O Ibn Umm Khālid. Upon my life you are doing nothing but marrying women, and in the yard of your house there is the blood of one thousand two hundred Muslims yet to dry!."[13] When Khālid read the letter, he commented, "This must be the work of al-A'sar," meaning Umar ibn al-Khattāb.

These are the strong facts that made me shun this type of Companions, and their followers who support them and defend them eagerly and invent various texts and stories to justify the deeds of Abū Bakr, Umar, Usmān, Khālid ibn al-Walīd, Mua'wiyah, Amr ibn al-As and their brethren. O Allah! I am innocent of the deeds and the sayings of those people who opposed Your rules, violated Your prohibitions and trespassed on Your territories. I am innocent of their followers and their supporters despite their full knowledge of the latter's misdeeds. Forgive me for my previous support for them because I was ignorant, and Your Messenger said, "He who doesn't know (the ignorant) cannot be excused for his ignorance." O Allah! Our leaders have led us astray and veiled the truth from us and presented us with distorted pictures of those renegade Companions had led us to believe that they were the best people after Your Messenger. There is no doubt that our forefathers were victims of the deception and the intrigues of the Umayyads and later the Abbasids.

O Allah! Forgive them and forgive us because You know what is in our inner souls. They loved and respected those Companions out of goodwill, assuming that they were supporters

---

[12] Haykal in his book, *Al-Siddīq Abū-Bakr*, p 151.

[13] *Tārīkh-Tabarī*, vol. 3, p. 254; *Tārīkh al-Khamīs*, vol. 3, p. 343.

of Your Messenger, may Your blessings and peace be upon him and upon those who love him. You know, my Lord, their and our love for the purified family, the Imāms whom You cleansed and purified, and at their head, the master of all Muslims, the commander of the believers, chief of the singularly radiant, Imām of all those who fear Allah, our lord Imām Ali ibn Abī Tālib.

O Allah! Let me be one of their followers who have committed themselves to their cause and followed their path. Let me be on their ship and help me to hold on to their strong link. Let me enter their doors and assist me in dedication to their love, help me to follow their words and their deeds, and let me be grateful for their virtues. O Allah! Let me be with them, for Your Prophet said, "Man is assembled together (on the Day of Judgment) with those whom he loves."

THE PROPHETIC TRADITION OF THE SHIP

The Messenger of Allah said, "Behold! My Ahlul Bayt are like the Ark of Noah, whoever embarked in it was saved, and whoever turned away from it was drowned."[14]

He also said, "My Ahlul Bayt are like the Gate of Repentance of the children of Israel; whoever entered therein was forgiven."[15]

Ibn Hajar cited the above tradition in his book *Al-Sawā'iq al-Muhriqah* and gave the following commentary: The idea behind comparing them with the Ark (ship) is to say that whoever loves them and reveres them as a sign of his gratitude for their graces, and whoever is guided by their learned people, will be saved from the darkness of contradictions.

On the other hand, whoever decides to stay behind, will sink in the sea of ingratitude and will be destroyed in the wilderness of tyranny. The reason for comparing Ahlul Bayt with the Gate of Repentance is that Allah--the Most High--made the Gate of Repentance (the Gate of Jericho or Jerusalem) a sign of His forgiveness. Similarly, Ahlul Bayt are the means of Repentance for this nation.

---

[14] *Al-Mustadrak* by al-Hakim, vol.3, p.151.

[15] *Al Sawā'iq - Al Muhriqah* by Ibn Hajar, pp. 184 and 234.

I wish I could ask Ibn Hajar if he was one of those who went on board the ship and entered the door and was guided by the religious leaders (*Ulama*), or was he one of those who order what they do not do in practice, and contradict their belief. There are many of those unfair people when I ask them or argue with them they say, "We are in a more favorable situation *vis-à-vis* Ahlul Bayt and Imām Ali than others, we respect and appreciate Ahlul Bayt, and nobody can deny their graces and their virtues."

Yes, they say with their tongues what is not in their hearts, or they respect them and appreciate them but follow and imitate their enemies who fought them and contradicted them, or even perhaps on many occasions do not know who Ahlul Bayt are, and if you ask them who Ahlul Bayt are, they answer you immediately, they are the Prophet's wives from whom Allah kept the dirt away and purified them." When I addressed the question to one of those people, he solved the puzzle by giving me the following answer: "All the Sunni people and al-Jama'ah follow Ahlul Bayt." I was surprised and said, "How could that be?" He answered, "The Messenger of Allah said that we should take half of our religion from this Humayra, meaning Ayeshah, therefore we took half off the religion from Ahlul Bayt."

On this basis one could understand their respect and appreciation for Ahlul Bayt, but when you ask them about the twelve Imāms they would only know Imām Ali, Imām Hasan and Imām Husayn from them, and they would not accept the Imāmate of Imām Hasan nor of Imām Husayn. Besides, they respect Mu'awiyah ibn Abī Sufyān who poisoned Imām Hasan and killed him (they call Mu'awiyah, "The writer of the Revelations"), and they also respect Amr ibn al-As in the same way as they respect Imām Ali.

This is nothing but contradictions and confusion and an attempt to cover the right with the wrong and the light with darkness. For how could the heart of the believer contain the love of Allah and the devil at the same time, and Allah said in His glorious Book: "*You shall not find a people who believe in Allah and the Latter day befriending those who act in opposition to Allah and His messenger, even though they were their (own) fathers, or their sons or their brothers or their kinsfolk; these are they into whose hearts he has impressed faith and whom He has strengthened with an inspiration from Him: and He will cause them to enter gardens beneath which rivers flow abiding therein; Allah is well-pleased with them and they are well-pleased with Him; these are Allah's party: now surely the party of Allah are the successful ones."* (Qur'an 58:22) Allah also said: "*O you who believe! Do not take my enemy and your enemy for friends, would you offer them love while they deny what has come to you of truth?*" (Qur'an 60:1)

THE PROPHETIC TRADITION ON LIVING LIKE HIM

The Messenger of Allah said: "Whoever wishes to live and die like me, and to abide in the Garden of Eden after death should acknowledge Ali as his patron and follow Ahlul Bayt after me, for they are my Ahlul Bayt and they have been created out of the same knowledge and understanding as myself. Woe unto those followers of mine who will deny the Ahlul Bayt their distinctions and who will disregard their relationship and affinity with me. May Allah never let them benefit from my intercession?"[16]

As you can see, the above tradition is one of those clear sayings which do not require any interpretation, nor indeed gives any scope for the Muslims to choose, rather, it eliminates any excuse. If he does not follow Imām Ali and acknowledge Ahlul Bayt, the Prophet's Family he will be deprived of the mediation of their grandfather, the Messenger of Allah.

It is worth noting here that at the early stage of my research, I felt doubtful about the authenticity of this tradition and I thought it carried a great threat to those who are not in agreement with Ali and Ahlul Bayt, especially when the tradition does not allow any scope for interpretation. I became rather worried when I read the book *Al-Isābah* in which Ibn Hajar al-Asqalānī gives the following commentary on this tradition:

> I based the tradition on what Yahya ibn Ya'la al-Muhāribī had said, and he is feeble. In fact Ibn Hajar removed some of the doubt that remained in my mind, for I thought that Yahya ibn Ya'la al-Muhāribī fabricated the tradition and could not be

---

[16] *Tārīkh Ibn Asākir*, vol. 2, p 95; *Mustadrak al-Hakim*, vol.3, p.128; et el.

a reliable transmitter. But Allah--Praise be to Him the Most High--wanted to show me the whole truth. I read a book entitled *Ideological Discussions on the Writings of Ibrahim al-Jabhan.*[17] This book clarified the situation and it became apparent to me that Yahya ibn Ya'la al-Muhāribī was a reliable transmitter of hadith and the two Shaykhs, Muslim and al-Bukhārī, depended on what he transmitted. I myself followed his case and found that al-Bukhārī cited a few traditions transmitted by him regarding the battle of al-Hudaybiyah, and they were put in Volume 3, Page 31. Muslim also cited a few traditions in his *Sahīh* vol. 5 in a chapter entitled *The Boundaries,* on page 119. Even al-Dhahabi, with all his restrictions, considered him a reliable transmitter, together with the Imāms of al-Jurh and al-Ta'dīl (criteria applied to ahādīth to find out the reliable and unreliable transmitter), and of course the two Shaykhs (Muslim and al-Bukhārī) used him as a reliable reference. So why all this intrigue, falsification and deception about a man who was considered to be a reliable transmitter by the authors of *al-Sahih*? Is it because he told the truth regarding the necessity to follow Ahlul Bayt, and was therefore branded by Ibn Hajar as feeble and weak?

It seems that Ibn Hajar was unaware of the fact that his writings would become subject to the scrutiny of some highly dedicated scholars and that he would be accountable to them for all what he had written. These scholars were able to uncover his prejudice and ignorance because they were guided by the light of the Prophet and Ahlul Bayt.

I realized later that some of our scholars try hard to cover the truth so that the affairs of the Companions and the caliphs, who were considered to be their leaders and mentors, remain unknown. We see them trying to interpret the correct tradition in

---

[17] *Munaqashah Aqadiyya fi Maqalat Ibrahim al-Jabhan,* p.29.

their own ways and give them different meanings, or they deny the traditions that contradict their creed, even if they were mentioned in their own books and *Sahih*. At times they remove half or one-third of the prophetic tradition to replace it with something else! Or they may throw doubts about the reliable narrators (of the tradition) because they raise issues that are not to their liking, and on a few occasions they publish them in the first edition (of a book) but remove it from the subsequent editions without giving any indication to justify their action, in spite of the full knowledge of the intelligent readers as to why the saying has been removed!

I have become aware of all these things after conducting meticulous research and investigation, and I have convincing proof to support what I am saying. I wish they would stop giving me all these excuses to justify the actions of those Companions who turned back on their heels, because their views seem to contradict each other and contradict the historical fact. I wish they would follow the just path, even if it was a bitter one, then they would leave their minds and the minds of others in peace.

They claim that some of the early Companions were not reliable transmitters of the Prophet's tradition; therefore they removed what they did not like, especially if these traditions included some of the last instructions of the Messenger of Allah before his death. Al-Bukhārī and Muslim both write about the fact that the Messenger of Allah advised three things on his death-bed:

--Remove all the polytheists from the Arabian Peninsula

--Reward the delegation in the same way as I have done and the narrator then said, "I forgot the third."[18]

It is possible that those Companions who were present at the death-bed and heard the three instructions forgot the third one, when we know that they used to learn by heart a whole epic after hearing it once? No. It is politics that forced them to forget it and not to mention it again.

This is indeed another of those comedies organized by the Companions, because there is no doubt that the first instruction of

---

[18] *Sahīh al-Bukhārī*, vol.3, p.121; *Sahīh Muslim*, vol. 5, p.14.

the Messenger of Allah was to appoint Ali as his successor, but the narrator did not recite it.

The person who is involved with the investigation about this issue will inevitably sense the undoubted recommendations for the succession of Imām Ali despite all the attempts to cover it or to remove it. Al-Bukhārī cited it in his *Sahīh* in a chapter entitled *Al-Wasaya* (The Legacies or the Recommendations), Muslim also cited it in his *Sahīh* and said that the Prophet recommended Imām Ali for the succession in the presence of Ayeshah.[19] Look how Allah shows His light even if the oppressors try to cover it.

I repeat here what I said before; if those Companions were not reliable enough to transmit the recommendations of the Messenger of Allah, then we cannot blame the followers and those who came after them.

If Ayeshah, the mother of the faithful, could not bear mentioning the name of Imām Ali and could not wish him any good--as Ibn Sa'd writes in his *Tabaqāt*,[20] and al-Bukhārī in his *Sahīh* in a chapter entitled *The illness of the Prophet and his death*, and if she prostrated herself to thank Allah when she heard the news of Imām Ali's death--then how can we expect her to mention the recommendation in favor of Imām Ali, when she was known, publicly and privately, for her animosity and hatred toward Ali and his sons and towards all the Family of the Prophet. Behold! There is no might or power except in Allah the Most High, the Great.

---

[19] *Sahīh Bukhārī*, vol. 3, p. 68; *Sahīh Muslim*, vol. 2, p 14.
[20] *Tabaqāt Ibn Sa'd*, Part 2, p. 29.

Chapter: 15

KNOWLEDGE OF THE AHLUL BAYT

By

Maulana Sayyid Muhammad Rizvi[1]

INTRODUCTION

The universal *wilayat* is in a way linked to the knowledge that Almighty Allah has bestowed upon the person holding the *wilayat*. The universal *wilayat* of Imām Ali, for example, is described in the Qur'an by the words "the person who has knowledge of the Book."

What is 'ilmu 'l-ghayb? Our means of gaining knowledge are through the senses that Allah has created in us. "*And Allah brought you forth from the wombs of your mothers while you did not know anything; and He made for you the ears, the eyes, and the hearts (i.e., minds) so that haply you may be thankful.*" (16:78)

We see things through our eyes and listen to sounds by our ears, and then we analyze the information in our minds and deduce the conclusion.

There is another kind of knowledge that can not be acquired by human senses; it comes from God. This kind of knowledge is known as *'ilmu 'l-ghayb*, the knowledge of the unseen, or about the future events or the inner thoughts and intentions of a person, etc.

"*Ghayb*" is the opposite of "*shuhūd* – the present, the seen." Sometimes the *ghayb* is absolute (e.g., the inner most intentions of a person) and at other times it is relative (e.g., what a person has hidden inside his house, it is 'unseen' for outsiders). The term "*ghayb* – unseen, hidden" is used from the perspective of the created beings only. For Allah there is no difference between *ghayb* and *shuhūd*. The Qur'an describes Allah as: "*....Knower of the unseen and the seen.......*" (39:46; 62:8).

---

[1] Reproduced from his book, *Shi'ism – Imāmate & Wilayat* (Chapter: Seven), published by Al-Ma'arif, Canada, 1999.

THE QUR'AN AND 'ILMU 'L-GHAYB

According to the Qur'an, the only independent source of *'ilmu 'l-ghayb* is Allah: *"And with Him are the keys of the ghayb, no one knows it except Him......"* (6:59); *"Say, 'Those who are in the heavens and the earth do not know the ghayb except Allah.'"* (27:65); and *"And to Allah belongs the ghayb of the heavens and the earth."* (7:49, 18:26). The importance of these verses is that the knowledge of *ghayb* belongs to Allah; He knows the *ghayb* by Himself.

Can anyone else have access to 'ilmu 'l-ghayb? Almighty Allah, out of His infinite grace and wisdom, bestows the *'ilmu 'l-ghayb* upon whomsoever He chooses. The Qur'an says: *"(My Lord) knows the ghayb and He does not expose His ghayb to anyone except to one with whom He is pleased from the messenger......"* (72:26-27); *".......And Allah is not about to inform you about the ghayb, but Allah chooses from His messengers whomsoever He pleases [for the ghayb]."* (3:179); and *"He knows what is before them and what is behind them, and they cannot comprehend anything of His knowledge except what He pleases."* (2:255) The importance of these verses is that Allah bestows *'ilmu 'l-ghayb* to some created beings.

When you put all the verses about the knowledge of the unseen together, you get the overall conclusion that (1) Allah is the only original and independent possessor of *'ilmu 'l-ghayb,* and that (2) whosoever from the angels, prophets, messengers, Imāms and other virtuous—persons that have *'ilmu 'l-ghayb* is totally dependent on Allah's discretion and power. [2]

After commenting on the last verses of Surah 72, Allama at-Tabātabā'ī reaches this conclusion:

"The exclusive possession of the *'ilmu 'l-ghayb* by Almighty Allah is in the sense of originality that we have explained, and so He, the Almighty, knows the *ghayb* by Himself while the others know the *ghayb* by Him informing them about it. And so it becomes clear that what has been mentioned in His words about others not having the *'ilmu 'l-ghayb* actually means 'not having it by themselves and independently,' it

---

[2] For an excellent discussion on the Qur'anic verses on *'ilmu 'l-ghayb* and their relevant ahādīth, see Ahmad Mutahharī and Ghulam Raza Kardan, *'Ilm-e Payambar wa Imām dar Qur'an*, Qum: Dar Rah-e Haq, 1366 A.H.

does not deny what others know (of the ghayb) through revelation......"[3]

'ILMU 'L-GHAYAB OF THE PROPHETS

The Qur'an not only talks about the possibility of others having access to the *'ilmu 'l-ghayb,* it actually gives various examples of those who had been given the *'ilmu 'l-ghayb* by Almighty Allah.

1. While counting the miraculous powers that he possessed, Prophet 'Isa says: *"I will inform you of what you are eating and what you store in your houses........."* (3:48)
2. In reference to Prophet Yusuf, we have these verses: *"And thus does your Lord choose you and teaches you the interpretation of words."* (12:6, 21); *".........And when they agreed to put him into the bottom of the pit, We revealed to him that (a time shall come when) you will inform them of this affair of theirs........."* (12:15); and *".......I shall inform you two of its interpretation before comes to you (the food): this is from what my Lord has taught me......."* (12:37)
3. Prophet Sulaymān was taught the language of the birds: *"And Sulaymān......he said, 'O men! We have been taught the language of the birds."* (27:16)
4. According to the Qur'an, Allah had bestowed *'ilmu 'l-ghayb* upon the Prophet of Islam as can be seen in the following verses:

> Referring to the events of the past, Allah says, *"These are the news of the ghayb that We reveal unto you......."* (11:49)
> Referring to the story of Prophet Yusuf, Allah says: *"These are the news of the unseen (ghayb) that We reveal unto you...."* (12:102)
> Allah informed the Prophet about the on-going war between the Eastern Roman Empire and the Sasanid Persian Empire: *"The Romans are vanquished in a nearby land; and they, after being vanquished, shall overcome (the Persians) within a few years..."* (30:1-4)

---

[3] At-Tabātabā'ī, *al-Mīzān*, vol. 20, p. 131-132.

On the conquest of Mecca at the hand of the Muslims, Allah said, *"Certainly Allah had shown to His Apostle the vision with truth: you shall most certainly enter the Sacred Mosque (in Mecca), if Allah pleases, in security......"* (48:27)

The Prophet is also informed about the inner most thoughts of the hypocrites: *".....And they say in their own hearts, 'Why does not Allah punish us for what we say?'....."* (58:8)

As you can see, these examples cover all aspects of *ghayb:* history of the past, events of the future, language of the birds, and also the intentions of other people. The Prophet is described as someone *"who was not niggardly of the ghayb,"* (81:24) he used to share the information with others.

Before we end this section, let me remind the readers that the knowledge of *ghayb* of a human being or an angel is not his own but is always and constantly dependent upon the will of Allah. That is why the Messengers were instructed to say that they do not posses *'ilmu l-ghayb.* (6:50; 11:3) It is for the same reason that Prophet Muhammad was instructed to say: *"Had I knowledge of the ghayb, I would have acquired much good, and evil would not have touched me."* (7:188) This is not a denial of having *'ilmu 'l-ghayb;* it is affirmation of the belief that whatever knowledge he has is according to the wish and pleasure of Almighty Allah.[4]

'ILMU 'L-GHAYB OF THE IMĀMS

Imām Ali was also blessed with the *'ilmu 'i-ghayb* as attested by verse 13:43 discussed in the last chapter on *wilayat.* It was on the basis of the "knowledge of the Book" that Imām Ali has the universal *wilayat.* Moreover, according to Shi'a ahādīth, Allah had instructed the Prophet to convey whatever knowledge was given to him to Ali bin Abi Talib. After all, the Prophet *"was not*

---

[4] For a precise and clear picture on the knowledge of God (which is absolute and unchanging, and is described as *"al-lawh al-mahfūz –* the protected tablet") vis-a-vis the knowledge of chosen human beings and angels (which is not necessarily absolute, and is described as *"lawhu 'l-mahw wa 'l-ithbāt –* the tablet that can be erased and re-written"), see S. Saeed Akhtar Rizvi, *The Justice of God,* p. 21-26. The book clearly explains that *bada'* (change) does not occur in the knowledge of God, it an only occur in the knowledge of humans and angels.

niggardly of the ghayb." The other Imāms, as successors of Ali, also had access to *'ilmu 'l-ghayb.*[5] Shaykh al-Muzaffar explains the Shi'a position on this issue as follows:

> "We maintain that the powers of the Imāms to receive inspiration have reached the highest degree of excellence, and we say that it is a Divinely-given power. By this means the Imām is able to understand information about anything, anywhere, and at any time, and he understands by means of this Divinely-given power at once, without recourse to methodological reasoning or guidance from a teacher. When he desires to know about some matter, it is reflected in his pure mind as if in a polished mirror. It is clear from the histories of their lives that, like the Prophet, the Imāms were not trained or taught by anyone at all, not even in reading and writing, from their childhoods to the maturing of their mind. No author or teacher was seen to instruct any one of them, but they were incomparable masters of knowledge, so that they never asked about any problem without being able to answer it immediately, and they never required time to consider a question before replying."[6]

Soon after the people accepted him as their leader, Imām Ali came to the mosque dressed in the turban and robe of the Prophet, and sat on the pulpit. Then he said: "O People, ask me before you lose me for this is the basket of knowledge, this is the breath of the Messenger of Allah, and this is what the Messenger of Allah fed me. Therefore, ask me for I have the knowledge of the first ones and the last ones. By Allah, if a cushion is set up for me so that I may sit on it, I shall give verdicts to the people of Tawrat according to their Tawrat until it will say, 'Imām Ali is true; he has not lied. He has given you the verdict according to what Allah has revealed in me.' And I shall give verdicts to the people of the Injīl according to their Injīl until it will say, 'Ali is true; he has not lied. He has given you the

---

[5] Al-Majlisī, *Bihāru 'l-Anwār*, vol. 26, chapters 1, 3 and 5 as quoted in Rizvi, *The Justice of God*, p. 21-26.

[6] Al-Muzaffar, M.R., *The Faith of Shi'a Islam*, p. 33-34.

verdict according to what Allah has revealed in me.' And I shall give verdicts to the people of the Qur'an according to their Qur'an until it will say, 'Ali is true, he has not lied. He has given you the verdict according to what Allah has revealed in me.' You read the Book (i.e., the Qur'an) at night as well as day; so is there anyone you who know what was revealed in it? If it had not been for a verse in the Book of Allah, I would have informed you of what has happened (in the past, what will happen, and what shall happen until the Day of Resurrection. And that is the verse: '*Allah erases and confirms what He wishes, and with Him is the Mother of the Book. [Ra'd 39]*.....'"[7]

This last passage is significant; in it, Imām Ali claims to have the access to '*ilmu 'l-ghayb* but also acknowledges that it is totally dependent upon the will of Almighty Allah.

Here we shall just quote one or two examples from the life of Imām Ali. Jundab bin 'Abdullah al-Azdi narrates the following:

> I took part with Ali in the battles of Jamal and Siffīn. I never had any doubts about fighting against those who fought him until I took part in the battle of Naharwān (against the Kharijites). Then doubts came to me about fighting against these people. I said, "It is our reciters of the Qur'an and our choice men whom we are killing. This matter is dreadful."
>
> In the morning I went for a walk (taking) a vessel of water with me, until I left the lines (of the army). Then I fixed my spear in the ground, fitted my shield on it and shaded myself from the sun. While I was sitting, Imām Ali came along. He said to me, "O' Brother from (the tribe of) al-Azd, do you have water for ritual purification with you?"
>
> "Yes," I answered and I gave him the vessel.
>
> He went aside so that I could not see him. Then he came back after he had purified himself. He sat down in the shade of the spear. Suddenly a horseman appeared asking for him. I said, "O! Imām Ali there is a horseman who wants you."
>
> "Make a sign to him (to come here)," he told me.

---

[7] Al-Mufīd, *al-Ikhtisās*, p. 235; a shorter version of this narration may also be seen in *al-Irshad*, p. 34 (in English, p. 21). For other references on this claim of Imam Ali that "Ask me before you lose me," see al-Amīnī, *al-Ghadīr*, vol. 6, p. 193-194; vol. 7, p. 107-108.

I made a sign and he came. He said, "O'! Imām Ali, the people (i.e., the Kharijites) have crossed the river."

"No," he retorted, "they have not crossed."

"Yes, by God, they have crossed." The man insisted.

"No," he retorted, "they have not crossed."

Then another man came. He said, "O'! Imām Ali, the people have crossed."

"No", he replied, "they have not crossed."

"By God," the man said, "I did not come to you until I saw the standards and the baggage on that side."

"By God," he declared, "they have not done so. (What you want) is to kill them and shed their blood."

Then he rose and I rose with him. I said to myself, "Praise be to God, who has given me insight into this man and enabled me to recognize his affair. He is one of the two men: he is either a bold liar or he has an evidence (for his authority) from his Lord and a covenant from his Prophet. O God, I give You a solemn undertaking which You can ask me about on the Day of Resurrection. If I find that the people have crossed, I will be the first to fight against him, the first to thrust my spear into his eye. If the people have not crossed, then I will go forth with him and fight alongside him."

We returned to the lines (of the army) and we found that the standards and pieces of baggage were as they had been (before).

Then Ali took me by the scruff of the neck and pushed me. Then he said, "O' Brother of (the tribe of) al-Azd, has the matter become clear to you?"

"Yes, Imām Ali." I replied.

"Your business is with your enemy," he said.

I killed one man from the Kharijites and then I killed another. I and another of them were exchanging blows. I struck him and he struck me. We both fell together. My comrades carried me back. By the time I recovered consciousness, there were none of the Kharijites left.

After quoting this incident, Shaykh al-Mufid makes the following comment: "In it, Imām Ali provides information about the unseen, gives clear evidence of his knowledge of the inner conscience (of man) and his knowledge of what is in men's souls. The evidence in it is outstanding which could not be equaled by evidence of a similar nature in terms of the greatness of the miracle and its clear proof."[8]

Now I would like to quote another example from the forthcoming book of my father where he has also discussed the issue of prophetic foresight. He writes: "There are numerous, well-documented prophecies of the Prophet and Imām Ali which were fulfilled later.....An important historical event is referred to in Sermon 128 in *Nahjul-Balāgha*. Sayyid Razi gives this sermon the caption 'From the Sermon describing the attributes of the Turks.' He quotes portions describing fierce invaders, their features, their clothes, the invincibility and their killing of multitudes. Now Sayyid Razi died in 406/1016, two hundred and forty-two years before the fall of Baghdad in 1258. Ibn Abil Hadid, who wrote the *Sharh* (commentary of *Nahjul-Balagha)* died seventeen years before the fall, he identifies the invaders with the Mongol hordes who had in his days already conquered Khurāsān, Iran and Syria. He describes the havoc they created in the neighboring countries up to 643/1245. He says: 'And know that this prophecy of the unseen by Ali, we have seen it by our own eyes and it has happened in our time. And the people, since the early days of Islam, were waiting for its fulfillment, until the firm decree (of Allah) made it appear in our day.' There are no clear details in his version of the sermon of who the conquered were. But this same sermon in its full form was in the hands of the learned Shi'a and had been since Ali's day. Allama al-Hillī was born eight years before the fall of Baghdad to Hulagu Khan. His father, Sadidu'd-Dīn Yūsuf al-Hillī was the most learned man of his time in *fiqh*, Principle of jurisprudence and theology."

Referring to the prophecies of future events by Ali, Allama writes: "And among them is his prophecy of the foundation of Baghdad and the Kingdom of the Abbasids and their circumstance in which the Mongols shall take away the kingdom from them. My father has narrated it, and that (prophecy) was the

---

[8] Al-Mufid, *al-Irshad*, p. 317-319; in its English translation, see p. 239-240. This narration can also be seen in the following Sunni sources: Muttaqi al-Hindi, *Kanzu 'l-'Ummal*, vol. 11, p. 289 quoted from at-Tabarani's *al-Wasit;* Ibn Abi 'l-Hadid, *Sharh Nahji 'l-Balagha*, vol. 2, p. 271.

reason for the citizens of Kūfā, Hilla and the two sacred cities (Karbala and Najaf) being saved from the massacre.

"When Hulagu reached Baghdad, and before he conquered it, the majority of the people of Hilla fled away to the deserts, except a few of them. Among those who remained was my father (may Allah have mercy on him), Sayyid Majddu'd-Dīn bin Tawūs, and the faqīh, Ibn Abi 'l-'Izz. They decided to write to the sultan (Hulagu) that they accepted his rule and were under the Il Khanid authority. They sent the letter with a Persian man. Hulagu sent a firmān (order) with two person, Nikalah and 'Ala'uddīn, saying, 'if your hearts are as your letter shows, then come to us.' The two officers came (and conveyed Hulagu's message). However, the others (who had signed the letter) were afraid to go as they did not know what the result would be. Therefore, my father (may Allah have mercy on him) asked the officers, 'Would it be enough if I alone come there?' They said, 'Yes.' Therefore, he went with them. When my father came before the Sultan (and it was before Baghdad was conquered and the caliph killed,) he asked my father, 'How is it that you ventured upon writing to me and coming to my court even before you knew how the matter between me and your king would be decided? How can you be sure; perhaps he would make peace with me and I would go away?'

"My father (may Allah have mercy upon him) said, 'We took that step because we have been told of the prophecy of Imām 'Ali that he said in his Sermon of Zawra':

'....And what would make you know what Zawra' is? A land of deep-rooted splendor. Strong buildings will be built in it and its inhabitants will increase in number; and there shall be therein servants and treasurers.
'The children of Abbas will make it their dwelling place and a showplace for their vanities; it shall be their house of amusement and sport; there shall be in it overpowering oppression, frightful fear, debauched leaders, sinful rulers, and embezzling ministers; these shall be served by the natives of Fars and Rum. They shall not perform any good even after knowing it and shall not leave any evil even

after knowing it. Their males shall satisfy their lust with males, and the females with females.

'Then there shall be the overwhelming grief, long weeping and destruction, and crying for the inhabitants of Zawra' from the assault of the Turks. And they are a people of small eyes, their faces like hammered shields, their clothes are iron, they are hairless, beardless. There will lead them a king who will come from whence their (the 'Abbasids') kingdom had begun. He will be of a very loud voice, powerful authority and high courage; he will not pass by a town but that he will conquer it, and no standard will be raised against him but that he will put it down. Woe unto him who would become his enemy, he shall remain like it until he is victorious.'

"After quoting the sermon, my father said, 'As these qualities had long been described to us and we found the very qualities in you, we put our hope in you and came towards you.'

"Thereupon the Sultan was satisfied and he wrote for them (i.e., the citizens of the four towns) a firmān, in the name of my father (may Allah have mercy upon him) giving tranquility to the hearts of the people of Hilla and the nearby towns.

"Clearly the leading Shi'a had the Sermon in a form which gave details of who the vanquished were—the 'Abbasids. It is inconceivable that Imām Ali would give such details of the victor without any reference to the vanquished. They believed so completely in its authenticity that they took such an irreversible step as to correspond with and go in person to the court of Hulagu. As for Sayyid Razi, one can understand his omission of details about the conquered. He did not omit them because of lack of high literary merit but because he lived in Baghdad under the very nose of those who were to be so signally vanquished, the 'Abbasid Caliphs."[9]

Jundab's personal example during the lifetime of Imām Ali and al-Hilli's example of the seventh Islamic century, clearly prove that the Imāms had access to *ilmu 'l-ghayb* by the blessing of

---

[9] The forthcoming book of Allama Sayyid Saeed Akhtar Rizvi on Shi'a faith and history. He cites al-Hilli's *Kashfu*, p. 28 as the source for the narration.

Almighty Allah, and that this belief is not "certain extravagant claims made for them by their fanatical associates."[10]

In the words of Shaykh al-Mufīd, "(The evidence for) this kind (of miracle) by Imām Ali is such that it can only be denied through stupidity, ignorance, slander and obstinacy."[11]

'ILMU 'L-GHAYB AND PERSONAL LIFE

So why did not the Prophet or the Imāms use the *'ilmu 'l-ghayb* to avert tragedies in their personal lives? This is a very commonly asked question in regard to the *'ilmu 'l-ghayb*. I always use an example I had seen in my childhood in East Africa. I remember seeing vehicles assigned to government officials with the sign "For Official Use Only" clearly visible on them. The *ilmu 'l-ghayb* given to the prophets and Imāms is just like that: "For Official Use only" it is not for use in their personal lives.

Recently, in response to a question from a Philippines Shi'a, my father wrote: "Allah had given fore-knowledge of many future events to the Prophet and the Imāms. But at the same time they were strictly ordered not to use that knowledge in their dealings with the people as if they did not know what was going to happen in the future. They had to live with the people on the level of the common people. They were not to use their super-natural knowledge or power for their own benefit or for averting any harm from themselves. (In fact, it was a very tough test for them to know that a certain man or woman would harm them or their children and then behave with him/her in the normal way.) That is why Imām Ali did not punish or imprison Ibn Muljim, although he knew that the latter would assassinate him."[12]

---

[10] Abdulaziz Sachedina writes about the evolution of Imamate as follows: "The Imams were now believed to possess divine knowledge which enabled them to predict future events.....The highly speculative aspects of the doctrine of the Imamate should be attributed to the circumstances in which the Imams manifested political quietism but did not object to certain extravagant claims made for them by their fanatical associates. These claims included the possession of esoteric knowledge inherited through designation by the Imam." (*Islamic Messianism*, p. 18-19)

[11] Al-Mufīd, *al-Irshād*, p.314; in English, see p.236.

[12] In the forthcoming *Your questions Answered*, vol. 8.

Shaykh Muhammad Ridhā al-Ja'farī explains, "The Prophets and the Imāms, it should be well observed, share with the rest of humanity the means for obtaining knowledge which Allah has given: the senses, the intellect, etc. They also possess a special power or means which other people do not have.

"In the carrying out of the commands of Allah's *sharī'ah* in which all have a responsibility, and likewise in ordinary behavior, the Prophets and the Imāms only make use of the first way of knowing, the commonly available means: the second means is only made use of by them in duties and works which are connected with their positions of prophethood and Imāmate. Thus in matters like knowing the beginning of the month, passing judgment, finding out if something is unclean or pure, etc., they make use of the means, such as the sighting of the moon, and so forth, which everyone else employs.

"Also the knowledge that Prophets or Imāms have concerning, for example, the time of their death, can not be the basis for action for them. What they volitionally do must be determined by the means available to everyone. Such knowledge thus has a spiritual aspect to it related to the Encounter with Allah, and the reason for it must be sought on this level, but it is not for the purpose of influencing and controlling events on the level of ordinary understanding."[13]

The same applies to the universal *wilayat:* the Prophet or the Imāms do not use it for their personal interest; it is only used for proving the truth of the faith.

THE CONCEPT OF *AL-QUR'AN AN-NATIQ*

"*Al-Qur'an an-nātiq*" means the "speaking Qur'an." This is a famous title given to the Shi'a Imāms to describe their proximity to the Qur'an; they are the custodians of the Qur'anic message and its interpretation; they are the embodiment of the Qur'anic values

---

[13] See the explanatory note of Shaykh Muhammad Ridhā al-Ja'farī in al-Kulaynī, *al-Kāfī* (Arabic with English translation), vol. 1, Part Two, Book 4 (iii) p. 259. Sayyid Muhammad Ridhā al-Jalālī has extensively dealt with this question and its responses by the Imāms themselves and the Shi'a 'ulama' of the last ten centuries. See *Ilmu 'l-Aimma bi 'l-Ghayb wa 'l-I'tiradh 'alayhi bi 'l-Ilqai ila 't-tuhlika wa 'l-ijabat 'anhu 'ibaru 't-ta'rikh, Turathuna*, no. 37 (Shawwal, 1414) p. 7-107.

and its ideals. This concept is based on the various sayings of the Prophet in which the Qur'an and the Ahlul Bayt are shown to never separate from one another.

The famous hadīth of *thaqalayn* says: "I am leaving two precious things behind among you: the Book of Allah and my Ahlul Bayt. The two shall not separate from one another until they come to me at the foundation of Kawthar (on the Day of Resurrection)."[14] In another hadīth, Umm Salama, the wife of the Prophet, quotes him as follows: "Imām Ali is with the Qur'an and the Qur'an is with Imām Ali, they shall never separate from one another until they reach to me at the Foundation (on the day of Resurrection)."[15]

Abū Sa'īd al-Khudrī reports that one day we were sitting waiting for the Prophet Muhammad to come out. He came to us while we saw that the strap of his shoe was broken; he gave it to Ali to repair. Then he said, "One of you will wage war for the interpretation (*ta'wīl*) of the Qur'an just as I waged war for its revelation (*tanzīl*)." Abū Bakr said, "Am I the one?" The Prophet said, "No." Then Umar said, "Am I the one?" The Prophet said, "No, but the one who is repairing the shoe."[16]

Imām Ali himself said, "Ask me before you lose me, for by the One who split the grain and created the soul, if you ask me as to which verse was revealed at night time or at day time, whether it is of Meccan or Medinite (era), during journey (of the Prophet) or while in Medina, whether it is abrogator or abrogated, whether it is clear or allegorical and whether you need its interpretation or context of its revelation — I shall inform you about it."[17]

It is based on these facts supported by the Sunni sources that the Shi'as use the title *"al-Qur'an un-Nātiq"* for their Imāms. As we

---

14 At-Tirmidhī, Sahīh, vol. 5 (Beirut : Dar al-Fikr, n.d) p. 328-329, hadīth # 3874, 3876; as-Suyūtī, *ad-Durru 'l-Manthūr*, vol. 6, p. 7, 306; Ibnu 'l-Maghazilī ash-Shāfi'ī, Mamaqib 'Ali bin Abī Tālib, p. 234, hadīth # 281.

15 Al-Hakim, *al-Mustakrak 'ala 's-Sahīhayn*, vol. 3 (Beirut : Dar al-Ma'rifa, n.d) p. 124; al-Khuwarazmi, *al-Manaqib*, p. 110; *Majma' uz-Zawā'id*, vol. 9, p. 134 as-Suyūtī, *Tārīkhu 'l-Khulafā'*, p. 173

16 An-Nasa'ī, *Khasā'isu Amiri 'l-Muminīn 'Ali bin Abī Tālib*, p. 134; Muhibbu 'd-Dīn at-Tabarī, *Dhakhairu 'l-Uqba*, p. 139.

17 Al-Mufīd, *al-Ikhtisās*, p. 236.

saw above, Imām Ali himself claims to have the true and inner meanings of the Qur'anic verses. This claim and belief has been there from the earliest days of Shi'aism. So it is incorrect to place the beginning of this concept in the latter period by saying that "the belief that the Imāms were the 'speaking (al-nātiq) Qur'an,' who knew the esoteric interpretation of the Book, most probably began during al-Bāqir's time."[18]

CONCLUSION

The beginning of Islam is not separate from the beginning of Shi'aism; it started with the Prophet of Islam, Muhammad al-Mustafa, and has been preserved in its origin form by the Imāms of Ahlul Bayt.

The Prophet presented the message of Islam in the *da'wat dhu 'l-'ashi'ra* and also introduced Imām Ali as "my brother, my successor, and my caliph." And then just a few months before his death, in the biggest gathering of his life, at Ghadeer Khum, the Prophet clearly appointed Imām Ali as the *mawlā* (the master, the leader) of the *umma*. In between the *da'wat* and Ghadeer Khum, the Prophet introduced Imām Ali to the people in various occasions. The appointment of Imām Ali for Imāmate and Khilafat was explicit and clear.

Imām Ali and the Imāms from among his descendants are the Ahlul Bayt in the Qur'anic term. Loving and honoring them is an Islamic duty of all Muslims. The Ahlul Bayt have been vested by Allah with the *wilayat* in the broadest sense of the word, and that also includes the *ilmu 'l-ghayb*.

---

[18] Abdulaziz Sachedina, *Islamic Messianism*, p. 15.

Chapter: 16

DIVINITY OF THE IMĀMS

By

Imam Muhammad Jawad Chirri[1]

The mercenary writers have tried more than one way to insult the followers of the Members of the House of Prophet Muhammad. Among these shameful ways is the allegation that the Shi'a Muslims believe that the Imāms from the Members of the House of the Prophet control the atoms of the universe. These writers declare that such a belief is a belief in the divinity of the Imāms.

They tried to prove this accusation by another allegation. They accused the revolutionary Islamic leader, Imām Khomeini, of saying in one of his books or lectures that the Imāms from the Members of the House of the Prophet control the atoms of the universe.

I have never read such a statement in the books or lectures of Imām Khomeini. However, let us assume that he indeed said this. But let us try to understand his words instead of deliberately trying to misunderstand them.

Did the revolutionary leader mean that the Imāms have an independent authority over the atoms of nature separate from the authority of God Almighty? Did he mean that the Imāms are able, by their own power, to change the course of nature? Could he not have meant that the Imāms are so absolutely obedient to God and that because of their purity and obedience to Him, He responds to their prayers? Therefore, if they ask Him to change a natural course, their prayers are answered.

There is no doubt that Imām Khomeini does not think that the Imāms have power independent from the Almighty. He is too

---

[1] Reproduced from his book, *The Shiites under Attack*, (Chapter 3: *Do the Imams Have Any Authority on the Universe?*) published by the Islamic Center of America, Michigan, 1986.

pure and righteous to voice such a thing, write it, or think it. He is one of the most righteous, pure, and obedient to the Almighty.

If Imām Khomeini had said that the Imāms can control the atoms of the universe, he undoubtedly meant that the Imāms of the House of the Prophet Muhammad had ascended in their obedience and worship to God to such a high degree that they could have asked the Almighty to transform the atoms of one object into the atoms of another, and He would have granted their request. Furthermore, if they had asked Him to revive a dead person, God would have brought him back to life. Is this a belief in the divinity of the Imāms?

Those who attribute such a statement to Imām Khomeini and consider it a deviation from the Islamic course should give the matter serious thought. They should test such a statement with the contents of the Qur'an. The Great Book informs us of the miracles of the Prophets of God.

".....And what is that in thy right hand, O Moses? He said: This is my staff. On it, I lean, and with it, I beat branches for my sheep, and in it I find other uses. God said: Cast it down, O Moses! He cast it down and behold! It became a snake, slithering. God said: Grasp it and fear not. We shall return it to its former state. And draw thy hand to your side; it will come forth white without harm. That will be another miracle." (20:17-22)

This means that the dead cells which composed the rod of Moses were transformed into living cells. Then those living cells miraculously went back to dead cells. In chapter *Al-Shu-ara*, we read these words of the Almighty: *"We revealed to Moses: Strike the sea with thy staff. It parted, and each part was like a huge mountain."* (26: 67) Does this not mean that God made the sea obedient to Moses to such a degree that Moses was able to divide the water of the sea into two solid parts, each of them as huge as a mountain in height and size?

THE QUR'AN INFORMS US OF JESUS

In *Aal-Umran*, we read that the Almighty informed us about Jesus: *"And we will make him a messenger to the children of Israel (with this message): I come to you with a sign from your Lord. Lo! I fashion for you out of clay the likeness of a bird, and breathe into it, and it becomes a bird, by Allah's leave. I heal those born blind, and the lepers, and I raise the dead by Allah's leave ...." (3: 49)*

Here we see that the Almighty enabled Jesus to transform a piece of clay into a living bird that could fly like other birds. Is this the work of Moses or Jesus? Would the Qur'an invite us to deify someone other than God?

THE QUR'AN INFORMS US OF MUHAMMAD

In regard to the Prophet Muhammad, we read God's word in the chapter of The Moon:

"The hour (of judgment) is near, and the moon has been split. But if they see a sign, they turn away and say: This is prolonged magic."(54: 1-2) This verse informs us that Allah split the moon in response to His Messenger Muhammad's prayer, and this never happened before the time of Muhammad.

TREE WALKED TO THE ORDER OF MUHAMMAD

We find in *Nahjal Balāghah* that Imām Ali reported that he was with the Prophet when the chieftains of Quraysh challenged him and asked him to order a nearby tree to uproot and walk to him. They said that this would be visible evidence of his prophethood.

The Messenger of God spoke to the tree saying: "Tree, if you believe in Allah and the Hereafter and know that I am a Messenger of God, uproot and walk until you stand in front of me, with permission of God." The tree, obeying the Prophet, uprooted and walked to him while making a loud noise like the wings of a flying bird.

When the chiefs saw the tree standing in front of the Prophet, they asked him to make half the tree come forward and keep the other half in its original place. When he did that, they said: "Let the half that came to you go back to the other half. He did."[2]

Ibn Hushām reported similar to this: "Rukanah Al-Muttalibi was the strongest man in Mecca. He met the Messenger outside Mecca and the Messenger invited him to Islam. Rukanah said: 'If you can prove that you are a true messenger, I will follow you.'

---

2 *Nahjal Balāghah,* part 2, pp. 158-9.

The Messenger said: 'What do you say if I wrestle you down? Will that make you believe that I am a true prophet?' Rukanah said, 'Yes.' The Prophet wrestled him down twice. Rukanah said: 'Muhammad, this is really amazing. Did you really wrestle me?' The Prophet said: 'I will show you more amazing things than this if you obey God and follow my way.' Rukanah said: 'What is it?' The Prophet said: 'I will call this tree which you are looking at, and it will come to me.' Rukanah said: 'Call it' and the Prophet called it. The tree came until it stood in front of him. The Prophet said to it: 'Go back to your place,' and it went to its original place."[3]

These miracles which occurred in response to prayers of the Messenger of God testify, as documented in the Qur'an, that Allah empowers His great servants to perform miracles by His permission. In other words, He responds to the prayers of His Messengers by creating miracles.

What happened through the prophets does not indicate that they had any touch of divinity. On the contrary, it testifies that those prophets were true servants of God. They ascended to the highest degree of servitude to Him, and their obedience to Him was absolute. Had they been otherwise, they would not have been able to perform any miracles, and no prayer by them would have been answered. They obeyed God completely and He responded to their prayers.

ARE THE IMĀMS LIKE THE PROPHETS?

It may be said that miracles are conceivable when they are attributed to messengers of God. However, the Imāms of the Members of the House of the Prophet are not prophets. They were men of knowledge and righteousness, but none of them ascended to the degree of prophethood.

This is true, but the Imāms from the House of the Prophet were non-prophets because the prophethood was concluded by the Messenger of God, Prophet Muhammad. Had the Messenger not been the last of the prophets, it would have been possible for the Imāms, or some of them, to be prophets. Probably other people could have become prophets as well.

---

[3] Ibn Hushām, *Al-Sīrah, Al-Nabawiah*, part 1, page 391.

The evidence of this is that the Prophet said to Imām Ali: "You are to me like Aaron was to Moses except that there shall be no prophets after me."[4] This means that Imām Ali was like Aaron in everything except the prophethood.

If any of the Sunni scholars think that we are exaggerating by saying that Ali and the Imāms from his children were qualified for the prophethood if the Messenger had not been the last of the Prophets, they should remember that prominent Sunnite scholars reported similar to this concerning Omar.

The hadīth-recorder Ahmad Ibn Hajar Al-Haithami in his book *Al-Sawā'iq Al-Muhriqah*, page 96, documents that Imām Ahmad, Al-Taramathi, Al-Hakim, and Al-Tabaranī reported that Aaqābad Ibn Malik said that the Messenger of God said: "Had it been possible to have a prophet after me, that prophet would have been Umar."

Why should anyone think that it would be an exaggeration to say that Allah would make nature and the atoms of the universe obedient to the Imāms of the House of the Prophet when we do not consider it an exaggeration to say that Umar could have been a prophet if Muhammad had not been the final Prophet?

---

4 Al-Bukhārī, his *Sahīh*, part 5, page 24.

Chapter: 17

TRADITIONS APPOINTING IMĀM ALI AS SUCCESSOR

By

Abū Tālib At-Turābī[1]

The Shi'as are criticized for saying that Prophet Muhammad had recommended that the Imamate and the caliphate were for Imam Ali and his sons, and that the Prophet's companions had opposed his testament.

The Answer: Among both Shi'as and Sunnis it has been established that the Prophet had appointed Ali to be the Caliph and Imam after him. At the Well of Khum (Ghadeer Khum), he proclaimed Imam Ali to be his successor in the presence of groups of Muslims coming back from his last Hajj. He made sure that everyone heard this in spite of the big crowds on that day. The news had reached everyone and everywhere. The chain of transmission of the news of Ghadeer Khum in Sunni books has been uninterrupted and certain.

We have collected 256 sources of the tradition on al-Ghadeer from the books of our Sunni brothers mentioned in our book *al-Jami' li Barāhīn Usūlul-I'tiqādāt*. We have adequately explained that the tradition clearly meant to appoint Ali as leader and Imam after the Prophet. Here we quote it in brief:

Ibn Asākir said in his book *The History of Damascus* Vol. p. 45: Abū Bakr Muhammad bin al-Husayn bin al-Marziqi told us that Abul-Husayn Muhammad bin Ali bin al- Muhtadi told us that Abul-Hasan Ali bin Umar bin Muhammad bin al-Hasan told us that al-Abbās bin Ahmad told us that Nasr bin Abdur-Rahmān Abū Sulaymān al-Washa' told us that Zayd bin al-Hasan al-Anmati told us that Ma'rūf bin Kharbūth al-Makkī told us that he had heard from Abut-Tufayl Aamirbin Wathīla that Hudhayfa bin

---

[1] Reproduced from his book, *Spurious Arguments about the Shi'a*, Ansariyan Publications, Qum: Iran, 2001.

Useid said, "When Prophet Muhammad had come back from his last Hajj (farewell Hajj), he ordered his Companions to stop at some trees which were near each another in the desert. He came and did his prayer under the trees. Then he stood up and said:

"O people, Allah the Most Kind the Omniscient has told me that no apostle lives to more than half the age of him who had preceded him. I think I am about to be called (die) and thus I must respond. I am responsible and you are responsible, then what do you say?' They said, 'We witness that you have informed, advised and striven. May Allah bless you.' He said, 'Do you not bear witness that there is no God but Allah and that Muhammad is His servant and Apostle, and that His Heaven is true, His Hell is true, death is true, the Resurrection after death is true, that there is no doubt that the Day of Judgment will come, and that Allah will resurrect the dead from their graves?' They said, 'Yes, we bear witness.' He said, 'O Allah, bear witness.' Then he said, 'O people, Allah is my Lord and I am the lord of the believers. I am worthier of believers than themselves. Of whomsoever I had been Guardian, Ali here is to be his Guardian. O Allah, be a supporter of whoever supports him (Ali) and an enemy of whoever opposes him.' Then he said, 'O people, I will go ahead of you and you will arrive at my pond (in Heaven) which is wider than the distance between Basra and San'a. It has receptacles as numerous as the stars, and two cups of gold and two of silver. I will ask you about the two weighty things that I have left for you when you come to me to see how you dealt with them. The greater weighty thing is Allah's book—the Qur'an. One end is in Allah's hand and the other is in your hands. Keep it and you will not deviate. That other weighty thing is my family and my descendents. The Most kind the Omniscient had told me that both of them would not separate until they come to my Pond.'"

The aforementioned account has been a summary of the tradition.

We will now cite some of its sources along with the names of the companions who had heard it form the Prophet, as quoted from the books of our Sunni brothers. After omitting names that have been repeated the following is what we have gathered from their books:

-134-

1. Narrated by Zathan, from thirteen persons, mentioned in (Ahmad's book *Musnad*) vol. 1, p. 84.

2. Ziyad bin Abū Ziyad, from twelve persons, who had fought in the battle of Badr. (Ahmad's *Musnad*) vol. 1, p. 88.

3. Sa'īd bin Wahhāb, from five or six persons (an-Nasāi'ī's book *al-Khasā'is*) p. 21 and Ahmad's *Musnad* vol. 5, p. 366.

4. Sa'id bin Wahhāb, from six persons--*Al-Khasā'is* p. 26 and 40.

5. Sa'īd bin Wahhāb, from six persons in *The History of Damascus*, vol. 2, p. 28.

6. Sa'īd bin Wahhāb, from thirteen persons--*Majma'uz-Zawayid*, vol. 9.

7. Sa'īd bin Wahhāb and Zayd bin Yathigh, from twelve persons--*Musnad*, vol. 1, p. 118.

8. Sa'īd bin Wahhāb and Zayd bin Yathigh, from some persons --*Kifayat at Tālib*, p. 18.

9. Zayd bin Yathigh, from six persons--*Al-Khasa'is*, p. 26.

10. Amr Dhi Mur, Sa'īd bin Wahhāb and Zayd bin Yathigh, from thirteen persons--*The History of Damascus*, vol. 2, p. 18.

11. Amr Dhi Mur and Sa'īd bin Wahhāb, from six or seven persons--*The History of Damascus*, vol. 2, p. 19.

12. Sa'īd bin Wahhāb and Abd Khayr, from some persons--*The History of Damascus*, vol. 2, p. 20.

13. Zayd bin Arqam, from sixteen persons--*Musnad*, vol. 5, p. 370.

14. Abut-Tufayl, from many persons--*Musnad*, vol. 4, p. 370.

15. Abut-Tufayl, from thirty persons--*Musnad*, vol. 4, p. 370.

16. Abut-Tufayl, from seventeen persons--*Al-Isābah*, vol. 4, p. 156.

17. Abū zumayla, from some persons--(Ibn abul-Hadid's book, *Sharh Nahjul-Balāgha*).

18. Abdur-Rahmān bin Abū Leyla, to twelve people--*Musnad*, vol. 1, p. 118.

19. Abdur-Rahmān bin Abū Leyla--*The History of Damascus*, vol. 2, p. 9.

20. Also Abdur-Rahmān bin Abū Leyla--*The History of Damascus*, vol. 2, p. 9.

21. Amr bin Sa'd, from six persons--*Al-Khasa'is*, p. 21.

22. Umayra bin Sa'd from twelve persons--*Hilyatul-Awliya'*, vol. 5, p. 26.

23. Umayra, from eighteen persons--*The History of Baghdad*, vol. 2, p. 13.

24. Umayra, from eight persons--*The History of Baghdad,* vol. 2, p. 13.
25. Amr Dhi Mur, from some persons--*Al Khasā'is* p. 40.
26. Abū Qulaba, from more than ten people--*Al-Kuna wa al-Asma',* vol. 2, p. 61.
27. Abū 'Ishāq as-Subay'i from more than ten people--*Mushkil ul-Athār,* Vol. 2, p. 307.
28. Abū Hurayra, Anas and Abū Sa'īd from nine persons and other besides--*Majma'uz-Zawā'id,* vol. 9, p. 708.
29. Umar bin Abdul-Azīz, from some persons--*Hilyatul-Awliya',* vol. 5, p. 364.
30. Abd Khayr, Amr Dhi Mur and Habbatul-Urani, from twelve people--Ibnul-Maghazili's *Manāqib* p. 20.
31. Al-Asbagh bin Nabata, from some persons--*Al-Isāba,* vol. 4, p. 80.
32. Riyah bin al-Hārith, from some of the Ansār--*Musnad,* vol. 5, p. 419.
33. Riyah bin al-Hārith, from some people--*Musnad,* vol. 5, p. 419.
34. Salama, Abū at-Tufeil from Hudhayfa bin Useid al-Ghifārī-Ahmad's *Manāqib.*
35. Salama from Hudhayfa bin Usayd, at-Tirmidhī's *Sahīh,* vol. 13, p. 165, *The History of Damascus,* vol. 2, p. 45.
36. Ma'rūf, from Hudhayfa bin Usayd al-Ghifārī.
37. As'ad bin Zurāra, from his father--*Muwazihul-Awhām,* vol. 1, p. 91.
38. Isa bin Talha, from Talha bin Abdullāh--*Al-Kāfi ash-Shāfi,* p. 95.
39. Sa'd bin Abū Waqqās--*The History of Damascus,* vol. 2, p. 53.
40. Umar bin al-Khattāb--*The History of Damascus,* vol. 2, p. 80.
41. Malik bin al-Huwayrith--*The History of Damascus,* vol. 2, p. 80.
42. Habashi bin Junada--*Al-mu'jam ul-Kabīr,* p. 127.
43. Amr Dhi Mur--*Al-Bidayah wa an-Nihayah,* vol. 5, p. 210.
44. Abdullāh bib Bamil- al- Isābah, vol. 2, p. 374.
45. Talha- Al-Kāfi ash-Shāfi, p. 95.
46. Habba bin Juwayn al-Urani- Usdul-Ghaba, vol. 1, p. 376.
47. Hamid bin Imara--*Majma'uz-Zawā'id,* vol. 9, p. 107.
48. Bishr bin Harb, from Jarīr--*Al-mu'jam ul-Kabir* of At-Tabarānī, p. 127.
49. Hamid at-Tawīl, from Anas-Ibnul- Maghazili's Manāqib.
50. Sa'd bin Malik--*Mustadrak us-Sahīheyn,* vol. 3, p. 116.
51. Abul-Hamra'--*Arjah ul-Matālib,* p. 581.

52. Mūsa bin Ayyūb, from Abū Hurayra--*The History of Baghdad,* vol. 8, p. 290.

53. Al-Bazzar, from Abū Hurayra--Al-Khawarizmī's *Manāqib,* p. 94.

54. Ibrahim bin al-Husayn, from Abū Hurayra--*The History of Damascus,* vol. 2. p, 72.

55. Abū 'Ishāq al-Khitabī, from Abū Hurayra, vol. 2, p. 74.

56. Mansūr bin abul-Aswad, from Abū Hurayra, vol. 2, p. 74.

57. Abū Ya'la, from Abū Hurayra--*The History of Damascus,* vol. 2, p. 74.

58. Abdullah bin Adiy, from Abū Hurayra--*The History of Damascus,* vol. 2, p. 75.

59. Habshun, from Abū Hurayra--*The History of Damascus,* vol. 2, p. 75.

60. Ali bin Shu'eib, from Abū Hurayra--*The History of Damascus,* vol. 2, p. 76.

61. Ad-Daqqaq, from Abū Hurayra--*The History of Damascus,* vol. 2, p. 77.

62. Samra bin Jundub--*The History of Damascus,* vol. 2, p. 71.

63. Shuriet bin Anas--*The History of Damascus,* vol. 2, p. 72.

64. Abū Leyla bin Sa'id--*Al-Jarh wet-Ta'dil,* vol. 4, p. 431.

65. Qubaysa, from Jabir bin Abdullah--*The History of Damascus,* vol. 2, p. 65.

66. Qubaysa, from someone else--*The History of Damascus,* vol. 2, p. 63.

67. Muhammad bin al-Munkadir, from Jabir bin Abdullah--*The History of Damascus,* vol. 2, p. 65.

68. Abū Salama, from Muhammad bin al- Munkadir--Ibnul-Maghazili's *Manāqib,* p. 25.

69. Abdullah bin Muhammad bin Aqil, from Muhammad bin al-Munkadir--*Kifayatu at-Talib,* p. 14.

70. Abdullah bin Muhammad bin Aqil, from someone else--*The History of Damascus,* vol. 2, p. 62.

71. Abdur-Rahmān bin Bahman--*The History of Damascus,* vol. 2, p. 63.

72. Ibn Abbas bin Burayda--*Al Khasa'is,* p. 21.

73. From another direction to Ibn Abbās from Burayda--*Al Khasa'is,* p. 21.

74. Tāwūs, from Burayda--*Al- Mu'jamu s-Saghīr,* vol. 1, p. 71.

75. From another direction, to Tawus, from Burayda--*Hilyatul-Awliya'*, vol. 4, p. 23.

76. Sa'id bin Ubayda, from ibn Burayda, from his father--Ahmad's *Musnad*, vol. 5, p. 358.

77. Sa'id bin Ubayda from another direction--*Musnad*, vol. 5, p. 358.

78. Sa'id bin Umayr, from ibn Burayda, from his father--*Al Khasa'is*, p. 21.

79. Al-Mansur, from his father, from his grandfather, from Ibn Abbas--*The History of Baghdad*, vol. 12, p. 366.

80. Umar bin Maymun, from Ibn Abbas--*Musnad*, vol. 1, p. 331.

81. Aamir bin Wathila--*Talkhis ul-Mustadrak*, vol. 3, p. 109.

82. Aamir bin Wathila from another direction--*Al Khasa'is*, p. 24.

83. Abdur-Rahmān bin Abū Leyla-- *The History of Baghdad*, vol. 14, p. 236.

84. Abdur-Rahmān bin Abū Leyla from another direction--Ibn Kathir's *Tafsīr*, vol. 2, p. 14.

85. Abdur-Rahmān bin Abū Leyla from a third direction--*Tafsīr*, vol. 2, p. 14.

86. Jundu' bin Amr bin Mazin--*Usdu l-Ghaba*, vol. 1, p. 308.

87. Tawus, from his father--Ahmad bin Hanbal's *Manāqib*, (Manuscript).

88. Abū Leyla bin Sa'id, from his father--*Al-Jarh wa at-Ta'dil*, vol. 4, p. 431.

89. Ya'la bin Murra--*Usdu l-Ghaba*, vol. 3, p. 233.

90. Abū Ayyub--*Al-mu'jam ul-Kabir*, p. 157.

91. Abū Ayyub from another direction--*Usdu l-ghaba*, vol. 5, p. 6.

92. Abū Bastam, Usama's freed slave--*The History of Damascus*, vol. 2, p. 86.

93. Alqama, from Abū Sa'id-al-bukhari's book *The History of Bukhari*, vol. 2, p. 194.

94. Al-Abdi, from Abū Sa'id-Al-Khawarizim's *Manāqib*.

95. Bint Ka'b (Ka'b's daughter) from Abū Sa'id--*Al-Bidayah wa an-Nihayah*, vol. 5, p. 208.

96. Al-Abdi, from Abū Sa'id--Khawarizmi's *Manāqib*.

97. Ali bin Khadim, from Abū Sa'id--*The History of Damascus*, vol. 2, p. 69.

98. Abū Ubayd, from Ibn Maymun, from Zayd bin Arqam--*Musnad*, vol. 4, p. 372.

99. Auf, from Ibn Maymum, from Zayd bin Arqam--*Al Khasa'is*, p. 22.

100. Shu'ba from Ibn Maymun, from Zayd bin Arqam--*The History of Islam*, vol. 2, p. 196.

101. From another direction to Shu'ba, from Zayd bin Arqam--*The History of Damascus*, vol. 2, p. 42.

102. Ibn Wathila, from Zayd bin Arqam*Mustadrakus- Sahiheyn*, vol. 3, p. 109.

103. Al-Hakam bin Abū Sulayman, from Zayd bin Arqam- Ibnu l-Maghazili's *Manāqib*, p. 23.

104. Al-Hasan bin Kathir, from Zayd bin Arqam--*Faza'ilu as-Sahaba*, of As-Sam'ani, (Manuscrip).

105. Yahya bin Ja'da, from Zayd bin Arqam--*The History of Damascus*, vol. 2, p. 41.

106. Abdul-Malik, from Zayd bin Arqam- Ahmad's *Musnad*, vol. 4, p. 370.

107. Atiya al-Aufi, from Zayd bin Arqam--*The History of Damascus*, vol. 2, p. 39.

108. From another direction to Atiya--*Musnad*, vol. 4, p. 370.

109. Abū at-Tufayl, from Zayd bin Arqam--*Al Khasa'is*, p. 21.

110. From another direction to Abū at-Tufayl, from Zayd bin Arqam--*Al-Mu'jamu l-Kabir*, p. 127 (Manuscript).

111. from another direction to Abū at-Tufayl, from Zayd bin Arqam--*Kifayatu at-Talib*, p. 13-14.

112. From another direction to Abū at-Tufayl, from Zayd bin Arqam- ibn Kathir's *Tafsīr*, vol. 2, p. 14.

113. Abū Maryam or Zayd bin Arqam--*Al-Bidayah wa an-nihayah*, vol. 7, p. 348.

114. Abū Surayha or Zayd bin Arqam--*The History of Damascus*, vol, 2, p. 36.

115. Hudhayfa bin Usayd or Zayd bin Arqam--*Al-Mu'jamu l-Kabir*, p. 157 (Manuscript).

116. Abū Abdullah ash-Shami from Zayd bin Arqam--*The History of Damascus*, vol. 2, p. 38.

117. Abuz-Zuha, from Zayd bin Arqam--Ibnul-Maghazili's *Manāqib*, p. 20.

118. Zayd's wife, from Zayd bin Arqam--Ibnul-Maghazili's *Manāqib*, p. 16.

119. Habibu l-Iskafi, from Zayd bin Arqam--*The History of Damascus,* vol. 2, p. 41.

120. Abū 'Ishaq, from Zayd bin Arqam--*The History of Damascus,* vol. 2, p. 41.

121. Yazid bin Talha--*Al-Bidayah wa an-Nihayah,* vol. 5, p. 108.

122. Abū 'Ishaq as-Subay'i from al-Bara' bin Aazib--*Al-Kuna wa al-Asma',* vol. 1, p. 160.

123. Abd bin Thabit, from al-Bara' bin Aazib- al- Khawarizmi's *Manāqib,* p. 93.

124. Al-Bara' bin Aazib from another direction--*Fara'idus-Samtein, vol.* 1, p. 64.

125. Al-Bara' bin Aazib from a third direction--*Fara'idu-Samtein,* vol. 1, p. 65.

126. Al-Bara' bin Aazib from a fourth direction--*Musnad,* vol. 4, p. 28.

127. Al-Bara' bin Aazib from a fifth direction--*Musnad,* vol. 4, p. 281.

128. Al-Bara' bin Aazib from a sixth direction--*Musnad,* vol. 4, p. 28.

129. Al-Bara' bin Aazib from a seventh direction--*Al-Bidayah wa an-Nihayah,* vol, 5 p. 208.

130. Al Bara'bin Aazib from an eighth direction--*Al-Bidayah wa an-Nihayah,* vol. 5, p. 208.

131. Al Bara'bin Aazib from a ninth direction--*Al-Bidayah wa an Nihayah,* vol. 5, p. 208.

132. Al-Bara' bin Aazib from a tenth direction--*The History of Damascus,* vol. 2, p. 48.

133. Al-Bara' bin Aazib from a eleventh direction--*The History of Damascus,* vol. 2, p. 50.

134. Al-Bara' bin Aazib from another direction--*The History of Damascus,* vol. 2, p. 50.

135. Abū 'Ishaq, from al-Bara' bin Aazib and Zayd bin Arqam--*The History of Damascus* vol. 2, p. 52.

136. Hudhayfa bin al-Yaman-al-Hasaqani's *Du'atul'Hudat.*

137. Ammar bin Yasir--*Fara'idus-Samtein* vol. 1, p. 195.

138. Fatimah (Prophet's daughter)--*Arjahul-Matālib* p. 448 and 571.

139. Abdullah bin Mas'ud-ibnul-Maghazili's *Manāqib* p. 23.

140. Amr Dhi Mur, from Imam Ali--*Mizanul-I'tidal* vol. 2, p. 303. *The History of Damascus* vol. 2, p. 30.

141. From another direction to Amr Dhi Mur, from Imam Ali--*Fara'idus-Samtein* vol. 1, p. 67.

142. Abū Maryam and one of Imam Ali's companions-Ahmad's *Musnad*, vol. 1, p. 152.

143. Umar bin Ali, from Imam Ali--*Al-Bidayah wa an-Nihayah*, vol. 5, p. 221.

144. Aamir bin Wathila, from Imam Ali-Khawarizmi's *Manāqib*, vol. 1, p. 41.

145. Salmān, from Imam Ali-Khawarizmi's *Manāqib*, vol. 1, p. 41.

146. Zayd bin Wahhāb and Abd Khayr, from Imam Ali-bin Kathir's *Tafsīr*, vol. 2, p. 14.

147. Al-Husayn bin Ali, from Imam Ali--*The History of Damascus*, vol. 2, p. 26.

148. Umar bins Ali, from Imam Ali--*The History of Damascus*, vol. 2, p. 28.

149. Abū at-Tufayl, from Imam Ali--*The History of Damascus*, vol. 2, p. 20.

150. Zayd bin Arqam, from Imam Ali--*The History of Damascus*, vol. 2, p. 20.

151. Some persons, from ibn Abū Awfa--*Al-Kuna* of al-Bukhari, p. 66.

152. Atiyah, from ibn Abū Awfa-ibnul--Maghazili's *Manāqib*, p. 24.

153. Umayra bin Sa'd-ibn al--Maghazili's *Manāqib*, p. 26.

154. Amr bin al-Aas-Khawarizim's *Mamaqib*, p. 125.

155. Abdur-Rahmān bin Saabit, from Abū Waqqas-Ibn Maja's *Sunan*, vol. 1, p. 58.

156. Aamir bin Sa'd from Sa'd bin Abū Waqqas--*History of Islam*, of ath-Thahabi, vol. 2.

157. Ayman, from Sa'd bin Abū Waqqas--*Al Khasa'is*, p. 4.

158. Ayeshah bint Sa'd from Sa'd bin Abū Waqqas--*Al Khasa'is*, 24-25.

159. From another direction to ('Aa'isha bint Sa'd).from Sa'd bin Abū Waqqas-Al-Bidayah wa an-*Nihayah*, vol. 5, p. 208.

160. Abū at-Tufeil, from Abū Qudama--*Usdul-Ghaba*, vol. 5, p. 276.

161. Ya'la, from Aamir bin Leyla--*Usdul-Ghaba*, vol. 3, p. 93.

162. Ya'la bin Murra, from Yazid or Zayd bin Shuraheel--*Usdul-Ghaba*, vol. 2, p. 233.

163. Hudhayfa bin Usayd and Aamir bin Leyla bin Zamra--*Usdul-Ghaba*, vol. 3, p. 92.

164. Aamir bin Leyla from another direction --*Usdul-Ghaba*, vol. 3, p. 93.

165. Abū Amra, from Amir bin Mahz--*Usdul-Ghaba*, vol. 3, p. 307.

166. Abū Zaynab--*Usdul-Ghaba*, vol. 3, p. 307.

167. Sahl bin Hunayf--*Usdul-Ghaba*, vol. 3, p. 307.

168. Khuzayma bin Thabit--*Usdul-Ghaba*, vol. 3, p. 307.

169. Abdullah bin Thabit al-Ansari--*Usdul-Ghaba*, vol. 3, p. 307.

170. Habashi bin Junada--*Usdul-Ghaba*, vol. 3, p. 307.

171. Ubayd bin Aazib--*Usdul-Ghaba*, vol. 3, p. 307.

172. Nu'Man bin Ajlan--*Usdul-Ghaba*, vol. 3, p. 307.

173. Thabit bin Wadi'--*Usdul-Ghaba*, vol. 3, p. 307.

174. Abū Fuzala al-Ansari--*Usdul-Ghaba*, vol. 3, p. 307.

175. Ibn Umar --*The History of Damascus*, vol. 2, p. 83.

176. Miqdad bin Amr--*Usdul-Ghaba*, vol. 5, p. 6.

177. Miqdad bin Amr--*Usdul-Ghaba*, vol. 5, p. 6.

178. Zurr bin Hubaysh, from Abdullah bin Badil bin Waraqa'--*Al-Kashshi's men*, p. 45.

179. Al-Asbagh, from Ubayd bin Aazib al-Ansari--*Usdul-Ghaba*, vol. 3, p. 307 and vol. 5, p. 205.

180. Amr bin al-Aas-Khawarizmi's *Manāqib*, p. 126, *Al-Imama wa as-Siyasa*, p. 93.

181. Qays bin Sa'd bin Ubada--*Al-Kashshi's Rijal*, p. 45.

182. Ibn Abbas-Ahmad's *Musnad*, vol. 1, p. 331.

183. Jabir bin Samra--*Kanzul-Ummal*, vol. 6 p. 398 from Ibn Abū sheiba.

184. Sulaym bin Qays, from some persons, one of them was Abi Dharr--*Fara'idus-Sametein*, vol. 1, p. 315.

185. Hasan bin Thabit --*Fara'idus-Samtein*, vol. 1, p. 73.

186. Habib bin Badil bin Warqa'--*Usdul-Ghaba*, vol. 1, p. 368.

187. Qays bin Thabit bin Shamaas --*Usdul-Ghaba*, vol. 1, p. 367.

188. Hashim bin Utba--*Usdul-Ghaba*, vol. 1, p. 368.

(The Ghadeer tradition was mentioned in the books of the Sunnis in other ways and by Companions other than those mentioned above. Unfortunately, we could not find the names of all its narrators.)

189. Al-Hafiz bin uqda mentioned it in his book *Al-Wilāyah*, chap. *At-Tarā'if*, p. 140 and Abū Bakr al-Ju'abī in his book *Al-Manāqib*, vol. 3, p. 25 narrated by Abū Bakr bin Abū Quhafa.

190. Al-Hafiz bin uqda in his book, *Al-Wilāyah*, chap. *At-Tarā'if*, p. 142.

191. Abū Bakr al-Ju'abī in his book *Al-Manāqib*, vol. 3, p. 26 narrated by Ubei bin Ka'b.

192. Ibn Uqda in *At-Tarā'if*, p. 142 by Asma' bint Umays al-Khatha' miya.

193. Ibn Uqda -*At-Tarā'if*, p. 142. by Umm Salama (the Prophet's wife).

194. Ibn Uqda-*At-Tarā'if*, p. 142. by Jibila bin Amr al-Ansari.

195. Ibn Uqda, *At-Tarā'if*, p. 141 and Abū Bakr al-Ju'abī in his book *Al-Manāqib*, vol. 3, p. 26 by Immam Husayn bin Ali.

196. Abū Bakr al-Ju'abī, *Al-Manāqib*, vol. 3, p. 26 by Khalid bin al-Walid.

197. Ibn Uqda in his book *Al-Wilāyah*, — chap. *At-Tarā'if*, p. 142 by Ad'id bin Sa'd bin Ubada.

198. Ibn Hajar in his book *Al-Isāba*, vol. 2 p. 255 narrated by Aamir bin Umayr an-Nimyari.

199. Ibn Uqda, *Al-Wilāyah*, chap. *At-Tarā'if*, p. 142 by 'Aa'isha bint Abū Bakr.

200. Ibn al-Maghazili, *Al-Manāqib* p. 27 by Abdur-Rahmān bin Auf.

201. Ibn Uqda and al-Khawarizmi in his book *Maqtal*, p. 48 by Abdur-Rahmān bin ya'mur ad-Daylami.

202. Ibn Uqda, *Tarā'if*, p. 141 by Abdullah bin Abū Abdul-Asada al-Makhzumi.

203. Ibn Uqda, *Tarā'if*, p. 142 by Abdullah bin Bashir al-Mazini.

204. Ibn Uqda, *Tarā'if*, p. 141 by Abdullah bin Ja'far.

205. Ibn Uqda, *Tarā'if*, p. 141 by Uthman bin Affan.

206 .Ibn Uqda, *Tarā'if*, p. 142 by Abū Wasma Wahshi bin Harb.

207. Ibn Uqda, *Tarā'if*, p. 142 by Abū Juhayafa Wahhāb bin Abdullah.

208. Mentioned by Abū Hatim, Ibn Asaakir and Muhibbud-Dīn at-Tabari in book *Arjahul-Matālib*, p. 339 by Ibn Shurayh.

209. Abū Bakr al-Ju'abī, *Manāqib*, vol. 3, p. 24 and Ibn Uqda, *Tarā'if*, p. 141 by Rifa'a bin Abdul-Munthir.

210. Ibn Uqda, *Tarā'if*, p. 141 and Ibnul-Maghazili, *Manāqib*, p. 27 by az-Zubeir bin al-Aiwa.

211. Ibn Uqda, *Tarā'if*, p. 142 by Zayd bin Abdullah.

212. Ibn Uqda, *Tarā'if*, p. 142 by Sa'd Junada.

213. Abū Bakr al-Ju'abī, *Manāqib*, vol. 3, p. 26 by Sa'd bin Ubada.

214. Ibn Uqda, *Tarā'if*, p. 141 by Salmān al-Farisi.

215. Ibn Uqda, *Tarā'if*, p. 141 by Salama bin Amr bin al-Aqua'.

216. Ibn Uqda, *Tarā'if*, p. 142 by Abū Umama as-Sadiy bin Ajlan al-Bahili.

217. Ibn Uqda, *Tarā'if*, p. 142 by Zumayra al-Asadi.

218. Ibnul-Maghazili, *Manāqib*, p. 27 by al-Fazl bin Muhammad from Sa'id bin Zayd.

219. Ibn Hajar, *Isāba, vol.* 2 p. 255 by Musa bin Aqtal from Aamir bin Umayr.

220. Ibn Hajar, *Isāba*, vol. 3, p. 257 by Aamir bin Leyla al-Ghifari.

221. At-Tabarānī, *Ihya'ul-Mayyit, by* Abdullah bin Huntub.

222. Khawarizmi, *Maqtal*, p. 48 by Abdullah bin Rabi'a.

223. Khawarizim, *Maqtal*, p. 48 by Amr bin Shurahil.

224. At-Tabarānī, *Kanzul-Ummal*, vol. 6, p. 154 and Ahmad bin Hanbal, by Amr bin Murra.

225. Ibn Uqda, *Tarā'if*, p. 141 ad Abū Bakr al-Ju'abī, *Manāqib*, vol. 3, p. 26 by Abul-Haytham bin at-Tayhan.

226. Ibn uqda, *Tarā'if*, p. 141 and Abū Bakr al-Ju'abī, *Manāqib*, vol. 3, p. 26 by Abū Rafi'.

227. Ibn Uqda, *Tarā'if*, p. 142 and Khawarizmi, *Meqtal*, p. 48 by Abū Thuwayb.

228. Ibn Uqda, *Tarā'if*, p. 142 by Umm Hānī.

229. Ibn Uqda, *Tarā'if*, p. 142 by Zayd bin Haritha.

230. Ibn Uqda, *Tarā'if*, p. 142 by Abdullah bin Abū Awfa al-Aslamī.

231. Ibu Uqda, *Tarā'if*, p. 141 by Abdullah bin Umar bin al-Khattab.

232. Ibn Uqda, *Tarā'if*, p. vol. 3, p. 142 by Abdur-Rahmān bin Mudlaj.

233. Abū Na'īm, Hilyatul-Awilya', chap. *Al-Yanabi'* p. 38 by seventeen persons, one of them was Adiy bin Hatim.

234. Abū Na'īm, *Hilyatul-Awliya'*, chap. *Al-Yanabi'* p. 38 by seventeen persons, one of them was Uqba bin Aamir.

235. Ibn Uqda, *Tarā'if*, p. 141 by Umar bin Abū Salama.

236. Ibn Uqda and Khawarizmi in his Maqtal, p. 48 by Imran bin Husayn.

237. Ibn Uqda, Khawarizmi, *Maqtal*, p. 48 by Amr bin al-Hamq.

238. Ibn Uqda, *Tarā'if*, p. 142 by Fatima bint Hamza.

239. Ibn Uqda, *Tarā'if*, p. 141 by al-Miqdad bin Amr.

240. Ibn Uqda, *Tarā'if*, p. 141 by Abū Barza Fazla bin Utba.

241. Ibn Uqda, *Tarā'if*, p. 142 by Atiya bin Bisr.
242. Abū Bakr al-Ju'abī, *Manāqib*, vol. 3, p. 26 by Ubada bin as-Samit.
243. Abū Bakr al-Ju'abī *Manāqib*, vol. 3, p. 26 by Abdullah bin Unays.
244. Abū Bakr al-Ju'abī *Manāqib*, vol. 3, p. 26 by Urwa bin Abū al-Ja'd.
245. Abū Bakr al-Ju'abī *Manāqib*, vol. 3, p. 26 by Amr bin Hurayth.
246. Abū Bakr al-Ju'abī *Manāqib*, vol. 3, p. 26 by Abdul-Al'a bin Adiy.
247. Abū Bakr al-Ju'abī *Manāqib*, vol. 3, p. 26 by Uthman bin Hunayf.
248. Abū Bakr al-Ju'abī *Manāqib*, vol. 3, p. 26 by Bashir bin Abdul-Munthir.
249. Abū Bakr al-Ju'abī *Manāqib*, vol. 3, p. 26 by Qays bin Aasim and by Abū kahil on the same page.
250. Abū Bakr al-Ju'abī *Manāqib*, vol. 3, p. 26 by Abū Rifa'a.
251. Abū Bakr al-Ju'abī *Manāqib*, vol. 3, p. 26 by Hubab bin Utba.
252. Abū Bakr al-Ju'abī *Manāqib*, vol. 3, p. 26 by Jundub bin Sufyan.
253. Abū Bakr al-Ju'abī *Manāqib*, vol. 3, p. 26 by Khabbab bin Samra.

QUR'ANIC VERSES ON HOMAGE AT GHADEER

The First Verse: Allah says: *"O Apostle! Deliver what has been revealed to you from your Lord; and if you do it not, then you have not delivered His message, and Allah will protect you from the people; surely Allah will not guide the unbelieving people."* (5: 67) This Qur'anic verse had descended in order to reveal Imam Ali's guardianship. This fact has been mentioned in the books of the Sunnis. The author of *Al-Ghadeer* has quoted this in vol. 1, p. 214-223 from thirty of their books.

The Second Verse: Allah says: *"This day have I perfected for you your religion and completed My favor on you and chosen for you Islam as a religion."* (5:3) Al-Amini, in his book *Al-Ghadeer*, vol. 1, p. 230, has quoted the narrations that confirm that this verse concerned the divine leadership of Imam Ali from sixteen books of the Sunnis.

The Third Verse: Allah says: *"A questioner asked about a chastisement about to fall for the unbelievers. There is none to avert it from Allah, the Lord of the ways of Ascent."* (70:1-3) This verse was revealed because someone, when he heard the Prophet saying, "Of whomsoever I had been guardian, Ali here is to be his guardian," said, 'O Allah, if what Muhammad is saying is true, let heaven send stones upon us.'" A little after that Allah sent down a stone on his head and killed him. Then Allah revealed this verse to Prophet Muhammad. Al-Amini quoted that in his book *Al-Ghadeer*, vol. 1 p. 239-246 from thirty of the books of the Sunnis.

COMPANIONS PAY HOMAGE TO IMAM ALI

At-Tabari said: "Then people began to say, 'yes, we have heard and obeyed the order of Allah and his Messenger with our hearts'. The first of those who shook hands with Prophet Muhammad and Imam Ali were Abū Bakr, Umar, Usmān, Talha, az-Zubeir, the rest of the Muhajirs (emigrants), the Ansar (helpers) and the public. They continued this until the Prophet led them in the congregational *Zhuhr* (noon) Prayer and the *Asr* (afternoon) Prayer combined. They kept on doing this until he led them in congregational *Maghrib* (sunset) Prayer and the *Isha* (evening) Prayer both of them also combined. Thus they carried on paying homage and shaking hands for three days". The author of *Al-Ghadeer* quoted, in vol. 1, p. 272, the news of Umar bin al-Khattab congratulating Imam Ali from sixty Sunnis books.

THE LINGUISTIC MEANING OF MAWLĀ

The Arabic word (Mawlā) means to take charge of something and to achieve it. The author of *As-Sihāh* says: "The ruler is the Mawlā i.e. he takes charge of the country. A man is Mawlā i.e. he takes charge of something, for example, selling. One says that someone was the Mawlā i.e. took charge of something, and was given charge of it. For example the commander made someone take charge of something or someone was put in charge of selling something, and he took charge of the job."

The author of *An-Nihāyah* says: "Wilāya --guardianship — means administration with ability and action. Whoever takes charge of something becomes its Mawlā –guardian. Umar's saying to Ali, 'You have become the Mawlā (guardian) of every believer', means taking charge of every believer's affairs."

The author of *al-Qamus* says: "Wilāya --guardianship-- means policy, command and authority. Being the Mawlā i.e. taking charge of something means being responsible for it. To take charge of the orphan means to be responsible for his affairs..."

The author of *Lisān ul-Arab* says: "Sībawayh says, 'Wilāya stands for the guardianship of someone; taking charge of his affairs and fulfilling his needs. The Mawlā (guardian) of a woman is he who undertakes the responsibility of contracting marriage on her behalf; she cannot get married without his agreement. Prophet Muhammad says: 'For women who got married without the permission of their guardians, their marriage is invalid.'"

Thus, the real meaning of this word (Mawlā) is to take charge of a matter and to carry it out. The various uses of the expression simply express this basic fact, such as saying the word 'man' for Zayd, Amr and Bakr. Allah is called Mawlā because He is the ruler of the affairs of Man.

The master is addressed as Mawlā because he is in charge of his slave, and the slave is also called Mawlā because he is in charge of carrying out his master's affairs. Likewise, neighbors, cousins, allies and sons-in-law are called Mawlā because they help those who need their help. So, it has a common literal meaning. So, the meaning of Prophet's saying (Of whomsoever I am guardian, Ali here is to be his guardian) is that over whomsoever I took charge of his affairs, Ali will take charge of his affairs.

This is clear concerning the leadership, imamate and guardianship of the nation. Since Prophet Muhammad was the leader, guardian and commander of the nation, so also will Imam Ali.

This is the real meaning of the word according to the opinions of the linguists. If one rejects this meaning in preference for the other manifold meanings of the word 'Mawlā,' it would be a word that would be common in expression, but having various meanings independent from each other. In this case there would be no doubt that the meaning that agrees with the tradition would be the first one.

Some senior scholars have discussed this subject in their books. Abū Ubayda says in his book *Gharībul-Qur'an:* "Mawlā means worthier." He cited al-Akhtal's poetic verse to Abdul-Malik bin Marwan as his evidence.

Al-Anbari said in his book *Tafsīrul-Mushkil fil-Qur'an:* "Mawlā means the worthier."

Az-Zajjaj and al-Farra' said, as mentioned in al-Fakhr ar-Razi's book *At-Tafsīr,* vol. 29, p. 227, Egyptian edition that "Mawlā means worthier."

It was mentioned that Abul-Abbas al-Mubarrid said that the meaning of Mawlā was worthier and most deserving.

Az-Zamakhshari said in his *Tafsīr,* vol. 4, p. 66, Egyptian edition: "In fact, Mawlā means your place, where it would be better for you to be."

Al-Halabī, in his book *At-Taqrīb,* said: "Mawlā, in fact, means worthier and the other expressions are derived from it. The master is a Mawlā because he is worthier to manage his slaves' affairs and to bear with their faults. The slave is a Mawlā because he is worthier to obey his master. So too are the freed slave, the helper who is more worthy of helping whom he helps, the ally to be more worthy of supporting his allies, the neighbor to be more worthy of helping his neighbor and defending him, the son-in-law to be more worthy of his relatives, the imam to be more worthy of whom he leads and the cousin to be more worthy of helping his cousins."

Since the word (Mawlā) means worthier, there is no excuse to turn it away from its real meaning and seek other ones.

FURTHER EVIDENCE OF AL-GHADEER SIGNIFICANCE

The First Evidence: The Prophet asked the people before appointing Imam Ali as guardian by saying, "Am I not worthier of yourselves than you are?" Then he said: "Of whomsoever I had been guardian, Ali here is to be his guardian."

The Prophet, in getting them to confess that he is worthier of themselves than they are, before he said, 'Of whomsoever I had been guardian, Ali here is to be his guardian', clarifies one of two things: either (1) to confirm the matter and that they confessed to. In this case the following would therefore become a fact which would be that Mawlā, then, means worthier and nothing else. Thus the Prophet's saying would mean, "Am I not worthier of yourselves than you are? Whoever's self I had been worthier than, Ali here is to be worthier of his self than he is;" or (2) forcing them not to deny what he wanted after this by appointing Ali a commander and a ruler over them. Therefore, Mawlā, here, means authority and leadership and nothing else.

In both cases, the hadīth means that Imam Ali had the right to dispose of their affairs and that they had to obey him and not to prevent him from this.

Moreover, many Sunni and Shiite scholars have quoted the Prophet's saying, 'Of whomsoever I had been guardian, Ali here is to be his guardian,' after his saying, 'Am I not worthier of yourselves than you are?' with slight differences in wording. Here are the names of some of such scholars:

1. Abū Hātim, 2. Abū Mūsa, 3. Abū Na'īm, 4. Abū Ya'la, 5. Abul-Faraj, 6. Ad-Darqutni 7. Ahmad bin Hanbal 8. Al-Aasimi 9. Al-Anbari, 10.Al-Ayji, 11. Al-Badkhashi, 12. Al-Bayhaqī, 13. Al-Bayd āw ī, 14. Al-Hakim, 16 Al-Hamawini 17. Al-Hasakani, 18. Al Haythami19. Al-Jazari 20. Al-Kanji, 21. Al-Khali, 22. Al-Khatib, 23. Al-Khawarizmi, 24. Al-Maqrizi, 25. Al-Maybadi, 26. Al-Mulla, 27. Al-Qati'i, 28. Al-Wassābī, 29. An-Nisā'ī, 30. Ash-Sharīf, 31. Ash-Shaybānī, 32. Ash-Shaykhānī, 33. As-Saharniwari, 34. As-Sajistānī, 35. As-Sam'ānī, 36. As-Samhudi, 37. As-Suyūtī, 38. Asilud-Dīn, 39. Ath-Tha'labi, 40. Ath-Thahabi, 41. At-Tabarānī, 42. At-Tabarī, 43. At-Taftazānī, 44. At-Tahawi, 45. At-Tirmidh ī, 46. Az-Zarandi, 47. Gazz Aughli, 48. Ibn Asākir, 49. Ibn Batta, 50. Ibn Hajar, 51. Ibn Hajar al-Makkī, 52. Ibn Kathīr, 53. Ibn Māja, 54. Ibn Uqda, 55. Ibnul-Athīr, 56. Ibnul-Maghazili, 57. Ibnus-Sabbagh, 58.Ibnus-Samān, 59. Kamālud-Dīn, 60. Muhibud-Dīn, 61. Shihabud-Dīn, 62. Waliyyudd-Dīn, and 63. Zia'ud-Dīn.

The Second Evidence: The second evidence is the Prophet's supplication to Allah for Imam Ali by saying, "O Allah, be a supporter of whoever supports him and an enemy of whoever opposes him, and help whoever helps him and betray whoever betrays him." This is mentioned at the end of the hadīth in many forms. It shows that the matter that the Prophet had conveyed concerning Imam Ali needed help and support and that Imam Ali would have enemies and betrayers. In addition, it shows that Imam Ali was infallible for he did not set about doing anything unless it was for the sake of Allah's pleasure.

The Third Evidence: Various narratives show that the Qur'anic verse: *"This day have I perfected for you your religion and completed My favor on you and chosen for you Islam as a religion,"* (5:3) had been revealed for this occasion. That main reason for perfecting the religion and completing the Divine favor upon the Muslims must be among the principles of the religion, a principle by which the order of life and religion would be completed and through which the efforts of the Muslims would be accepted. Some narrators of the hadīth mentioned in some books confirm this point. They attest that the Prophet, after telling this hadīth continued by saying, "Allah is the greatest for the perfection of this religion and the completion of the favor, and for His contentment with my mission and the guardianship of Ali bin Abū Tālib." In other narratives, the following form is recorded: "...and the perfection of Allah's religion by Ali's guardianship after me."

The Fourth Evidence: Many narratives show that the Qur'anic verse — *"O Apostle! Deliver what has been revealed to you from your Lord; and if you do it not, then you have not delivered His message, and Allah will protect you from the people,"* (5:67) was revealed for this occasion (Ghadeer Khum), too. The verse showed the importance of this matter and it compared leaving this matter (informing of Imam Ali's guardianship) with leaving the Islamic mission as a whole. It also showed that it was the basic ingredient of the religion, but it was not about Divine Unity, prophecy or resurrection that the Prophet had informed of at the beginning of his mission. Nothing remained except the imamate of Ali, which the Prophet was hesitant to convey because he was afraid of the people. Therefore, Allah says, *"Allah will protect you from the people."* (5:67)

The Fifth Evidence: Many narratives have been mentioned in the reference books of hadīth concerning the Qur'anic verse, *"This day have I perfected for you your religion and completed My favor on you."* (5:3) They have explained that it had been revealed after the event of al-Ghadeer in which the Prophet informed that Imam Ali would be the guardian of Muslims. Likewise, the verse showed that the perfection of the religion and the completion of the Divine favor of Islam were achieved only after the declaration of Ali's guardianship and imamate.

The Sixth Evidence: The Prophet said in some narrations of this tradition, "Allah had sent me with a mission, which was challenging and I thought that the people would not believe me. Then Allah threatened me with Divine torment if I did not convey it."

The Seventh Evidence: This hadīth has confirmed in many ways, that the Prophet uttered this honorable saying after he had gotten the people to confess the Oneness of Allah and the Prophecy of Muhammad. This fact shows that this matter was very important for Islam and was considered as one of the fundamentals of faith after the oneness of Allah and the prophethood of Muhammad.

The Eighth Evidence: Before he had conveyed this important message, the Prophet had said: "I am about to be called (to die) and I am to respond." This shows that the Prophet was afraid of leaving something very important which he had to reveal before his death. It was nothing but Ali's guardianship.

The Ninth Evidence: The Prophet said after conveying the news of Imam Ali's guardianship: "Let him who is present inform him who is absent." This shows that he was very concerned that this matter should reached all the Muslims.

The Tenth Evidence: The Prophet said after conveying the news of Ali's guardianship: "O Allah! You are a witness that I have informed and advised." This shows that he informed of a great and important matter which he had made the Muslims for and had acquitted himself of this great duty.

The Eleventh Evidence: There is the factual evidence that is clear and copious confirming the purpose of this tradition. For example, when the Prophet stopped in the desert in the heat of the midday sun, the narrators of hadīth and historians mentioned that it was so hot that some people had to put cloths over their heads, some had covered their heads with their saddlebags, some sat in the shade of their camels and others sat in the shade of the rocks. Then the Prophet asked his Companions to erect a high platform of camel saddles and stones in order to see over all Muslims who were about seventy, eighty or one hundred thousand as some historians have said. The Prophet ordered the Muslims who had gone ahead to return and those who had been behind to join. Then he took Imam Ali with him up the platform, held his hand, and raised it until the white of the Prophet's armpit appeared to the on-lookers.

The Twelfth Evidence: People paid homage to Imam Ali, shook hands with him, and congratulated both him and the Prophet. It was mentioned that Umar bin al-Khattāb was the first to congratulate him. The hadīth of Umar's congratulation of Imam Ali has come down to us in more than sixty different forms. Abū Sa'īd an-Neisabūrī (died in 407 A.H.) mentioned in his book *Sharaful-Mustafa* about the event of Ghadeer according to a tradition narrated by Ahmad bin Hanbal from al-Bara' bin Aazib and another one narrated by Abū Sa'īd al-Khudrī that the Prophet said: "Congratulate me! Congratulate me! For Allah has favored me with Prophecy and favored my family with Imamate." Then Umar bin al-Khattāb met Imam Ali and said: "May you be blessed, you have become my guardian and the guardian of every believer; men and women."

At-Tabarī mentioned in his book *al-Wilāyah* a tradition narrated by Zayd bin Arqam that Prophet Muhammad had said: "Say that we have given a vow from ourselves and a word from our tongues and homage with our hands which we pass on to our offspring and to our families. We will never change that…"

The author of *Rawdatus-Safa* mentioned in vol. 1, p. 173, that Prophet Muhammad sat in a tent and let Imam Ali sit in another. He ordered people to congratulate Imam Ali in his tent. When the men had finished congratulating Imam Ali, the Prophet ordered his wives to go and congratulate Imam Ali.

Al-Ghazālī said in his book *Sir ul-'Ālamīn*, in the Fourth Essay: "The fact was crystal clear and the public had unanimously agreed on with the contents of the Prophet's speech when he said on that

Day in Ghadeer Khum: 'Of whomsoever I had been guardian, Ali here is to be his guardian.' Umar then said: 'Excellent, O Abul-Hasan (Imam Ali's surname)! You have become my guardian as well as that of every believer; man and woman.' Thus there was acceptance, approval and the appointment of his leadership. But later on this right was defeated by the passion for being in charge, for bearing the title of the caliphate, for the waving of ensigns and the snorting of horses in the wars and for conquering countries. All of this made them drink the cup of vanity and go back to the first discord. They threw the right behind their backs and sold it for a little price, and what a bad thing they had bought!"

The Thirteenth Evidence: The incident of al-Hārith bin an-Nu'mān al-Fihri is another piece of evidence. It has been mentioned by many historians, one of which was ath-Tha'labī in his *Tafsīr*. The Prophet in Ghadeer Khum, called for people to gather, then he took Ali's hand, and said: "Of whomsoever I had been guardian, Ali here is to be his guardian." The news spread everywhere and reached al-Hārith bin an-Nu'mān al-Fihri. He came on his camel until he reached a place called al-Abtah. He rode off and hobbled his camel. He came to the Prophet with some of Companions and said: "O Muhammad, you had ordered us, from Allah, to witness that there is no god but Allah and that you are His Messenger and we accepted. And you had ordered us to pray five times a day and we accepted. And you had ordered us to go to Mecca to perform the Hajj and we accepted. All of that did not please you until you raised your cousin's hand to prefer him among us and you said, of whomsoever I had been guardian Ali here is to be his guardian! Is this from you or from Allah?" The Prophet said: "I swear by Allah other than Whom there is no other God that this is from none other but Allah."

Al-Harith went towards his camel saying: "O Allah, if what Muhammad said was true then let the heavens shower us with stones or bring us painful torment." Before he could reach his camel, Allah hurled a stone at him that descended upon the crown of his head and exited out from the other side and killed him. It was mentioned in many traditions that the Qur'anic verses: "*One demanding demanded the chastisement, which must befall the unbelievers,....*" (70:1-3) had been revealed for this occasion.

The Fourteenth Evidence: Hasan bin Thābit asked permission from the Prophet to describe the event in poetry. His poems have been repeatedly narrated and mentioned in both Sunni and Shiite books. Hasan wrote:

Their Apostle called upon them on the Day of Ghadeer Khum,
What a caller he was, the best.
He said, "Who is your guardian and who is your Apostle?"
They said, and no one refrained,
"Your Allah is our Guardian and you are our Apostle,
You will not find anyone of us disobedient."
Then he said "O Ali, rise.
I have chosen you to be Imam and a guide after me.
Of him whose guardian was I, this is to be his guardian.
Be, for him, followers truthful."
Then he prayed "O Allah, help whoever helps him,
And be an enemy for Ali's enemy."

Ibn al-Jawzī and Abū Abdullah al-Kānjī ash-Shāfi'ī said that the Prophet said after hearing that poem, "O Hasan, you are still aided by Holy Spirit whenever you strive for us with your tongue."

Qays bin Ubada al-Ansārī said the following poem in the presence of Imam Ali during the battle of Siffīn,

I said, when the enemy had oppressed us,
'It is enough for us to rely on Allah, our Guardian,
And Ali, our Imam and our standard bearer,'
As it had been revealed in the Holy Qur'an.
When the Prophet said, of whomsoever I had been guardian.
This is to be his guardian, great and honorable.

The Fifteenth Evidence: Imam Ali came to the courtyard of Kūfa Mosque while the people were gathered there and asked about this tradition in order to refute his dissenters in the matter of caliphate. He said: "I ask anyone to bear witness before Allah if he had heard the Prophet say, on that day in Ghadeer Khum, "Of whomsoever I had been guardian, Ali here is to be his guardian." Some people then stood up and testified.

Accounts of Imam Ali's urgent appeal spread so widely that it reached a degree of wide transmission. Al-Hamawini said in his book *Farā'id as-Samtein,* 'Zayd bin Arqam, al-Bara' bin Aazib, Salmān and many others stood up and said, "We testify that we remember that the Prophet Muhammad was on the pulpit when he said: 'O people, Allah ordered me to appoint your Imam who is in charge of your affairs after me to be my inheritor and successor. He is to be obeyed by all believers according to Allah's order as in the Qur'an. Allah made obedience to him as same as obedience to me and He ordered you to take him as guardian.....etc.'"

The Sixteenth Evidence: Some books on hadīth have expressed the occurrence of this event as a nomination. The Prophet had nominated Imam Ali as guardian. It is clear that such a nomination was not just to show love for some physical object.

Chapter: 18

THE IMĀMS: SUCCESSORS TO THE PROPHET

By

Various Authors[1]

Eventually the inevitable occurred and the spirit of the Prophet flew to its eternal abode. For, in the words of the poet Nizāmī, 'he who has not died and will not die is only God.'

It was clear that with the death of this great man a storm would blow up over the peaceful ocean of Islam, and that turbulent waters would be churned up. The ambitious would try to benefit and to get as much as they could from this turbulence and commotion, to fish in these troubled waters. On the other hand, we know that the great mass of people believe anything they see; they have always been thus and have always been fuel for a fire that anyone may care to kindle. They need constant training and continual taking care of, and without an educator they cannot reach their own perfection.

Now we must ask if such a society in such conditions needs a leader who can take the reins of command in the place of the Prophet or not, so that the result of all the pains the Messenger of Allah took, should not be dissipated. Is there not a need for a knowledgeable, political authority who is thoroughly acquainted with the Divine laws and who can guide and lead the people on the right path in the right way?

The Shi'a belief holds that the generous Grace and Love of God and His infinite wisdom demand that after the Prophet the people should not be without a leader. Such a leader must be sinless and wise, so that his soundness of speech and action may be a guarantee and true sign of a superior man, someone selected by God. He must take the reins of the Muslim community in his hands and lead and guide them with extensive wisdom and

---

[1] Reproduced from the book, *Roots of Religion*, No Author, Noor-e-Isam Imambarah, Faizabad: India, 1986.

foresight, without error, and this he must take from the Prophet of Islam. Because there is no reason for God, Who was considerate of the people in the time of the Prophet to change His judgment and to withdraw His loving concern. How could it be possible that God, Who by His Grace created thousands of elaborate details for the protection and growth of our bodies, Who caused the eyebrows to grow so that the salty, bitter, tainted sweat of the forehead can not hurt the eyes, and Who made the eyelashes also so that under their outspread canopy the eyes, can be more beautiful and better protected, how can God, Who created these and many more known and unknown things, have neglected to appoint a godly successor to the Prophet? Does not the bringing into existence of the best of communities, which is the aim of Islam, need the selection of the best of leaders? Is not the appointment of a sinless leader, educator and Imām the basis of the contentment of society? Can Islamic society attain contentment and happiness without divine supervision and leadership?

So if there is a need for the divine, sinless leader, and Islamic society wants a divine educator, how can it be said that this matter has been ignored by Islam and that the people have been left to themselves? In short, the same philosophy which demands the appointment of the Prophet also precisely demands that God introduce and appoint a successor through the Prophet.

The Prophet of Islam said in the latter part of his life: "O People, I swear before Allah that I have explained what will make you nearer to heaven (contentment) and what will make you far from the Fire (error)." [2] With this explanation, how can it be said that the Prophet of Islam did not appoint his immediate successor?

IS THE QUR'AN NOT SUFFICIENT?

The great and mighty Qur'an is the fundamental basis for every kind of Islamic concept. Like a mighty rock, all the fruitful buildings of Islamic knowledge have been made steady on it. It is the clear spring from which all the streams of insight flow. The credibility and prestige of other religious foundation rest on it. But, on the basis of the proofs we shall give, one can not be content with the Qur'an alone to solve the problems of leadership,

---

[2] *Usūl Kāfi*, vol. 2, p. 74.

the differences which crop up in Islamic society or the satisfying of the needs of the Muslim people.

First, the Qur'an and its great and abundant contents need commentary and explanation. Since all the verses are not alike in clarity and openness, an unacquainted and unknowing readers in the first moments of their journey may become lost and not take the path to their destination. So the Prophet himself or those appointed by him who have a spiritual link with what is beyond the external world, must be a guide in this valley also, so that they can interpret and explain the Āyāt according to Allah's purpose. For if not, ordinary people will sometimes interpret incorrectly and will end up far from the truth. The great Prophet of Islam said that everyone who interprets the Qur'an according to his own opinions will have the place in the Fire.[3]

It is recounted that a thief was brought into the presence of the Abassid Caliph Mo'tasim so that he might have the punishment proscribed in the Qur'an administered. The command of the Qur'an is: "*Cut off the hand of thief.*" But Mo'tasim did not know from where the hand should be cut. He asked his Sunni *ulamā*. One of them said: "From the wrist." Another 'ālim said, "From the elbow." Mo'tasim was not satisfied. He was forced to ask Imām Muhammad a-Taqi, the 9th Imām who was present, and he replied: "Four fingers must be cut off." He asked, "Why?" The Imām replied, "Since Allah has decreed in the Qur'an: "*And that the places of sajdah are for Allah.*" (72: 18), that is the seven places of the body, of which one is the palm, which in *sajdah* contact the ground belong to Allah, they should not be cut off."[4] All those present accepted and were satisfied with his proof.

This kind of interpretation is in fact interpretation of the Qur'an by the Qur'an, and is peculiar to the descendents of the prophetic mission, and no one, to whatever degree he may be a master of interpretation, is able to succeed unless he has learnt from the Household of the Prophet and has taken them as his model.

---

[3] *Tafsīr as-Sāfi*, vol. I, p. 21.

[4] *Nūr ath-Thaqalayn*, vol. 5, p. 439.

Second, another proof is that what we have said concerning the need for correct interpretation of the Qur'an concerns only one side of the Qur'an, the exoteric meaning and the commands of the Qur'an. But in the shelter of these exoteric words and meanings, a deeper and wider aim, a spiritual profundity is concealed, especially in the sections on knowledge, beliefs and the virtues. The Prophet said: "The Qur'an has a beautiful outer meaning and a profound inner meaning."[5] He also said: "The Qur'an has profundity, and the profundity of that is deep too, up to seven inner meanings."[6] Truly, what all the Qur'an has, according to the words of the great exegetists, a hermeneutics and an inner meaning, and to arrive at them by thought and research alone is not possible. It is not explicable to all through words, for the ability to perceive and practice this is not given to all men. Only those near to God, the pure, those free from corruption, can comprehend this, and use it for the solution of the differences and incidents between men, and learn it, and then, by virtue of the immunity from error and mistake that they have from God, teach it to others.

These ones near to God, the slaves immune from error are the Prophet and the Household of the Prophet about whom the Qur'an said: *"Household of the Prophet; Allah desires only to put away from you abomination and to cleanse you."* (33: 33) There is also a hadīth that only the Prophet and his Household, who are the original ones to be addressed by the Qur'an, can perceive all the truths of the Book.[7] That is to say the Prophet who was addressed by Jibrā'īl and his Household, since they are the family of the Prophet, are more acquainted with the meaning of the Qur'an. It is because of this connection (the Qur'an and the Household) that the Prophet said to the people in the last days of his life: "I leave two things in your trust, the Book of Allah and my descendents; if you attach yourselves to these two you will never go astray."[8]

---

[5] *Usūl Kāfi*, vol. 2, p. 599.
[6] *Tafsīr Sāfī*, vol. 1, p. 39.
[7] *Tafsīr Mirat al-Anwār*, p. 16.
[8] *Ibn Haubab, Musnad*, Beirut, vol. 3, p. 17; *al-Ghadir*, vol. I, p. 55; and *Ghayat al-Marām*, p. 212.

Third, The Qur'an needs a sinless enforcing guarantor. Since the Qur'an is a fundamental law, a kind of constitution, it needs an enforcing guarantor and a power to implement it. But only he who is like the Prophet and is free from error and who understand and knows the Qur'an with competence can be the guarantor of its commands and laws. These special qualities are to be found in the beings of the Imāms, and the best witness to this is the few years of the leadership of Imām Ali who, despite the difficulties which beset his holding of the rein of government, carried out to the end the great and resplendent laws of Islam each and every one.

As a postscript, the summary and fundamental of this lesson can be found in a discussion which students following the sixth Imām, Ja'far as-Sādiq, had with one of the Sunni school in the presence of the Imām.

A man from Damascus was given a meeting with Imām Sādiq and said that he had come for a discussion with one of his students. The Imām said, "Introduce him to Hishām." Hishām was the youngest of his students.

"O Boy," said the man from Damascus, "ask me concerning the Imāmate of this man (Imām Sādiq)." Hishām was angered by his lack of manners and shuddered. But he concealed his temper and began.

"Is your Creator more kind and loving towards His slaves, or the slaves themselves?"

"The Creator."

"What has the loving Creator done for his slaves?"

"He has appointed a clear guidance and proof, to protect them from differences and disunity, and to establish friendship and unity among them. He has made clear to them their religious duties."

"Who is that guide?"

"The Prophet."

"Who is it after the death of the Prophet?"

"The Book of Allah and the Sunna of the Prophet of Allah."

"Can the Book of Allah and the Sunna of the Prophet prevent us from differences today?"

"Yes."

"So why do you and I who are both Muslims have a dispute, or in other words, why have you come here from Damascus as a result of this difference?"

The man from Damascus was silent and said no more.

Imām Sādiq said to him: "Why don't you speak up?"

"What shall I say?" He replied. 'If I say we have no difference, then I lie. And just as I said the Book of Allah and the Sunna of the Prophet should take away the difference between us, so this also is untrue, because, in many instances, the Book of Allah and the Sunna do not have a clear and obvious meaning that could dispel our differences."

So the man from Damascus said that he wanted to ask the very same question from Hishām. The Imām agreed.

"O Hishām. Who is the more loving towards people? God or the people themselves."

"God."

"Did he send them someone to protect the unity of Muslims and to take over their control, to explain to them truth and falsity?"

"Are you talking about the time of the Prophet, or about now?"

"In the time of the Prophet, it was him; no, tell me about now."

"Today it is this man who is seated here and to whom people come from every corner of the land, and who gives us news of the heaven and the earth; and this knowledge was bequeathed to him from his father and so on back to the Prophet."

"How can I verify and accept this statement for myself?"

"Go now and, ask him anything you like."

"That's right, there is no other excuse; only I must ask."

Then Imām Sādiq told him about his journey and of the things that happened to him on his way which only the man could know of. When he had explained so that no doubt remained for him, the man declared his belief in the Imām.[9]

---

[9] *Usūl Kāfi*, vol. 1, p. 171-173.

Chapter: 19

ATTRACTION TO IMĀM ALI AND HIS FAMILY

By

Abū Tālib At-Turābī[1]

Some spuriously criticize Shi'as for having an over excessive love for the Prophet's family and for their diminishing the dignity of the companions because they prefer Imām Ali and his family above all the other companions.

The Answer: Many traditions mentioned in Sunni books show that Imām Ali had been preferred above all the other companions. Prophet Muhammad says: "Of whomsoever I had been guardian; Ali is to be his guardian." He also said addressing Imām Ali: "You are to me as was Aaron to Moses, except that there will be no prophet after me."

The tradition of 'the bird' shows that Imām Ali was the most beloved of Allah after His Messenger, Muhammad. The Prophet said: "I am the city of knowledge and Ali is its gate."

The Prophet ordered all the doors of his companions that opened to the mosque to be closed except the door of Imām Ali.

The prophet said: "Ali and I are the fathers of this nation." "People are from various trees but I and Ali are from one tree." "There are three veracious people and Ali bin Abū Tālib is the best of them."

Many other ahādīth in this regard are mentioned in Sunni and Shi'a reference books. Some of these are:

1. The Prophet had instituted the bonds of brotherhood between his companions and said to Imām Ali, "You are my brother," as it was mentioned in Sunni books narrated by ibn Abbās, Sa'īd bin al-Musayyab, Zayd bin Abū Awfa, Anas bin Mālik, Zayd bin Arqam, Hudhayfa bin al-Yaman, Makhduj bin Zayd, Abū Sa'īd, Abdur-Rahmān bin Aweym and Abū Huraira.

---

[1] Reproduced from the author's work, *Spurious Arguments about the Shi'a*, Ansariyan Publications, Qum: Iran, 2001.

2. Ahmad bin Hanbal mentioned in his book *Fadā'il us-Sahāba* a tradition narrated by Akrima that was heard from ibn Abbas that the Prophet said: "There is no Qur'anic verse that begins with 'O you who believe,' without Ali being their (i.e. those who believe) head, leader, and their distinction. Allah has censured the Prophet's Companions in the Qur'an but He did not mention Ali save in praise." The same was also mentioned in *Dhakha'ir ul Uqba* p. 89, Egyptian Edition. It was also mentioned by at-Tabarani and ibn Abū Hātim in *As-Sawā'iq ul-Muhriqah* p. 125; Egyptian Edition, and *Tarīkh ul-Khulāfa* (*History of the Caliphs*) p. 116; Lahore Edition.

3. Abū Na'īm mentioned in his book *Hilyatul- Awliya'* vol. 1 p. 64; Egyptian edition, a tradition narrated by ibn Abbās that the Prophet had said: "Allah had not revealed any verse beginning with 'O you who believe,' unless Ali was its head and *amīr*."

4. Ahmad bin Hanbal sums it up for Imām Ali when he said; "No one of the Prophet's Companions had virtues like that of Ali bin Abū Tālib." This saying has been mentioned in many books; *al-Mustadrak, al-Istī'āb, al-Kāmil* of ibn ul-Athir, *Kifāyat ul-Tālib, ar-riyadun-Nazira, Tahthīb ut-Tahthīb, Fath ul-Bārī fi Sharh il-Bukhārī, Tārīkh ul-Khulāfa', as-Sīra al-Halabiyah, ar-Rawdul-Azhar, Is'āf ur-Rāghibīn* and others.

5. There is a tradition, which was agreed upon by the Sunni showing the preference of Fatima az-Zahrā, the Prophet's daughter, over all others. The Prophet said: "Fatima az-Zehrā is the chief of women of Paradise." This hadīth has been narrated by some companions: Hudhayfa bin al-Yamān as in *Sahīh at-Tirmidhī*, vol. 13, p. 197, 'Ayeshah as in *Sahīh al-Bukhārī*, vol. 4, p. 203, and Umm Salama in *Sahīh at-Tirmidhī*, vol. 13, p. 250.

6. There is also an agreement upon the tradition among Sunnis showing the preference of Imām Hasan and Imām Husayn. The Prophet said: "Hasan and Husayn are the masters of the young men of Paradise." This hadīth was narrated by some Companions of the prophet who were: Abū sa'īd al-Khudrī as in *Sahīh at-Tirmidhī*, vol. 13, p. 190; *Musnad* of Ahmad, vol. 3, p. 3; Hudhayfa as in *Sahīh at-Tirmidhī*, vol. 13, p. 197; and by Abdullah bin Umar in the *Sunan* of ibn Maja vol. 1, p. 56.

7. The Sura Al-Insān (76) of the Qur'an was revealed concerning Imām Ali, Fatima az-Zehrā, Imām Hasan and Imām

Husayn. In addition, the Qur'anic Verse of purification: "Allah only desires to keep away uncleanness from you, O People of the House, and to purify you with a thorough purification," (33:33) was revealed concerning them. This has been narrated by many of the Prophet's companions such as Wathīla bin al-Aqa, amr bin Abū Salama, 'Ayeshah, Umm Salama, Sa'd bin Abū Waqqās, Abū Sa'īd, Imām Ali, Ja'far bin Abū Tālib, Abū Barza, Sabīh, ibn Abbās, Anas, Abul-Hamra', Atiyah, Sahl bin Sa'd, Abū Hurayra, Burayda, Abdullāh bin Umar, Imrān bin al-Husayn, Salama bin al-Aqua', Ma'qil bin Yasār, and Abdullāh bin Az-Zubeir.

This has been mentioned by al-Haythamī in his book *Majma'uz-Zawā'id* and as-Suyūtī in his book *al-Jāmi'us-Saghīr* narrated by al-Bazzāz on p. 113 and by ibn Hajar in his *as-Sawā'iq ul-Muhriqa* on p. 184 and *Miftāh un-Naja* on p. 9, *Yanābī'ul-Mawaddah* on p. 187, *al-Fath ul-Kabīr* on p. 133, *Arjahul-Matālib* on p. 330, *as-Sayf ul-Yamānī al-Maslūl* on p. 9.

It has also been narrated by Aamir bin Wathīla, which was mentioned by al-Hāfiz ad-Dulabī in his book *al-Kuna wal-Asmā'* vol. 1, p. 76. It was narrated by Salama bin al-Aqua' which was mentioned by *ibnul-Maghazilī* and ash-Shāfi'ī in his book *al-Manāqib*, and mentioned in other Sunni books like *Arjah ul-Matālib* on p. 330 and *Yanābī'ul-Mawaddah* on p. 28. Also, it was narrated by Imām Ali, which was mentioned by Muhibbud-Dīn at-Tabarī in his book *Dhakhā'ir ul-Uqba* on p. 20 from Ibn as-Seri.

Chapter: 20

THE TWELFTH IMĀM: MUHAMMAD AL-MAHDĪ

By

Various Authors[1]

The Imām, the just Guide, Imām Mahdī was born half-way through the month of Sha'ban in the year 255 A.H. in the town of Samarra, and in 260 A.H., when his great father died, he reached the exalted position of the Imāmate. His name (Muhammad) and his agnomen (Abu'l-Qasim) are the same as the Prophet's. His father, the 11th Shi'a Imām, was Imām Hasan al-'Askarī, and his mother, the great lady Nargis.

For various reasons, the twelfth Imām, from the first day of his life, did not appear publicly, and for about seventy years people were in communication with him through the intermediary of his special representatives, in order of succession: Usman ibn Sa'īd, Muhammad ibn Usman, Husayn ibn Rūh, and Ali ibn Muhammad as-Samarrī. This period of seventy years is known as the minor occultation (al-*ghaybat as-sughrā*), and at the end of that period the major occupation (*al-ghaybatal-kubrā*) began.

During the major occultation till the time of his re-appearance, no one has been his special representative, and there will be no one in the future, and the people have the duty to refer to the *fuqahā*, those excelling in knowledge of the *sharī'ah*, and the narration of ahadīth who are specialized in the matters of the religion.

BELIEF IN IMĀM MAHDĪ, AND UNIVERSAL REFORM

The belief in the re-appearance of the expected Imām Mahdī, the universal reformer, is not confined to the Shi'a Muslims. Other Islamic groups and even non-Islamic groups like the Jews and the Christians and some of the great world intellectual figures believe in the appearance of a great spiritual reformer. In Psalm 37 is written:

---

[1] Reproduced from the Book, *Roots of Religion*, No Author, Noor-e-Islam Imambara, Faizabad: India, 1986.

"......Trust in the Lord and do good; so you will dwell in the land, and enjoy security.

......For the wicked shall be cut off: but those who wait for the Lord shall possess the Land.

......But the weak shall possess the land, and delight themselves in abundant prosperity.

......The Lord knows the days of the flawless, and their heritage will abide forever.

......For those blessed by the Lord, shall possess the land, but those cursed by Him shall be cut off.

......The righteous shall possess the land, and dwell upon it for ever........"

THE QUR'AN AND BELIEF IN IMĀM MAHDĪ

In the Qur'an a time is promised when the worshippers of Truth, the world's people of righteousness, will take over the power and government of the world and the glorious *din* of Islam will reign all over the earth. Various following Āyāt have been revealed which exegetically point to Imām Mahdī:

"For We have written in the Psalms, after the Remembrance, 'The earth shall be the inheritance of My righteous servants.'" (11: 105)

"Allah has promised those of you who believe and do righteous deeds that He will surely make you successors in the land, even as He made those who were before them successors, and that He will surely establish their religion for them, and will give them in exchange, after their fear, security: "They shall serve Me, not associating with Me anything." (24: 55)

"It is He who has sent His Messenger with the religion of truth, that he may lift it above every religion, though the unbelievers be averse." (61: 9)

"Yet We desired to be gracious to those that were abased in the land, and to make them leaders, and to make them the inheritors." (28: 5)

The above Āyāt clearly show that in the end the world will fall to the hands of Allah's worthy and righteous servants and that they will become the leaders of the people of the world. Then Islam will be victorious over all religions.

BELIEF IN IMĀMA MAHDĪ AND SUNNI AUTHORITIES

On this subject, the scholars of the Sunni school have related many ahādīth from the Prophet of Islam, through narrators whom they themselves trust. From among them are such ahādīth which tell that the Imāms are twelve persons and that they are all from the Quraysh.

Imām Mahdī, the promised one, is from the family of the Prophet and is a descendent of Imām Ali and Fatima az-Zehra, and in many of these ahādīth it is mentioned that he is from the line of Imām Husayn.

They have mentioned and recorded hundreds of ahādīth about the Imām Mahdī in more than seventy books by their own valued and dependable authorities of which following are a few examples:

1. *al-Musnad* of Ahmad bin Hanbal (d. 241 A.H.)
2. *Sahīh of al-Bukhārī* (d. 256 A.H.)
3. *Sahīh* of al-Muslim ibn Hajjaj Nishapūrī (d. 261 A.H.)
4. *Sunan* of Abī Dāwūd Sajistānī (d. 275 A.H.)
5. *Sahīh* of Muhammad ibn 'Isa at-Tirmidhī (d. 279 A.H.)

The authors of the above most authoritative books of the Sunnis, died either before the birth of the Imām of the Age (255 A.H.) or shortly after his birth. The years of their death are:

1. *Mūsabīh as-Sunnah* of al-Baghawī (d. 516 A.H.)
2. *Jāmi' al-Usūl* of ibn Athīr (d. 606 A.H.)
3. *Al-Futuhat al-Makkiyyah* of Muhyi'd-dīn ibn al-'Arabī (d. 638 A.H.)
4. *Tadhkira al-Khawās* of Sibt ibn al-Jawzī (d. 654 A.H.)
5. *Farā'id as-Simtayn* of al-Hamawī (d. 716 A.H.)
6. *As-Sawā'iq al-Muhriqah* of Ibn Hajar al-Haythamī (d. 973 A.H.)
7. *Yanābī' al-Mawaddah* of Shaykh Sulaymān al-Qunduzī (d. 1293.)

Some of the Sunni scholars have written books especially about the Imām of the Age. Some of these are:

1. *Al-Bayān fī Akhbār Sahib az-Zamān* of Al-Ganji ash-Shāfi'ī.
2. *'Iqd ad-Durar fī Akhbār al-Imām al-Muntazar* of Shaykh Jamāl ud-dīn Yūsuf al-Dimashqī.

3. *Mahdī Al ar-Rasul* of 'Ali ibn Sultan Muhammad al-Harawi al-Hanati.

4. *Kitāb al-Mahdī* of Abū Dāwūd.

5. *'Alamāt al-Mahdī* of Jalāl ud-dīn as-Suyūtī.

6. *Manāqib al-Mahdī* of Hafiz Abū Nu'aim al-Isfahani.

7. *Al-Qawl al-Mukhtasar fī 'Alamat al-Mahdī al-Muntazar* of Ibn Hajar.

8. *Al-Burhān fī 'Alamāt al-Mahdī Akhir az-Zamān* of Mulla 'Ali al-Muttaqī.

9. *Arba'ūn Hadīth fī al-Mahdī* of Abul 'Ala al-Hamadānī.

THE HIDDEN REFORMER

We have at hand these three hundred ahādīths from the Prophet and from the five Imāms about the Imām of the Age. From these it is clear that the Imām of the Age is the ninth son of Husayn ibn Ali. His father is Imām Hasan Askarī, his mother Nargis Khātūn. His name is the same as that of the Prophet of the time; his first name is al-Mahdī. It was to happen that he would be born during his father's lifetime in Samarra and that his father would die when he would be young, that he would live even to this day, and as long as God wished it. Then he will re-appear and the world will be filled with justice at a time when there is injustice everywhere and that is why he is now hidden from the sight of men.

And when he comes--may his appearance be honored--with his back towards the Ka'bah's edifice, he will lean against the wall and cry out and call for his followers, who will number 313 persons. Prophet Isa will come from the heaven down to the earth, and will pray in a prayer led by al-Mahdī. The Imām of the Age will cause the commands of Islam to reach all over the world, and the earth will be like heaven.

There are very many ahādīth related by the Shi'a and Sunni scholars on many aspects connected with this great Imām, and these are mentioned in books like *Bihar al-Anwar* and *Muntakhab al-Athar*.

First we shall indicate here the topics of some of these ahādīth (with number given in parentheses) which the authors of *Muntakhab al-Athar* wrote down in his book and then we shall give the text of some of them.

1. A hadīth in which is it related that the Imāms are twelve, the first being Ali, the last being al-Mahdī. (58)
2. A hadīth which gives news of the appearance of al-Mahdī. (657)
3. A hadīth which identifies him as being from family of the Prophet. (389)
4. A hadīth which says that his name and agno-men are the same as the Prophet's. (48)
5. A hadīth which says al-Mahdī is a descendent of Imām Ali. (214)
6. A hadīth which says he is a descendent of Fatima az-Zehra. (196)
7. A hadīth which says he is a descendent of Imām Husayn. (175)
8. A hadīth which says he is the ninth descendent of Imām Husayn. (148)
9. A hadīth which says he is a descendent of Imām Zain al-'Ābidīn. (175)
10. A hadīth which says he is a descendent of Imām Bāqir. (103)
11. A hadīth which says he is a descendent of Imām Ja'far as-Sādiq (103)
12. A hadīth which says he is a descendent of Imām Mūsa Kāzim. (101)
13. A hadīth which says he is a descendent of Imām Ridā. (95)
14. A hadīth which says he is a descendent of Imām Javad. (90)
15. A hadīth which says he is a descendent of Imām Hadi. (90)
16. A hadīth which says he is a descendent of Imām Hasan al-'Askarī. (146)
17. A hadīth which says that the name of his father is Hasan. (147)
18. A hadīth which says that he will fill the world with justice. (123)
19. A hadīth which says his occultation will be prolonged. (91)
20. A hadīth which relates the extent of al-Mahdī's life. (318)

21. A hadīth which says that Islam will rule over the world through him. (47)

22. A hadīth which says he will be the twelfth and the last Imām.

When looking at the above mentioned and other ahādīth, it should be kept in mind that the ahādīth mentioning Imām al-Mahdī have been narrated most frequently, and that there are few subjects in Islam which have been mentioned in ahādīth so often. Thus, in this light, anyone who believes in Islam and its Prophet must necessarily declare his belief in the existence of the promised Imām Mahdī who is now in occultation. Now we shall relate some of these ahādīth.

1. The author of *Yanābī' al-Mirada* relates that the Prophet said: "Al-Mahdī is a descendent of mine. He will be in concealment, and when he manifests himself, the earth will become filled with justice, just as it was previously filled with injustice."

2. In this book it is also related that Salmān al-Farisī said: "I went to the Prophet, when Husayn ibn 'Ali was sitting in his lap and the Prophet was kissing his eyes and mouth, and he said: 'You are a noble one, the son of a noble one, and the brother of a noble one; you are the Imām, the son of the Imām, and the brother of the Imām. You are the Proof, son of the Proof and the brother of the Proof; you will be the father of nine Proofs of whom the ninth will be Qā'im.'"

3. Ibn 'Abī Dalaf says: "I heard from Imām Ali ibn Muhammad (the 10th Imām) that he said: 'The Imām after me will be Hasan, my son, and after him his descendent the Qā'im, who will fill the earth with justice, when it was previously filled with injustice.'"

4. Hudhayfah said that the Prophet said: "If no more than one day is left of the world, Allah will make that day so long that a man, descendent of mine, whose name is my name, will appear." Salmān asked: "O Prophet of Allah, which descendent will he be?" The Prophet put his hand on Imām Husayn and said that it would be one of his descendents.

5. Mas'adah relates from Imām Sādiq that he said: "The Qā'im will be born of Hasan (the eleventh Imām, Imām

Hasan al-'Askarī), and Hasan will be son of Ali (the tenth Imām, Imām Ali al-Naqī), and Ali will be son of Muhammad (the ninth Imām, Imām Muhammad Taqī), and Muhammad will be born of Ali (the eighth Imām, Imām Ali ibn Mūsa) and Ali will be son of this child (he pointed to Imām Mūsa ibn Ja'far, the seventh Imām). We are twelve Imāms, all pure and noble birth. I swear by Allah, if there remain of the world no more than one day, Allah will make that day so long that ˈthe Qā'im of us, the Household of the Prophet, will appear."

THE OPINION OF SOCIOLOGISTS

The world's foremost intellectuals are of the opinion that the wars, massacres, murders, prostitution, and all the evils of this age which are daily on the increase are because there is no equilibrium between man's material and spiritual requirements. The man of today has turned his back on moral virtues and spiritual riches, although he has conquered the sea, the desert and space, and has taken himself to the moon.

It is obvious that by relying on force and power he can not establish order and justice in the world, and that only with technology and the material sciences the happiness of humanity will not be secured. Man has no other resort than to strengthen his social relations on the basis of faith and virtue, and to save himself from the vortex of dangers with the guidance of a great world reformer, to establish a rule based on justice together with peace, security and sincerity. In this state of affairs, human society is moving quickly towards preparation for the rising up of the Imām of the Age.

THE LENGTH OF IMĀM AL-MAHDĪ'S LIFE

We believe that the lengthening of a man's life is not impossibility, because it is explicitly said in the Qur'an that: *"We sent Nuh to his people, as he lived among them a thousand years all but fifty."* (29: 14)

What is more, research undertaken in the biological sciences has corroborated the possibility of lengthening the human life-span. Even great scientists are of the opinion that food and drugs may be prepared which can prolong man's life.

The late Ayatullah Sadr, a learned scholar of Qum (1882-1953), and father of the well-known Imām Mūsa Sadr of the Lebanon in his book *"al-Mahdī"*, quoted from a scientific article written in 1959 which stands as a witness to what we have said above. Here we shall give a summary of it.

"Authoritative scientists say that all the basic tissues of the animal body can live forever, and it is possible for a man to live for a thousand years, provided that it doesn't happen that the thread of his life is not severed. These scientists do not speak on the basis of guess work or surmise, for they have arrived at their conclusion through scientific experiment.

"A professor at Johns Hopkins University has said that it has been proven that the human body has the potentiality for extended life. Apparently the first person to carry out these experiments on parts of an animal's body was Dr. Jack Lubb, and after him Dr. Warren Lewis, who, together with his wife, proved that parts of bird fetuses could be kept alive in buffer solutions. These experiments were systematically continued until Dr. Alexis Karel, as a result of further experimental work, established that parts of animals subjected to experiments did not degenerate, and even that they lived longer than the animal from which they had been taken. In January 1912 he started his experiments and by dint of self-sacrifice and removing the numerous difficulties, he discovered the following facts:

1. "Unless complications such as lack of nutrition or attack by microbes intervened, living cells would continue living forever.
2. "These cells which continued to live also grew and multiplied.
3. "The growth and division of these cells could be controlled by the nutrition given to them.
4. "The passing of time did not affect them and did not make them age or lose strength. Not even the smallest effect of ageing was seen. Each year they grew and multiplied exactly as in previous years. So why does man die? Why is his span of life rarely more than a hundred years? The part of the human or animal body are numerous and various, and there is also a perfect relationship and unity between them; so that

the life of some of them depends on the life of others, and the failure or death of parts of human or animal bodies is the consequence of the death of the other parts. Sudden deaths which are the result of infection are for this reason, and it also provides the reason for the average limit of man's life being around seventy to eighty years. Of course, what experiments have shown is that the cause of death is not the arrival at seventy or eighty years of age, but that the fundamental causes are diseases and accidents which may attack one of the body's organs and put it out of work; then the death of this part causes a break in its relation to other parts and the death of all the organs ensues.

"Thus if science could eliminate these accidents or obstruct their harmful effects, there would be no impediment to the prolongation of life."

So if we know that a greatly extended life is not an impossibility, there is no hindrance to prevent God, the All-powerful, from keeping a man safe and sound for thousands of years, because the regulations of a man's life is in the hands of God. He can bring a new harmony into existence which has precedence over the usual order of things, just as He did in the case of all the miracles. The miracles of the prophets, the cooling of the fire for Ibrahim al-Khalil, the turning into a serpent of Prophet Mūsa's staff, the bringing to life of the dead through Prophet 'Isa, and so forth, are all against the usual flow of things, but God brought another order into existence by His own power and a miracle occurred; all Muslims, and Jews and Christians, believe in these miracles.

Similarly for the length of the life of the Imām of the Age there remains no place for any kind of objection, because if someone says that such a length of life is impossible, his claim can not be at all accepted after the stipulation of the Qur'an concerning the length of Prophet Nūh's life, and also after the latest revelations of biology.

If it is said that it is possible, but against the normal natural order of things, it can be retorted that the length of life of the Imām of the Age is against the natural order just as the miracles of the prophets, and is carried out according to the will of God. Someone who believes in the power of God and the occurrence of the miracles of the prophets can not have the slightest objection to the length of the Imām's life.

THE OCCULTATION OF IMĀM OF THE AGE

The Prophet of Islam sometimes hinted to people concerning the occultation of the twelfth Imām, and other five Imāms also reminded people of this matter. The news of the occultation of the Imām of the Age was so well known even before his birth, that everyone who believed in the birth of the Imām also believed in his prolonged occultation. Let us look at some of the indications that have come down to us from many ahādīth on this subject.

1. The Prophet said: "The Qā'im of my descendents will become hidden, as the result of a covenant between me and him, and then people will say that Allah has no need of the family of Muhammad, and some will doubt his birth. So everyone who is aware of his time must act according to his religion, and must not let *Shaytān* enter him by faltering lest he be thrown out from my people and my religion."

2. Imām Ali said: "Our Qā'im has an occultation which will be of great devotion....Beware! Everyone who is firm in his religion, and does not become hard-hearted from the lengthening of the occultation of this man (and turn away from his religion) will find himself on the same side as me on the Day of Resurrection." Then he said: "Our Qā'im when he rises has no responsibility for anyone's allegiance to him, and for this reason his birth will be secret and he will be hidden."

3. Muhammad ibn Muslim said that he heard from Imām Ja'far as-Sādiq that he said: "If you hear of the occultation of your Imām, do not deny it."

4. At-Tabarsī wrote: "The ahādīth of the occultation were recorded by the Shi'a narrators in books which were composed in the time of Imām Bāqir and Imām Sādiq. Of these entire reliable narrators one was Hasan ibn Mahbūb. About a hundred years before the time of the occultation, he wrote a book called "*al-Mashaykhah*....and mentioned the ahādīth about the occultation in it. One of them is: "Abū Basir said: 'I said in the presence of Imām Sādiq that the Qā'im of the

family of Muhammad will have two occultations; one prolonged, one short'. The Imām replied: 'Yes, O Abū Basīr, one of those occultations will be longer than the other.'"

Therefore, the Prophet of Islam and the other Imāms reminded people that the occultation of the Imām of the Age went together with the announcement of the existence of the Prophet himself, and that belief in the Imām's occultation went together with belief in the Prophet's existence.

Shaykh Sadūq narrated from Al-Sayyid al-Himyarī: "I had some exaggerated idea about Muhammad ibn al-Hanafiyyah, and believe that he was hidden, till Allah enlightened me through Imām Sādiq and saved me from the Fire. I was guided to the true way, whereby after the Imāmate of Ja'far ibn Muhammad had been proved to me by evidence and demonstration, I said one day to him: 'O son of the Prophet of Allah, tell me some ahādīth from your forefathers about occultation and the truth of it.' He replied: 'The occultation will occur for my descendent in the sixth generation, and he will be the twelfth Imām after the Prophet of Allah, the first one being 'Ali ibn Abī Tālib, and the last the Qā'im of the Truth, the Continuance of Allah on earth, and the Lord of the Age...'"

WHY IS IMĀM OF THE AGE IN CONCEALMENT?

The existence of the Imām and the successor of the Prophet was necessary for a number of reasons, such as differences, explaining the laws of Allah, and giving spiritual, inward guidance, and that Allah, the Merciful, appointed Imām Ali and after him eleven descendents, one after the other, as Imāms after the Prophet of Islam.

It is obvious that the duties of the Imām of the Age, in all the aspects of the Imāmate, are the same as that of his predecessors. If there were no hindrance, it would be necessary that he be clearly manifested, so that people might prosper from all the benefits of his existence. So why was he hidden from the very first?

Basically, there is no need to look for the philosophy or reasons behind his occultation so as to believe in the rule of Allah, for there is no obligation on us to know the basic reason for it, just as we remain ignorant of the metaphysics behind many other things. It is sufficient that we know on the basis of the many ahādīth and true proofs that God, the All Mighty, sent his own proof, but that, for various reasons, He kept him hidden behind the curtain of occultation.

It can also be found from some ahādīth that the basic and fundamental reason for the occultation will become known after the appearance of Imām al-Mahdī. Abdullah al-Fadl al-Hashimī says: "I heard from Imām Ja'far as Sādiq that he said: 'The occultation will be indispensable for the Lord of Power, so that the people of vanity will fall into doubt about him.' I asked: 'Why? He said: 'For a reason which I am not at liberty to declare.' I asked: 'What will his rule be?' He replied: 'The same rule as existed in the occultations of previous proofs. It will not be disclosed until after his appearance, just as the rule of the works of Khidr was not known (meaning the drilling of a hole in the boat, the killing of the youth, and the repairing of the wall in the story of Khidr in the Qur'an) until Mūsa and Khidr decided to part company. O Fadl, the subject of the occultation is a command of Allah and a secret of His secrets, and since we acknowledge Allah to be Wise, we must accept that all his acts are done with Knowledge and Wisdom, even if the reason for them is not known to us.'"

Of course the benefits of Imām al-Mahdī's occultation can be covered, and these have been indicated in some of the ahādīth. For example:

1. A test of people is one of the benefits of the occultation of the Imām of the Age: on one side, a group without faith, whose inner feelings become evident; on the other side, those in the depths of whose hearts faith have taken root, their hope of deliverance, their patience in adversity, their faith in the unseen becoming more perfect, their worthiness becoming known, and degrees of spiritual reward falling to them. Mūsa ibn Ja'far said: "When my fifth descendent becomes hidden, persevere in your religion, so that no one may turn you away from it. There will be an occultation for the Lord of that Age, when a group of believers in him will relinquish their belief. This occultation is a test by which Allah will test his slaves."

2. The second benefit is the protection for the Imām against being killed. From a study of the leaders of Islam, and their

situation vis-à-vis the Umayyad and Abbasid Caliphs, we can clearly see that if the twelfth Imām manifested himself they would surely kill him like his forefathers or poison him. Because when they heard and knew that there would arise from the family of the Prophet, from the descendents of Imām Ali and Fatima az-Zehra someone who would destroy the government of the oppressors, and that person would be a child of Imām Hasan al-'Askarī, the Abassids planned to kill him. But Allah protected him and his enemies lost hope. Zurārah relates from Imām Sādiq that he said: "There will be an occultation prior to the appearance of the Qā'im." Zurarah asked: "Why?" He said: "So that he may escape being killed, and that occultation will continue till the ground for his appearance and triumph over the rule of the oppressors is ready."

3. The third benefit that can be gleaned from the ahādīth is that by this means Imām al-Mahdī will be saved from having allegiance made to him by the oppressors, caliphs, and usurping rulers. When he appears no one will swear allegiance to him, so that he can freely expose the truth and establish a just and righteous rule.

THE PURPOSE OF THE HIDDEN IMĀM

We have said above that God appointed the Imām of the Age to be a guide amongst people; however it is the people who are the obstacle to his appearance, and whenever they are ready for a single, divine world rule, formed on true justice observing rights, truths and realities, putting into practice all the laws of Islam without any dissimulation or fear, Imām Mahdī will openly declare himself. So, with regard to Allah, the Merciful, there is not the slightest lack of favor or mercy, for the fault lies with the people that the Imām is hidden and the appearance of his rule is delayed. Still, it must be remembered that the benefits of the existence of the Imām are not limited to outward guidance among people, for the pure existence of the Imām has other benefits which are not necessarily evident among people.

The most important benefit of the Imām's existence is that he is the intermediary for Divine Favor. For, on the basis of the evidence scholars have produced and also according to the numerous ahādīth which speak about the Imāmate, if there were no Imām, the relation between the world and its Creator would no longer exist, because all of the favors of Allah come through the Imām to the rest of humanity. In many ahādīth it is said very clearly that the earth will not remain without an Imām.

The Imām is the heart of the world of existence, the leader, the preceptor of mankind, and for this reason his presence or his absence makes no difference. What is more, the spiritual guidance of the Imām towards worthy individuals will always be there, although they may not see him, especially as it is mentioned in ahādīth that Imām Mahdī comes and goes in among the people in the meetings of the believers without anyone understanding. Thus the guarding of Islam and the protection of the worthy is well undertaken by the Imām, even during the time of his occultation. In reality the hidden Imām is like the sun behind a cloud from whose light and heat existent things may profit, although the ignorant and the blind may not see it.

Imām Sādiq also said in answer to the question: "How can people benefit from a hidden Imām?" The Imām replied, "Just as they do from the sun when it is behind a cloud."

We would now like you to look at this excerpt from the writings of Henri Corbin, the famous French scholar:

"I believe that the Shi'a sect is the only religion which maintains eternally the link of Divine guidance between God and his creation, and continually keeps alive the union of wilayat. The Jewish religion finished prophethood, which is the relationship between God and the world of man, with Moses, and do not acknowledge the prophethood of Jesus or Muhammad. Thus they have severed this link. The Christians, also, stopped with Jesus, and the Sunni Muslims stood still with Prophet Muhammad. With the seal of prophethood among the latter, they admit of no further link being maintained between the Creator and creation.

"Only the Shi'a faith believes that the prophethood ended with Prophet Muhammad, but that walayat, which is this link of guidance and progression, continues to live after him and forever.

"Indeed, only among the Shi'a does this reality between the world of man and the Divinity remain forever."

Belief in the Imām of the Age means that the link between people and the unseen world is inseparable, and someone who believes this must always remember Imām Mahdī and await the appearance of this hidden reformer.

Of course, waiting for the Imām of the Age does not mean that all Muslims and Shi'as should fold their arms and take no measures in the way of furthering the aims of Islam, only waiting for him to appear. For, as the great Shi'te scholars have been saying from the earliest times, all Muslims and Shi'as have the duty to make every effort in the path of establishing and strengthening Islamic knowledge and laws in the face of injustice and evil, to struggle against this with all their possibilities; or, in other words, to strive till the preparation for a just rule has been made, till society has been so harmonized that all those with complaints have seen justice; and if there is any oppression or cruelty reigning among people, to protest against it, and continue in this way. Every Muslim has the duty to sacrifice himself in the way of Eman and Islam, and to always be prepared to welcome the promised Imām Mahdī, that is, so order his life that it may not be a contradiction of the project of the Imām, so that he can take his place in the ranks behind him and fight against his enemies.

Chapter: 21

THE GUIDANCE OF TRUTH

By

Dr. Muhammad Al-Tījānī al-Samāwī[1]

In a small village in the south of Tunisia, during a wedding ceremony, an old lady sat in the middle of a group of ladies listening to them talking about a married couple. The lady expressed her astonishment about what she heard, and when she was asked why, she said that she had breast-fed both when they were babies. The ladies spread the news quickly among their husbands who investigated the matter. The woman's father testified that the old lady had actually breast-fed his daughter, and the man's father also testified that his son was breast-fed by the same old lady.

Inevitably the two tribes were agitated by the news and started fighting each other, and each tribe accused the other of being the cause of this tragedy which would bring the wrath of Allah on them. What made it worse was the fact that the marriage had taken place ten years earlier and had produced three children. As soon as the woman heard the news she fled to her father's house and refused to eat or drink anything, and she attempted suicide for she could not bear the shock of being married to her brother and giving birth to three children without knowing the real situation.

As a result of the clashes between the two tribes, many people were injured until one particular Shaykh intervened and stopped the fighting and advised them to consult the learned scholars and ask them for their opinion in the matter and hopefully they could reach a solution.

The people concerned embarked on their journey around the big town asking the learned people for a solution to their

---

[1] Reproduced from his book, *Then I was Guided*, (Chapter: *The Guidance of Truth*), Message of Peace Inc. (Pyame Aman), Bloomfield, New Jersey: U.S.A., 1991.

problems. However, every time they explained the case to a learned scholar and asked him for advice, he told them that the marriage was void and the couple should be separated for as long as they lived, in addition to freeing a slave or fasting for two months and various other legal opinions.

Eventually, they arrived at Gafsa and asked the learned people there but the answer was the same, because all the Mālikīs prohibit the marriage between a couple if they were fed even one drop of milk from the same woman. They do so by following Imām Mālik who treated milk and alcohol on the same level and said, "When a great quantity of whatever makes you drunk is prohibited, then a small amount of it must also be prohibited." Thus, the marriage between the couple who was breast-fed with one drop of milk from the same woman must be prohibited. One of the men who was present at the hearing told them privately to come and see me, and he said to them, "Ask al-Tījānī on these matters for he knows all the *Madhāhib*, and on many occasions I had seen him arguing with these learned scholars and beating them with his logical reasoning."

That is what the husband of that woman told me when I took him to my library where he told me the whole case in detail, and said to me, "Sir, my wife wants to commit suicide and our boys are neglected and we do not know how we can solve this problem, and people led us to you hoping that you might have an answer to our problem, especially since I see all these books in your possession, which I have never seen before in my life."

I brought him some coffee and thought about the case for a little while then I asked him about the number of times that he was breast-fed from that old woman. He said, "I do not know, but my wife was breast-fed by her twice or three times, and her father testified that he took his daughter two or three times to that old woman."

I said, "If that is right, then there is no problem and your marriage is legal and valid." The poor man fell on me kissing my hands and head, saying, "May Allah bring you good news for you opened the gates of peace to me." Before even finishing his coffee or asking me for any reference, he asked permission to leave my house and hurriedly went out to tell his wife and children and the rest of his family about the good news.

But the day after he came back with seven men and introduced them to me saying. "This is my father, this is my father-in-law, the third is the mayor of the village, the fourth is the Imām of the Friday prayers, the fifth is the religious adviser, the sixth is the chief of the tribe and the seventh is the headmaster of the school, and all of them came to investigate the case of the breast-feeding and how you considered the marriage to be valid."

I took the whole party to the library, and greeted them and offered them coffee for I expected a lengthy debate with them.

They said, "We came to discuss with you how you legalized a marriage in which the couple were breast-fed from the same woman. Such a marriage has been forbidden by Allah in the Qur'an and by His messenger who said that it (marriage) is forbidden between a couple who has been breast-fed (by the same woman) in the same way as it is forbidden between a couple who is related (brother and sister). Imām Mālik has forbidden it too."

I said, "Gentlemen, you are eight and I am one, and if I speak to all of you, I will not be able to convince you and the discussion might well lose its aim. I suggest you choose one man from among you to discuss the matter with me, and you will act as an arbitrator between us." They liked the idea and chose the religious advisor as their representative because they thought he was more knowledgeable and more able than anybody else. The man started his deliberation by asking me how I allowed something that had been forbidden by Allah, His Messenger and by all the Imāms.

I said, "God forbid! I never did such thing. But Allah forbade the marriage (in case of common breast-feeding) by stating it briefly in a Qur'anic verse and did not specify the details; rather, He left it to His Messenger to explain how and how much."

He said, "Imām Mālik forbids the marriage when one drop of milk has been taken through breast-feeding."

I said, "I know that. But Imām Mālik is not an absolute authority over all Muslims, and what do you say about the opinions of other Imāms?"

He said, "May Allah be pleased with them they all followed the steps of the Messenger of Allah."

I said, "What is then your reasoning before Allah about following Imām Mālik who contradicted a text by the Messenger of Allah?"

He looked bemused and said, "Praise be to Allah! I did not know that Imām Mālik could contradict the Prophetic texts."

The rest of the men looked even more puzzled and were amazed at my daring criticism of Imām Mālik, which they had never heard before. I continued by asking, "Was Imām Mālik one of the Companions?"

He replied, "No." I asked, "Was he one of the Followers?" He replied, "No, but he followed the earlier Followers." I asked, "Who is nearer, him or Imām Ali ibn Abī Tālib?" He replied, "Imām Ali ibn Abī Tālib was one of the rightly guided caliphs." One of the men added, "Our master Ali is the gate to the city of knowledge." I said, "Why did you leave the gate to the city of knowledge and follow a man who was neither a Companion nor a Follower, and he was born after the civil war and after the city of the Messenger of Allah had been sacked by Yazīd's forces who killed the best of the Companions and violated all aspects of human morality and changed the Messenger's tradition to some heretical doctrines of their own make. How could then for any man have confidence in these Imāms who pleased the authorities because they preached in accordance to their policies?"

Another man started talking saying, "We heard that you are a Shi'a, and that you worship Imām Ali." His friend, who sat next to him kicked him, and said, "Be quiet, are you not ashamed of yourself saying that to such a learned man? I have known many learned scholars in my life, but I have never known any of them to possess a library like this one. Furthermore, this man's argument is based on knowledge and he sound sure about what he is saying."

I answered, "Yes that is right, I am a Shi'a, but the Shi'as do not worship Imām Ali, but instead of following Imām Mālik, they follow Imām Ali because he is the gate to the city of knowledge, as you yourselves said."

The religious adviser asked, "Did Imām Ali permit the marriage between couples who have been breast-fed by the same woman?"

I answered, "No, he forbids it if the babies were breast-fed fifteen full and consecutive times by the same woman, or what could produce flesh and bone."

The woman's father was very pleased to hear what I had said, and his face lit then he said, "Praise be to Allah! My daughter was breast-fed on two or three occasions by that old woman. The saying of Imām Ali is a solution to our predicament and a mercy on us from Allah after we had lost hope."

The religious adviser said, "Give us the authentic reference to the saying (of Imām Ali) so that we may feel satisfied. I gave them *Minhāj al-Salihīn* by al-Sayyid al-Khū'ī, and he read aloud the chapter concerning breast-feeding and what it entails.

The men were very pleased, especially the husband, who was afraid that I might not have the reference. They asked me to lend them the book so they could take it to their village and use it as a reference for their reasoning. I lent them the book, and then they left me full of praises and apologies.

As soon as they left my house they met a sinister man who took them to some wicked religious leaders and they for their part frightened them and warned them that I was an "Israeli agent" and that the book *Minhāj al-Salihīn* was all lies, that the people of Iraq were blasphemous and hypocrites, that the Shi'as were *Majūs* who permitted the marriage between brothers and sister and that was why I allowed that man to continue with his marriage to his "sister"– having been breast-fed by the same woman. In the end they persuaded the men to change their minds and forced the husband to take legal action with regard to his divorce in Gafsa's Magistrate court. The judge asked them to go to the Capital Tunis and approach the Mufti of the Republic, for he might have a solution to the problem. The husband left for the Capital and waited there for a whole month until he was able to have an interview with him.

During the interview the husband explained the case in detail then the Mufti asked him about the religious scholars who accepted the marriage as being correct and legal. He told him that none of them thought so except one called al-Tījānī al-Samāwī. Al-Muftī took a note of my name and said to the husband, "Go back to your village and I shall write to the judge in Gafsa."

Shortly after that a letter from the Mufti of the Republic arrived, and the husband's lawyer read it and found that the Mufti ruled that the marriage was void.

The husband, who looked very tired and exhausted, was informed by his lawyer about the contents of the letter. He later came to see me and apologized for all the inconveniences that he had caused me.

I thanked him for his feelings towards me, but expressed my surprise regarding the Mufti's rule to consider the marriage in this case as void. I also asked him to bring the Mufti's letter to the Magistrate court in Gafsa so that I could publish it in the Tunisian press and show that the Republic's Muftī did not really know much about the four Islamic *Madhahib* and did not understand the juridical differences between them regarding the issue of brotherhood by breast-feeding. However, the husband told me that he could not see the file on his case, and therefore was unable to bring me the letter, and then he departed.

A few days later I received an invitation from the judge asking me to bring the book and other proofs that allow the marriage between two people who have been breast-fed by the same woman. I chose a number of references and prepared the chapters regarding brotherhood by breast-feeding, so that I could produce the evidence quickly.

I went to the court at the agreed time and I was received by the clerk who took me to the judge's office, and I was surprised to see the District Magistrate and the Republic's Attorney as well as three other judges. I noticed that the judges were wearing their official regalia, as if they were sitting to pass judgment; I also noticed that the husband was sitting at the end of the court room, facing the judges.

I greeted everyone, but they looked at me with disdain, and when I sat down the chief judge asked me, "Are you al-Tījānī al-Samāwī?" I answered, "Yes." He asked, "Are you the one who passed a judgment in which you legalized the marriage in this case?"

I answered, "No I did not pass a judgment, rather, the Imāms and the religious scholars of Islam passed that judgment by accepting the marriage as being correct and legal."

He said, "That is why we summoned you, and you are now in the dock. If you cannot support your claim with the appropriate proof, then we will have to send you to prison, and you will never come out of there as a free man."

I knew then that I was actually in the dock, not because I had passed a judgment on that particular case, but because some of those sinister religious leaders had told the judges that I was a troublemaker and that I cursed the Companions and campaigned for the support of Ahlul Bayt. The chief judge asked them to bring two witnesses against me then he would have the authority to throw me in prison.

In addition to that, the Muslim Brotherhood took advantage of my judgment in this case and spread rumors that I had legalized the marriages between brothers and sisters, and that is, as they claimed, what the Shi'as believe!

I became absolutely sure about that when the chief judge threatened to throw me in prison, so I was left with nothing but to challenge him and to defend myself with all my courage and I said to the chief judge, "Can I speak frankly and without any fear?" He replied, "Yes you can do that, for you have no lawyer."

I said, "First of all, I would like to say that I have not appointed myself to pass judgment (Fatwa) but this is the woman's husband before you, so ask him. He came to my house and asked me, and it was my duty to provide him with whatever information I had. I asked him how many times his wife had been breast-fed by that old lady, and when he said that it was only on two occasions, I gave him the answer according to Islamic law. I was not trying to interpret Islam, nor indeed was I trying to legislate."

The chief judge said, "What a surprise! Now you claim that you know Islam and that we do not know it!"

I replied, "God forbid! I did not mean that. But everyone here knows the Mālikī *Madhhab* stops here. What I did was to search in the other Islamic *Madhāhib* and find a solution to this case."

The chief judge asked, "Where did you find the solution?"

I said, "Sir, may I ask you a question before I answer?"

He replied, "Ask what you like."

I asked, "What do you say about the Islamic *Madhāhib*?"

He replied, "They are all correct for they all follow the teachings of the Messenger of Allah, and there is mercy in their differing."

I said, "Well, have mercy on this poor man (pointing to the woman's husband) who has been away from his wife and children for the past two months, when one of the Islamic *Madhāhib* has a solution for his problem."

The chief judge reacted angrily, "Give us your proof and stop all this nonsense. We allowed you to defend yourself, now you have become a lawyer defending others."

I took out from my briefcase the book entitled *Minhāj al-Salihīn* by al-Sayyid al-Khū'ī, and said, "This is the *Madhhab* of Ahlul Bayt, and in it there is the absolute proof."

He interjected by saying, "Forget about the *Madhhab* of Ahlul Bayt, we do not know it, and we do not believe in it." I was expecting such an answer, so I had brought with me, after having done some research, a number of references from the Sunni Traditionists and al-Jamā'ah, and I arranged them according to my knowledge. I put *Sahīh al-Bukhārī* in the first line, then *Sahīh Muslim*, then *al-Fatāwa* by Mahmūd Shaltūt, then *Bidāyat al-Mujtahid wa Nihayat al-Muqtasid* by Ibn Rushd, then *Zād al-Masīr fi Ilm al-Tafsīr* by Ibn al-Jawzī and many other Sunni references.

When the chief judge refused to look at al-Sayyid al-Khū'ī's book, I asked him which books he trusted.

He said, "*Al-Bukhārī and Muslim*."

I took *Sahīh al-Bukhārī* and opened it at the specific page, then said, "Here you are Sir, read it."

He said, "You read it."

I read, "So and so told us that Ayeshah, the mother of the believers, said that the Messenger of Allah in his lifetime only prohibited the marriage, if the couple were breast-fed on five occasions or more by the same woman."

The chief judge took the book from me and read it himself then gave it to the Attorney General, and he too read the hadith then he passed the book to the other judges. In the meantime, I showed the chief judge *Sahīh al-Bukhārī*, pointing out to him the same hadīth, then I opened *al-Fatāwa* by al-Azhar's Shaykh Shaltūt who mentioned the differences between the Imāms about breast-feeding issue, some of them prohibited the marriage if the breast-feeding was on fifteen occasion, others said seven or even five except Mālik who contradicted the text and prohibited the marriage if there had been one drop of milk taken by the couple from the same woman. Shaltūt added, "I tend to favor the middle solution and say seven or more."

After having looked at the references, the chief judge turned to the woman's husband and said to him, "Go now and bring your father-in-law to testify that your wife was breast-fed twice or three times by the old woman, then you can take your wife with you today."

The poor man was delighted. The Attorney General and the other judges excused themselves and left the court, and when I was alone with the chief judge he apologized to me and said, "Forgive me for the wrong information I have been given about you, now I know that they are biased and envious people who wish to harm you."

I was very glad to hear about that quick change of heart and said, "O, Sir, Praise be to Allah Who made me victorious through you."

He said, "I heard that you have a great library, and have you got *Hayāt al-Haywān al-Kubrā* by al-Damiri?"

I said, "Yes".

He asked, "Could you lend me the book, for I have been looking for it for the past two years?"

I said, "It is yours Sir, whenever you want it."

He said, "Have you got time to come to my library sometimes, so we could discuss various issues, and hopefully I may benefit from you." I said, "God forbid! I will benefit form you. You are more senior to me, both in age and in position. However, I have four days off-duty during the week, and I am at your service then."

We agreed to meet every Saturday, for he did not have court hearings on that day. After he asked me to leave with him the *Sahīhs* of al-Bukhārī and Muslim and *al-Fatāwa* by Mahmud Shaltūt to copy the relevant texts from them, he stood up and saw me out of his office. I came out full of joy and thanking Allah, praise to Him for that moral victory. I entered the court full of fear and threatened with imprisonment, but came out with the chief judge becoming a good friend of mine and asking me to meet him for discussion so that he could benefit from me. It is the grace of Ahlul Bayt's way. It does not let down those people who keep to it, and it is a safe refuge for whoever comes to it.

The woman's husband talked about what happened to the people of his village, and the news spread to the neighboring villages when the wife returned to her husband's house, and the case ended with the marriage being legal. The people started saying that I was more knowledgeable than anybody even the Republic's Mufti.

The husband came to my house with a big car and invited me and my family to his village and told me that the people there were waiting for me and they would slaughter three calves to celebrate the occasion. I apologized to him for not being able to accept his invitation because I was busy in Gafsah and told him that I would visit them some other time, if Allah wished.

The chief judge also talked to his friends and the case became famous. Thus, Allah prevailed on the cunningness of those wicked people, some of them came to apologize, and others were enlightened by Allah and became one of the faithful. This is truly the grace of Allah. He gives it to whoever He likes. Allah is the Most Gracious. Our last word is to say: Thanks to Allah, Lord of Creation, and May Allah bless our master Muhammad and his purified Household.

PART THREE: WAHHĀBĪSM

Chapter: 22

WAHHĀBĪSM AND ITS REFUTATION

BY

Ayyub Sabri Pasha[1]

Wahhābīsm was established by Mohammad ibn 'Abd al-Wahhāb. He was born in Huraimila in the Najd in 1699 and died in 1791. Formerly, he had been to Basra, Baghdad, Iran, India and Damascus with the view of traveling and trading, where he found the vicious books written by Ahmad Ibn Taimiyya of Harran (1263-1328), [d. in Damascus], the contents of which were incompatible with the Ahl al-Sunna.

Being very cunning and talkative, he became known as ash-Shaikh an-Najdī. In order to increase his fame, he attended the lectures of Hanbalī 'ulamā' in Medina and later in Damascus and wrote many books when he returned to the Najd. His book *Kitāb at-tawhīd*[2] (was annotated by his grandsons, 'Abd ar-Rahmān, and was interpolated and published in Egypt with the title *Fath al-majid* by a Wahhābī called Mohammad Hamid. (I rebutted his corrupt writings and published them in my book, *Advice for the Wahhābis in 1970*). Mohammad ibn 'Abd al-Wahhāb's ideas deceived the villagers, the inhabitants of Dar'iyya and their chief, Mohammad ibn Sa'ūd. The number of those who accepted his ideas, which he called Wahhābīsm, increased and he imposed himself as the *qādī*

---

[1] The Wahhābīs are one of the groups who name themselves as Muslims while, in fact, they strive to demolish Islam. The author of this chapter is an Ahl As-Sunna Scholar who served as a Rear-Admiral in the time of the thirty-fourth Ottoman Sultan Abd Al-Hamid Khan II (1842-1918), and buried in the shrine of Sultan Mahmūd, in Istanbul. Ayyub Sabri Pasha (d. 1890) wrote a history book in which he told about Wahhābīsm in full detail (*Mir'at al-Haramain*, pp. 99 vol. III, (five volumes in Turkish), Matba'a-i Bahriye, Istanbul, 1301-06 A.H.). This chapter is excerpted from the English translation of his book.

[2] Meccan scholars wrote very beautiful answers to *Kitāb a-tawhīd* and refuted it with sound documents in 1221. The collection of their refutations, titled *Saif al-Jabbār*, which was later printed in Pakistan, was reproduced by Isik Kitabevi in Istanbul in 1395 (1975).

and Mohammad ibn Sa'ūd as the *amīr* (ruler). He declared it as a law that only their descendants should succeed them.

Mohammad's father, 'Abd al-Wahhāb, who was a good (Sunni) Muslim, and the ulamā in Medina understood from Mohammad's words that he would start a heretical movement and advised everybody not to talk with him. But he proclaimed Wahhābīsm in 1737. To deceive the ignorant and lead them astray, he spoke ill of the *ijtihāds* of the *ulamā* of Islam. He went so far as to call the Ahl as-Sunna *Kāfir*. He said that he who visited the shrine of a prophet or of a *walī* and addressed him as "Ya Nabī Allah! (O Allah's Prophet) or as, e.g. "Ya 'Abd al-Qādir!" would become a polytheist (*mushrik*).

In the view of the Wahhābī, he who says that anybody besides Allah did something becomes a polytheist, a *kāfir*. For example, he who said, "Such and such medicine relieved the pain," or "Allah accepted my prayers near the tomb of such and such prophet or *walī*," would become a disbeliever. To prove this idea, he puts forth as documents the Āyat, "*Iyyaka nasta'īn*" (Only Thy help we ask) in the Surah al-Fātiha and the Āyāt telling about *tawakkul*. (The correct meanings of these Āyāt by the Ahl as-Sunna ulamā and the concepts of *tawhīd* and *tawakkul* are written in detail in the chapter "*Tawakkul*" of Sa'adate Abadiyeh by the author. Those who know the correct meaning of *tawhīd* will understand that the Wahhābīs, who consider themselves *muwahhids*, are not *muwahhids* but another group of those who, under the mask of *tawhīd*, want to break the Ahl-at-tawhīd to pieces and to make reform in Islam.)

MEANING OF MAJAZ

At the end of the second part of the book *Al-Usūl al-arba'a fī tardīd al-Wahhābiyya*, Hadrat Hakim as-Sirhindi al-Mujaddidi writes: "The Wahhābīs and the non-*madhhabite* people can not comprehend the meanings of '*majāz*' (allegory, symbol) and '*isti'āra*' (metaphor). Whenever somebody says that he did something, they call him a polythesist or a disbeliever though his expression is a *majaz*. [3]

---

[3] *Majāz* is the use of a word not in its usual or obvious literal meaning but in a sense connected to its meaning. When a word special to Allahu ta'āla is used for men in a majāzī sense, the Wahhābis take it in its literal meaning and call the one

"Whereas, Allahu ta'āla declares in many Āyāt of the Qur'an that He is the Real Maker of every act and that man is the maj āz ī (symbolic, so-called) maker. In the 57th Āyat of the Surah al-An'ām and in Surah Yūsuf, He says, *'The decision (hukm) is Allah's alone,'* that is, Allahu ta'āla is the only Decider (Hakim). In the 64th Āyat of the Surah an-Nisā', He says, *'they will not be* [considered to be true] *believers until they make thee* [the Prophet] *judge* (yuhakkimunaka) *of what is in dispute between them.'* The former Āyat states that Allahu ta' āla is the only Real Hakim, and the latter states that man can be metaphorically said to be a hakim. ("Every Muslim knows that Allahu ta'āla alone is the One who gives life and takes life, for He declares, *'He alone gives and takes life,'* in the 56th Āyat of the Surah Yusuf and *'Allah is the One who makes man dead at the time of his death,'* in the 42nd Āyat of the Surah az-Zumar. In the 12th Āyat of the Surah as-Sajda, He said as a majāz, *'the angel who is appointed as the deputy to take life takes your life.'")*

"Allahu ta'āla alone is the One who gives health to the sick, for the 80th Āyat of the Surah ash-shu'arā' says, *'When I become sick, only He gives me recovery,'* He quotes Prophet 'Isa in the 49th Āyat of the Surah al-Imrān as saying, *'I heal him who is blind and the abrasa* (A *skin-diseased person, albino or vitiligo, with complete or partial whiteness of the skin), and I bring the dead back to life by Allah's permission.'* The one who gives child to man is actually He; He declares in the 18th Āyat of the Surah Mariam that (the Archangel] Jabirā'īl's words, *'I will give you a pure son,'* was *majazi.*

"The real protector of man is Allahu ta'āla. The 257th Āyat of the Surah al-Baqara states this openly; *'Allah is the Walī* (Protector, Guardian) *of those who believe.'* And by saying, *'Your walī is Allah and His Prophet,'* and *'the Prophet protects the believers more than they protect themselves,'* in the 56th and 6th Āyāt of the Surahs al-Ma'ida and al-Ahzāb respectively, He means that man, too, though symbolically, is a walī. Similarly, the real helper is Allahu ta'āla, and He also said 'mu'in' (helper for men metaphorically: He said in the third Āyat of the Surah al-Ma'ida, *'Help you one another in goodness and piety (taqwat).'* The Wahhābīs use the word *'mushrik'*

---

who uses it metaphorically a polytheist and disbeliever; they are unaware that such words are used for men in metaphorical senses in the Qur'an and Hadīth.

(polytheist) for those Muslims who call somebody an 'abd (servant, slave) of someone other than Allah, for example, "Abd an-Nabī' or "Abd ar-Rasūl'; however, in the 32nd Āyat of the Surah an-Nūr, it is declared: *'Give in marriage your unmarried women and those pious ones among your male and female slaves.'* The Real Rabb (Trainer) is Allahu ta'āla, but someone other than Allah can also be called *'rabb'* metaphorically; in the 41st Āyat of the Surah Yusuf it is said, *'Remember me in the presence of your rabb.'"*

MEANING OF ISTIGHĀTHA

'Istighātha' is what the Wahhābīs oppose most: to ask help or protection of someone other than Allah,' which they call polytheism. It is true that, as all Muslims know, *Istighātha* is only for Allahu ta'āla. Yet it is permissible to say metaphorically that one can do *istighātha* of someone, for, it is declared in the 15th Āyat of the Surah al-Qasas: *"People of his tribe did Istighātha of him against the enemy."* A hadīth says, *"They will do Istighātha of Adam at the place of Mahshar."* A hadīth written in Al-hisn Al-hasin, says, *"He who needs help should say, 'Oh Allah's servants! Help me!'"* This hadīth commands that one should (in case) call for help of someone not near him."[4]

The author refutes the Wahhābīs and other non-*madhhhabite* people also in his Arabic work *Tā'rīkh an-Najāt*, published in India in 1350 A.H. This book was also translated in Urdu and it was photographically reproduced by Isik Kitabevi, in 1976. To ask for *shafā'a* and help from the Prophet and *awliyā'* does not mean to abandon Allah or forget that He is the Creator. It is like expecting rain from Allah through the cause or means (*wasita*) of clouds, expecting cure from Allah by taking medicine, expecting victory from Allah by using cannons, bombs, rockets and airplanes. These are causes. It is not polytheism (*shirk*) to stick to these causes.

The prophets always clung to causes. As we go to a fountain to drink water, which Allah has created, and to the bakery to eat bread, which again Allah has created, and as we make armaments

---

[4] Hakim al-Ummat Khwaja Mohammad Hasan Jan Sahib as-Sirhindi al-Mujaddidi, *Al-usūl al-Arba'a* (in Persian), India, 1346 (1928), photographic reproduction by Isik Kitabevi, Istanbul, 1395 (1975).

and drill and train our troops so that Allah would give us victory, so we set our hearts on the soul of a prophet or a *walī* in order that Allah would accept our prayers. To use radio in order to hear the sound which Allah creates through the means of electro-magnetic waves does not mean to abandon Allah and have recourse to a box, for, Allah is the one who has this peculiarity, this power, to the installation in the radio box. Allah has concealed His Omnipotence in everything. A polytheist worships idols but does not think of Allah. A Muslim, when he uses causes and means, thinks of Allah, who gives effectiveness and peculiarities to the causes and creatures. Whatever he wishes he expects from Allah. He knows that whatever he gets comes from Allah. The Wahhābīs do stick to and make use of means in worldly affairs. They satisfy their sensual desires by any means, but they call it 'polytheism' to procure means for winning the next world. What conception of *tawhīd* is this?

Because those words of Mohammad ibn 'Abd al-Wahhab were all right with sensual desires, those who did not have religious knowledge were easily taken in. They claimed that the Ahl as-Sunna 'ulamā and Muslims of the right path were disbelievers. Amirs found Wahhābīsm just right with their desires to increse their lands and territories. They forced the Arab clans to become Wahhabi. They killed those who did not believe them. Villagers, from fear of death, obeyed the amir of Dar'iyya, Mohammad ibn Sa'ud. To become soldiers of the amir well suited their desires to attack the property, life and chastity of non-Wahhābīs.

Mohammad ibn 'Abd al-Wahhab's brother, Shaikh Sulaymān, was an Ahl as-Sunna alim. This blessed person refuted Wahhābīsm in his book, [5] and worked against the dissemination of its heretical tenets. Mohammad's teachers, who realized that Mohammad had opened a way leading to evil, refuted his deviant books. They announced that he had gone astray. They rebutted Wahhabism through Āyāt and ahādīth. Yet all these increased the Wahhābīs' resentment and hostility against Muslims.

---

[5] *As-sawā'iq al-ilāhiyya fī 'r-raddi 'ala 'l-Wahhābiyya*, Printed by Nuhbat al-ahbār, Baghdad, in 1306 [1889]; reproduction by Isik Kitabevi, Istanbul, 1396 [1975].

The heretical tenets of Wahhābīsm spread not through knowledge but through cruelty and bloodshed. Of the cruels that stained their hands with blood in this way, the amir of Dar'iyya, Mohammad ibn Sa'ud, was the most stony-hearted. This man, who was the ancestor of the amirs of today's Saudi Arabia, was of the Banū Hanīfa clan and was one of the descendants of those who had believed Musaylama al-Kadhdhāb as a prophet.

ONENESS OF ALLAH

The Wahhābīs talk as if they were sincere in believing in the Oneness of Allah and thus escaping disbelief, and as if all Muslims had been polytheists for six hundred years, and the Wahhābīs have been trying to save them from *kufr*. To prove themselves right, they put forth the fifth Āyat of the Surah al-Ahqaf and the 106th Āyat of the Surah Yunus. All the Qur'an's commentaries unanimously write that these two Āyāt and many Āyāt like these have all been sent down aiming at polytheists. The first of these Āyāt is: *"No one is more deviated than he who abandons Allah and prays to things which will never hear till the end of the world."* And the other is: *"Tell the Meccan polytheists, 'I was commanded not to pray to things, useful or harmful, other than Allah. If you pray to anyone but Allah, you will be torturing and doing harm to yourselves!'"*

The Wahhābis, in their book, *Kashf ash-shubhāt*, misinterpret the third Āyat of the Surah az-Zumar, in which Allah declares, *"Those who accept things other than Allah as guardians say, 'If we worship them, we worship them to that they might help us approach Allah and intercede for us.'"* This Āyat quotes the words of polytheists who worship idols. The Wahhābīs liken Muslims who ask for *shafā'a* (intercession) to such polytheists and intentionally say that polytheists also believed that their idols were not creative and that Allah alone was the Creator. In the interpretation of this Āyat, the book *Rūh Al-bayān* says, "Human creatures are created with the ability to acknowledge the Creator who created them and everything. Every human creature feels the desire to worship his Creator and to be drawn towards Him. Yet, this ability and desire are worthless, for, the *nafs*, the Satan or bad companions might deceive man, and as a result, this innate desire being destroyed, man becomes either a polytheist or an unbeliever in the Creator and in the Last Day like atheist freemasons. The valuable thing is the *ma'rifa* that ensues from *tawhīd*. Its sign is to believe the prophets and their books by following them, that is, it is such an instance of being drawn towards Allah. It was in its creation for the Satan to prostrate, but it refused to prostrate in a manner unsuitable to its creation, and philosophers became *kāfirs* because they wanted to approach Allah not by following the prophets but their own reason. Muslims, to approach Allah, adapt themselves to the *Sharī'a*, thus their hearts get filled with spiritual light, and the attribute *jamāl* (beauty) [of Allah] manifests itself to their spirits. Polytheists, to approach Allah, follow not the Prophet or the *Sharī'a* but their *nufūs* and *bida'h*, and thus their hearts get darkened and spirits get obscured. Allah, at the end of this Āyat, tells that they lie in their statement, 'We worship idols so that they shall intercede for us.' As it is easily understood, it is very unjust of the Wahhābīs to take the 25th Āyat of the Surah Luqmān which says : *"If you ask disbelievers, 'Who created the earth and the skies?' they will say, 'Certainly Allah created, '"* and the 87th Āyat of the Surah az-Zukhruf which says, *"If you ask those who worship things other than Allah, 'Who created these?' they will say, 'Certainly Allah created,'"* as documents and to say, "Polytheists, too, knew that the Creator was Allah alone. They worshipped idols so that they would intercede for them on the Day of Judgment. For this reason, they became polytheists and disbelievers."[6].

These words of the Wahhābīs are very wrong and very unsound, for we Muslims neither worship the prophets or *awliyā'* nor say that they are companions or partners of Allah. We believe that the prophets and *awliyā'* were creatures and human beings and that they are not worth worshipping. We believe that they are the beloved creatures of Allah and Allah will pity His human creatures for the sake of His beloved. It is Allah alone who creates harm and profit. He alone is worth worshipping. We say that He pities His human creatures for the sake of His beloved. As for

---

[6] This Āyat was interpreted (*tafsīr*), and it was proved that the Wahhābīs misinterpreted this Āyat, also by Jamil Sidqi as-Zahawi, an 'alim from Iraq, in his work *Al-fajr as-Sadiq fi ar-raddiala munkiri 't-tawassuli wa ' l-karamati wa 'l-bawariq* (Egypt, 1323/1905; photographic reproduction by Isik Kitabevi, Istanbul, 1396/1979). Jamil Sidqi taught *'ilm alkalam* at the University of Istanbul. He died in 1355/1936. The 1956 edition of *Munjid* gives a picture of him.

polytheists, though they say that their idols are not creative, they believe that they are worth worshipping and that is why they worship them. Because they say that idols are worth worshipping, they become polytheists. Otherwise, they would not become polytheists for saying that they wanted to intercede. To ask the shafa'a of idols is superstitious, a false belief. It is unlawful in Islam to believe so, yet it is not polytheism.

It is seen that the Wahhābīs' likening of the Ahl as Sunna to idolatrous disbelievers is quite wrong. All the Āyāt they put forth were sent for idolatrous disbelievers and polytheists. The book, *Kashf ash-shubuhāt* gives wrong meanings to Āyāt and uses sophisms and says that the Ahl as Sunna Muslims are polytheists. It recommends that non-Wahhabite Muslims should be killed and that their property should be confiscated.

Abdullāh ibn Umar transmitted the two ahādīth which say, "They have left the right course. They have imputed to Muslims the [meaning of the] Āyāt descending for disbelievers," and "Of what I fear, on behalf of my umma, the most horrible thing is their interpretation of the Qur'an according to their own opinions and their out-of-place translations." These two ahādīth notified that the Wahhābīs would appear and, by misinterpreting the Āyāt that had descended for disbelievers, they would refer them to Muslims.

Another person who, realizing that Mohammad ibn 'Abd al-Wahhāb had heretical ideas and later would be harmful, advised him was Mohammad ibn Sulaeman al-Madanī (died in Medina in 1194/1779), one of the great *ulamā* of Medina. He was a Shāfi'ī faqīh and wrote many books. His annotation on Ibn Hajar al-Makki's *At-tuhfat almuhtāj*, a commentary to the book *Minhāj*, has won a great fame. In *Al-fatāwa*, his two-volume book refuting Wahhābīsm, he said, "O Mohammad ibn 'Abd al-Wahhāb! Don't slander Muslims! For Allah's sake I advise you. Yes, if someone says that someone other than Allah creates actions, tell him the truth! But those who cling to causes (*wasīla*) and who believe that both causes and the effective power in them are created by Allah can not be called disbelievers. You are a Muslims, too. It is better to call one Muslim 'disbeliever' than calling all Muslims. He who leaves the crowd will go astray, more easily. The 114th Āyat of the Surah an-Nisā' proves my word right: *'We will drag the person who, after leaning the way to guidance, opposes the Prophet and deviates from the believers' path along the direction to which he has deviated and then we will throw him into Hell the terrible.'"*

WRONG TENETS OF WAHHĀBĪSM

Though the Wahhābīs have innumerable wrong tenets, their religion is based on four principles:

BASIS OF BELIEF

They say that rites, *'ibādāt*, are included in *Emān* and that he who does not perform a fard (obligatory action, for example, ritual salāt because of laziness, or zakāt because of stinginess, though he would believe it to be a fard or an obligatory action) will become a disbeliever and he must be killed and his possessions must be distributed among the Wahhābīs.

Ash-Shehristānī wrote: "The Ahl as-Sunna *ulamā* have unanimously said that *'ibādāt* are not included in *Emān*. He who dos not perform a *fard* because of laziness, though he believes it to be a *fard*, does not become a disbeliever. There has not been unanimity only for those who do no perform ritual *salāt*; according to the Hanbalī madhhab, he who does not perform *salāt* because of laziness becomes a disbeliever."[7] In the Hanbalī madhhab, it was said that only he who did not perform *salāt* became a disbeliever. It was not said for other kinds of *'ibādāt*. Therefore, it would be wrong to consider the Wahhābīs as Hanbalī in this respect. Those who do not belong to any of the four *madhhabs* are not of the Ahl as-Sunna. We explained before that those who do not belong to the Ahl as-Sunna cannot be Hanbalī, either.

ASKING FOR SHAFA'A

They say that he who asks for *shafā'a* from the souls of the prophets or *awliyā'* or visits their tombs and prays by considering them as intermediaries becomes a disbeliever, and that the dead do not have any sense. If the one who talked to a dead person in a grave would be a disbeliever, our Prophet, great *ulamā* and the *awliyā'* would not have prayed in this manner. It was our Prophet's custom to visit the Baqī' Cemetery in Medina and the

---

7 *Al-milal wa 'n-nihal*, Turkish version, p 63, Cairo, 1070 A.H.

martyrs of Uhud. In fact, it is written on the 485th page of the Wahhabite book *Fath al-majid* that he greeted and talked to them.

Our Prophet always said in his prayers, *"Allahumma innī as'aluka bi-baqqi's-sailina 'alaika"*, (O my Allah! I ask Thee for the sake of those persons whom Thou hast given whenever they asked) and recommended to pray so. When he buried Fatima, the mother of Imām' Ali, with his own blessed hands, he said, *"Ighfir li-ummi Fatimata binta Asad wa wassi' alaiha mad-halaha bi-baqqi nabiyyika wa 'l-anbiya' illadhina min qabli innaka arhamu 'r-rahimin"*. (O Allah! Forgive Mother Fatima bint Asad, her sins! Widen the place she is in! Accept this prayer of mine for the right (love) of Thy Prophet and of the prophets who came before me! Thou art the Most Merciful of the merciful!) In a hadīth given by An-Nasā'ī and At-Tirmidhī, it is told that the Prophet ordered a blind man, who asked him to pray for his cure, to perform abultion and *salāt* of two *rak'āt* and then to say, *"Allahumma inni as'aluka wa atawajjahu ilaika bi-nabiyyika Mohammad in nabi 'r-Rahma, ya Mubammadu inni atawajjahu bika ila Rabbi Fi hajatihadbebi li takdiya li, Allahuma fa-shaffi'hufiyya."*. In this prayer the blind man was commanded to put Prophet Mohammad as an intermediary so that his prayer would be accepted. As-Sahāba often recited this prayer. This prayer is also quoted in the book. *Al-hisn al-hasīn* with its references and, in its explanation, is interpreted as, "I turn towards Thee through Thine Prophet." These prayers show that it is permissible to put those who Allah loves as intermediaries and to pray to Allah by saying "For their sake."

Shaikh 'Ali Mahfūz (d. 1361/1942) one of the great *ulamā* of Jāmi'a al-Azhar, praised Ibn Taimiyya and 'Abduh much in his book *Al-ibda'*. Nevertheless, he wrote: "It is not right to say that the *awliyā'* dispose worldly affairs after death, such as curing the ill, rescuing those who are about to be drowned, helping those who are against the enemy and having the lost things be found. It is wrong to say that, because the *awliyā'* are very great, Allah has left these tasks to them and they do what they wish and that he who clings to them will not go wrong. But, among His *awliyā'* Allah blesses the ones who He wants, whether they are alive or dead, and through their *karamāt* He cures the ill, rescues him who is about to be drowned, helps him who is against the enemy and makes the lost things be found. This is logical. Also the Qur'an teaches these facts."[8]

Hazrat 'Abd al-Ghanī an-Nabulusī wrote that a hadīth qudsī, which al-Bukhārī reported from Abu Huraira, says: *"Allahu ta'āla declared, 'My human servants cannot approach through the fard. If my human creatures do the supererogatory' ibādāt, I like them so much so that they hear with Me, see with Me, and I give them whatever they ask of Me. If they turst in Me, I protect them.'"* The supererogatory' *ibādāt* mentioned here are (as written in *Maraq al-falah* and At-Tahtawi's annotation) the *sunna* and supererogatory *'ibādāt* done by those who do the *fard' ibādāt*. This hadīth shows that he who, after doing the *fard 'ibādāt*, does the supererogatory ones will earn Allah's love and his prayers will be accepted."[9]

Whether alive or dead, when such people pray for others, they get what they wish. Such people hear even when they are dead. As they did not when they were alive, they do not turn down those who ask empty-handed, but they pray for them. For this reason, a hadīth declares, "When you are in trouble in your affairs, ask for help of those who are in graves!" In actual fact, "Muslims are still Muslims when they are dead just as when they are asleep. Prophets are still prophets after death just as when they were asleep; because, it is the soul who is a Muslim or a prophet. When man dies, his soul does not change. This fact is written in the book *'Umdat al-'aqā'id* by Imām 'Abdullah an-Nasafi (edited in London in 1259 A.H./1843). Likewise, the *awliyā'* are still *awliyā'* when they are dead just as when they are asleep. He who does not believe it is ignorant, stubborn. We have proved in another book of mine that the *awliyā'* possess *karamāt* after they die, too."[10]

The Hanafi scholar Ahmad ibn Sayyid Mohammad al-Makki al-Hamawi and the Shafi'i scholars Ahmad ibn Ahmad as-Suja'i and Mohammad ash-Shawbari al-Misri wrote booklets in which they proved with evidences that the *awliyā'* possessed *karamat*,

---

[8] Sheikh 'Ali Mahfuz, *Al-ibda'*, p. 213, Cairo, 1956; 'Abdullah ad-Dasuqi and Yusuf ad-Dajwi, professors at Jami' al-Azhar, wrote eulogies at the end of *Al-ibda'*.

[9] Abd al-Ghani an-Nabulusi, *Al-hadiquat an-nadiyya*, p. 182, Istanbul, 1290 A.H.

[10] Ibid. p. 290.

that their *karamat* continued after their death, and the *tawassul* and *Istighātha* at their graves was permitted (*ja'iz*). [11] And "a true hadīth which the hadīth scholars Hudhaima, ad-Dara Qutni and at-Tabarani conveyed from 'Abdullah ibn' Umar, declares: 'It became wajib for me to intercede for those who would visit my shrine.' 'Imām al-Manawi, too, quoted this hadīth in his book *Kunuz ad-daqa 'iq*. In addition, he wrote the hadīth. 'After my death, visiting my shrine is like visiting me when I am alive,' from Ibn Hibban, and the hadīth, 'I will intercede for him who visits my shrine,' from at-Tabarani. The following two *marfu'* ahādīth, the first one quoted by Imām al-Bazzar from 'Abdullah ibn' Umar and the second one written in *Sahīh* of Muslim and quoted from 'Abdullah ibn' Umar, are known by almost every Muslim: 'It became halal for me to intercede for those who would visit my shrine,' 'On the Day of Judgment I shall intercede for those who would come to Medina to visit my shrine.'" [12]

It is great good news that it is said in the hadīth, "He who carries out the hajj and then visits my grave will have visited me when I am alive," which was quoted by at-Tabarani, ad-Dara Qutni and (Abd ar-Rahman) Ibn al-Jawzi. The hadīth, "The one, who does not visit me after carrying out the hajj will have hurt me," which ad-Dara Qutni quotes, alludes to those who neglect to visit the Prophet's shrine after hajj though they do not have any excuse.

Abd al' Aziz, the rector of the Islamic University of Medina, wrote in his *Tahqiq wa Idah*, "None of the (above) ahādīth [recommending the visit] has any *sanad* (support) or document. The Shaikh al-Islam Ibn Taimiyya told that all of them were *mawdu*." He denies it like all Wahhābīs, despite the fact that the *'asnād* of these ahādīth are written in detail in the eight volume of az-Zarkani's commentary to *Al-mawāhib* and at the end of the fourth volume of as-Samhudi's *Wafa' alwafa'*. In these books, it is also written that these ahādīth were *hasan* and that Ibn Taimiyya's

---

[11] These three booklets were published together with Hadrat Ahmad Zaini Dahlan's *Ad-durar-as-saniyya fī 'r-raddi' ala I-Wahhābiyya* in Cairo in 1319 (1901) and 1347 (1928); photographic reproduction by Isik Kitabevi, in Istanbul, in 1369 (1976).

[12] *Mir'at al-Medina* (Mir'at al-Haramain), p. 106.

comment was groundless. The rector and instructors of the Medina University thus try to calumniate the writings of Ahl as-Sunna ulamā and to spread the Wahhābī tenets all over the world with their books.

The Wahhābīs, in order to make Muslim and non-Muslim nations believe that they are the real Muslims, follow a new policy: They have founded an Islamic center called the *Rabita al-Alam al-Islami* in Mecca and gathered the ignorant, hired men of religious profession they have chosen from every country, to whom they pay salaries of hundred of dollars. Because these ignorant men of religious posts have no knowledge about the books of the Ahl-as-Sunna scholars, they use them as tools. From this center to the whole world, they disseminate the heretical tenets of Wahhābīsm, which they call the "fatwas of world Muslim unity."

There are many ahādīth telling that the Prophet is alive in his tomb in an unknown life. Their being numerous signifies that they are sound. Of these ahādīth, the following two are written in six famous books of the ahādīth: "I will hear the *salawāt* recited at my shrine. I will be informed with the *salawāt* recited at a distance." "If a person recites *salawāt* at my shrine, Allah sends an angel and informs me of this *salawāt*. I will intercede for him on the Day of Judgment."

If a Muslim goes to the grave of a dead Muslim, whom he knew when he was alive, and greets him, the dead Muslims will recognize and reply him. A hadīth communicated by Ibn Abi'd-dunya declares that a dead Muslim recognizes and answers the one who greets him and gets happy. If a person greets the dead people whom he did not know, they become pleased and answer him. While good Muslims and martyrs recognize and answer those who greet them, is it possible that the Prophet would not? As the sun in the sky illuminates the whole world so the Prophet answers all simultaneous greetings simultaneously.

A hadīth says, "After my death, I will hear as I do when I am alive." Another hadīth given by Abu Ya'la says, "Prophets are alive in their graves. They perform ritual salāt." Ibrahim ibn Bishar and Sayyid Ahmad ar-Rifā'ī and many *awliyā'* said that they had heard the reply when they had greeted the Prophet.

The great Muslim scholar Jalāl ad-dīn as-Suyūtī wrote the book *Sharaf al-muhkam* as an answer to the question if it was true that Sayyid Ahmad ar-Rifā'ī had kissed the Prophet's blessed hand. In this book he proved by reasonable and traditional evidences that the Prophet was alive in his shrine in an incomprehensible life and that he heard and answered greetings. He also told in this book that on the Mi'rāj Night the Prophet saw Prophet Musa (Moses) worshipping in his grave.

A hadīth, which Ayeshah related, says, "I suffer the pain of the poisonous meat I ate at Khaybar. Because of that poison my aorta almost fails to function now." This hadīth shows that, in addition to the prophethood, Allah has given the status of martyrdom to the Prophet, the highest of mankind. Allah declares in the Qur'an, in the 169th Āyat of the Surah al-'Imrān, *"Never regard those who have been killed on the way to Allah as dead! They are alive in Allah's view. They are nourished."* No doubt this great Prophet, who has been poisoned on the way to Allah, is on top of the honorable status defined in this Āyat.

The hadīth given by Ibn Hibban says, "Prophets' blessed bodies never rot. If a Muslim recites *salawāt* for me, an angel conveys that *salawāt* to me and says, 'so and so and son of so and so recited *salawāt* and greeted you.'"

The hadīth given by Ibn Māja says, "On Fridays recite *salawāt* for me repeatedly. The salawāt will be communicated to me as soon as it is recited." Abu'd-darda', one of those who were in company of the Prophet at that moment, asked, "Will it be communicated to you after you die, too?" The Prophet said, "Yes, I will be informed of it after my death, for, it is harām for the earth to cause the prophets to rot. They are alive after death, and they are nourished."

Umar, after the conquest of Quds (Jerusalem), went into the Prophet's shrine and visited his grave and greeted him. 'Umar ibn Abd al-'Azīz, who was a great *walī*, usually sent officials from Damascus to Medina and had them recite *salawāt* at the Prophet's shrine and greet him. Abdullah ibn' Umar, after returning from each travel, would go direct to the Prophet's shrine-(Hujrat as-Sa'āda, the room where the graves of the Prophet and of his two immediate caliphs are). First he would visit the Prophet, then Abu

Bakr as-Siddīq and then his father and greet them. Imām Nafi' said, "More than a hundred times I saw Abdullah ibn' Umar go into the Prophet's shrine and say, *'As-Salamu' alaika ya Rasulullah!'"* One day Imām Ali went into the Masjid ash-Sharif and when he saw the grave of Fatima az-Zehra he wept, and when he saw the Prophet's grave he wept the more, and said, *"As-salamu' alaika ya Rasulullah' and 'As-salamu' alaikuma."*

According to al-Imām al-A'zam Abū Hanīfa one should carry out the hajj first and then go to Medina and visit Rasulullah. So is written in the fatwa of Abū 'I-Laith as-Samarqandi. Qadi 'Iyad, author of the book *Shifā',* Imām an-Nawawī, a Shāfi'ī alim, and Ibn Humam, a Hanafī alim, said that they had formed *ijma' al-Umma* on that it was necessary to visit the Prophet's shrine. Some *'alims* said that it was wajib. As a matter of fact, it is a *sunna* to visit graves, a fact which is also written in the Wahhabite book *Fath al-majid.*

The 63rd Āyat of the Surah an-Nisā' declares : *"If they, after tyrannizing over their nufūs, come to you (the prophet) and beg Allah's(My) pardon, and if My Messenger (you) apologizes on behalf of them, they will certainly find Allah as the Receiver of Repentance and Merciful."* This Āyat indicates that the Prophet will intercede and his *shafā'a* (intercession) will be accepted. Also, it commands us to visit the Prophet's shrine and ask for *shafā'a.*

A hadīth says: "It is suitable to set off on a long journey only with the view of visiting three mosques." This hadīth points out that it is reward-deserving to go on a long journey with the purpose of visiting the Masjid al-Harām in Mecca, the Masjid an-Nabī in Medina and the Masjid al-Aqsa in Jerusalem. For this reason, those who go on hajj but do not visit the Prophet's shrine, in the Masjid an-Nabī, will be deprived of this reward.

A hadīth says, "Do not make a (place of) festival of my shrine." Hazrat 'Abd al-'Azim al-Munziti, a hadīth alim, explained this hadīth as: "Do not consider it enough to visit my shrine only once a year, like on feast days. Try to visit me every time!" As a matter of fact, it is not permitted to perform ritual *salāt* at the cemetery. It was said that this hadīth might come to mean "For visiting my shrine, do not fix a certain day like a feast." Jews and Christians, during their visit to their prophets, habitually assembled together, played instruments, sang songs and acted ceremoniously. These ahādīth imply that we should not make merry with forbidden things on feast days; we should not play reeds or drums or gather to act ceremoniously during our visit. We should visit and greet, pray and leave silently without staying long.

Al-Imām al-A'zam Abū Hanīfa said that visiting the Prophet's shrine was the most valuable *sunna,* and there are some scholars who said that it was wājib. For this reason, visiting the Prophet's shrine is allowed as a vow in the Shāfi'ī madhhab. In fact, Allah, in His word, "if I had not created you, I would not have created anything,"[13] points out that the Prophet is the Habibullāh (Allah's Darling) and that He loves him very much. Even an average person will not refuse something asked for the sake of his darling. It is easy to have a lover do something for the sake of his beloved. If a person says, "O my Allah! For the sake of Thy Habīb, Muhammad, I ask of Thee,' this wish of his will not be refused. The trivial worldly affairs, however, are not worth rutting the Prophet's sake as a means."[14]

As-Sayyid Ahmad bin Zaini Dahlan, Mufti of Mecca, was a great *'alim* and the *Shaikh alkhutaba'* in the Shāfi'ī madhhab. He wrote many works. He explained the real purposes of the Wahhābīs and proved through Āyāt and ahādīth that they were deviated, in his books *Khulāsat al-kalam fī bayāni umara'I balad al-Harām, Fi'r-raddi 'ala 'l-Wahhabiyyati atha'u madhhabi Ibn Taimiyya and Ad-durar as-saniyya fī 'r-raddi 'ala 'l-Wahhābiyya. In Khulāsat al-kalām,* he told how they deceived the ignorant ones of Muslims and refuted them one by one. He proved that their words were lies and slanders. He wrote: "It is acceptable and permissible to pray through the mediation of the Prophet when he is dead as it was done when he was alive. Likewise, it is shown in the hadīth that it is also permissible to pray through the mediation of the awliyā' and pious Muslims. (The writings on the 167, 170, 191, 208, 248, 353, 414, 416, 482, 486 and 505th pages of the Wahhabite book *Fath al-majid* are lampoons against Muslims).

---

[13] This hadīth qudsī is quoted also in Hadrat al-Imām ar-Rabbānī's *Maktubāt,* vol. III, 122nd letter.

[14] *Mir'at al-Madina,* p. 1282.

The Ahl as-Sunna *ulamā* say that it is Allah alone who gives the effectiveness, who creates, invents, gives use or harm and annihilates. He does not have a partner. Neither prophets nor any other living or dead person can create effectiveness, use or harm. However, since they are the beloved servants of Allah, we bless ourselves with them.

INTERCESSION BY DEAD

The Wahhābīs believe that the living can affect but the dead can not. It is written on the 70, 77, 98, 104, 239, 248, 323, 503 and 504th pages of their book *Fath al-majid*: "He who asks a dead person or a living one who is absent for something becomes a polytheist. Man can be asked for what is within his power. It is not permissible to ask for what are within Allah's power alone." It is written on its 70th page: "A living person can pray for the things that have been asked of him, and Allah accepts it and creates that thing. To ask a dead or an absent person means to ask for what is not within his power, which is polytheism." It is written on its 136th page: "To bless oneself with the graves of pious Muslims is polytheism like worshipping the idols named *al-Lat* and *Manat*." It is written on its 208th page: "It is polytheism to ask the dead people for what one needs or to pray through the dead." It is ignorance to ask a dead person without being permitted by Allah, and they are not designated as intermediaries for interceding or for being permitted to intercede. The prerequisite of intercession is *Emān*. But the person who asks the dead to intercede is a polytheist. In fact, the book contradicts itself as it is written on its 200th page that "The skies fear Allah. Allah creates sense in skies. They perceive."

It has been declared in the Qur'an that the earth and the skies praise and laud Allah. As-Sahāba heard the pieces of stone praise and laud Allah when the Prophet took them in his hands, the pillar called Hannana in the Masjid moan, and the food praise and laud Allah. It shows their stupidity to say that the prophets and *awliyā'* do not have sense, while on the other hand, to say that mountains, stones and pillars have sense and conscience. The Wahhābīs become polytheists by saying that the living can be made intermediaries but the dead cannot be made intermediaries. For this statement means that the living hear and affect but the dead do not hear or affect, and that those other than Allah can affect, and they, too, call those who believe so polytheists. The reality is that the dead and the living are intermediaries. It is Allah alone who affects, and they, too, call those who believe so polytheists. The rumor telling that al-Imām al-A'zam prohibited to pray through the mediation of the Prophet, which is written in Ālūsī's Qur'an commentary, is mendacious, for no *alim* has ever reported such news form al-Imām al-A'zam. The *ulamā* told that it was permissible. The words *tawassul, tashaffu', Istighātha* and *tawajjub* have the same meaning. They are all permissible. It is declared in the *Sahīh* of al-Bukhārī, "On the Day of Judgment, people will ask for Prophet Adam's intercession first." Hazrat Bilal ibn Harith, one of the notables of as-Sahāba, visited the Prophet's grave and said, "O Rasulallah! Pray on behalf of your umma that it shall rain!" And it rained. Disbelievers who said that idols would intercede for them worshipped idols. But the believers who ask for intercession do not worship the prophets or *awliyā'*. It is declared in the Qur'an, *"Intercession can be done only with His permission,"* and *"Only the accepted people will be interceded for!"*

How does the person who asks for intercession know that the Prophet will be permitted to intercede for him? Moreover, how does he know he is one of the accepted and ask for intercession? These words both disagree with ahādīth and contradict the book itself, because the same book says on its 208th page, "The prerequisite of intercession is *emān*." In the prayer which we are ordered to recite after the *adhan*, it is mentioned that Allah has promised our Prophet the Attributes of Fadila and Wasila. He declared that he would intercede for those who recite this prayer, for those who say *salawāt* and for those who visit his grave.

Similarly, many more ahādīth show that our Prophet has been permitted to intercede for whomever he likes. The hadīth, "I will intercede for those who have committed big sins," shows that he will be permitted to intercede for anybody who has *Emān*. Of the forty ahādīth on the 130th page of *Shawajid al-haqq*, the thirteenth one says, *"I will say, 'O Allah! Put those who have Emān as much as a mote of mustard in their hearts into Paradise.' They will enter Paradise. Then,*

I will tell those who have something little in their hearts to enter Paradise." Al-Bukhari wrote this hadīth; too.

Istighātha means *tawassul*, to put someone as an intermediary, to ask for his help, and for his prayer. To ask someone for *shafa'a* means to pray to Allah so that one can leave the world with *Emān* in one's last breath for His sake. It is written at many places of the Wahhabite book *Fath al-majid*, particularly on the 323rd page that it is polytheism to ask an absent person for his intercession. Allah orders to war against polytheists. Whereas, the Prophet used to tell (himself), "O Muhammad! I am turning towards my Allah by putting you as an intermediary." After his death, as-Sahāba frequently said this prayer. A hadīth communicated by at-Tabarani declares, "If a person who is left alone in a desert loses something, he shall say, 'O Allah's servants! Help me!' For, Allah has servants whom you do not see." Ibn Hajar al-Makkī said in his commentary to *Idah al-manasik* that this prayer had been proved many times. As reported by Abū Dāwūd and many others, one evening when he was on a journey, the Prophet said, "O my Allah's earth! Against your evils I trust-myself to Allah."[15]

Al-Imām al-A'zam Abū Hanifa said, "I was in Medina when Shaikh Ayyub as-Sahtiani, who was a well-known pious Muslim, went into the Masjid ash-Sharif. I followed him. Hazrat Shaikh faced the Prophet's tomb and stood with his back to the *qibla*. Then he went out." Hazrat Ibn Jama'a wrote in his book *Al-mansak al-kabīr*, "While visiting, after performing a *salāt* of two *rak'as* and praying near the *minbar* (pulpit), one should come to the *qibla* side of the Hujrat as-Sa'ada and, the Prophet's blessed head being on one's left, should stay two meters away from the wall of al-Marqad ash-Sharif (the Prophet's shrine), then leaving the *qibla* wall behind and turning slowly till he faces the Muwajahat as-Sa'ada, should greet. This is so in all the *madhāhib*."

Abd al-Ghanī an-Nabulusī, while explaining the twenty-third of the "Disasters Caused by the Tongue," writes: "It is *makruh* to say, while praying, for the right of the prophets, or for the right of (such and such living or dead) *wali* and to ask Allah for something

---

15 *Khulasat al-Kalām*, Bāb as-Salām, Mecca, 1305; Isik Kitabevi, Istanbul, 1395 (1975).

-211-

by saying so, for, it has been said that no creature has any right on Allah, that is, Allah does not have to do whatever anybody would like. It is right, yet Allah promised His beloved servants and recognized a right for them on Himself, that is, He will accept their wish. He declared in the Qur'an that He gave a right to His human servants on Himself, for example, *"It has become a right on Us to help the believers."* It is declared in *Al-fatāwa al-Bizaziyya* that: "It is permitted to ask for something for the sake of a prophet or a dead or living walī by mentioning his name." *(Al-Hadīqa).*

As it is seen, Muslim scholars said that it was permissible to pray to Allah through the right and love which Allah had given to His beloved ones. And no scholar has said that it would be polytheism to pray with the idea that men have rights on Allah. Only the Wahhābīs say so. Though the Wahhābīs praise *Al-fatāwa al-Bizaziyya* in their book *Fath al-majid* and put forth his *fatwas* as documents, they oppose him in this respect. Also, Hadimi, while explaining the "Disasters Caused by the Tongue," wrote: "For the right of Thy prophet, and during the wars he asked for Allah's help for the right of the poor among the Muhajirun. Also there were many Muslim *ulamā* who prayed for the sake of those people whom Thou hast given whenever they asked Thee and for the right of Mohammad al-Ghazālī and who wrote these prayers in their books." *(Hadimi, Bariqa, Istanbul, 1284).*

The book *Al-hisn al-hasin* is full of such prayers. It is written in *Ālūsī's Ghaliyya,* too, that when Prophet Adam asked to be forgiven for the right of the Prophet, Allah declared, *"He (Muhammad) is the one I like most among Mine human creatures. I forgave thee for his right. If it hadn't been for Muhammad, I wouldn't have created thee."*

The Wahhābīs write: "Imām Zain al-'Abidin saw a man praying near the Prophet's grave and interrupted him by telling him the hadīth, 'Recite *salawāt* for me. Wherever you are, your greeting will be communicated to me.'" It narrates the event incorrectly and goes on, "Hence, it is forbidden to go near a grave and pray and recite *salawāt,* which is sort of making graves places of festival. It is forbidden for those who go to perform ritual *salāt* in the Masjid an-Nabī to approach the tomb with the view of greeting. None of the Sahāba did so. They prevented those who wanted to do so. No other deed but the *salawāt* recited and the greetings said by his umma will be communicated to the prophet."[16] He also writes that the Saudi government placed soldiers near the Prophet's shrine in the Masjid an-Nabī to prevent Muslims from doing so.[17]

Hazrat Yūsuf an-Nabhani, at many places of his book on Wahhābīsm, refutes these lies: "Imām Zain al-'Ābidīn did not forbid the visitation to the blessed shrine of the prophet. But he forbade unsuitable and unlawful behaviors during visiting. His grandson, Imām Ja'far as-Sadiq, used to visit the Prophet's shrine, and standing near the pillar which stood in the direction of the Rawda, greet and say, 'his blessed head is on this side'. *'Do not make [a place of] festival of my shirne,'* means 'do not visit my shrine on certain days like feast days. Visit me every time.'"[18]

Abū 'Abdullah al-Qurtubī writes in his *at-Tadhkira* that "the deeds of the Prophet's umma are communicated to him every morning and every evening." (pp. 88, 106) "Caliph Mansūr, during his visit to the Prophet's Shrine, asked Imām Malik, 'Shall I face the tomb or the *qibla?*' Imām Mālik said, 'How could you turn away your face from the Prophet? He is the cause of your and your father Adam's forgiveness!'" (pp. 89, 116) "The hadīth, *'visit shrines!'* is a command. If a *harām* is committed during the visit, not the visit itself but the *harām* should be forbidden." (p. 92) Imām an-Nawawī says in his *Adhkār*, "It is a *sunna* to visit the shrines of the Prophet and of the pious Muslims and to stay long near such places of visitation." (p. 98) Ibn Humām, in his *Fath al-qadīr*, quotes the hadīth transmitted by ad-Dara Qutni and al-Bazzar which says, "If someone visits my shrine only with a view to visit me and not to do anything else, he has the right to be interceded by me on the Day of Judgment." Allah favored the *awliyā* with *Karamāt*. Their *Karamāt* are witnessed frequently even after their death. They are able to be helpful after death, too. It is permitted to have them intercede with Allah. But one should ask help of them in a lawful manner. It is not permitted to say, 'I will give that much...for you if you give me what I request,' or 'if you cure my sick relative', which is often uttered by the ignorant. However, this can not be regarded as an act causing *kufr* or

---

[16] *Fath al-Majid* p. 259.
[17] Ibdi., p. 234.
[18] *Shawāhid al-baqq*, p.80, 3rd. Edition, Cairo, 13854 (1965).

polytheism, because even the utterly ignorant does not think that the *walī* would create. He wants the *walī* to be the cause in Allah's creating. He thinks that the *walī* is a human creature whom Allah loves, and says, 'Please ask Allah to favor men with what I wish; He will not reject your prayer.' As a matter of fact, the Prophet said, "There are many people who are considered low and worthless but who are Allah's beloved creatures. When they want to do something, Allah certainly creates it." This hadīth is also quoted on the 381st page of the Wahhabite book *Fath al-majid*. Obeying such ahādīth Muslims want the *awliyā'* to intercede. Imām Ahmad, ash-Shāfi'ī, Mālik and al-Imām al-A'zam Abū Hanīfa said that it was *jā'iz* (possible, permissible) to attain *baraka* (blessing) through the shrines of the pious. "Those who say that they are of the Ahl as-Sunna or that they belong to one of the Ahl as-Sunna *madhāhib* has to say as those Imāms said. If not, one may decide that they are not of the Ahl as-Sunna but liars." (p. 118)

It is written on the subject of going on hajj on behalf of someone else, in the book *Al-fatāwa al-Hindiyya,*[19] that "It is permissible to devote the *thawāb* of an '*ibāda* to anybody. Therefore the *thawāb* of *salāt*, fast, alms, pilgrimage, of recitation of the Qur'an, *dhikr*, of visitation of the tombs of the prophets, martyrs, *awliyā'* and pious Muslims, of giving a shroud for a corpse and of all charities and good deeds can be devoted." It is understood from this passage, too, that visiting the graves of the *awliyā'* does bring *thawāb*.

SHOWING RESPECT TO GRAVES AND MOSQUE

The Wahhābīs say, "It causes *kufr* (infidelity) and *shirk* (polytheism) to build a dome over a grave, to light oil-lamps for those who worship and serve in shrines and to vow alms for the souls of the dead! The inhabitants of al-Harāmain (Mecca and Medina) have worshipped domes and walls up to now." Building a dome over a grave is *harām* if it is for ostentation or ornamentation. If it is for protecting the grave from destruction, it is *makruh*. If it is intended to protect it from a thief or an animal, it is permissible. But it should not be made a place of visiting, that is, one should not say

---

[19] Prepared by Shaikh Nizām Mu'īn ad-dīn an-Naqshabandī and others in the time of Mohammad Aurangzayb 'Alamgīr ibn Shah Jahan of the Gurganiyya State (reigned 1068-1118/1658-1707); printed in Cairo in 1310; 3rd ed. 1393 (1973).

that it should be visited at certain times; yet one should have *tawassul* of and recite Qur'an for the dead when one passes by a grave.

It is not *makruh* to bury a corpse in a building that has been built before. As-Sahāba buried the prophet and his two caliphs in a building. None of them stood against it. The hadīth informs that their unanimity could not be heresy. The great Islamic scholar Ibn 'Abidīn wrote: "Some scholars said that it was *makurh* to put a covering cloth, a skullcap or a turban over the graves of pious Muslims or *awliyā*." The book *Al-fatāwa al-hujja* says that it is *makruh* if it is intended to show everybody the greatness of the one in the grave and lest he should be insulted and so that those who visit him will be respectful and in good manners. Deeds, acts that are not prohibited in *al-adillah ash-Shar'iyya* should be judged in view of the intention involved. It is true that in the time of as-Sahāba neither domes were built over graves, nor sarcophagus (stone or wooden) and clothes were put on graves. But none of them was against the interment of the Prophet and his two caliphs in a room.

For this reason, and for carrying out the commands of, *'Do not step on graves* and *'Do not be disrespectful to your dead'*, and because they were not prohibited, they can not be bid as though they were done afterwards. All fiqh books communicate that right after the farewell *tawaf* (the act of going round the Ka'ba during the Hajj) it is necessary to go out of the Masjid al-Harām as an act of respect towards the Ka'bah.

As-Sahāba, because they respected the Ka'ba in every point, did not use to do so. The posterity, being unable to show that much reverence, our ulamā declared that it was necessary to show respect by exiting the Masjid walking backwards. Thus they made it possible for us to be respectful like as-Sahāba. Likewise, it became permissible to cover the graves of the pious and of the *awliyā'* with cloth or to build domes over them in order to be respectful like as-Sahāba. The great savant 'Abd al-Ghanī an-Nabulusī explains this in detail in his book *Kashf an-nūr.* [20]

---

[20] Ibn 'Abidīn, *Hashiyatu Durr al-mukhtār (Radd al-mukhtār)* p. 232, Vol. V Bulaq, 1272; *Kashf an-nūr* and Jalāl ad-dīn as-Suyūtī's *Tanwīr al-halak fī imkani ru'yati 'n-Nabī jiharan wa 'l-malak* were edited together the third time with the title *Al-minhaj al-wahhabiyya*, Isik Kitabevi, Istanbul, 1974.

In the blessed city of Medina, there were many shrines called "Mashhad" in the Baqī' Cemetery. The Wahhābīs destroyed all of them. Except the Wahhābīs, no Islamic 'ālim has said that it would be polytheism or *kufr* to build domed tombs or to visit tombs. Except these deviated people, no one has ever been seen demolishing tombs.

At the end of the book, *Halabi-i kabīr*, it is written, "If a person decides his land to be a cemetery and if there is empty space in it, it is permissible for one to build a domed tomb in it with a view to burying corpses. When there is not any other empty space left, this tomb shall be demolished and graves shall be dug (at its ground). For, this is a place belonging to the *awqāf*, devoted to be a cemetery." If building domed tombs had been known to be polytheistic, or if domed tombs had been considered to be idols, it would have been always necessary to demolish them. The famous Wahhabite book says: "The one who intends to get blessed *(tabarruk)* with a tree, stone, grave or the like becomes a polytheist. Graves have been idolized by building domes over them. The people of the *Jāhiliyya* Ages, too, worshipped pious persons and statues. Today, all such and more excessive acts are committed at shrines and graves. To attempt to get blessed with the graves of pious persons is like worshipping the idol al-Lat. These polytheists suppose that the *awliyā'* hear and answer their prayers. They say that they approach the dead by making vows and giving alms for graves. All these acts are major polytheism. The polytheist is still a polytheist even if he would call himself another name. Praying the dead respectfully and affectionately, slaughtering animals, making vows and other similar acts are all polytheistic whatever they call it. The polytheists of the present time, using the words 'ta'zim' (respect) and *tabarruk*, say permissible for what they do."[21]

ANSWERS TO OFFENSIVE LAMPOONS OF WAHHĀBĪS

I have already translated in my various books the answers given by Muslim scholars to such offensive lampoons of the Wahhābīs against the Ahl as-Sunna Muslims. In the following, a passage from the book *Al-usūl al-arba'a fī tardīd al-Wahhābiyya* is translated to show to the vigilant reader that the Wahhābīs deceive and deviate themselves and take Muslims to ruination:

---

[21] Op cit., p. 133.

RESPECT TO ALLAH'S INDICATIONS

"The Qur'an, hadīth, the sayings and acts of the *Salaf as-salihīn* and most of the *'ulamā'* documents point that it is permissible to show *ta'zīm* (respect, honor) to somebody other than *Allahu ta'āla*, The 32nd Āyat of the Surah al-Hajj states : *'When one shows honor (yu'azzim) to Allah's sha'ā'ir* this behavior is out of the heart's *taqwa. 'Sha'ā'ir'* means 'indications, signs'. Hadrat Abd al-Haqq ad-Dahalwi said, *'Sha'ā'ir* is the plural of *sha'ira*, which means indication (*'alama*). Anything that reminds *Allahu ta'āla* when seen is an indication of *Allahu ta'āla'*. The 158th Āyat of the Surah al-Baqara says: *'As-Safā and al-Marwa are among the sha'ā'ir of Allah.'* As understood from this Āyat, the hills as-Safā and al-Marwa are not the only indications of *Allahu ta'āla*. There are other indications as well. And not only the similar places but 'Arafat Muzdalifa and Mina should be cited to be the indications. Shah Walī-Allah ad-Dahlawi says on the 69th page of his work *Hujjat-Allahi 'l-bāligha*, 'The greatest indications of Allahu ta'āla are four: the Qur'an, the Ka'aba, the prophet and the ritual prayers'. And on the 30th page of his book *Altaf al-Quds*, he says, 'To love the indications of *Allahu ta'āla* means to love anything that reminds Allahu ta'āla. To love the *awliyā'* of Allahu ta'āla is the same'. (The hadīth quoted in IbnAbi Shaiba's Musnad and al-Manawi's Kunuz ad-daqā'iq says: 'Allahu ta'āla is remembered when *awliyā* are seen.' So the *awliyā'*, too, are among the indications. While the two hills near the Masjid al-Harām in Mecca, namely as-Safa and al-Marwa, between which the Prophet Ismā'īl's mother Hazrat Hajara had walked, are among the indications of *Allahu ta'āla* and can cause one to remember that blessed mother, why should not the places where the prophet Muhammad, who is the most superior of the creatures and the Darling of *Allahu ta'āla*, was born and brought up and the places where he worshipped, migrated, performed *salāt* and passed away and his blessed shrine and the places of his Ahlul-Bayt: Household of the prophet and companions be counted among the indications? Why do the Wahhābīs destroy these places? When the Qur'an is read attentively and equitably, it will be easily seen that many Āyāt express *'ta'zīm'* for the Prophet. In the Surah al-Hujurat it is declared: *'O those who believe! Do not pass yourselves beyond Allah and His prophet! O those who believe! Do not speak louder than the prophet's voice! Do not call him as you call one another! The reward for the deeds of those who would do so will vanish!*

Allah fills with taqwa hearts of those who lower their voices in the presence of Allah's Prophet; He forgives their sins and gives much reward. Those who shout at him from the outside are thoughtless; it is better for them to wait till he comes out.' It is apparent to the one who reads and thinks over these five Āyāt equitably how much *Allahu ta'āla* praises the *ta'zīm* that will be shown to His Beloved Prophet, and how importantly He commands the umma to be respectful and modest towards him. The degree of this importance can be judged by that the reward for all the deeds of those who would speak louder before him is of no avail. These Āyāt came as a penalty for the seventy people of the Banū Tamīm tribe who had called the Prophet shouting disrespectfully from the outside in Medina. Today, the Wahhābīs say that they belong to the Banu Tamīm tribe. It should have been for this that the Prophet said, *'The violent and torturous people are in the East,'* and *'The Satan will arouse disunion from there,'* pointing to a direction towards the Najd. Another name used for the Wahhābīs is Najdis, for they have spread out the Najd country (on the Arabian Peninsula). The disunion predicted in the above hadīth came out twelve hundred years later: the Wahhābīs came from the Najd to the Hijaz, plundered Muslims' possessions, killed the men and enslaved the women and children. They committed the worse evils that disbelievers yet committed.

"In the above Āyāt, the repetitive phrase *'O those who believe,'* shows that all Muslims of all centuries till the Last Day are commanded to be respectful towards the Prophet. If the command had been only for his companions, *'O the Companions of the Prophet,'* would have been said. As a matter of fact, the phrases, *'O the wives of the prophet,'* and *'O the people of Medina,'* are Qur'anic. The same phrase, *'O those who believe,'* is used in the Āyāt stating that ritual prayers, fast, pilgrimage, zakāt and other *ibadas* are *fard* for all Muslims of all times till the Last day. So, the Wahhābīs' idea that the Prophet was to be respected when he was alive; neither respect is to be shown to nor help is to be asked from him after his death, is groundless in view of these Āyāt. The above Āyāt indicate that *ta'zīm* towards others besides *Allahu ta'āla* is also necessary. The 104th Āyat of the Surah al-Baqara states: *'O those who believe! Do not say, 'Ra'ina' (to the prophet), but say, 'Look upon us. You be listeners (to Allah's command).'* Believers used to say, *'Ra'ina'* also meant to swear, to blemish in the Jewish language, and the Jews used this words for the Prophet in this sense. Because it also had this bad meaning, *Allahu ta'āla* forbade the believers to use this word and protected His Prophet against the possibility of being disrespected. In order for this respect to be shown till the end of the world, he said, *'O those who believe!'*

BLESSED PLACES OF THE PROPHET

"In the 33ʳᵈ Āyat of the Surah al-Anfāl, *Allahu ta'āla* declares, *'Allah will not punish them while you are with them,'* and promises not to punish them till the end of the world. This Āyat refutes the Wahhābīs' claim that the Prophet went away and become soil.

"They destroy the blessed places inherited from the Prophet. They say these places make people polytheists. If it were polytheism to pray to *Allahu ta'āla* at sacred places, *Allahu tal'ala* would not have ordered us to go on Hajj; the Prophet would not have kissed the *Hajar al-aswad* while he was performing *tawaf;* nobody would pray at 'Arafat and Muzdalifa; stones would not be thrown at Mina, and Muslims would not walk between as-Safā and al-Marwa. These sacred places would not have been so respected. When Sa'd ibn Ma'ādh, the head of the Ansār, came to where they assembled, the Prophet said, *'Stand up for your leader!'* This command was intended for all of them to do honor to Sa'd. It is wrong to say, Sa'd was ill. It was intended that he should be helped off his riding-animal, because the order was for all of them. If it were intended for helping him, the order would have been for one or two persons; only for Sa'd would have been said, and there would have been no need to say, *'for your leader'.*

"Every time he went from Medina to Mecca for hajj, Abdullah ibn 'Umar stopped and performed *salāt* and prayed at the sacred places where the Prophet had sat. He would get blessed (tabarruk) with these places. He used to put his hands on the Prophet's *minbar* (pulpit) and then rub them on his faces. Imām Ahmad ibn Hanbal used to kiss the *Hujrat as-Sa'ada* and pulpit to get blessed by them. The Wahhābīs, on the one hand, say that they belong to the Hanbali madhhab and, on the other, regard as polytheism what the Imām of this madhhab did. Then, their claim to be Hanbalī is a lie. Imām Ahmad ibn Hanbal put Imām ash-Shāfi'ī's shirt into water and drank the water to obtain blessings. Hazrat Khālid ibn Zaid Abū Ayyūb al-Ansārī rubbed his face against the Prophet's blessed grave and when someone wanted to lift him up, he said: 'Leave me! I came not for the stones or soil but for the audience of the Prophet.'

"As-Sahāba used to get blessed with the things that belonged to the Prophet. They received blessings from the water he used in ablution and from his blessed sweat, shirt, scepter, sword, shoes, glass, and ring, in short, from anything he used. Hazrat Umm Salama, the mother of the faithful, kept a hair from his blessed beard. When ill people came, she would dip the hair into water and have them to drink the water. With the blessed glass, they used to drink water for health. The *Ulamā* of hadīth and fiqh permitted such actions, while the Wahhābīs regard them as polytheism and disbelief.[22] In the times of as-Sahāba and the Tābi'oūn, and even till the end of the first millennium, there were many *awliyā'* and *sulaha'* (plural of *salih,* the pious). People used to visit and receive blessings from them as well as attaining their prayers. There was no need to make intermediary *(tawassul)* of the dead or to get blessed *(tabarruk)* with lifeless things. That these actions were rare in those days does not mean that they were forbidden. If they had been forbidden, there would have been those who would prevent them. No *'ālim* prevented them.

"As the Last Age has set in, however, *bid'as* and disbelief have increased, the youth have been deceived by the enemies of Islam in the disguises of religious authorities and scientists, and because irreligiousness and apostasy have suited their purposes, dictators and the cruel, the slaves of their *nufūs,* have given great support to this current. The number of *ulamā* and *awliyā* has decreased, even there has been seen none in the last decades, and it has become a must to get blessed with the graves of and the things inherited from the *awliyā*. To the unanimity of the Ulamā[23] of Islam, this lawful practice itself should not be prevented even though prohibited behaviors *(harāms)* have been introduced into it as it has been the same with every hadīth and religious affairs, but the *bid'as* introduced should be removed."

---

[22]*Al-usūl al-arba'a,* Part One.
[23] The writings of the Ulama on this subject are quoted in Ahmad bin Zaini Dahlau's *Ad-durar as-Saniyya fi 'r-raddi'ala 'l-Wahhābiyya,* Egypt, 1319 and 1347; photographic reproduction by Isik Kitabevi, Istanbul, 1395 (1975).

PART FOUR: FIQH AND BELIEFS

Chapter: 23

DEDUCING RELIGIOUS RULING: IJTIHĀD

By

Maulana Syed Rizwan Rizvi

Ijtihād means to seek or research; it is a science which deals with deducing religious rulings. The word Ijtihād is derived from the root word *'juhud'*[1] which means striving or exerting, and reflects on the mujtahedin and their hard work in explaining the laws of Islam. In the rich Islamic history and in particular the Shi'a history this method has been adopted; by the ulama from the very beginning, from the time of the infallible Imāms.[2]

The phenomenon of Ijtihād is unique to Shi'a sect. For other sects of Islam the doors of Ijtihād were closed for ever after the passing of their four Imāms, namely, Abū Hanīfa, Mālik, Shāfi'ī, and Hanbal. For them the religious rulings have not undergone any change since their Imāms' times, which in a way was responsible for giving rise to today's extremism and fundamentalism.

Mujtahid is a jurist competent enough to deduce precise inferences regarding the commandments from the holy Qur'an and the Sunna of the holy Prophet by the process of Ijtihād. Technically as a term of jurisprudence it signifies the application by a jurist of all his faculties to the consideration of the authorities of law with a view to finding out what in all probability is the law. In other words Ijtihād means making deductions in matters of law, in the cases to which no express text is applicable.[3]

The same way we seek an expert's advice in making some of the important decisions in our life; for example: When one is not feeling well, he or she refers to a physician to get the best medical help possible. Why doesn't that person treat himself on his own? What is the need to refer to an expert? Answers to these questions

---

[1] *Farhang Navin*, p. 126.
[2] Imam Khomeini, *Ar-Rasā'il*, vol. 2, p. 125.
[3] Baqir Sadre, *A Short History of Ilmul Usūl*, ISP, 1948.

are intuitive these days. Health is the most important thing in anyone's life. If you are not healthy you cannot do anything. So to stay healthy we seek medical help and don't rely on our own decisions. We put our faith in someone else who has more knowledge than us in that particular field. Moreover, when one wants to build a house, he or she refers to the expert in that field; an engineer, to help him build his house. Any field it might be we rely on expert's advice because that person has worked hard to attain a degree in his respective field.

Islamic jurisprudence is no different than any other field of life, in fact more important than anything else. Therefore, we have been given three choices when it comes to performing our duties as a Muslim.

We can become mujtahid that is to spend several years in Islamic seminary and attain the level of Ijtihād and act according to our own verdicts (*fatāwa*). If that's not possible one must act on *Ihtiyāt* that is he should act on such precaution which assures him that he has fulfilled his religious obligation. For example, if some mujtahids consider an act to be harām, while others say that it is not, he should not perform that act. Similarly, if some mujtahids consider an act to be obligatory (*wājib*) while others consider it to be recommended (*Mustahab*), he should perform it.[4] To act on precautionary measures (*Ihtiyāt*) one must have almost the same amount of knowledge as a mujtahid.

If one can neither be a mujtahid nor act on precautionary measures (*Ihtiyāt*), the third option is to follow a mujtahid. The same way we follow experts in other matters of our life. Since not every one of us has the ability or strength to become mujtahids, the easiest thing to do is to put our faith in someone who is a mujtahid and follow them. The one who follows a mujtahid is known as a *Muqallid*. This is where the concept of *taqlīd* comes into play. *Taqlīd* in religious laws means acting according to the verdicts of a mujtahid. It is necessary for a mujtahid who is followed, to be male, *Shi'a Ithnā 'Asharī*, adult, sane, of legitimate birth, living and just ('*ādil*).[5]

---

[4] Ayatollah Sistani, *Islamic Laws*, p. 1.
[5] Ibid. p. 2.

As mentioned before it is certainly not an easy thing to become a mujtahid, which makes us understand their elevated status. That is the reason they take all the responsibility of our actions in their verdicts.

So if we follow one of their verdicts and act according to it, but in the end it wasn't what Allah demanded from us, we will not be held accountable for our actions in that particular *mas'alah*, rather the Mujtahid will be questioned. The Prophet, Muhammad said: علماء أمتى كانبياء بنى اسرائيل Scholars of my nation are like the Prophets of *Bani* Israel (in their knowledge).

Muqallid has a few conditions of his own: he must be mature, sane ('*āqil*) and capable. Therefore, a person who is mature, *aqil* and is capable of performing the obligatory actions has a responsibility towards the *wajibāt* and harām set by Allah. If he disobeys these commands, he will face the consequences in the hereafter. But if he performs these obligatory actions he deserves the rewards. Thus, a child, a person who is insane and someone who isn't capable of performing the actions required by the *sharī'ah*, isn't considered to be *mukallif* and doesn't have to do *taqlīd*. Since nothing is *wājib* on him. But if he still performs any of these obligatory actions he will be rewarded by Allah.[6]

There could be more than one Mujtahids, but one must ascertain the most knowledgeable among them (*A'alam*) to follow. There are different ways to determine this.

One way is having enough knowledge of our own to determine the most knowledgeable, secondly, by asking two persons, who are learned and just and possess the capacity to identify a Mujtahid or the A'alam. Third way is when a number of learned scholars who possess the capacity to identify a Mujtahid or an A'alam, certify that a particular person is a Mujtahid or an A'alam, provided that one is satisfied by their statement.

Once a Mujtahid has been identified and one starts to follow him, there are few ways to acquire their verdicts.

1. When a person hears from the Mujtahid himself.

---

[6] Fallahzadeh, Muhammad Hussain, *Amozish Fiqh*, p. 2.

2. When the verdict of the Mujtahid is quoted by two just persons.

3. When a person hears the verdict from a person whose statement satisfies him.

4. By reading the Mujtahid's book of Masā'il, provided that, one is satisfied with the correctness of the book.[7]

---

[7] Op.cit. p. 3.

Chapter: 24

HIDING TRUE FAITH: TAQIYAH

By

Allama Sayyid Saeed Akhtar Rizvi[1]

The author of the book, *What is Shi'aism* writes under the heading Taqiyah: "Nifāq or hypocrisy is a principle of the Shi'a religion. They technically term such hypocrisy as Taqiyah which means the permissibility to conceal one's true belief for the sake of expediency."

It is easy to give a wrong meaning to a word and then heap abuses on it. Taqiyah is a Qur'anic term and it means permission of hiding one's true faith, not for the sake of expediency, but when there is danger to one's own life, property or honor or to that of another believer. This principle is initiated by Qur'an, was followed by many respectable Sahābah, and is accepted by all Muslims, Shi'as and Sunnis alike. But the writer of that booklet is outside the circle of Islam; therefore, he does not know these things. He does not realize that Islam is not only the Shi'a religion but the religion of all Muslims. I would like to give here only a few references from the Qur'an, action of Sahābah, Tafāsīr, traditions, and writings of respected Sunni scholars.

FROM THE QUR'AN

"He who disbelieves in Allah after his belief in Him, (is the liar) *except he who is compelled while his heart remains steadfast with the faith* (has nothing to worry). *But he who opens his breast for infidelity, on these is wrath of Allah, and for them is a great torment."* (Qur'an, 16:106) This verse of the Qur'an refers to the incident when the respected Sahābī, Ammār bin Yāsir had to utter some words against Islam to save himself from the Qurayshite infidels. The Qurayshites had brutally martyred Yāsir and his wife Sumaiyah

---

[1] Reproduced from his book *Wahhābīs Fitna Exposed*, a Pyame Aman Publication, Message of Peace Inc., Bloomfield, New Jersey: U.S.A., 1999.

just because of their faith. They were the first martyrs of Islam. When the parents were killed, Ammār pretended to renounce Islam and thus saved his life. Someone told the Prophet that Ammār had become *Kāfir*. The Prophet said "Never; verily the flesh and blood of 'Ammār is saturated with True faith." Then Ammār came to the Prophet bitterly weeping that he had to utter evil words against Islam, in order that he could slip away from the clutches of the infidels. The Prophet asked him: "How did you find your heart?" Ammār said: "Steadfast in Faith." The Prophet told him not to worry and advised him to repeat those words if the infidels again asked him to do so. And it was not only the Prophet who liked the choice of Ammār. Even Allah confirmed his action in the verse quoted above. This event is mentioned in almost all books of Tafsīr, under this verse.[2]

Another Āyat: *"Let not the believers take the disbelievers as their friends rather than the believers; who ever shall do this then he has no relation with Allah, except when you have to guard yourselves against them for fear of them; and Allah cautions you of Himself, for unto Allah is the end of your journey. Say whether you conceal what is in your hearts or manifest it, Allah knows it; and He knows all that is in the heavens and all that is in the earth; and verily Allah has power over all things."* (Qur'an, 3:28-29) The reason of this permission is given in this very Āyat: *"Say whether you conceal what is in your hearts or manifest it, Allah knows it."* Here Allah assures the Muslims that Faith is a spiritual thing, connected with heart; and if your faith inside your heart is unimpaired, then Allah is pleased with you whether you manifest that faith or hide it. It is all the same with Allah, because He knows your hidden secrets, and even when you hide your faith from unbelievers, Allah knows it and recognizes it.

FROM BOOKS OF TAFSĪR

There are other verses too; but we do not want to spend much time on this topic here. Now some statements from the books of Tafsīr. Imām as-Suyūtī writes, *inter alia*, under the above verse: "And Ibn Jarīr and Ibn Abī Hātim have narrated through Al-Awfī

---

[2] For example, *Tafsīr Ad-Durru 'l-manthūr* of Imām as- Suyūtī, vol. 4, p. 123; *Tafsīr Al-Kashshāf*, of az-Zamakhsharī, Beirut ed. Vol. 2, p. 430; and *Tafsīr Kabīr*, of Imām ar-Rāzī.

from Ibn Abbās (that he said about this verse): 'So Taqiyah is by tongue. Whoever is compelled to say something which is disobedience of Allah and he speaks it because of those people's fear while his heart remains steadfast in the faith, it will do him no harm; verily Taqiyah is with tongue only.'

"....And Abd ibn Hāmid has narrated from al-Hasan (al-Basrī) that he said: 'Taqiyah is lawful up to the day of resurrection.' And Abd ibn Hāmid has narrated form Abū Raja that he was reciting, *illa an tattqqu munhum taqiyatan,* and Abd ibn Haimd has narrated from Qatadah that he was reciting (likewise).... Taqiyatan - with *ya.*"[3]

So you see here the name 'Taqiyah' is favorably mentioned in the Qur'an. And this unknown writer says it is hypocrisy!

Imām Fakhruddīn ar-Rāzī has mentioned some rules concerning Taqiyah under this verse. Rules third to sixth which are relevant to our discussion are given here:

> *Third Rule:* Taqiyah is allowed in matters related to manifestation of friendship or enmity: and it is also allowed in matters connected to professing (their) religion. But it is certainly not allowed in matters which affect other persons, like murder, fornication, usurpation of property, perjury, slander of married women or informing the unbelievers about the weak points in the Muslims' defense.
>
> *Fourth Rule:* The Qur'anic verse apparently shows that Taqiyah is allowed with dominant unbelievers. But according to the Madhhab of Imām Shāfi'ī if the condition between (various sects of) the Muslims resembles the condition between the Muslims and the polytheists, then Taqiyah (from the Muslims too) is allowed for the protection of one' life.
>
> *Fifth Rule:* Taqiyah is allowed for protection of life. The question is whether it is allowed for the protection of property; possibly that too may be allowed, because the Prophet has said: "The sanctity of a Muslim's property is like the sanctity of his blood"; and also he has said: "Whoever is killed in defense of his property, is a martyr"; and also because man greatly needs his

---

[3] *Ad-Durru'l-manthūr,* vol. 2, pp. 16-17.

property; if water is sold at exorbitant price, *wudhū* does not remain *wājib* and one may pray with *tayammum* to avoid that small loss of property; so why should not this principle be applied here? And Allah knows better.

Sixth Rule: Mujāhid has said that this rule (of Taqiyah) was valid in the beginning of Islam, because of the weakness of the believers; but now that the Islamic government has got power and strength, it is not valid. But Awfī has narrated from al-Hasan (al-Basrī) that he said: "Taqiyah is allowed to the Muslims up to the Day of Resurrection." And this opinion is more acceptable because it is wājib to keep off all types of harm from one's self as much as possible.[4]

FROM AHADITH

Imām Al-Bukhārī has written a full chapter, *Kitābul Ikrāh*, on this subject of compulsion, wherein he writes *inter alia*: "And Allah said 'except when you have to guard yourselves against them for fear of them.' And it is Taqiyah."

And Hasan (Basrī) said: "Taqiyah is up to the Day of Resurrection.... And the Prophet said: 'Deeds are according to intention.'[5] That is why the Prophet has categorically said: 'He who has no Taqiyah has no religion.'"[6]

It is clear that the principle of Taqiyah is a part of the religion of Islam initiated by the Qur'an, confirmed by the traditions of the Prophet, fully agreed by the Sunni scholars and *mufassirīn*, and followed by respectable Sahābah. And now look at this ignorant man saying that Taqiyah is *nifāq* or hypocrisy! Certainly he himself is not only a *munāfiq* (hypocrite) but an out-right *Kāfir* who accuses the Prophet and respected Sahābah of propagating and practicing *nifāq!!* *Astaghfirullāh!* Remember that according to the hadīth of the Prophet this enemy of Taqiyah is not Muslim at all (has no religion).

---

[4] Imām Ar-Rāzī, *Tafsīr Mafātihu 'l- ghayb*, Beirut, 3rd.ed. vol. 7, p.13.
[5] *Sahīh Al-Bukhārī*, Egypt ed. vol. 9, pp. 24-25.
[6] Mulla Ali al-Muttaqī, *Kanzu 'l-Ummāl*, Beirut, 5th ed., 1405-1985, vol. 3 p. 96, hadīth no 5665.

The fact is that Taqiyah is opposite of *nifāq*. Remember, *Emān* and *Kufr*, when seen with their declaration can be divided into four categories only:-

(1) Correct belief of Islam, by heart and its declaration in words. This is open *Emān* (faith).

(2) Belief against Islam by heart and expression of that anti-Islamic belief in words. This is open *Kufr* (infidelity). These two categories are opposite to each other and cannot combine in one place.

(3) Belief against Islam in heart but declaration of Islam in words. This is *nifāq* (hypocrisy).

(4) Correct belief of Islam by heart but declaration of anti-Islamic belief in word. This is Taqiyah: and these two categories (*nifāq* and Taqiyah) are, likewise, opposite to each other and can never be found in one place. In other words, he who opposes Taqiyah is *munāfiq* like that unknown writer.

Imām ar-Rāzī too has clearly described this contrast in his Tafsīr in the following words:

"This points to the fact that (in these matters) consideration is given only to what is hidden in the heart. A hypocrite who shows faith and hides disbelief is a disbeliever, while a believer who under compulsion shows disbelief and hides faith is a believer: and Allah better knows what is hidden in the hearts of all.[7]

Before closing this chapter, I would like to ask this unknown author why not he has disclosed his name in his booklet. Is it not Taqiyyah? And that too without any justification? Kenya is a free country and there is no danger to his life, honor or property if he has written his name as the author. So Taqiyyah is a shameful thing if it is done by a non Wahhābī to protect his life, from Wahhābīs, barbarism; but very admirable if done by a Wahhābī without any reason.

---

[7] *Tafsīr Mafātihu'l-ghayb*, under verse 19:20

Chapter: 25

TEMPORARY MARRIAGE: MUT'A

By

Dr. S. Manzoor Rizvi[1]

Islam being a practical religion has attempted to solve all human problems in the most practical manner. The problem of sex is unquestionably a very important one and Islam has done its best to meet the requirements in this direction, taking into consideration all the conditions that are likely to arise in man's every day life.

As is well-known a Muslim man is allowed to marry four wives, of course, provided he satisfies all conditions laid down by the Law in this regard. In addition to this, Islam also allowed Mut'a, actually meaning a temporary marriage which is absolutely religious in character. While Mut'a has the possibility of limiting the duration of the marriage from the beginning, Nikah is expected to be permanent. But even with the permanent Nikah, a man can terminate his commitment of Nikah by giving a divorce whenever he wants, under the circumstance allowed by the law. In Mut'a it is compulsory to fix the period and this period is fixed by the mutual consent of the man and the woman concerned, and the woman has every right to dictate her terms. Just as in Nikah, in Mut'a also Mehr is to be fixed and on this count Nikah and Mut'a are identical, because the woman can demand whatever Mehr she wants. The laws of inheritance for the children born of Mut'a and of Nikah are identical although with regard to the rights of the woman, the laws are different. In short, Mut'a and Nikah both are religiously allowed in Islam and can be performed by the utterance of the *sigha* particularly meant for each type of marriage. Nikah is the common form of marriage, while Mut'a is an uncommon form of marriage. This is perhaps due to the fact that

---

[1] Excerpted from the title *Shiaism Explained* (various chapters), Peermahomed Ebrahim Trust, Karachi: Pakistan, 1972

Nikah is generally supposed to be a permanent marriage, while in Mut'a it is absolutely essential to specify the duration of marriage. However, if provided for in the contract, the woman can claim such rights as are normally permissible in Nikah.

QUR'ANIC VERSE ON MUT'A

It appears that the institution of Mut'a was found necessary for special circumstances, such as wars, a sailor's or traveler's life, etc. Its purpose is mainly to save Muslims from doing sin. If the institution of Mut'a is brought into practice, the woman could dictate her terms and agree or disagree to enter into Mut'a with the person demanding the same. Moreover, if the children are born due to such a Mut'a the father will be responsible for their maintenance and also the laws of inheritance will apply. If these rules are strictly followed in practice, there will be nothing like adultery or debauchery and such controlled marriage under the circumstance will solve the sex problem of the soldiers and there will be no chaos or disorder in society. The Qur'an says : *"And as such of them ye had Mut'a with them, give them their dowries as fixed reward; and it shall not be a sin on you, in whatever ye mutually agree (to very) after the fixed reward: Verily God is All-Knowing, All-Wise."* (4:24)

MUT'A IN PRACTICE DURING PROPHET'S TIME

Mut'a as a timed marriage and combining of Hajj with Umrah, were both practiced during the time of the Prophet and also during the time of the first Caliph and also for some time during the caliphate of the second Caliph who later made these haram. As stated in *Sahīh Muslim* and other reliable Sunni books, in which Umar was reported as saying that both were enforced during the time of the Prophet but he forebode it and would punish those who practiced them.

If Mut'a were not made *harām* by Umar as an innovation of his own, adultery and debauchery would not have been as rampant as they became after its prohibition. In Shi'a school of thought Mut'a is permissible as it was permissible in the times of Prophet.

In the fiqh followed by Shi'as, whatever the Qur'an and the Prophet dictate can not be changed by anyone whosoever he or she may be. *Haram-e-Muhammad* is haram and *Halal-e-Muhammad* is halal till the Day of Judgment.

The charge of fornication against Mut'a is unfounded because, contrary to the conditions of fornication, the child born out of a Mut'a is entitled to the same rights as the child born out of a Nikah and the wife at the time of the contract can demand certain rights including the rights of inheritance.

The same laws also necessary in Mut'a are also necessary in Nikha: women wait for the period of *Iddah* that is laid down by law before they can enter into any contract for marriage or Mut'a in order to determine the parentage of any child that the women might have conceived. Therefore, if one ponders very carefully over the laws and restrictions laid down by religion in respect of Mut'a, one will visualize that it is religiously as perfect as Nikah and if one would go further into its philosophy, one would find some special advantages also in this institution which are not available in Nikah.

The laws pertaining to Mut'a are pure and holy just as the laws of Nikah are pure and holy. These good laws are disfigured by people many a time and their sanctity is destroyed by the misuse of the power given under the law. This does not mean that the Law is bad. If a person goes on performing Nikah and goes on giving divorce, it does not mean that Nikah is bad. Similarly, if a man or woman goes on performing Mut'as without observing the laws, it does not mean that Mut'a is bad. Thus, if the rules are strictly followed in Nikah or Mut'a these institutions are blessings for mankind.

Even Ibne-Umar the son of the Caliph Umar, refused to subscribe to the validity of Umar's prohibiting or declaring a thing like Mut'a as illegal which was pronounced lawful by the Prophet. (Trimidhī B.H.) It is reported of Imām Ali having declared, "If Umar had not declared Mut'a as unlawful only some unfortunate fellow would have committed adultery."

It is reported that Jābir Ibne Abdullāh Ansārī had said: "We practiced Mut'a during the time of the Prophet, during the Caliphate of Abū Bakr and until half the term of Umar's regime as a Caliph when Umar declared it as unlawful and punishing those who practiced Mut'a. (*Durr al-Manthūr, Tafsīr al-Kabīr, Kashāf, Ma'alimaut-Tanzīl Mustadrak* etc.)

The Sunni Malīkī School holds Mut'a as lawful. It is now left for any intelligent reader to judge for himself and to follow the Qur'an and hold Mut'a as lawful or to follow Umar against the decision of the Word of God

Given below are a few references of Sunni books on Mut'a:

(1) *Sahīh Bukhārī* by Sahābī Abdullāh Ibne Masūd, vol. 2, p. 759, published by Mujtabai Press, New Delhi.
(2) *Sahīh Bukhārī*, vol. 1, p. 450, published by Mujtabai Press, Delhi.
(3) *Kanzul-Ummāl* by Mulla Muttaqī, vol. 8, p. 295.
(4) *Tafsīr Mazharī* by Qazī Sana'ullāh Panipati.
(5) *Masnad* Ibne Hanbal, vol. 4, p. 438, printed in Egypt.
(6) *Tafsīr Durr al-Manthūr*, Allama Jalāluddīn Suyūtī (Confirming the statement of Imām Ali).
(7) Sharhe- Bukhārī, vol. 9, p. 138 (Statement of Abū-Alzahra).

THREE CARDINAL POINTS OF MUT'A

1. In case someone is stuck in some corner of the world away from his wife, Mut'a allows him to fulfill his sexual desire by marrying for a limited time. When he leaves that corner of the world he would not have to go through the rigors of divorce process associated with permanent marriage.

2. In case of Mut'a one may have a provision of abstinence (abstaining from sexual relations) depending on the individual's particular situation. In a regular marriage such a provision would make the marriage null and void.

3. Mut'a carries with it all the legal bindings of the Shari'ah.

Chapter: 26

AUTHENTIC BOOKS ON AHĀDĪTH

By

Dr. S. Manzoor Rizvi

Once Hitler told his Prime Minister that it looked like the world specially German started believing in all what he said. The Prime Minister replied that if he continued to lie with the same force he himself would start believing in his own lies.

The same can be said about the books of ahādīth of Ahle Sunnah e.g., *Sahīh Bukhārī*, *Sahīh Muslim* and other seven books. People believe that these books are true collection of all genuine ahādīth. The fact is that thousands of ahādīth in these books were extracted from hundred of thousands of ahādīth and many were left out because they were outright lies or at least doubtful. The ahādīth included in these could be equally wrong. One of the proof of this assumption is that each time a new edition of these books particularly Bukhārī and Muslim are brought out some of the ahādīth are omitted because these might have been found doubtful.

The problem with the collection and compilation of ahādīth among Ahle Sunna is due to the late start of the work. It was forbidden to collect ahādīth during the time of the first three caliphs. The work of compiling ahādīth started during the caliphate of Mua'wiyah, at least 30 years after the death of the Prophet, when a few factories were established to mint ahādīth in total disregard to the saying of the Prophet that, "One who ascribe wrong statement to me will go to hell."

In Shi'aism the collection of ahādīth started by Imām Ali during the lifetime of the Prophet and continued thereafter. This collection known as *Sahīfa-e-Ali* has been in mentioned in *Bukhārī*. (See *Babe Kitāb-ul-Ilm*, vol. 1, printed in Cairo in 1314 A.H.) Jalāluddīn Suyūtī (died in 911 A.H.) writes: "Among Sahāba and Tabe'īn there was a difference of opinion about collecting ahādīth. Some were of the opinion that it was wrong to collect ahādīth and some were saying that ahādīth should be collected. Imām Ali and his son, Imām Hasan deemed it right and started working on it."[1] There are four types of ahādīth: Sahīh; Muwassaq; Ahasan; and Daīf. To assess the authenticity of any hadith Muslim ulema use the science. There are many books written on this science but the best Shi'a book is *Kitāb-Arrerya Fī Ilmed Daraya* written by Zain Shaheed (died in 655 A.H.). The best book in Ahle Sunna is *Tadrīb-al-Rāwī* by Jalāluddīn Suyūtī who died in 911 A.H.

SHI'A BOOKS OF AHĀDĪTH

Given here are books which are much more authentic as some of these were started before or immediately after the death of the Prophet: *Sahīfa* by Imām Ali; *Sahīfia Sajjādia* by Imām Zain-ul-Abidīn; *Tafsīr of Qur'an* by Imām Mohammad Bāqir; and *Risālathe-Ela-Al-Shi'a* and *Tawhīd*, both written by Imām Ja'far Sādiq. Books on ahādīth compiled by companions are: *Al-Sanan wal-Ahkām wal-Qadāya* by Abū Rafe' Qibli Misrī, a close companion of the Prophet who died in 30 A.H.; *Mansak* (on Hajj) by Jābir Ibne Abdullāh Ansārī who died in 78 A.H.; and *As-Saqia* by Salīm ibne Qais Bilāl-Al-Ansārī.

In the second century there were about 400 books published on this subject by Shi'a Ulema. Presently there are four famous Shi'a books on ahādtīh collectively known as *Kitāb-ul-Arba'a* and these are: (1). *Al-Kāfī* by Shiekh Mohammad bin Yaqūb Kuleini Baghdadī who died in 329 A.H. This book has a total number of 16,121 ahādīth; (2).*Mun Lā Yahduruhu'l- Faqīh* by Al- Husain bin Mūsa bin Bābweh Qummī who died in 381 A.H. The book contains 5,963 ahādīth; (3). *Tahzībul- Ahkām* by Shiekh Abū Ja'far Mohammad bin Al-Hasan At-Tūsī who died in 460 A.H. The book has 12,590 ahādīth; and (4).*Al-Istibsār* also written by At-Tūsī and has 5,521 ahādīth.

Shi'as are fair in their treatment of ahādīth. The criteria for judging the hadīth are two-fold: hadīth contents should not go against the Qur'an; and the sources of hadīth should be authentic. For Ahle-Sunna there are no such criteria and for them whatever is given in *Sihāh Sitta* especially in *Sahīh Muslim* and *Sahīh Bukhārī* is always correct.

---

[1] *Tadrīb-al-Rāwī*, vol. 1, p. 96, printed in Cairo in 1383 A.H.

Chapter: 27

COMPANIONS OF THE PROPHET

By

Allama Sayyid Saeed Akhtar Rizvi

One of the "proofs of Shi'a's kufr" is given by some writers in these words: "The Shi'as believe in wickedly reviling the Shaikhain (i.e. Sayyidina Abū Bakr and Sayyidina Umar (Radhiallahu 'anhu) and launch false charges against the chastity of Sayyidina (sic.) Ayeshah (R.A.)"

Before writing anything on this proof it is necessary to mention that no Shi'a has ever said, written or transmitted anything "against the chastity" of Ummu l-mu'minīn Ayeshah. This man probably does to know that the word, Chastity, is generally used for "abstaining from unlawful sexual intercourse." We, the Shi'as, cannot think in such terms about any "Mother of the believers" or for that matter about any wife of any Prophet be she the wife of Nūh or of Lūt. Of course, we cannot stop the Wahhābīs from indulging in such obscene talk. The Shi'as will whole-heartedly agree that any one who launches a charge against the chastity of Umu 'l-mu'minīn 'Ayeshah is *kāfir*. Obviously, such a charge will go against the clear verdict of the Qur'an and will therefore be tantamount to disbelief in the book of Allah.

Coming to the position of the companions of the Prophet, there is a basic difference between the outlook of the Sunnis and that of the Shi'as.

First, let us see what the meaning of a "Companion" is. According to the Sunni books, a companion is a person who after accepting Islam had seen the Prophet, at least once, even if he had not had any talk with the Prophet, nor heard any hadīth from him nor fought under the Prophet in any *jihad;* provided he died as a Muslim. This definition includes those who could not see the Prophet because of blindness.[1]

---

[1] Ibn Hajar Al-'Asqalānī, *Al-Isābah*, p. 10.

And this name is applied to all who professed Islam, even if faith had not entered their hearts yet, even if they were hypocrites. In other words, almost the whole of Arabia was full of the companions.

Now, according to the Sunni belief all the companions were just and pious. They ascribe a tradition to the Prophet which forms the basis of their belief: "My companions are like the stars, which one of them you follow you should be guided aright." Therefore they believe that all the companions were just *('ādil)*. This view is diametrically opposed to the Qur'an and the ahādīth of the Prophet, leave aside the fact that the historical events totally disprove it.

OPPOSED TO QUR'AN AND AHĀDĪTH

As for the Qur'an, the criterion of excellence is the individual's faith, good deeds and piety, as is seen in hundreds of verses, no matter whether that person was a companion or not. Also the Qur'an says in 9th surah *at-Tawbah* (revealed in 9 A.H., just about 1½ years before the death of the Prophet: *"And from among those who are round about you of the Arabs there are hypocrites. And from among the people of Medina; they are stubborn in hypocrisy; you (O Prophet!) do not know them; We will chastise them twice, then shall they be turned back to a grievous chastisement."* (9: 101)

Perhaps someone might say that this verse concerns the hypocrites. But the hypocrites too were counted among the companions, especially so when hypocrisy of many of them was not known even to the Prophet. However, we quote here only a few verses (out of many) which are addressed to the believers among the companions:–

1. *"O you who believe! What (excuse) have you that when it is said to you: Go forth in Allah's way, you should incline heavily to earth; are you contented with this world's life instead of the hereafter? But the provision of this world's life compared with the hereafter is but little. If you do not go forth, He will punish you with a painful punishment and bring in your place a people other than you and you will do Him no harm; and Allah has power over all things."* (9: 38-39)

2. *"Say: if your fathers and you sons and your brethren and your mates and your kinfolks and property which you have acquired and the slackness of trade which you fear and dwellings which you like,*

are dearer to you than Allah and his Messenger and jihad in His way, then wait till Allah brings about His command, and Allah does not guide the transgressing people." (8: 27)

3. *"O you who believe! Be not disloyal to Allah and the Messenger, nor be unfaithful to your trusts while you know."* (47: 38)

4. *"Even as your Lord caused you to go forth from your house with the truth, though a party of the believers was surely averse. They disputed with you about the truth after it had become clear, (and they went forth) as if they were driven to death while they looked at it."* (9: 25)

5. *"Behold! you are those who are called upon to spend in Allah's way, but among you are those who are niggardly, and whoever is niggardly is niggardly against his own soul; and Allah is Self-sufficient and you are the needy; and if you turn back He will bring in your place another people, then they will not be like you."* (8: 5-6)

As for the ahādīth of the Prophet, the following few are given here to clarify the issue:–

1. It has been narrated by the companions, Talha Ibn 'Abdullah, Ibn 'Abbās and Jabir ibn 'Abdullāh that the Messenger of Allah conducted funeral prayer on the martyrs of Uhud; and the Messenger of Allah said: "I am witness for these." Abū Bakr said: "O Messenger of Allah! Is it not that our brothers had accepted Islam as we did, and did *jihad* as we did? He i.e. the Prophet said: "Certainly! But they did not eat anything from their reward, and I do not know what you will do after me." Abū Bakr wept and said: "Are we going to remain after you!" [2]

2. Imām Bukhārī narrates from al-'Ula' ibn al-Musayyab from his father that he said: "I met (the Companion) al-Bara' ibn 'Azib and said: 'Blessings to you! You remained with the Prophet and did his *bay'ah* under the tree.' He said: 'O son of my brother! You do not know what we have done after him!'"[3].

3. The Companion, Ibn 'Abbās narrated that the Prophet said *inter alia* in a hadīth about the Day of Judgment: "And verily

---

[2] Al-Waqidi, *Kitābu 'l-maghāzī*, vol. 1, p. 310.
[3] *Sahih al-Bukhārī*, Vol. 5, p. 195; Imām Mālik, *Al Muwatta*, Vol. 2 p. 462.

some people of my *umma* will be brought and taken to the left side (i.e. the side of the Fire): so I will say: 'O my Lord! (they are) my companions.' But I will be told: 'Certainly you do not know what they did after you; they continued to turn back on their heels right from the time you left them.' Then I will say as had said the good servant (i.e. the Prophet 'Isa: 'and I was a witness of them so long as I was among them, but when Thou didst take me (away) Thou wert the watcher over them and Thou art witness of all things...'"[4].

4. The Prophet said: "Surely you will be taken to the left side on the day of *Qiyamah* (Resurrection), so I will say: 'Where to?' and will be told: 'To the Fire, by Allah! Then I'll say: 'O my Lord! They are my companions.' Then it will be told: 'Surely you do not know what they did after you; verily they had gone out of Islam since the time you had departed from them.' Then I'll say: 'to hell with them! To hell with them who changed after me!' And I do not think anyone will be saved from them except (a few) like unattended cattle."[5].

Ahādīth of similar meaning have been narrated from the companions, Abū Bakrah[6] and Abū 'd-Darda.[7]

In spite of hundreds of verses and traditions criticizing many of the companions, the Sunnis refuse to look critically at individual companions to verify whether a particular companion really deserved to be followed or not. For them, every one of them deserves to be followed. Their method of argument runs on the following lines. They will take a verse praising some companions and then apply it to all of them without pondering on its provisos and restrictions. For example: "*Certainly Allah was pleased with the believers when they gave allegiance to you under the tree, and He knew what was in their hearts, so He sent down tranquility on them and rewarded them with a near victory.*" (Qur'an, 48:18). If you ponder on this verse, you will find that it is not a blanket declaration of

---

[4] *Musnad* Ahmad ibn Hanbal, Egypt ed. Vol 1, p. 235. The verse quoted is from *Surah Al-Mā'idah*, verse 117.

[5] *Sahih al-Bukhārī*, vol. 7. p. 209; vol. 4, pp. 94 and 156; *Sahīh Muslim*, vol. 7, p. 66.

[6] *Musnad* Ahmad ibn Hanbal, vol. 5, p. 50.

[7] *Majma'u 'z-zawāid*, vol. 9, p. 367.

pleasure with all those who did *bay'ah* for all times to come. In other words, it does not say that Allah was pleased with those who gave allegiance to you. It restricts it to the *believers* and that too for a certain time, "when they gave allegiance...." Clearly, those who did not do *bay'ah* or who were not true believers are beyond the limit of this verse. Not only that; a preceding verse puts this verse in clear perspective: *"Surely those who swear allegiance to you do but swear allegiance to Allah; the hand of Allah is above their hands. Therefore whoever breaks* (this allegiance) *he breaks it only to the injury of his own soul, and whoever fulfils what he has covenanted with Allah, He will grant him a mighty reward."* (Qur'an 48:10)

So there is another most important proviso here: Those who have done *bay'ah* should not break it. Why this proviso, if all the companions who had done *bay'ah* under the tree, were immune from breaking it? The *bay'ah* under the tree was on one specific term that "they would not flee from battle ground."[8]

And the Qur'an itself is the witness that almost all of them broke it in the battle of Hunayn, two years after the said *bay'ah*. Allah says: *"Certainly Allah helped you in many places, and on the day of Hunayn, when your great numbers made you vain, but they* (i.e. number) *availed you nothing and the earth became too small for you notwithstanding its spaciousness, then you turned back retreating."* (Qur'an, 9: 25)

The books of traditions and history clearly say that in the battle of Hunayn, in which ten thousand companions (including all those who had done *bay'ah* under the tree) had participated, all of them fled away except four who remained steadfast, three of them were from the Prophet's clan, Banū Hāshim ('Ali ibn Abī Tālib, 'Abbās ibn 'Abdul Muttalib and Abū Sufyān ibn al-Hārith ibn 'Abdul Muttalib) and one from another clan ('Abdullāh ibn Mas'ūd).[9] According to other traditions, 'Aqīl ibn Abī Tālib, Zubayr ibn al-'Awwām, 'Abdullāh ibn Zubayr ibn 'Abdul-Muttalib and Usāmah ibn Zayd also remained steadfast.

The Prophet told his uncle, Abbās, to call the Muslims back. He wondered as to how his voice would reach the fleeing herd.

---

8 *Musnad* Ahmad ibn Hanbal, vol. 3, p. 192; *Tārīkh Tabarī*, vol. 3, p. 87.
9 *Tārīkh al-Khamīs*, vol. 2, p. 113; *As-Sīrah Al-Halabiyah*, vol. 3, p. 255.

The Prophet said that Allah would cause his voice to reach them, no matter how far they might have gone. So, Abbās called them in these words as the Prophet had taught him: "O group of the *Ansār* (helpers), O People of the tree of *samurah*" (where they had done the above mentioned *bay'ah* two years earlier).[10].

By this fleeing from the battlefield, all of them (except the four or eight named above) broke their allegiance, and can not be included in the good-news of Allah's pleasure. But the Sunnis refuse to look at these clear signs. This is a vast topic, but I have merely shown the basic difference in the outlooks of the Sunnis and the Shi'as.

However, we do not "wickedly revile" anyone; we only repeat what the Qur'an, the ahādīth, and the history say. And we use the same words for each group which the Qur'an and ahādīth have for them.

GROUND FOR DECLARING *KĀFIR*

But let us suppose, just for the sake of argument, that the accusation of this unknown writer against the Shi'as is correct and that they really abuse the Shaykhayn; and then let us see if this really is a ground to declare that they are kāfirs.

Ibn Taymiyyah, the Shaykhul Islam of the Wahhābīs, quotes a group of Sunni scholars as follows:–

"And merely abusing someone other than the Prophets does not necessarily make the abuser *kāfir;* because some of those who were in the time of the Prophet (i.e. the companions) used to abuse one another and none of them was declared *kāfir* because of this (practice): and (also) because it is not *wājib* (compulsory) to have faith particularly in any of the companions; therefore abusing any of them does not detract from the faith in Allah and His books and His messengers and the Last day."[11].

Even more clear is the wording of Mulla 'Ali al-Qari who writes in his *Shrahal-Fiqh-al-akbar*: "To abuse Abū Bakr and 'Umar

---

[10] Ibn Sa'd, *At-Tabāqāt Al-Kubra*, Beirut, n.d., vol. 4, pp. 18-19.
[11] Ibn Taymiyyah, *As-Sarimu 'l-maslūl*, 1402/1982, p. 579 (published by 'Alama 'l-Kutub).

is not *kufr*, as Abush-Shakur as-Salimi has correctly proved in his book, *at-Tamhīd*. And it is because the basis of this (claim that reviling the Shaykhayn is *kufr*) is not proven, nor its meaning is confirmed."

"It is so because certainly abusing a Muslim is *fisq* (sin, moral depravity) as is proved by a confirmed hadīth, and therefore the Shaykhayn (Abū Bakr and Umar) will be equal to other (Muslims) in this rule; and also if we suppose that someone murdered the Shaykhayn, and even the two sons-in-law (i.e. Uthmān and Ali), all of them together, even then according to *Ahlus-sunnah wal Jamā'ah*, he will not go out of the Islam (i.e. will not become *kāfir*): and we know that abusing is less serious than murder....."[12] We have quoted here from three old editions printed in Turkey and India. Now a new edition had been printed by *Darul Kutubil 'Ilmiyah*, Beirut, in 1404/1984 which claims to be "the First Edition" and from which four pages (including the above text) have been omitted. The deleted portion contains also the declaration that those who believe that Allah has a body are definitely *kāfir* according to *Ijma'* without any difference of opinion. Obviously this statement expels the Wahhābīs out of Islam because they believe that Allah has a body, as described earlier.

Then two and a half pages contain the debate whether it is permissible to do *la'nah* on Yazīd. Mulla 'Ali Qari has quoted some Sunni scholars as saying that Yazīd became Kāfir the moment he ordered the killing of Imām Husain; but he (Mulla 'Ali Qari) himself allow only the *la'nah* in these words: "May Allah curse him who killed Husayn or was pleased with it." Even this was unpalatable to the Wahhābīs who call Yazīd *"Amīru 'l-mu'minīn"!* The white lie that the Beirut edition is the "First" and this *Tahrīf* by omission is one more proof how honest and trustworthy the Wahhābīs are. And the omission has left a sentence hanging in the air—its subject is omitted while the predicate is intact. Wahhābī scholarship indeed!

---

12 Mulla 'Ali Qari, *Sharh Al-Fiqh Al-Akbar*, (1) Matba' Uthmaniyah, Istanbul, 1303, p. 130, (2) Matba' Mujtaba'i, Dehli, 1348, p. 86, and (3) Matba' Aftab-e-Hind, India, no date, p. 86.

SHI'AS' OPINION ABOUT HAFSA AND AYESHAH

Some people spuriously criticize the Shi'as cursing the wives of Prophet Muhammad, especially Ayeshah (daughter of Abū Bakr; the first caliph) and Hafsa (daughter of Umar; the second caliph), and that they ascribe adultery to them, Allah forbid!

The Answer: This is a great calumny. When did the Shi'as ascribe adultery to Ayeshah and Hafsa? This is definitely not true. In fact, they condemned their disobeying Allah and His Messenger and they have determined that they both indeed had disobeyed and broke the order of Allah and His Messenger. The Qur'an has confirmed this. Allah says: *"If you both turn to Allah, then indeed your hearts are already inclined (to this); and if you back up each other against him, then surely Allah it is Who is his guardian, and Jibril and the believers that do good, and the angles after that are the aiders."* (66: 4)

The Shi'as are unhappy with Ayeshah for encouraging Talha and az-Zubeir to break their homage to Imām Ali, when she gathered a group of hypocrites, mounted a camel, and set out with Talha and az-Zubeir to fight Imām Ali. Indeed, they fought him and were unjust to him.[13]

---

[13] The last three paragraphs are excerpted from the book, *Spurious Arguments about the Shi'a*, written by Abū Tālib At-Turābī. The book was published by Ansariyan Publications, Qum, Iran in 2001.

Chapter: 28

SHI'AS AND THE PROPHET'S COMPANIONS

By

Imam Muhammad Jawad Chirri[1]

Muslim scholars differ in answering two questions pertaining to the companions of the Messenger of God: (1) Who are the companions of the Prophet Muhammad; and (2) Are all companions of the Prophet righteous?

PROPHET'S COMPANIONS

Most of the Sunni scholars consider all those who adopted Islam during the time of the Prophet, saw the Prophet, and prayed with him to be of his companions. However, it seems that the Messenger himself did not agree with these scholars. Al-Tabarī in his *History* part 3, page 68, reported that there was an argument between Khālid Ibn Al-Walīd and Abdul Rahmān Ibn Awf when Khālid killed some members of Banū Juthaimah. The Messenger of God sent Khālid as a missionary for Islam (not as a fighter). Khālid exceeded the order of the Messenger and killed a number of men from Banū Juthaimah after he gave them the assurance of no-harm.

Some men from Banū Juthaimah had killed Al-Fakih Ibn Al-Mugheerah Al Makhzumī, uncle of Khālid, and Awf Ibn Abd-Awf, father of Abdul Rahmān, before the conquest of Mecca. Now Khālid acted in revenge in spite of the Prophet's orders. In their heated dialogue, Abdul Rahmān said to Khālid: "You followed the method of the pre-Islamic era." Khālid said: "I only avenged the killing of your father." Abd Al-Rahmān: "You lie. I already killed the killer of my father, but you avenged the killing of your uncle."

Their heated argument led to a verbal abuse on the part of Khālid. When the Prophet found out about it, he said to Khālid: "....Khālid, leave my companions alone. By God, should you have a piece of gold the size of Uhud Mountain, and you spend it in the

---

[1] Reproduced from his book, *The Shiites under Attack*, (Chapter 8: *Are the Shiites Negative towards the Companions?*), Islamic Center of America, Chicago, 1986.

path of God, your charity would not compare to a morning or evening trip in defense of Islam by any one of my companions."[2]

This statement of the Prophet indicates that Khālid was not considered a companion of the Prophet because he told him to leave his companions alone.

Thus, the Prophet clearly indicated that Khālid was not one of his companions. Yet, this statement was uttered by the Prophet after the conquest of Mecca (which took place two years after Khālid adopted Islam, shortly after the pact of Al-Hudaibiyah). The exclusion of Khālid from the community of the Prophet's companions means the exclusion of thousands of companions who adopted Islam during the time of the Prophet, who met the Prophet, and who prayed behind him.

RIGHTEOUSNESS OF PROPHET'S COMPANIONS

The righteousness of all the companions and their worthiness of confidence are matters about which the Shi'as and the Sunnis argue. The majority of the Sunni scholars believe that all the companions are righteous and worthy of our confidence. The Shi'a scholars are selective.

The Sunni scholars cite Qur'anic verses for substantiating their claim: "*Muhammad is the Apostle of God; and those who are with him are firm against unbelievers, compassionate towards one another. You see them bowing and prostrating, seeking grace from God and His satisfaction......The mark of prostration shows on their faces.....Allah has promised those among them who believe and do righteous deeds forgiveness, and a great rewards.*" (48:29) Thus, the Almighty described the companions of the Messenger as firm against the unbelievers; merciful among themselves; and that they bow and prostrate. The mark of their prostration shows on their foreheads; and that Allah promised those who believe and do righteous deeds forgiveness and a great reward.

All these descriptions substantiate the piety and virtue of the companions. The verse, however, does not include all the companions. It only includes the companions who were firm against the unbelievers, merciful among themselves.

_____

[2] Ibn Hushām, in his *Sīrat of the Prophet*, part 2, page 421.

Thus, the companions who were not firm against the unbelievers or were unmerciful to the believers would not be included by the verse.

It would be only logical to say that those who shed the blood of Muslims without justification in civil wars such as Talhah, Zubeir, and Mu'awiya are not included in this Qur'anic statement, plus all companions who joined them in their unrighteous wars against Imam Ali, and those who divided the Muslims and destroyed their unity. Furthermore, the end of the verse clearly indicates that the praise was not to include all the companions because it declares that only those who believed in Islam and did good deeds will be entitled to forgiveness and great rewards.

One of the verses which is offered as evidence of the righteousness of all the companions of the Prophet is the following: *"And the early Muslims from the Meccan migrants and the Medinite Ansār (the helpers) and those who followed them with their good deeds, Allah is well pleased with them, and they are well pleased with Him; and He has prepared for them gardens beneath which rivers flow, to dwell therein forever. That is the mighty achievement."* (9:100)

This verse, however, speaks of the virtue of the migrants and Medinites who adopted Islam at the early state of the Islamic era. Thus, it does not include the thousands of the companions adopted Islam after the Hudaibiyah truce or after the conquest of Mecca. These were not from the early Muslim. Their Islam took place about twenty years after the proclamation of Islam and about eight years after Hijrah.

Another verse which is cited for the righteousness of all companions is: *"Allah was well pleased with the believers when they swore allegiance unto thee beneath the tree; He knew what was in their hearts, and He sent down tranquility to them and rewarded them with a speedy victory...."* (48:18) This verse also does not include all the companions who declared their Islam after signing the Hudaibiyah pact which took place during the sixth year after Hijra. The declaration of the allegiance to the Prophet under the tree took place shortly before signing the pact. The companions who gave allegiance under the tree at Hudaibiyah were about fourteen hundred. It is worthy to mention that a number of students of the companions (such as Sa'īd Ibn Al-Musayah and Al-Shi'abī and Ibn Sirīn) said that the early migrants were those who prayed to the two Qiblas (Al-Masjid Al-Aksa and Al-Ka'bah).[3]

SUBSTANTIATING RIGHTEOUSNESS OF COMPANIONS

Some scholars tried to substantiate the righteousness of the companions through a number of ahādīth:

> 1. It is reported that the Messenger of God said, "None of those who attended the battle of Badr or the pact of Hudaibiyah will enter Hell."
> 2. It is also reported that the Prophet said: "None of those who gave their allegiance under the tree (during the event of Hudaibiyah) will enter the Fire." *(Abd-Bir, page 4).*

The two ahādīth do not substantiate the righteousness of any companions except the companions who were present at Badr and Hudaibiyah. Putting them together, their number would not reach two thousand, while the number of the companions was much bigger. Those who attended the conquest of Mecca were ten thousand, and those who went with the Prophet to Tabūk were about twenty-five thousand. Thus, the majority of the companions of the Prophet would not be included in these two ahādīth.

THE OPINIONS OF THE SELECTIONISTS

The Shi'a Muslim scholars did not put all the companions in one rank; nor did they say that all of them were righteous. Some of them were righteous to the highest degree. Some of them were truthful and worthy of confidence, but they were not entirely righteous. Some of them were not known to be righteous or unrighteous, and some of them were known to be devious.

QUR'ANIC VERSES SUPPORT THE SELECTIONISTS

These scholars who view that some of the companions were neither righteous nor in a place of confidence support their view with a number of Qur'anic verses: *"And they say: 'obedience'; but when they leave thee, some of them spend the night planning other than what they say to you. Allah records what they plan by night. Disregard them and put thy trust in Allah. Allah is Sufficient Trustee."* (4:81)

---

[3] Abū Omar Yūsuf Ibn Abd-Bīr, *Al-Istī'āb* part 1, pages 2-3.

This verse declares that a number of those who were residents of Medina were Muslims, and they prayed with the Prophet and attend his gatherings and heard the Messenger commanding the Muslims to do some good deeds. They used to say to the Prophet: "We heard you and we will obey you;" but when they left him, they did not obey the Messenger.

We find in chapter nine of the Qur'an many verses which indicate that some of the companions of the Messenger were people of hypocrisy, and the Messenger did not know their hypocrisy. Some of these verses are:

1. *"And among those around you of the wandering Arabs are hypocrites and among the people of Medina there are some who persist in hypocrisy whom thou (O Muhammad) know not. We know them and We shall chastise them twice; then they will be relegated to a painful doom."* (9:101)

2. *"O Prophet! Combat the disbelievers and the hypocrites and be hard on them. Their abode is Hell, a hapless journey's end. They swear by Allah that they said nothing (wrong), yet they did say the word of disbelief. They disbelieved after they declared their Islam, and they sought revenge only because Allah and His Messenger enriched them of His bounty....."* (9:72)

3. *"Among them are men who made a covenant with Allah (saying): If he gives us of His bounty we will give alms and become of the righteous. Yet, when He gave them of His bounty, they hoarded it and turned away, averse. So He made a consequence (to be) hypocrisy in their hearts until the day when they shall meet Him, because they broke their word to Allah and because they lied."* (9:75-77)

4. We also find in chapter 33, "The Confederates". *"And when the hypocrites and those in whose hearts is a disease say 'Allah and His Messenger promised us nothing but delusions.' And when a party of them said: 'Oh folk of Yathrib! There is no stand possible for you, therefore, go back.' And some of them even ask permission of the Prophet, saying: 'Our homes are exposed to the enemy, and they lay not exposed.' They only wished to flee."* (33:12-13)

The chapter of *Al-Munāfiqūn* is a clear evidence that a number of Muslims (who declared their Islam at the time of the Prophet and lived with him in Medina and prayed with him were hypocrites.

They came to the Prophet to defend themselves by taking an oath in the presence of the Prophet that they did not betray him and they were liars. They had believed in Islam then deserted it and Allah sealed their hearts. The verse says: *"When the hypocrites come to thee (O Muhammad), they say: 'We bear witness that thou art indeed Allah's Messenger. And Allah knows that thou art indeed His Messenger, and Allah bears witness that the hypocrites indeed are speaking falsely. They made their oaths a shield so that they may turn (men) from the way of Allah. Verily, evil is that which they wanted to do. That is because they believed and then disbelieved, therefore, their hearts were sealed so that they understand not.'"* (63:1-3)

These numerous verses which are in many of the Qur'anic chapters testify clearly that many of the people who declared Islam during the time of the Prophet and who lived and prayed with him were hypocrites. What testimony could be bigger than the testimony of the Qur'an?

These hypocrites were living with the rest of the companions, and their names were not known. Therefore, it is impossible to avoid taking ahādīth from them or know how many they were. Historians, among them Al-Tabarī in his *History*, part 2, page 504, and Ibn Hushām in his *Al-Sīrah Al-Nabawiyyah*, part 2, page 64, reported that when the Messenger went with his army to Uhud, he had with him one thousand companions. But Abdullah Ibn Abū Salūl left the Prophet and went back to Medina accompanying three hundred from the Medinites. Islamic history did not inform us of the names of any of the three hundred except the name of their chief, Abdullāh Ibn Abū Salūl. Knowing that the situation was so, how can we not avoid taking ahādīth from these hypocrites who were not separated from the good companions through any mark of distinction?

COMPANIONS SHEDDING BLOOD OF MUSLIMS

We should not forget that there were among the companions some prominent men such as Talhah, Zubeir, Mu'awiyah, Amr Ibn Al-Aws, al-Nu'mān Ibn Bashīr, and Simarah Ibn Jundab who shed Muslim blood. These should not be considered in a place of confidence after they shed the blood of thousands of Muslims in order to reach their worldly goals. Allah declared in His book: *"And whoever kills a believer deliberately, his reward is Hell forever, and the wrath of God is upon him, and He cursed him and prepared for him a great punishment."* (4:73) Thus, if a person kills a believer, his abode will be the Fire and the wrath of Allah is upon him, and He curses him and prepares for him a great chastisement. This will be the fate of people such as Mu'awiyah, Amr Ibn Al-Auss, Talhah, and Zubeir who shed the blood of more than forty thousand Muslims.

It would be very illogical to consider people who committed so many sins righteous and their reports acceptable. There are people who say that these men who committed such sins are from the companions whom Allah likes because they were from the early Meccan and Medinite Muslims, and they were among the ones who gave their allegiance to the Messenger under the tree of Hudaibeyah. These are from among the ones whom Allah was pleased with; and whoever Allah was pleased with one time, He will never be angry with. This would be clear when we look at the end of the verse which gives the early Muslims of Mecca and the Medinite the good tidings that they will have gardens under which rivers flow, wherein they will dwell forever.

But this verse and the verse of allegiance under the tree of Hudaibiyah did not include men such as Mu'awiyah and Amr Ibn Al-Auss because they were neither from the early Muslims nor from the early migrants from Mecca to Medina; nor were they from the people of the allegiance under the tree of Hudaibiyah. Amr Ibn Al-Auss adopted Islam after Hudaibiyah and Mu'awiya adopted Islam after the conquest of Mecca.

Furthermore, we cannot find in the Qur'an any verse that declares that whomever God has been pleased with, God will not be angry with. It is inconceivable that Allah will give a permanent immunity against punishment to a person who did a good deed, such as being of the early Muslims or early migrants from Mecca to Medina, and that Allah will forgive his shedding the blood of thousands of believers without any justification. If it were so, it would mean that a companion could cancel all the Qur'anic rules and the instructions of the Prophet. Certainly, we can not believe this when we remember that Allah said to His own Messenger Muhammad: *"Say: surely I fear (if I disobey my Lord) the chastisement of a grievous day."* (6:15)

If a companion can interpret the Qur'anic verses and the Prophet's words the way he wants, he may be able to give a verdict that the five daily prayers are only desirable and not imperative. He may say "I understand from *Aqīmu 's-Salāt* (offer prayer) that the prayer is only desirable. Nor do I understand from the word *salāt* that it has to contain bowing and prostrating, or reading from the Qur'an or the declaration of the *Shahādah*. It would be sufficient in the prayer to supplicate the Lord to forgive or to give sustenance or to prolong life because the word *Salāt* used to mean supplication before Islam.

DEVIATION OF MANY OF COMPANIONS

The Messenger informed the Muslims that many of his companions will deviate after him. Al-Bukhārī in his *Sahīh*, part 2, page 149, reported that the Prophet said: "A number of my companions will come to drink from the basin. When I recognize them, they will be taken away from my sight. I would say: 'My Lord, these are my companions.' And Allah will say: 'You do not know what they innovated after you.' "

The same source, page 150 recorded that Abū Hāzim reported that Sahl Ibn Sa'd reported that the Prophet said: "I shall come to the Houdh (basin of water) before you. Whoever meets me there will drink water. And whoever drinks of it will never be thirsty afterwards, Groups will come to me, and I will recognize them and they will recognize me and they will be screened from me." Abū Hāzim said: "Al-Nu'mān Ibn Ayyash heard me and said: 'I testify that Abū-Sa'īd Al-Khidrī said and I heard him adding to it the following: I will say: 'May God put away from me whoever deviated after me.'" Similar to this is reported by Muslim in his *Sahīh*, part 15, pages 53-54. Al-Bukhārī reported in the section of Al-Houdh that Abū Huraira reported that the Messenger of God said: "On the Day of Judgment a group of my companions will come to the Houdh (Basin), and they will be prevented from drinking out of the basin. I will say: 'My Lord, these are my companions.' He will say: 'certainly you do not know what they innovated after you. They deserted their religion.'"

Al-Bukhārī reported in his *Sahīh*, part 4, page 169, that one reporter quoted Ibn Abbās as saying that the Prophet said: "You will be resurrected bare footed, unclothed, and uncircumcised." Then he read: "As We started the first creation, We shall resurrect it, a promise on our part. Certainly We shall fulfill it. Certainly a number of my companions will be taken to the left side, and I will say: 'My companions, my companions.' Allah will say: 'They continued deserting their faith after you left them.' I will say as the good servant of God (the Messiah) said: 'And I was a witness on them as long as I was with them.....'"

Muslim in his *Sahih*, part 10, page 59, reported that the Messenger of God said: "I will be the first one to come to the Basin, and I shall be challenged about some people and I will lose them, then I will say: 'My Lord, these are my companions; these are my companions.' I will be told: 'You do not know what they innovated after you.'"

Muslim in his *Sahih*, part 10, page 64, recorded that Anas Ibn Mālik reported that the Prophet said: "Men from among the people who accompanied me shall come (on the Day of Judgment) to the Basin. When I see them and they are brought to me, they will be taken away from me. I will say: 'My Lord, these are my companions.' It will be said to me, 'you do not know what they innovated after you.'"

Chapter: 29

THE INCIDENCE OF PAPER AND PEN

By

Dr. S. Manzoor Rizvi

The Prophet took his last breath on a Monday. Four days before his death on Thursday an incident happened that changed the history of Islam.

The Prophet was sick and lying in his bed and was surrounded by his companions including Umar ibn Khattāb. According to the historians, Imām Ali was not present. The Prophet asked his companions to give him a pen and a paper so that he would write something, presumably for the umma that it would not go astray. A slight commotion followed among the companions as some were inclined to give what the Prophet wanted and others did not. Umar ibn Khattāb said at this juncture that the Prophet was delirious and they did not want any written note as the Qur'an was sufficient for them to guide. The Prophet was annoyed and asked them to leave him alone

The narrators of the incidence are Abdullāh ibn Abbās (who was 14 or 15 years old) and Umar ibne Khattāb. This happening has been reported at different places in *Sahīh Bukhārī, Sahīh Muslim* and *Kanzul-Ummāl*.

DISCUSSION

This unhappy incidence had a far reaching impact on the history of Islam. Following issues are worthy of consideration:

1. The incidence is reported by all books written by Ahle Sunna. It is also confirmed that Umar Ibn Khattāb made those remarks.
2. It is said that by not giving a chance to the Prophet to write some thing a great opportunity was lost for achieving the unity of the umma.
3. The incident helped in nurturing a mentality in what they preach and what they do in action. It is easier to say that the

Qur'an is sufficient for us but hard to follow what Qur'an is asking to follow. The Qur'an clearly says that take what the Prophet gives you and stays away what he asks you to shun.

4. The Qur'an became subjected to personal interpretation by taking what one likes and leaving what one does not like.

5. It is beyond doubt that the Prophet wanted to write something which Umar ibne Khattāb did not like and acted against the wishes of the Prophet. From Shi'as perspective the Prophet wanted to write about his successor and reiterate the appointment of Imām Ali as the Caliph. When the Prophet was in his death-bed the most important matter he must be desirous to write as his last will for the benefit of umma could not be less important than any other issue except the Caliphate. By denying him the opportunity the issue of caliphate was made a matter of dispute for all times to come.

6. The seekers of the Right Path believe that the Prophet must be wanting to pen down the caliphate of Imām Ali so that no one could defy him in future.

7. It is a shame that the Prophet was denied the opportunity of expressing his last will by his close friends.

8. The disunity and chaos in the Muslim fold could be attributed directly to this incidence.

Chapter: 30

SAQĪFAH: HISTORICAL AND RELIGIOUS PERSPECTIVES

By

Dr. S. Manzoor Rizvi[1]

The Saqīfah of the Banī Sa'ādah, a meeting place near Madina witnessed the first gathering of the Ansār and the original Madinite immediately after the Prophet died to choose his successor. The meeting turned out to be the saddest happening in the Islamic history which derailed the development of Islam in a direction not originally intended. The Prophet had settled the issue of his succession before he left this world. The Saqīfah meeting challenged the very basic tenants of the prophethood, the status of the member of his progeny and the future course of the Islamic polity of governess. We discuss here the Saqīfah meeting from the religious perspective and what transpired at the meeting.

RELIGIOUS PERSPECTIVE

The Muslims maintain that without any doubt and in all certainty the Prophet of Islam is without sin and/or error. If it were otherwise, they say Allah could not have commanded unconditional obedience to him (the Prophet). So his command is Allah's command and it is an absolute necessity to obey him.

What is more, we can see on the basis of the Āyāt quoted below, that the Prophet had the right of jurisdiction over every one's idea or opinion, and that his command on social and other matters had to be carried out. The Qur'an says:

"The Prophet has a bigger claim on the believers than they have themselves."(33:6)

"It is not for any believer, man or woman, when Allah and His Messenger have decreed a matter, to have a choice in the matter."(33:36)

---

[1] Excerpted from the book, *Roots of Religion* (Chapter 27: *A Brief History of Saqīfah*), No Author, Noor-e-Islam Imambara, Faizabad: India, 1986.

An examination of these Āyāt and their explanation make it clear that the decree of the Prophet in every matter, even in personal matters, is binding, since the Āyāt were revealed concerning an individual matter, viz. the marriage of Zayd and Zainab. Zainab was the daughter of the Prophet's uncle, and Zayd was a slave whom the Prophet freed. The Prophet of Islam, so as to break the pre-Islamic custom whereby the noble and rich were not prepared to marry outside their own, ordered Zainab to marry Zayd. The false pride and inappropriate arrogance which had been inherited from pre-Islamic times forebode her to take Zayd as a husband.

But this Āyat which follows makes it clear that even in a personal matter the Prophet's command was to be obeyed, so Zainab married him and was content.[2]

"But no, by thy Lord! They will not believe till they make thee judge between them, then they shall find in themselves no impediment touching thy verdict, but shall surrender in full submission."(4:64)

IS THE PROPHET SUBJECT TO MAJORITY OPINION?

Some Sunnis claim that in social matters the opinion of the majority is over-ruling to the degree that the Prophet himself must obey. A deeper look at the Āyāt mentioned above makes it clear that this is invalid. Now we shall proceed in an investigation of their evidence and claims and then answer them. The evidence is Āyat 159 of Surah al-Imrān:

"It was by some mercy of Allah that thou was gentle to them; hadst thou been harsh and hard of heart, they would have scattered from among thee. So pardon them, and pray forgiveness for them, and take counsel with them in the affairs; and when thou art resolved but thy trust in Allah, surely Allah loves those who put their trust." (3:159)

This Āyat clearly explains that the Prophet is not subject to the opinion of the majority. In other words, the right of jurisdiction belongs to the Prophet even in social matters, and he has a duty, after consultation, to put his view into practice, not the opinion of others, since it says: *"Take counsel with them in affairs, and when thou art resolved, put thy trust in Allah."*

---

2 *Tafsīr Nūr ath-Thaqalayn*; vol. 4, p. 280.

If it had been otherwise, and the views of others were to be acted upon, it should have said: *"When the opinion of people has been obtained on a matter, accept it and carry it out."* But we see that the Āyat was not revealed in this sense. What is more, there is evidence in history against the view of the Sunnis: for instance, in the peace of Hudaibiyah.

The Prophet of Islam left Medina to visit the Ka'bah. Near Mecca, the representative of unbelievers of the Quraysh met with him and said that the Quraysh were not prepared to admit him into Mecca. He replied that he had not come for war but only to visit Ka'bah.

After much discussion, the Quraysh were prepared to make a treaty, and the Prophet, with some special conditions, agreed, although the Muslims were not happy with the agreement and wanted to enter Mecca that day.[3] The Prophet then told the Muslims; "I am the slave of Allah and His Prophet will never turn away from the command of the Allah, nor will He let me go."[4] Here, an honest reasonable question would be as follows: What then is the meaning of the Prophet consulting with people at all?

His consultations were part of a policy both of respecting and showing the value of the views of the people, and of using reason and thought in the way of progress of Islam. Also, when faced with some obstructions by some of the tribal leaders, consultations were held with them because by the value which they gave to consultation and by the fact that they saw themselves sharing in the work they desisted from their destructiveness. However, in this kind of counsel meeting the Prophet never subjected himself to the majority opinion and if he paid attention to the opinion of some person or group, it was in fact because that was also his opinion.

CONSULTATION AFTER PROPHET'S DEATH

We have seen and understood that it has been proved that the opinion of the Prophet was above the view of every one, even the view of the majority, and that it was the view of the Prophet, as was

---

[3] *Sīrah*; Ibn Hishām, vol. 3, p.321
[4] *Tārīkh of Tabarī*, vol. 3, p. 1546

Allah's command that he selected Imām Ali to be his successor on the day of Ghadeer and informed the people of his decision.

So, consultations aimed at appointing a successor after the Prophet's death are clearly against the wishes of Allah and his Prophet and are completely useless; however, abandoning this reality, we now want to ask whether after the Prophet's death consultative meetings were held, and if so, whether the majority opinion was upheld? To answer and explain the aforementioned question, we shall take a look first of all at some history and the circumstances of the Saqīfah of Banī Sa'ādah according to reliable historical documents.

WHAT HAPPENED AT SAQĪFAH

When the Prophet closed his eyes to the world, the Ansārs, the people who originally belonged to Medina, gathered in a building called the Saqīfah of the Banī Sa'ādah and pronounced that after the Prophet, government and wilāyat belonged to Sa'd ibn Ubadah. Sa'd was ill but was present in the meeting. He addressed the meeting and said: "O Ansār! There is no other group better than you in Islam. For the Prophet was thirteen years among the Quraysh, and he called them to abandon idols and their worship for one God; but, apart from a few individuals, they did not believe in him and did not let the religion grow. So Allah restored you to happiness; put him and his religion in your hands, entrusted support for him and his religion to you. You have always been loyal to this agreement, till He chose to take him away. Now you should make every effort, for it is your special right."

The Ansār said that he had spoken well, and that he should take the government and succession into his own hands. But some said: "What if the Quraysh want to dispute the matter with us?" "We shall tell them," said another group, "that they should choose a leader from themselves, and we shall choose a leader from among us." "This would be the first blow to break Islam," said Sa'd.

Umar was informed and he sent for Abū Bakr, who was out of Medina. Umar sent another message, in which he was informed that his presence was indispensable. When Abū Bakr came Umar said to him: "Do you not know that the Ansārs are gathered in the Saqīfah to choose Sa'd for the Caliphate?" So both of them hurried to the place. On the way they met Abū Ubaydah al-Jarrah, whom they took along with them. When they reached the Saqīfah, Abū Bakr rose up to address the crowd:

"Praise be to Allah, and blessings on his Prophet. Allah sent the Prophet to mankind so that they who worshipped many gods might worship One God. It was difficult for the Arabs to leave the religion of their fathers. Then Allah showed His preference for the Muhājirīn (those Muslims from Mecca who migrated with the Prophet), and brought them faith. They bore the difficulties with this great man with forbearance, so they are more deserved: after him in this matter. You, O Ansār!, say that after you no one is to be more preferred in the religion, so after the Muhājir no one has a higher degree than you--so we are the rulers, and you are the ministers and the counselors. We will not do any thing without consulting you."

Habāb ibn Mundhir stood up and said: "O Ansār! Beware! Take the reins of government in your hands; for the people are under your protection, no one can quarrel with you. Do not fall in the trap, so that what you have done is not ruined. If these people do not accept our authority, then we must have our own ruler, and they theirs."

"That can never be," said Umar. "The Arabs would never submit to your rule; they will not yield, for the Prophet was not from you."

Habīb stood up again and said: "O Ansār! You must decide! Do not listen to this man and his hollow talk. He wants to do away completely with your right. If they do not give up, you must throw them out of this town and take things over. I swear by Allah, you are more deserving."

"May Allah kill you!" said Umar.

"May He kill you!" said Habāb.

Abū Ubaydah stood up to come between them. "O Ansār!" he cried, "you were the first group of believers who believed and gave support, so you must not be the first to go astray."

Then Bashīr ibn Sa'd got up and said, "O Ansār! I swear by Allah that if we were the first in the jihad against the polytheists, and had priority in the religion, it was only because we wanted nothing but the will of Allah."

"Now!" cried Abū Bakr, "Do you wish to swear allegiance to both this Umar and this Abū Ubaydah al-Jarrah?"

"No!" some shouted. "We swear by Allah that you are the most deserving of the Muhājirīn, and we are not at par with you; so give your hands that we can swear allegiance to you."

Then, Umar and Abū Ubaydah *swore* allegiance to Abū Bakr. Bashīr ibn Sa'd, from the Ansār and the tribe of Aws, the great Medina tribe, followed them and swore allegiance.

When the people of the tribe of Aws saw Bashīr open the way and acknowledge the Quraysh to be more deserving than them, and the Khazraj, the other great tribe, wanted Sa'd ibn Ubadah as their leader, they spoke among themselves. "By Allah, if the Khazraj take the reins of power in their hands, they will always have preference. Let us rise up and swear allegiance to Abū Bakr."

Then Umar seized Sa'd ibn Ubadah by the collar and said to the people: "Kill him!"

Now You Judge

With the evidence that we shall present to you now, it will be seen that the story of Saqīfah was not only a consultation among some of the Muslims, but it was a plot to usurp the right to the Caliphate of Imām Ali and to put someone else in his place.

First, while on his way to Saqīfah, Umar sent word only to Abū Bakr and not to any one else. Abū Bakr was outside Medina, although he should have been in the house of the Prophet with the great ones among the companions of the Prophet and with Imām Ali. Umar did not tell anyone and leaving the corpse of that great man hurried to Saqīfah. If, truly, a plan had not been arranged, why did Abū Bakr not tell Umar that he had to tell the Banī Hāshim and the helpers of the Prophet that they should wait until the body of the Prophet was buried, and that afterwards they should proceed all together to decide about the successor to the Caliphate? Is consultation—*shūrā'*—like this? That three people should come from one of the tribes of the town, and, with the opinion of these people being controlled by one man, by his sweet words and by his threats and other means, deceive them and create differences between them, then by force and threat of killing enforce his point of view? [5] In consultation over such a great matter, should not at least the great companions and the Banī Hāshim be present?

Second, Saqīfah became like a football field; involuntarily bringing shouts and cheers from the people. After sweet words and self-advertisement, Abū Bakr said to the Ansār: "Swear allegiance to whomever you want --Umar or Abū Ubadah." There was no place for questions. One of these two must be the Caliph. The Caliphate became like a football which they then passed to Abū Bakr and said, as long as you have it, what more do you want? And the Sunnis call this childish ball game--the meeting and consultation of the people.

Third, Umar made clear that no consultation had taken place. Some years after the proceedings of Saqīfah, Umar said, at the time of his own Caliphate: "We have heard that one of you said that if Umar dies I shall swear allegiance to so-and-so. Someone said to him that the allegiance to Abū Bakr was without consultation and without reckoning. It is true that allegiance to Abū Bakr took place all at once without much thought or reckoning, but Allah protected us from mischief. However no one should give you the example of Abū Bakr to follow."[6] If there really had been a question of a consultation, and the great ones of the companions of the Prophet could have voted in freedom, allegiance to Abū Bakr would not have been "all at once without much thought or reckoning." It would not in this way have become famous; there would have been no mischief or danger in it.

Fourth, Umar said: "After the Prophet, Ali and Zubayr and their companions rose up against us, and assembled in Fatima az-

---

[5] Of course, there were many who did not swear allegiance to Abū Bakr: the Banī Hāshim, Abbās and his sons, Habāb ibn Mundhir, Salmān al-Farisī Abū Dharr, Miqdād, Ammār, Zubayr, etc. For reference see *Fusūl al-Muhimmah*, vol. 4 p. 1837.

[6] Tabarī, vol. 4, p. 1820-23.

Zehrā's house."[7] We ask whether this clear opposition can be ignored, especially as it is acknowledged by Umar.

Fifth, if the matter of the caliphate must be resolved on the basis of consultation, the Prophet would have certainly before death explained, or at least indicated the way it should be done. By the criterion of reason, would the Prophet explain only some very abstruse commands, but make no mention of such a great matter as this? The Prophet, during his lifetime, explained and carried out the minutest details of Islamic beliefs and actions. He never mentioned, according to any book that umma should decide their leader after his death. On the contrary, Imām Ali's successorship to the Prophet had been declared on several occasions. This is the reason why Shi'a does not believe in these Caliphates.

---

[7] Ibid.

Chapter: 31

FADAK

By

Dr. S. Manzoor Rizvi

One of the great tragedies happened during the first caliphate of Abū-Bakr, a few months after the death of the Prophet, was the confiscation of the land property of Fadak from the Prophet's daughter, Fātima az-Zehrā'.

Fadak was a fertile land near Khayber. After the conquest of Khayber the Prophet sent his emissary, Mrehissa ibne-Masūd to invite the people of Fadak to the fold of Islam. The people of Fadak, according to the prevalent custom offered part of the property to the Prophet and requested to be left alone. The Prophet accepted the offer.

According to the Qur'an when the Muslim army goes to Jihād (with all the principles of not attacking to grab land) and wins the war then whatever it gets out of the war with the enemy is divided among the warriors. In case the enemy surrenders without fighting and offers some land then the property belongs to the Prophet and the Allah. (Surah Hashr)

Since Fadak was given without a fight it was the property of the Prophet and the Allah. Then the Qur'anic verse came: *"And give to the near of kins his/her dues."*(17:26) The Prophet called her daughter, Fātima az-Zehrā' and gave Fadak to her and transferred the ownership in her name. It remained under her possession (from 7th Hijra year onward). When Abū-Bakr became Caliph he confiscated the property although the property had been used for meeting the needs of the poor of Hāshimite clan and not for the personal needs of Fātima az-Zehrā.'

Fātima az-Zehrā' asked for its return in the court of the Caliph. She was asked to produce witness to prove her ownership. She presented Umme-Aiman and Rabah (Prophet's slave) as the witnesses and these were rejected as the Caliph asked for presenting two men or two women and one man as witnesses. Imām Ali came forward as a witness but he was not accepted as witness as he was the husband. The witnesses of Imām Hasan and Imām Husayn were also turned down as they were minors. The land became the state property. Fātima az-Zehrā' was upset and she never talked to Abū Bakr after this incidence.

DISCUSSION

The Fadak incidence gave rise to a number of issues which made further dents in the differences between Shi'as and Sunnis. Some of these issues are listed below:

1. The Caliph quoted a hadīth during the hearing of the case in which the Prophet was claimed to have said that prophets neither inherited any thing nor left any thing for their families and what they left was for the poor. Fātima az-Zehrā' quoted examples from the Qur'an that inheritance is the Islamic law. She quoted the Qur'anic Āyāt in support of the fact that many prophets inherited and left inheritance for their children. The Caliph kept on repeating the hadīth against all her arguments. We all know that the Qur'an is above all ahādīth and if there is any conflict between the two the Qur'an will take precedence. It is also surprising that just before the death of the Prophet, Umar said in front of all that the Qur'an was sufficient for them and now the Caliph of Islam was giving preference to the hadīth over the Qur'an. (See Chapter 29: *The Incidence of Paper and Pen.*) The hadīth quoted by the Caliph was nullified by the witness produced by Fātima az-Zehrā'. The witness, Umme-Aiman was a slave given to the Prophet by his father Abdullah ibne Abdul Muttalib. The Prophet himself inherited the slave girl from his father.

2. The hadīth described by Abū Bakr is worth rejecting as it is contrary to the Qur'anic verse and its narrator is only one person in the entire umma. It is stated in some works namely, *Sahīh Bukhārī, Bābul Khums,* and *Bābul Maghāzī* that the Caliph himself negated his own argument by saying that the Allah commanded the Prophet to give his or her due and being his (Prophet's) successor Abū-Bakr took over the control of Fadak

3. Fadak incidence has been mentioned in all the major Sunni books including *Sahīh Muslim* and *Bukhārī*. Some books

for example *Insānul Ghayūr, Fī Sīrat ul Amīn Al-Mamūn*, (page 403), and *Sīrah al-Halabiyya* (vol.3, p.391) by Ali ibn Burhānuddīn mentioned that Abū-Bakr did write down on a paper giving the ownership to Fātima az-Zehrā' but before the paper could be passed over to her Umar grabbed it and torn it apart.

4. It is a strange fact of the history that the Christian accepted the witness of Imām Ali, Fātima az-Zehrā', and the two Imāms, Hasan and Husayn at the time of *Mubāhilla* and the Muslim Caliph did not accept their witness.

5. Hearing of Fadak case is the stigma on the face of the justice as the Caliph Abū Bakr was representing the State as a claimant, he was the prosecutor, he was the judge supposed to dispense justice, and he was the head of the State issuing order, all in one. How Fātima az-Zehrā' could under such circumstances, expect fair hearing and justice.

6. If Fadak was declared as the property of the State meant for the welfare of the general public why it was transferred by the third Caliph, Usman to Marwān. During the Caliphate of the fourth Caliph, Imām Ali did not take any action for its return as it was under the control of Marwān. It was Mamūn ar-Rashīd who returned the property to the family but Muttawakkil took it back and later wrote to the Governer in Medina, Qasam bin Ja'far to return Fadak back to the Prophet's family. The order was rescinded by Muttawakkil. Umar ibn Abdul Azīz also issued decree to return Fadak to the family of the Prophet. It can be seen that Fadak became controversial issue and several caliphs took different actions at different times which resulted in further widening the gulf between Shi'as and Sunnis. It became a source of torturing and marginalizing the family of the Prophet.

7. After the case of Fadak had been decided Abū Bakr and Umar visited Fātima az-Zehrā' not to apologize but to find out if she was angry with them. Fātima az-Zehrā' asked them whether they remembered the hadīth of the Prophet that whoever made Fātima az-Zehrā' angry made the Prophet angry and whoever made the Prophet angry made the Allah angry.

When they agreed to the authenticity of the hadīth she replied that she was angry and totally disappointed with them.

ADDITIONAL THOUGHTS

The two critical incidents, 'Paper and Pen' (see Chapter 29) and 'Fadak' are very significant and poignant moments in the history of Islam that literally and severely altered the very focus of Islam.

The incident of the 'Paper and Pen' clearly shows that a group of self-centered Muslims were ready to marginalize even the Prophet himself behind a veil of the 'Qur'an being sufficient.' This diversion was purposely designed so that the road would be clear for them to interpret the Qur'an to their own liking and to cover all their tracks as needed. This unfortunately shows the thinking and goals of some of the so-called elites of early Islam.

The incident of Fadak shows how the line of action would be drawn for the future so-called Islamic kingdoms and caliphates. In other words, their rule would be based on the principle of injustice, trampling of basic freedoms, marginalizing the rights of the people and false accusation. In the case of Fadak, Fatima Az-Zehra had the rightful ownership of the land, which was given to her by her father. It was forcibly and illegally confiscated by the Government as state property. This was an open and direct violation of personal rights, and a complete disregard of the legal system as laid out by Islam. Fatima Az-Zehra then took her case to court and requested for her inheritance as dictated by Islam and yet was denied under the pretext of a visibly forged hadith. She was also denied of the Khums which was also her right as a daughter of the Prophet.

These actions were a total and deliberate disregard of the justice system that Islam requires of any person especially for any Islamic State. The last Prophet set forth certain principles and always followed a clear rule of ethics and morality when it came to the rights and freedom of individuals and citizens. However, after his death, all these golden rules for the betterment of society and its inhabitants, were viciously trampled and discarded. Instead a new rule took place for the Islamic rule which is 'might is right.' Sadly, this continues till today as rights after rights for all are violated day after day.

PART FIVE: MUHARRAM MOURNING

Chapter: 32

MOURNING FOR THE MARTYRS OF KARBALĀ'

By

Allama Sayyid Saeed Akhtar Rizvi

On Ashore day (5th December, 1965) an article of mine was published in the *Standard*, Darussalam, Tanzania on the Tragedy of Karbalā'. A. Robley of Arusha (a Qadiani) in a letter to the editor protested that mourning for the dead was against the teaching of Islam. I sent a short reply and invited him to seek enlightenment by private correspondence. When he wrote a letter to me, I advised him to see Hājī Ali Mohammad Jaffar Sheriff (Arusha) for detailed reply. After being shown the references etc. on this subject, he asked Hājī Ali that the references should be given to him in writing. Hence the following letter, to which no reply was ever received is published now because it answers many question often put before us.

TEXT OF LETTER

Please refer to your conversation with Hājī about mourning for the martyrs of Karbalā' and your request that it should be recorded in writing.

First of all, let me emphasize that your whole approach to this issue is wrong. You are laboring under the presumption that everything to be lawful should be expressly allowed in Sharī'ah, while the dictum accepted in all the sects of Islam is that everything is lawful unless it is expressly forbidden. We can not declare an act unlawful just on the ground that it was invented after the Prophet. Otherwise we shall have to burn all books of traditions, commentaries of Qur'an, Fiqh of Imāms Abu Hanifa, Shāfi'ī, Mālik, and lbn Hanbal. Not only this, but we should have to think whether it is not harām to have the Qur'an in our houses which has been divided in thirty parts and its alphabets marked by dots, and pronunciations made clear by adding fat'ha, kasra, and Dharnma etc. Again, we shall have to ponder whether it was lawful for the First Caliph and Third Caliph to unify the different qirā'āt of Qur'an which were prevalent among the companions of the prophet

Then we note that the Prophet never used paper notes in place of coins. Is it not haram to use currency notes for charity, building mosques and other good deeds? It is alleged, though we say it is wrong, that the Prophet did not appoint anybody as his successor, and it is known that he never entrusted this duty to anybody else. What will be the legal status of those Caliphs who were elected by people to carry on the work of Prophet after the death of the Prophet?

I may here quote the universally accepted traditions of the Prophet that "Everything is allowed until it is forbidden," and, "all things are allowed so long as you do not get any law for or against it." These traditions are accepted by Sunnis and Shi'as alike. But, of course, you are neither Sunni nor Shi'a; and you are not bound to accept anything recorded in their books. But, then, you have no right to interfere in the internal matters of these Muslim sects.

Sheikhul Islam, Allama ibn Hajar Asqalani, in his *Sharh Sahīh Bukhārī (Bābul Iqtadae-hi-Sunanirrasul)* says: "Almost all Muslims divide Bid'at in five kinds; (1) Wājib Bid'at, *viz*, arranging Qur'an and preparing of Ilmul-Kalām against atheists and wrong religions and sects; (2) Sunna Bid'at, e.g. writing books of religion, establishing *Madāris* (schools) and *Musāfirkhānas* (rest houses); (3) Mubah Bid'at, e.g. different kinds of dishes of food; (4) Makrūh Bid'at, e.g. using good clothes and food so long as it does not reach the boundary of *Isrāf* (extravagance) ; and (5) Harām Bid'at, e.g. revolt against Imām and everything which is against the Sharī'ah and about which there is established proof of its being harām."

Imām Shāfi'ī also has said, which has been recorded by Allama Asqalani in the same book *Sharhe Sahīh Bukhārī*, that 'Bid'at is of two kinds: (a) Mamdūh (praiseworthy), and (b) Mudhmūm (condemned); what is in accordance with Sunna is Mamdūh and whatever is against Sunna is Madhmūm."

You see that it is not enough to say that such and such thing was not in the days of the Prophet and then declare that it is unlawful, because there are some innovations which are Wājib, Sunnat, Mubah, Makrūh and all these are lawful and halāl.

And, of course, there are some harām Bid'ats and we have to guard against every Bid'at of this type. One example of such Bid'at may be found in the traditions: "Whosoever innovates something and calls others to it or establishes a religion, certainly he ⁻goes out of Islam." I wonder what will be your reaction to this tradition and for such a Bid'at, because you have chosen to follow a religion which was invented 1,300 years after the Prophet of Islam!

Still it is not my intention to leave you in darkness, and, therefore want to make it clear that actually mourning for martyrs is not 'Bid'at (innovation} at all. Every history of Islam records that when the Prophet came to the corpse of his uncle, Hamza, he cried loudly and fainted. When recovered from the faint, he again began crying and calling "Hamza, Hamza; O! Uncle of the Prophet of God; O! Defender of the Prophet; Hamza, Lion of Allah and the Prophet". It is called Nauha in Arab language. Not only this, but when the Prophet came back to Medina, he heard crying voices from every house of Medina for their martyrs. The Prophet did not forbid it. On the contrary, he sadly said, "But there are no women to weep for Hamza." People of Medina hurried back to their houses and asked their womenfolk to go to the house of Hamza and weep and cry for him. When the Prophet heard their crying voices and was told that they were weeping for Hamza, the Prophet was so happy that he said, "May Allah be pleased with you, with your children, and with the children of your children." Wāqidī, in his history, records that after this incident, it became an established practice in Medina that whenever there was death, the women cried first for Hamza and then for their dead relative.

I think you will now be satisfied that the practice of mourning for martyrs was established by the Prophet himself, and the practice for mourning over Hamza was started in 3rd year of Hijra and the Prophet died in 11 A.H. and there is no record that he ever expressed his dislike against this practice. This is the answer to your query about mourning year after year.

So far as the particular case of Imām Husayn is concerned, I would like to quote some traditions and Āyāt to enlighten you:-

1. God says in Qur'an about Pharaoh and his army: *"Neither the sky nor the earth wept for them nor they were not given chance."*

Imām Muslim records in *Tafsīr* of this Āyat (Ad-Dukhān), "When Husayn was martyred, the sky as well as the earth wept on him and weeping of the sky its being red." (*Sahīh Muslim*)

2. Some fifty years before the event of Karbalā', the Prophet wept when he was told by the Angel that Husayn would be killed by the army of Yazīd in Karbalā. Then Gabriel asked, "O! Prophet of God, do you want me to give you some earth from his place of martyrdom?" The Prophet said, "Yes." Gabriel gave a handful of earth of Karbalā' and the Prophet began weeping uncontrollably. This tradition is recorded in *Mishkāt, Musnad* Ahmed bin Hanbal, *As-Sawā'iqul-Muhuhriqa* of Allame Ibn Hajar Makkī and *Sirrul Alamin* of Imām Ghazālī; and has been narrated by Imām Sha'abi, Imām Baihaqi, Imām Hakim and scores of other traditionalists. The Prophet gave that earth to his wife, Ummul Mu'minīn, Umme Salma, and told her, "When you see this earth turned into blood, know that Husayn has been martyred."

3. On the 10th Muharram, 61 A.H., Umme Salma was asleep in the afternoon when she saw the Prophet in her dream: He stood in tragic condition and his hair was dusty and disarranged and in his hand was a bottle full of blood. Umme Salma asked what it was. The Prophet said, "This is the blood of Husayn and his companions. I was collecting it since this morning." Umme Selma woke up and ran towards the bottle which contained the earth of Karbalā' and saw red blood flowing from it. Then she cried and called her relatives and started mourning for Husayn. This tradition is in *Musnad* of Imām Ahmed bin Hanbal, *As-Sawā'iqul-Muhriqa, Mishkātul Masābīh, Tirmidhī* and other books.

4. Sheikh Abdul Qādir Jilānī writes in his book *Ghunyatut-Talibīn,* (vol. II, page 62); "70,000 angels came on the grave of Husayn bin Ali after his martyrdom and they are weeping on him and will remain weeping up to the Day of Judgment."

5. *Matam (Beating of chests and Face):* It is recorded in *Madārij-un-Nubuwwat* (vol. II, page 163) that when Shaitan announced a lie that the Prophet was killed (in the Battle of Uhud), the Hāshimite women, including the Lady of Paradise--Fatima az-Zehrā--came out weeping, beating their chests and faces. The same book also records that after the death of the

Prophet, some of the companions wept and cried so much that they lost their eyesight. This is also recorded in *Kitāb Mathabata-Bis-Sunnah* (Page 119).

6. When the Second Caliph was informed of the death of Ibne Muqrim, he put his hand to his head and cried. (*Iqdul-Farīd*, vol. II, page 4).

7. When Imām Zain-al-Abidīn came back from Damascus, and people of Medina were informed that the family of the Prophet was outside Medina, the Medinites rushed to meet them and they were beating their heads, chests and faces. It should be mentioned that the practice of Medinites is one of basic laws in some sects of Ahle-Sunna.

Actually, the notion that mourning for Husayn and his companions or weeping, crying, beating of chests, etc. is unlawful, and is based on misinformation. People are misled by a tradition of Abdullah bin Umar, in which he alleges that the Prophet said that "dead man is punished if people weep for him." But wherever this tradition is recorded its correction and tradition by Ayeshah is also recorded. When she was told of this alleged reporting of Abdullah bin Umar, she said that "May God forgive him, he did not tell wrong (intentionally) but he has forgotten or is mistaken. The fact is that the Prophet passed by a corpse of a Jew and people were crying for her. The Prophet said that they are weeping over her while she is being punished."

You see the difference. The Prophet did not say that dead man is punished because of the action of weeping of people, and he could not have said it because the Qur'an says, "Nobody will carry weight of others," and it would be a gross injustice to punish the dead man for the action of the living relatives. What the Prophet meant was that a kāfir can not gain anything through the weeping of his relatives. Unfortunately, misunderstanding of Abdullāh bin Umar gave a chance to mischief-mongers to make a stand against the family of the Prophet, and against the natural human feelings.

What makes me wonder is the fact that they do not pay any heed to the correction by Ayeshah which is recorded side by side in every book of tradition. Does it not show that these people raise objection against the mourning of Imām Husayn, do not want to seek the truth. They just want to further their own interest at the cost of Islamic truth. Of course, there may be some excesses in some places in the customs of mourning but it does not justify an all-out attack upon the principles of Islamic mourning.

These are only a few of the traditions of the Prophet regarding propriety of mourning for Imām Husayn. As you have asked to know custom and rulings of our Imāms, I would like to quote here a few of the traditions of our Imāms. Even now it is not necessary to quote from our own books because so many Sunni scholars believe in this cause and they have given those narrations in their own books.

1. Mulla Ali Qari writes in his book *Sharhul Mishkāt*, (vol. v, page 604) that Imām Hasan (our second Imām and fifth Caliph of Sunnis) said, "Whosoever sheds one drop of tear from his eyes concerning us, Allah Ta'ala will give him Jannat." Same tradition is recorded in *Yanābī'ul Mawaddah* (page 153).

2. Majālis (gatherings to hear about events of Karbalā') were established just after Karbalā' by our fourth Imām, Ali Ibn Husain Zain-al-Abidīn and was developed by our Sixth Imām Ja'far Sādiq and our eighth Imām, Ali bin Mūsa Rezā.

Chapter: 33

COMMEMORATING MUHARRAM

By

Dr. S. Manzoor Rizvi[1]

RECOLLECTION OF GRIEF IS HUMAN NATURE

It is human nature that whenever hardship ends, recollecting those bad times reignites that pain and suffering. People often recollect their suffering in front of relatives and friends. It is on account of this natural instinct that people commemorate the important days of their ancestors or of religious leaders. Such days are observed internationally e.g. the 1st May, is observed to remember the oppressed workers of Chicago. Some anniversaries are only celebrated by friends and relatives, while days are celebrated by nations (such as Independence Day) and some days are commemorated internationally such as Remembrance days, for instance, to remember the victims of war.

To remember martyrs is not only the Sunna of the Prophet but also the practice of Sahāba. "It is narrated by Abū Hurariah that the Prophet used to visit the graves of martyrs every year. When he would reach the entrance of the mountain, he would say (to the martyrs), "*Asalamo Alaykum Bima Sabartum,*" which means 'Peace be on you due to your patience (and you have reached a pleasant place due to this).' Then after the Prophet, Abū Bakr also used to come (every year), and after him Umar used to do the same and then Usmān also did the same."[2] After this narration the word "every year" is recorded in the narrations of Wāqidī.

The Shi'as accordingly commemorate the memory of martyrs of Karbalā' every year. The Prophet and his companions used to visit the graves of Uhud's martyrs every year. Similarly, Shi'as visit the tomb of Imām Husayn every year during Muharram.

---

[1] Excerpted from the title *Shiaism Explained* (various chapters), Peermahomed Ebrahim Trust, Karachi: Pakistan, 1972

[2] *Al Bidāyah wa al-Nihāya*, vol. 4, page 45, published in Beirut.

If one can not implement this practice by practically visiting Karbalā' every Muharram there is no ground to abandon it altogether; we seek to do as much as we can to remember our ill-treated Imām. So we commemorate the day with processions, conference, and mourn to show our love and faith, as all cannot visit the tomb every year.

TEN DAYS OF MUHARRAM

The Qur'an says: *"By the dawn and ten nights, and the even and the odd, and the night when it departeth."* (79:1-4) We read in *Tafsīr Durre Manthūr* (vol. 6, p. 346) under the commentary of this verse: "Abū Uthmān says that three periods of ten days are venerable which are referred to in this verse. They are, first ten days of the month of Muharram, first ten days of the month of Zilhaj and last ten days of the month of Ramadan."

We read in *Kanz al Ummāl*, (vol. 4, p. 320) that the day of Ashura is Allah's day, a day of torment for the Ahlul Bayt when the beloved grandson of the Prophet was starved and martyred, a day when horse trampled his arrow-pierced body. Why Shi'as mourn Imām Husayn every year?

We read in the Qur'an, *"We verily sent Musa with our revelations, saying: Bring thy people forth from darkness unto light. And remind them of the days of Allah. Lo! Therein are revelations for each steadfast, thankful (heart)."* (14: 5) What are days of Allah? We read in Tafseer al Kabeer, (vol. 5, p. 219) that Allah's days refer to the great events that happened in favor of Musa. This was a day when the Bani Israel were stuck with troubles and problems and were entrapped by Pharaoh's injustice.

INSTANCES OF GRIEF

We read in *Biadaya wa al Nihaya*, (vol. 6, p. 360) that Umar said: "Whenever I venture out at sunrise I remember the death of my brother Zaid bin Khattab." If the Shi'as commemorate the martyrdom of Imām Husayn every year why do these *Nasibi* raise objections? Look at the words of your master, Umar who remembered the death of his brother throughout his life.

We read in *wasā'il ash-Shi'a*, (p. 139) that Imām Muhammad Bāqir left a will that he should be remembered and his memories be recalled by holding special ceremonies (Nudaba) for ten years. If performing Nudaba had been harām, the Imām would not have left a will to that effect.

We read in *Tārīkh-e-Yāqūbī,* (vol. 1, page 3) that Prophet Adam and Eve wept for their son Hābīl for so long that their tears turned into a stream. In *Rawdah ash-Shuhadah,* (p. 30) the same incident has been quoted by Husayn Wa'az Kashifi who adds: "Tears from Adam's right eye were flowing like the River Dajela and like the river Euphrates from his left eye."

Nāsibīs say that mourning on the death of one's dear ones should be restricted to three days, but this reference prove that the Father of Mankind wept for such a long period that tears became streams. If Adam wept for his son in such a manner then Nāsibīs should know that Shi'as love Imām Husayn more than their children and they likewise continually shed tears for the suffering of the Imām.

THE YEAR OF GRIEF

The annals of *Sīrah* are unanimous that the Prophet named the year in which Khadīja and Abū Tālib died as *'Ām al Huzn* i.e., the year of grief. The Prophet named the whole year as *'Ām al Huzn,* just to commemorate the loss of his uncle and beloved wife. Is this act of the Prophet a Sunna or not? Shi'as mourn their Imām for ten days and the Prophet mourned for an entire year. Even after the passage of a year the Prophet never got over this grief, and this was known to Ayeshah who wanted him to abandon his remembrance of his departed wife. We read in *Sahih Bukhari* Hadith No. 5:166 this narration from Ayeshah: "I did not feel jealous of any wives of the Prophet as much as I did of Khadīja though I did not see her, but the Prophet used to mention her very often, and whenever he slaughtered a sheep, he would cut its parts and send them to the women friends of Khadīja. When I sometimes said to him, 'You treat Khadīja in such a way as if there is no woman on earth except Khadīja,' he would say, 'Khadīja was such-and-such, and from her I had children.'"

The testimony of Ahl as-Sunna's leading lady is clear evidence that the Prophet never got over the grief of his wife and it is obvious that the *Dhikr* of Khadīja would also have taken place in presence of receptive ears. The process of *Dhikr* between a speaker and listener is called a congregation (Majlis). Shi'as likewise commemorate the death of Khadīja and Abū Talib and the martyrdom of Imām Husayn.

If Muslims have no issue with celebrating nights such as Me'rāj of our Prophet then there is no reason to abandon the remembrance of calamities because both grief and happiness are important in life. Offering condolence is a *mustahab* act so why the opposition? Conducting any *mubāh* or *masnūn* act carries no timing restrictions. It can be performed any time depending upon the circumstances and situations.

AHL AS-SUNNA'S YEAR OF MOURNING

According to Allama Shiblī Numānī, Imām Al Harmain, whose actual name was Abdul Malik having Ziauddin as his title, was considered a supreme scholar of his era and many renowned Ulema including Imām Ghazālī were his students. Imām Ghazālī, while mentioning the mourning over his teacher's death, writes in his authoritative work *Gunjīna Hidayat,* (which is an Urdu translation of *Kāmil Sa'ādat*) on page 3: "The Imām of Harmain died in 478 Hijrī. At that time all the market stalls in Nishapūr were closed and the pulpit in the Jami Mosque was broken, his students that numbered almost 400 destroyed their books and poems and mourned him for a whole year." The episode can also found in a biography of Imām Ghazālī.[3]

These were the people, who had an historical enmity with writing materials, but we have no idea why the pulpit was destroyed. Did these esteemed students (who were themselves scholars) have no knowledge of the verse on patience that today's Nāsibīs quote against the Shi'as. Whilst they have no opinion here but the moment the Shi'as mourn Imām Husayn in Muharram all sorts of articles against mourning are published.

The students of the Imām of Haramain mourned his loss for an entire year. Are we going to say that not even one of these four hundred students were aware that such mourning contravened the Qur'an and Sunna (as some claim). The closure of shops,

---

[3] *Al Ghazālī,* page 12-13, authored by Allama Shiblī Numānī.

abandonment of patience, destructions of the pulpit and destroying writing materials are all understandable and acceptable acts of mourning when Sunni Imām dies, but when the Shi'as mourn Imām Husayn they have exceeded the limits of the *sharī'ah*!

Sūfī saint, Shah Hassan Miyān Phulwārī Hanafī Qādrī has commented on mourning for Imām Husayn during Muharram. This Sūfī saint wrote his observations in the Sunni text of *Gham-e-Husayn,* (page 7): "The ten days of Muharram, for us Muslims are days of mourning and grief. To lament on the slaughtered Imām is certainly following in the Prophet's foot steps. I consider weeping and lamenting on Imām Husayn and making others to cry and weep as an act of great reward. I do not wish to talk or remember anything other than the tragedy of Imām Husayn during these ten days of Muharram. All the saints and holy men and Sūfī personalities in Hindustan have always openly expressed grief and sorrow and cried and wept profusely on the Day of Ashura." Hazrat Mualana Shah Muhammad Sulaymān Hanafī, Qādrī, Chishtī, the residing Saint of Phulwārī Sharīf always celebrated this grief and sorrow.

If expressing grief and sorrow, weeping for Imām Husayn and making others do the same is harām, then all the Sūfī saints and holy men of India and Pakistan would not have perpetually expressed this sorrow during their lifetimes. We read in *Uswa-e-Sūfia Uzzām,* (page 9) that Sheikh al Imām Makhdūm Aia'al Haq Pindavi used to mourn for all ten days of Muharram and would say: "How could one achieve sainthood when he does not mourn and weep on the family of the Prophet and perform Azadari for these pure personalities? One who doesn't have a heart of stone?" Thus Sunni saint has himself declared that if he does not perform Azadārī he can not be a saint *(walī)* and he who abstains from Mātam, is stone-hearted.

MOURNING ATTESTS TO SUPPORT FOR SUFFERING

The tragedy of Karbalā' took place in 61 Hijra. Before that incident, Islam was not divided among different sects. The killers of Imām Husayn had been excluded from the circle of Islam. Today, to carry out the *dhikr* of Imām Husayn is to support him and to oppose it is in effect to follow the path of Yazīd. In this connection, there is a very important hadīth: "I heard the Prophet say 'Verily my son (Husayn) will be killed in a land called Karbalā', whoever amongst you is alive at that time must go and help him.'"[4]

For Shi'as, mourning for their fallen Imām is an act of expression of support for him and hence is in complete accordance with the Sunna of the Prophet. If to remember Imām Husayn, carry out the *Dhikr* of his courageous actions and to mourn, lament and wail while falling deep into the sentiments of love is not evidence of Shi'as' support for him then what is it? To follow the path of Husayn is to share in his joys and tragedies. Azadārī is the means via which Shi'as show their support for the suffering of Imām Husayn. It is based on their love and affection for him. Token words by Nāsibīs such as 'we also love Imām Husayn' mean nothing. Love needs to be practical and as true lovers of Imām Husayn Shi'as deem it necessary to keep the remembrance of their beloved in their hearts. The names of a beloved are always on the lips of an adherent. People who want to bring the *dhikr* of Imām Husayn to an end by crying Bidha do so because they want to end his remembrance so as to cover up the sins of their Nāsibī ancestors who killed Imām Husayn.

MOURNING HUSAYN IS LIKE MOURNING PROPHET

Shah Abdul Azīz Muhadith Dehlavi while explaining the philosophy of martyrdom writes in the preface of his book *Sirr ash-Shahādatain*: "The martyrdom of Imām Husayn is in reality the martyrdom of his grandfather, the Prophet, Muhammad Mustafa." We therefore infer from this that mourning (Azadārī) for the leader of the martyrs, Imām Husayn is mourning (Azadari) for his grandfather, the Prophet, the most beloved of Allah's creation.

Allah desires that the martyrdom of Imām Husayn is conveyed to all. The renowned anti-Shi'a scholar al Muhammad Shah Abdul Azīz Dehlavi writes that "martyrdom is of two types, open and hidden martyrdom. Both types were distributed between the two grandsons of the Prophet. The hidden martyrdom (by poison) happened to be Imām Hasan's share since the state of his martyrdom

---

4 This hadīth has been taken from two sources : (1).*Khasā'is al Kubra*, vol. 2, page 125, Maktaba Nuroee Rizvi Publishers, Pakistan; and (2).*Yanābī' ul Mawwaddat* chapter 60.

was hidden and it was supposed to be kept secret and undisclosed. It was also foretold by the Prophet. The open type of martyrdom was attained by the younger grandson of the Prophet, Imām Husayn who was chosen for this type of martyrdom. Since this was to be disclosed as an unveiled martyrdom this news was revealed through Gabriel and the place of this martyrdom was foretold and the time was declared to be the beginning of the year 61 A.H.

"It was declared on numerous occasions. Ali also foretold the people about it when they were at the battle of Siffīn. When this tragedy occurred it was conveyed in a manner by Allah that the earth started to bleed and the sky turned red, angels and *jins* recited elegies for Imām Husayn, lions and other beasts kept roaming around the body of Imām Husayn in order to protect it and live snakes kept showing into and out of the nostrils of the assassins of Imām Husayn. This incident was made famous in numerous other ways. It was conveyed to those present and absent, that the greatest sacrifice and martyrdom had occurred.

"In fact Allah started this custom of mourning and weeping for Imām Husayn, so that he might be remembered and cried upon, and all those hardships should be remembered; even the reason behind all this is the same that this incident should earn fame and acknowledgement. This was achieved everyone present or absent, human or spirits, and the creatures came to know about this incident."5

These are the comments of a vehement opponent of the Shi'as. If the desire of Allah is that the martyrdom of Imām Husayn be conveyed to all then the Shi'as are implementing this will by retelling this event in every home, mosque, and street corner.

---

5 *Sirr ash-Shahādatain Dar Tehrīr ash-Shahādatain*, pp. 4-20, published in Lucknow: India. This publication is also available from the Pyame Aman Inc., (Bloomfield, New Jersey) in original text with English and Urdu translations.

Chapter: 34

EXPRESSIONS OF MOURNING

By

Dr. S. Manzoor Rizvi[1]

Prophet Noah was wailing and crying so frequently that this feature became his name. Noah in Arabic means the one who mourns and cries out to God at the suffering he receives at the hands of his nation. His bewailing is recorded in the Qur'an in the Chapter Noah. The Qur'an says: *"I called upon my people day and night. I called upon them publicly and privately. I called upon them loudly and in soft voice, but all they did by way of responding my call was to insert their fingers in their ears. My repeated call made them only run away from me so they would not listen."* (71:5-14) In another place the Qur'an records his wailing in these words, *"O my Lord! I am overcome. Do help (me) O lord."* (54:10)

On the death of Hamza, the Prophet cried and bewailed and said a Nauha and called upon the people of Medina to cry for the loss of a man like Hamza. Owais Qarnī had never seen the Prophet but on hearing the report that some teeth of the Prophet had broken in the fierce battle of Uhud, he broke all his teeth in token of his love to the Prophet. The Prophet praised this act of Owais Qarnī and prayed for him.

All Imāms of Shi'as are unanimous about mourning for Imām Husayn. When the prisoners of Karbalā' who were mostly women, were released after a year, and were returning from Damascus to Medina, they visited Karbalā'. As their caravan reached Karbalā', all of them including the 4th Imām and Jābir Ibn Abdullāh al-Ansārī, the companion of the prophet, cried, hit their faces and chests. Imām Ja'far Sādiq, according to *Bihār ul-Anwār*, confirmed that Rabāb did Mātam of Imām Husayn after his martyrdom. According to *Bihār ul-Anwār*, when the caravan returned to Medina all ladies of Medina come out of their homes

---

[1] This chapter is excerpted from the Urdu book, *Karbala Shanasi,* Allama Sayyid Saeed Akhtar Rizvi, Noor-e-Islam Imāmbarah, Faizabad: India, 1982.

-283-

open-headed crying while beating their chests and faces. After that they formed a huge procession and came to Imām Zain-al-Abidīn. The *Julūs* or the Muharram procession taken out by Shi'as is not in memory of the *Julūs* of Medina but in memory of the caravan of the Ahlul Bayt.

RELIGIOUS SANCTIONS OF MOURNING

Some authentic examples are given below to show that mourning by beating of head and chest was practiced and there was no prohibition at any time on such practices.

Chest Beating: Sa'īd bin Musayyah relates: "A Bedouin beating his chest and tearing his hair came to the Prophet loudly saying that he who remained away from virtues was ruined. The Prophet asked him the reason of what he was doing. The Bedouin replied that he had….with his wife while fasting during the month of Ramazan. The Prophet inquired if he could set free a slave; he replied in negative. The Prophet again inquired if he could fast continuously for two months. The man expressed his inability to do so. In the meantime a basket full of dates was brought to the Prophet who in turn asked the man to take the dates and give away in charity as an atonement of what he had done. The man said, 'O' Messenger of Allah! There is none needier than I.' The Prophet said: 'Eat yourself and observe one fast for lapse.'"[2] The incident should be considered in the light of the following facts:-

1. The Bedouin being a Muslim was *sahabi* (companion) of the Prophet.
2. He was beating his chest and tearing his hair in presence of the Prophet who neither objected to it nor reprimanded him for the same.
3. The action of the Bedouin was a result of spiritual pain he suffered as fast was invalidated.
4. This incident has been authentically recorded by Sunni traditionalists.

The tragedy of Karbalā' is more grievous and painful than the breaking of one's fast. Consequently, how the beating of the chest can be forbidden?

---

[2] *Mowtta* of Imām Mālik, Urdu Translation by Wahid-uz-zaman.

Mourning of Hazrat Bilāl: Describing the events of the fatal illness of the Prophet, Sheikh Abdul Haq Mohaddis Hanafī Dehlavi in his book *Madarij an-Nabuwwat* (vol. II, page 544) records: "Bilāl emerged beating his head and loudly wailing (from the room of Ayeshah)." Even in this case none of the companions raised any objection at the actions of Bilāl, the special Muezzin of the Prophet. Moreover, the Prophet was yet alive and not dead. This is the extreme extent of grief. Then how can similar actions for Imām Husayn are prohibited?

Mātam by Hazrat Sayyida: Sheikh Abdul Haq Muhuddith Dehlavi who is regarded as one of greatest scholars of the Sunnis has also recorded in his book *Madārij an-Nubawwat* that Fātima az-Zehrā' hearing the rumor of the martyrdom of the Prophet at Uhud came out of her house running and beating her head (vol. II, page 163). This shows that beating of head during the act of mourning for a martyr is allowed by the religion as Fātima az-Zehrā' was well aware of the religious code and was also infallible?

Mourning by Ayeshah: According to *Musnad Imām Hanbal*, Ayesha mourned the demise of the Prophet with other women by beating her head.[3]

Mourning by Owais-e-Qarnī: As almost all the Muslims know, Owais-e Qarnī had an immense love for the Prophet and when the news reached him that two teeth of the Prophet were broken in the battle of Uhud, he extracted all his teeth.[4] It should be realized that mourning by beating of chest head is decidedly milder form as compared with the extraction of all the teeth on the part of somebody like Owais-e-Qarnī, wherein a part of his body was lost for ever.

Smiting the head or face mentioned in the the Qur'an : When the Angels gave tidings to Prophet Ibrahim in his old age about the birth of a son to his wife Sarah, the Qur'an says: "*Then came forward his wife (Sarah) speaking then she smote her head and said 'an old and barren (Women).'*" (51:29) This is the English rendering of the Urdu translation of Sheikhul Hind Mahmūdul Hasan

---

[3] *Musnad Imām Ahmed Hanbal*, vol. VI, page 274.
[4] *Tazkiratul Awliyā'* by Sheikh Fariduddīn Attar, also *Ihsānul 'Uyūn* commonly knows as *Sīrate Halabiya*, vol. II, page 295.

Deobandi and Shah Abdul Qadir Muhuddis. Both have correctly translated the Arabic word *Fa-Sakkat* as *peeta* (smote) in Urdu. But they have misinterpreted the word *Wagh* which really means face, and not 'head,' as translated by them. However, it is evident that smiting the face was not an objectionable act in the sight of Allah, otherwise Allah would have at least reproached or reprimanded for doing so.

A QUESTION

Those who are against mourning for Imām Husayn and, for that matter, for any of the martyrs of Karbalā' usually ask a question whether the Prophet had ordered mourning for Imām Husayn? The answer is: Did the Prophet order Owais-e-Qarnī to extract all his teeth? Did the Prophet ask Ayeshah to mourn on his death by beating her face? Did the Prophet ask Fātima az-Zehrā' to beat her head at the rumor of his martyrdom at Uhud. No orders or sanctions are relevant in such situations. This was all done spontaneously out of love and sorrow for the Prophet who had not forbidden this.

One should not forget the fact that the Prophet had time and again directed to seek guidance from his Ahlul Bayt in all matters which led finally to the famous *Hadīth Thaqlain* declaring: "I leave behind me two weighty things; the Qur'an, the book of Allah, and my progeny, the Ahlul Bayt. If you remain attached to both of them you will never go astray..." The Ahlul Bayt of the Prophet are models of for us. They mourned for the martyrs of Karbala and we should follow them.

TABUT OR TAZIYAH

A section of Muslims never tired of calling Tābūt, Tāziyah, or 'Alam to be Bid'a and idol worship. They know that these objects are made to remind us of Imām Husayn. The principle underlying the making of these objects is the same as making of a mosque, which, in fact, is the replica of Ka'bah.

SANCTION FOR MAKING IMAGES

Allah has mentioned about Prophet Sulayman in the Qur'an: *"Those Jiins made for him whatever he willeth of (such as) huge buildings, statues, and basins (large as) reservoirs and (huge) cooking cauldrons immovable from their places."* (34:13)

Since the essentials of *Tawhīd* did not change from the time of Prophet Sulayman to the time of the prophethood of the last Prophet they are intact even today in each and every detail. Therefore, it is easy to arrive at the conclusion that according to the Qur'anic law the making of statues or the physical images of anything was neither prohibited during the time of the prophethood of Prophet Sulayman nor it is forbidden for the followers of Islam.

Beside, it must be remembered that there is a clear distinction between the idols whose worshippers are called polytheist and the statues which are not worshipped by their makers and their making is not therefore, in any way against the ideal of *Tawhīd* (Unity of God).

SHABĪH IN TIMES OF THE PROPHET

Religious sanction for making Shabīh (physical image) or a doll is clearly proved by the following incident, which took place during the prophethood of the Prophet.

The Prophet once entered his house after his marriage with Ayeshah and noticed a shelf on one of the walls covered with a curtain. He asked Ayeshah as to what was there in the niche behind the curtain. Ayeshah told him that there were some of her dolls with which she used to play at the house of her father and had brought them with her after her marriage with the Prophet. The Prophet removed the curtain and looked at the shelf and found some dolls there. The Prophet instead of pulling his face smiled at the sight and asked Ayeshah as to why the small doll horse she had kept with the other dolls had wings. Ayeshah promptly replied that it was because the horse of Prophet Sulayman had wings. According to Ayeshah the Prophet laughed at her reply and his teeth became visible.[5] (See next Chapter 35 for more details.)

The incident is a clear proof of the fact that the Prophet did not object to Ayeshah's keeping and even making of the images of girls and the horse according to the version of Abū Dāwūd as quoted by *Mishkāt*. The images were not naturally supposed to be

---

[5] *Mishkāt-Kitābun-Nikha*, (Hadīth 3105) from Abū Dāwūd.

idols for worship. The Prophet's smile rather laugh at the sight was also a sign of his pleasure and not of an objection to it. In the light of this, how could a Shabīh of the Imām Husayn or for that matter, a living horse called Zuljanah are objectionable in any way and the makers and those who present them to the view of general public could be blamed of innovations? It is significant that the Tāziyah and Zuljanah not only help commemorate the tragedy of Karbalā' but also impress the people.

IMITATION OF THE RIDING OF IMĀM HUSAYN

Those who object to Zuljanah which is only an imitation of the memorial of riding of Imām Husayn should ponder a little that by doing this, they commit the sin of raising an accusing finger to an act of the Prophet himself who happened to act as a camel for the riding of Imām Husayn several times. Umar happened to enter the house of the Prophet and seeing the Prophet imitating a camel remarked: "What a nice camel!" To this remark of Umar, the Prophet promptly retorted: "And what a nice rider, too!"[6] From this it is evident that the imitation of the memorial of riding of Imām Husayn and presenting its Shabīh (Zuljanah) to the view of the public is like following a tradition of the Prophet. As in the case of the Prophet it was not against the commandment of Allah, it is not against the religious law even today.

PLEASURE OF ALLAH AND THE PROPHET

The Prophet allowed Imām Husayn to ride over his back like the rider of a camel. This was in fact a pleasure of the Prophet himself and the pleasure of the Prophet being the pleasure of Allah according to a unanimously acknowledged tradition of the Prophet. The imitation of riding Imām Husayn has both the pleasure of the Prophet as well as the pleasure of the Allah.

There are some prejudiced people who say that the sight of Shabīh of Zuljanah causes the breaking of the *Nikah* (the religious wedlock). This is only a far fetched idea without any religious basis. Why don't such people ponder that had it been so, the

---

[6] Urdu Translation of *Kashful Mahjūb* entitled *Bayānul Matlūb*, chp.8, sec. 118, page 119, published by Ferozsons Ltd., Lahore: Pakistan.

Prophet would have stopped Umar from entering his (the Prophet's) house at a time when he was moving like a camel on the floor with Imām Husayn on his back, or why did he not ask him to cast away his eye's from the sight thereof, if there was any danger of the breaking of his *Nikah*? Besides, what would such people say about the Prophet imitating a camel?

KISSING OF SHABĪH

Worship is only for Allah and Allah alone, and if it is practiced for someone other than Allah it is polytheism. Kissing of something is a sign of love and regard for that thing or person and not for worship. It cannot be called polytheism. People kiss their children and they similarly kiss covers of the Qur'an, the lattice of the sacred sepulcher of the Prophet and the shrines of other great religious personalities among the Muslims but it is not objected to, because it is only done out of love, regard, and respect without distinction and is not therefore worship which is religiously restricted for Allah only. In view of this the Shabīh of sacred sepulcher of Imām Husayn, his Tāziyah or the memorial of his riding, Zuljanah is never the worship of the Shabīh. It is therefore, incorrect to call these actions on the part of any body to be polytheism. It is recorded in *Bukhārī* and *Muslim* that the Prophet kissed the dead body of Uthmān bin Maz'ūn. Can one say that the Prophet committed polytheism?

BLACK CLOTHS

Putting on black clothes on the 10th of Muharram, which is the day of the martyrdom of Imām Husayn is a sign of grief. The practice is not a deviation from the religious law. It is not even an innovation on the part of the Shi'as. The Prophet used to put on a black turban and a black sheet as a cover for his body. Wearing black cloths is not only a sign of immense grief on that particular day but also serve as following of the tradition of the Prophet.[7]

KISSING SOIL OF KARBALĀ'

Some of the Muslims call kissing the soil of Karbalā' as idolatry and vehemently oppose it as such. It may be explained

---

[7] *Nashiut Tayyib* by Maulana Ashraf Ali Thānwī, p. 181, published by Taj Co, Ltd., Karachi: Pakistan.

that the Shi'as are not emotional or sentimental in this regard as well as in performing other rites of their faith. They hold the soil of Karbalā' in the very esteem it demand from the lovers of Imām Husayn and look upon it with same reverence as they look upon any other thing which has an attachment with the sacred name of Imām Husayn. But did not the Prophet kiss this very soil when it was brought to him by the angels and he handed it over to Umme-e-Salma for preservation as mentioned earlier? We have also recorded the statement of Sheikh Abdul Qādir Jīlānī [8] to the effect that seventy thousand angels came down on the grave of Imām Husayn for mourning on the day of 'Āshūrā' and would continue mourning on his grave till the Day of Judgment. It is interesting to observe that angels are undoubtedly busy in worship in the heaven and they came down on the grave of Imām Husayn for mourning. If this statement is analyzed it can safely be said that: (i) mourning for Imām Husayn by the angles in the eyes of Allah is as good as worship on their part, (ii) the soil of Karbalā' is without doubt as sacred as the heaven itself before Allah. That is why He sent His angels to the soil of Karbalā' for mourning Imām Husayn.

In view of the above how could the kissing of such a sacred soil be listed as an act of idolatry? Moreover, is not the kissing of *Hajar-e-Aswad* among the most essential rites of Hajj? What for? The believers have been commanded by Allah to revere the stone so much so as to kiss it only because of the reverence attached by Allah Himself with the name of the founder of his house, Prophet Ibrahim who exalted His name on earth. Why the water of the spring of Zam-Zam is so sacred in the eyes of all the Muslim without any distinction of sect or beliefs? Is it not for the same reason?

SABĪL

Setting up Sabīls i.e. offering water or refreshing drinks to the thirsty is another thing which is called innovation by some Muslims and a Maulvi from Karachi has gone to the extent of calling such water or refreshing drinks offered on Sabīls as harām.

---

[8] *Ghuniyat-ul-Talebīn* by Sheikh Abdul Qādir Jīlānī, p.64, published in Egypt 1332 A.H.

There is no religious ban on putting up Sabīls. On the contrary, such humanitarian acts of generosity are generally appreciated by all religious and social organizations. How could anyone object to the offering of water or refreshing drinks in the name of, and in remembrance of the agonizing thirst of the one who offered the whole stock of water to the enemy forces headed by Hur, the then officer of the army of Yazīd? This very Hur realized his mistake later on and quitted the army of Yazīd to join the faithful band of Imām Husyan and drank the cup of martyrdom on the day of 'Āshūrā'.

'AZĀ KHĀNA

After the death of the Prophet, Imām Ali and Fātima az-Zehrā' built the first Azā Khāna to mourn the sad departure of the Prophet and the affliction perpetrated on the progeny of the Prophet. This 'Azā Khāna was called *Bait-ul-Huzn* and it was built next to *Jannatul Baqī'* in Medina.

ZANJEER MĀTAM

We have already told about Owais who had broken all his teeth on coming to know that a tooth of the Prophet had broken in the battle of Uhud. On hearing about it the Prophet appreciated the intensity of Qaranī's love and his devotion to the Prophet of Allah. Recently there surfaced some disagreement among some Shi'a Ulama about the Zanjīr Mātam, but no one, anyhow, has forbidden it, including Ayatuallāh Nā'īnī, Khū'ī, Khumainī and others. All of them agree on two things; it should not be the cause of humiliation to the religion and secondly, individual should not get hurt.

Among Sunni Ulama, there is a general rule from the companion of the Prophet, Ibne Mas'ūd, who says, "Whatever Muslims think good for them, is good for Allah.[9] Based on this, if Shi'as think it good as the symbol of their love to their Imāms, it should also be ok to others. Shedding the token-blood in memory and sympathy of those who had shed all their blood for the cause of truth and justices, is not condemnatory, if not compulsory.

---

[9] *Mustadark* by Hākim, *Sawā'iq-e-Muhriqa*, and *Tārīkh-e-Khulafā'*.

Azādārī is obligatory on all Muslims. It has been shown that the Prophet and his companions and Imāms all observed it. It is *Sha'āirallāh* as it reminds us of the Imām Husayn's struggle to establish the truth of Allah's religion. It reminds us of the Greatness and Glory of Allah for whom everything can be scarified. It gives us encouragement to struggle and improve our lives and serve to improve the Muslim community. It gives us strength to suffer for the welfare of humanity.

NAZR

If some one vows (Nazr) that he will hold a Majlis in commemoration of Imām's martyrdom, after his difficulty is removed or his important works is completed, it would be incumbent on him to fulfill his vow (Nazr). The Qur'an says: *"Fulfill your promise."* (Bani Israel: 24) In Surah Dahr the Qur'an says. : *"They fulfill their vows and are afraid of the day when fear will be spread far and wide."* (76: 7)

Nazr of Imām Husayn and other Imāms or martyrs in the path of Allah, derives its justification from the Prophet's hadīth that: "Reading *Surah al-Hamd* and *Surah Tawhīd* three times, carries the *thawāb* of reading the entire Qur'an. So if some one recites these Surahs on food with the spiritual benefit of reciting them to go to the person for whom is intended it will be good for the departed soul."

Chapter: 35

CREATING AND REVERING SYMBOLS OF MOURNING

By

Dr. S. Manzoor Rizvi[1]

The Qur'an says: *"Verily, Safā and Marwa are among the signs of Allah."*(2:158) With reference to this verse Allama Imām Fakhrrudīn Rāzī of Ahle-Sunna in his *Tafsīr Kabīr* writes: "The signs of Allah (*Sha'āir* Allah) are to be revered and treated with obeisance and veneration. Whatever symbols and signs are made to invoke remembrance of Allah constitute *Sha'āir* of Allah or sign of Allah as He himself gives an example of the Mounts of Safā and Marwa."

Comments: Since the love of Imām Husayn is obedience to Allah then all symbols, monuments, Tāziyah, Zarīh, Zuljanah etc. that indicate love and attachment to the Prophet and his Ahlul Bayt are all signs of Allah and they command respect. Showing disrespect to them or dishonoring them would be tantamount to shunning this verse of the Qur'an whether this insult is done by writing or spoken by the tongue!

The Qur'an says: *"O ye who believe violate not the (sanctity of) the monuments of Allah!"*(2:5) If mountain is a sign of Allah then certainly the image of a horse, cradle and standards are also signs of Allah. People who venerate Tāziyah are certain to get their sins erased by the blessings of the Prophet.

We read in *Sawā'iq al Muhirqah*, p. 147: "When king Timur was on his death bed, his face suddenly turned black and his countenance grew horrible. When his situation improved, his soldiers and his relatives asked him about the strange happening. Timur replied: "I saw Angles of Torture from Allah coming to me to chastise and punish me; hence I trebled from fear and my face contorted and blacked. But all of a sudden, I saw the Prophet came near me and commanded the Angles to go away declaring

---

[1] Excerpted from the title *Shiaism Explained* (various chapters), Peermahomed Ebrahim Trust, Karachi: Pakistan, 1972

that he had come to intercede on my behalf for my sins to be erased as I am the lover of his progeny and his descendents."

This proves that one who venerates and sanctifies Tāziyah is a lover of the holy progeny and the descendents of the Prophet and his act is held in high esteem by the Prophet to the extent that he considers it an act of beneficence and benevolence unto him. It is obvious that if 'Azādārī had been harām the Prophet would not have come to intercede on behalf of a perpetrator of sins and forbidden acts!

The Qur'an says: *"And (further) their Prophet said to them: 'A sign of his authority is that there shall come to you the ark of the covenant, with (an assurance) therein of security from your Lord, and the relics left by the family of Moses and the family of Aaron carried by angles. In this is a symbol for you if you indeed have faith.'"* (2:248)

These relics reached the hands of descendents of Prophet Moses and as a proof of it we rely on these esteemed Sunni works. : (1) *Tafsīr Kabīr*, vol. 2, pp. 506 – 507; (2) *Tafsīr Khazan*, vol. 1, p. 216; and (3) *Al Jamah la Hukam Al Qur'an* by Qurtubī 2nd edition, p. 247, published in Beirut.

Tafsīr Kabīr: "The Ashāb narrate that Allah sent some relics to Adam which contained pictures of the prophets and these relics were inherited by the children of Adam until these reached Prophet Yaqoob."

Qurtubī, in his commentary of this verse states: "This covenant was sent by Allah to Prophet Adam and it remained with him until it reached Prophet Yaqoob. After which it remained with Banī Isrā'īl. They kept overcoming their opposing armies due to blessing of this chest until they disobeyed Allah and were defeated by Amaliqans who took the chest from them."

It is from this verse and tradition Allah created these pictures of prophets and sent them to Prophet Adam who transferred it to his lineage. Hence, paying homage to the symbols/images of prophets stands as an established fact. Why do some of the Ahl as-Sunna remain silent when it comes to this matter? If Shi'as produce images of Karbalā' to commemorate the tyrannies faced by Ahlul Bayt, the aim is to recall the tragedy of Karbalā' in people's minds. The Shi'as' aim is not to worship these images. If Allah sent picture of prophets that were kept by the people to remember them why the objection when Shi'as create images to remember Karbalā'?

LEGAL JUSTIFICATION FOR IMAGE

The illegality of an image is greatly emphasized and it is compared to idol worship. There are a number of methods to know or teach somebody about a thing: (i) To mention it verbally; (ii) To make its image/diagram so as to get facts into people's mind. Imagery has a clear benefit in that it reminds people of an event. It acts as an effective tool to get key message to an audience. One of the key aims of commercial advertising is to get an audience to associate a specific image with key message about their products. If you look in Encyclopedia books, they are embellished with images next to text on the subject matter. Why are they there? Aren't words enough?

Images included within instructional or educational materials help increase our comprehension and understanding of concrete concepts. Accompanied with text or words, this dual coding type of theory facilitates our learning processes. For example, if we were teaching the concept of a volcano, either in a dormant or active stage, using words alone would be difficult to describe it. The process of an eruption could also be clarified with the use of visuals. Imagine the impact of a video shown to a group of learners who have seen this colossal natural event. Let us look at other real-life examples. Architects render illustrations of their building designs to show what the structure will look like before it is built, helping educate the clients on the building's important features. Doctors look at X-rays or CT scans to help them with diagnoses. What appears in the X-rays will help the doctors learn what type of problem the patient is experiencing, so they can prescribe and perform necessary treatment.

EXAMINE THE THEORY

Three important theories support the use of imagery with instruction. The information processing theory, developed by Atkinson and Shiffrins (1968), is the process by which information is perceived and transferred from short-term memory to long-term memory. Pavio's dual-coding theory defines two separate memory systems; one function as verbal memory and the other as imaginal memory that deals with visual processing. Mayer's multimedia theory suggests that visuals and words together help learner select, organize and integrate information in meaningful ways.

While the three theories stated above support the use of imagery, two design principles (Lohr, 2003, pp. 39-44) assist instructional designers in the process of creating visual aids. The first one, known as the figure/ ground principle, helps learners select important information. The second, the hierarchy principle, helps learners integrate information.

Levie and Lentz (1982) compared data from research with 155 experiments on learning with and without supporting illustration. They came to the conclusion using illustration that closely relates to the text helps the learner understand and remember.

Based along the same principles, imagery in Azadari (mourning) ceremonies acts as a means of educating the masses about the suffering of Imām Husayn. The image of Zuljanah (the horse of Imām Husayn) reminds us the time when Imām Husayn fell from the horse and it returned to his camp without its rider. It notified the women of Ahlul Bayt that the Imām had been martyred.

Displaying the image of an 'Alam (standard) also serves the purpose of educating the masses that are not familiar with the tragedy of Karbalā'. These are used in the *Julūs* (mourning processions). The image of 'Alam (the flag) purports to bring to our memories the time when Imām Husayn brought back the 'Alam of his slain brother Hazrat Abbās after his death and the distraught women and children mourned and wailed to see the standard. If one looks at the 'Alam carefully, we see that it is made up of three components: (i) Scarves; (ii) The symbol of a "hand" on the top of the flag; and (iii) A water flask. All three act as sharp reminders to the tragedy of Karbalā', and have a direct correlation to that event. The scarves symbolize the humiliation that the women of the Prophet's household were subjected to. The grand daughters of the Prophet had their scarves forcefully removed by the soldiers of Yazīd's army after the martyrdom of the Imām. The hand represents the slain arms of Abbās, the brother of Imām Husayn. The water flask represents the thirst experienced by Imām Husayn, his family and loyal companions. It focuses one's mind to the harsh blockade so severe that Yazīd's forces turned down Imām Husayn's request for water even for his six-month old son.

The purpose behind the image of the cradle is to remember the martyrdom of Ali Asghar, the infant son of Imām Husayn. Anyone upon seeing a horse in a procession will ask about its role in 'Azādārī. This is where education plays such a pivotal role.

The horse represents the final moments of the Imām Husayn as he left his family enclave to engage in Jihad, never to return again. Upon his martyrdom, the horse of our Imām returned back to the tents wherein the ladies of the household were waiting anxiously. An empty saddle in effect confirmed that Imām Husayn was martyred.

All these things carry a strong message to all the generations wherever 'Azādārī is carried out and they remind everyone of these events which are attached to these symbols. All of these images are meant to remember the afflictions faced by the Prophet's family. The Shi'as do not consider these images as God nor do they worship them. Only Allah is worthy of worship. The Shi'as kiss these images as a mark of respect as the poet in this Arabic poem has said: *I kiss the place where my beloved lives not because I love this place but because I love the person who lives here.* In the same way kissing an image demonstrates love and respect for Ahlul Bayt and if enemies of the Prophet still shut their eyes and insist on calling it worship of images then they are advised to first look at them. We will present some references, which will show that "worship" of images takes place in their own camp not in ours only.

THE IMAGE OF ZULJANAH

The Qur'an says: *"By the (Steeds) that run with panting (breath) and strike sparks of Fire."* (100:1-2) In this verse, Allah speaks of the high standing of the warriors by swearing upon the horses used in Jihād. This shows that when a warrior of Jihād is praised, Allah also loves and praises his horse. When the Shi'as remember the warriors of Karbalā' who fought against the oppression of Banū Ummaya they also talk about those faithful horses that withstood a barrage of arrows and spears. The images of the horse of Imām on the 10th of Muharram portray the hardship of the martyrs of Karbalā'. Preparing images to preserve remembrance of an incident is not forbidden in Islam.

KISSING THE IMAGE OF GRAVE

On page 868 of *Majma' ul Bahrain*, the Shi'a author writes on a Sunni reference: "It is written in *Kifiyat ul shābī* that a man came to the Prophet and said, 'O Prophet of Allah I have sworn that I would kiss the door of paradise, what should I do now.' The Prophet said to him to go and kiss his father's forehead and mother's feet. He said what if his parents were not alive? The Prophet replied, 'kiss the graves of your parents.' He said 'I do not know where their graves are.' The Prophet said, 'draw two lines on earth and consider them the graves of your parents and then kiss them.'" This tradition clarifies that there is nothing wrong in making images of the graves of ones parents. The rank of Imām Husayn is no doubt, higher than one's parents. Then why there is objection to making image of Imām Husayn's grave.

IMAGES OF ABŪ BAKR AND UMAR

Tārīkh Khamīs, vol. 2, p. 172 provides a mapped illustration of the graves of the Prophet, Abū Bakr, and Umar. We then read this written commentary underneath: "It is written in *Khulasathul Wafa* that first is the grave of the Prophet and Abū Bakr's head is near the shoulder of the Prophet and Umar's head is near the feet of the Prophet." The Ahlul Sunna have created a map of the grave of Umar and Abū Bakr, but ironically when the Shi'as create an image of Imām Husayn's grave this tantamount to Shirk and Bid'ah.

THE IMAGE OF COIN

Bashārat ul Dārain is a book that has been written against the Shi'as on mourning rituals in Muharram. The cover depicts the image of an Islamic coin, which is the copy of the original Islamic coin. The aim is to highlight the high rank of the three caliphs so as to create feeling of love towards them. The images that the Shi'as make are not for the purpose of worshipping them. Worship is only of Allah. These images are only meant to portray the hardships and tyranny faced by Ahlul Bayt so as to arouse love for them and hatred for their enemies in the hearts of Muslims.

THE IMAGES OF PROPHETS

We read in the Qur'an: *"They worked for him as he desired, (making) arches, images, basons as large as reservoirs, and (cooking) cauldrons fixed (in their place): 'Works ye, sons of David, with thanks!' But few of My servants are grateful."* (34:13) From this verse three points are clear:

1. Allah made jinns the subordinates to Prophet Sulayman.
2. Whatever the jinns did for Prophet Sulayman was in accordance with Allah's wishes.
3. These jinns made statues/sculptures for him.

The statues/sculptures are the translation of the word *Tamāthīl*, as has been confirmed by Sunni scholars of *Tafasir*. Allama Baydhawī in his *Tafsīr* volume 2, p. 173 states: "*Tamathīl* are the pictures and replicas, which were the pictures of angles and prophets so that other people may contemplate worship after observing them."

In *Mu'alim ul-Tanzīl*, p. 737, we see the commentary of Allama Baydhawī's statement as follow: "Those jinns used to make the picture of angels, prophets and the pious people in the mosques so that they could see them worship more."

The same statement can also be located in *Tafsīr Kashāf*, vol. 2 p. 445 and *Tafsīr Durre Manthūr*, vol. 5, p. 228. These statements show that in obedience to Allah's commands, the jinns created picture of prophets and angels for Prophet Sulayman in order to provide the people with inspiration and increase their urge for worshipping Allah. Tāziyahs are the replicas of Imām Husayn's shrine, which cause the increase in mourning and crying for Imām Husayn, which we have already proven to be an act of worship.

What better logic or proof can possibly be given to prove that forming replicas (Shabīh) is as valid as this! Allah ordered the jinns to make such replicas for Prophet Sulayman. When it is permissible for Prophet Sulayman to have images created for him and it does not negate the Qur'an in any sense then it is also permissible for the Shi'as to create images that identify the tragedy of Karbalā' because Allah says in the Qur'an: *"Those were the (Prophets) who received Allah's guidance; copy the guidance they received; Say: 'No reward for this do I ask of you: This is no less than a message for the nations.'"*(6:91)

Accordingly, today the Muslims make images following the practices of the Prophet Sulayman and weep by looking at them just in the manner in which the Prophet would weep. Not only are Shi'as acting in accordance with the Sunna of Prophet Sulayman they are also obeying Allah because Allah would order the jinns to make these replicas.

When it is proved from the Qur'an that the jinns created 'images' upon the order of Prophet Sulayman then why is there objection from Mullahs when Shi'as prepare images of a standard, cradle or Zuljanah in order to bring to their remembrance the sufferings of Imām Husayn.

Those who say that 'Azādārī is idol worship must look into own books first. Was Prophet Sulayman an idol worshiping (*Mazallah*), because he prepared pictures of angels and prophets?

Thus it is very clear that the purpose of images in Muharram is not to worship them but to bring to remembrance the sufferings of Imām Husayn and his family and thus pay homage to them for his patience and firmness in the face of extreme difficulties and tyranny. If still someone thinks it is idol worship it is only because of his malice for the progeny of the Prophet.

THE HORSE OF AYESHAH

Ayeshah narrated: "When the Apostle of Allah arrived after the expedition to Tabūk or Khaybar (the narrator is doubtful about the name), the draught raised an end of a curtain which was hung in front of my store-room, revealing some dolls which belonged to me. The Prophet asked: 'What is this?' I replied: 'My dolls.' Among them he saw a horse with wings made of rags, and asked: 'What is this I see among them?' I replied: 'A horse.' He asked: 'What is this that it has on it?' I replied: 'Two wings.' He asked: 'A horse with two wings.' I replied: 'Have you not heard that Sulayman had horse with wings?' Thereupon the Apostle of

Allah laughed so heartily that I could see his molar teeth." (*Sunan Abū Dāwūd*, Book 41, Number 4914)

Ayeshah was not an infant at the time that she kept this image. We read in *Muruj al Dhahab*, book 2, p.294, that Ayeshah was married two years before the Hijrat. The battle of Hunayn was fought in 8th Hijra. Adding 8 to 9 makes 17 years, so when Ayeshah made the horse she was seventeen years old, hence a mature adult. If we accept the common Sunni defense that Ayeshah was a mere child at the time then we have to accept that the house of the Prophet remained a place of idols for eight years after the Hijra. Moreover Ayeshah herself said that she was eighteen years old when the Prophet died.

It is quite evident from the above mentioned story that the explanation given by Ayeshah for her toy, was based on its resemblance with the Sulayman's horse and hence she placed it inside the house of the Prophet while deeming it the replica of Sulayman's horse. Yet the Prophet neither rejected her notion nor did he prohibit the replica to be placed in his house. In fact he smiled which was an act of satisfaction with that act of Ayeshah.

Now the interesting thing is that the horse with wings or a 'Flying Horse' is called Zuljanah in Arabic. Hence we can say that the foundation of making replica of Zuljanah was established inside the House of Prophet by his wife. Hence, if Shi'as make the replica of Zuljanah, it is not illegitimate because Shi'as don't worship that horse (as propagated by Nāsibīs) rather it is made deeming it only an honorable sign of history.

AHLUL SUNNAH CREATING IMAGES

Ibne Kathīr whilst discussing the events that occurred in 363 Hijrī states in *al Bidāyah wa-l Nihāya*, vol. 11, p. 275: "In 363 Hijrī a fight broke out between the Ahl as-Sunna and the Rafida. The Ahlul Sunna through a lack of commonsense, or a complete omission of commonsense were not willing to make peace. One group amongst them placed a woman on a camel and made her Ayeshah and made men, Talha and Zubayr. They then declared their opponents the Sahāba of Ali, and said: "Now we shall fight the Sahāba of Ali."

Comments: Just see that Nāsibīs create an image of Ayeshah when the need arises. When Shi'as create an image of Imām Husayn deeming it necessary for the remembrance, these Mullahs suddenly suffer from indigestion. The narration also sheds light on the fact that whenever these Nāsibīs wanted to display their enmity towards the family of the Prophet they would use the family of Abū Bakr as their means of approach.

KISSING HOOFS OF IMĀM RAZĀ HORSE

When Imām Ali Razā came to Khurasān and reached Nishāpūr, Abū Dhara Rāzī and Muhammad bin Muslim Tūsī came to welcome him along with other scholars and people were in such a condition that some were screaming, some were crying, some were throwing dust on their heads and some were kissing the hooves of the horse. (*Sawā'iq-e-Muhriqah*, pp. 679-680, *Dhikr Imām Ali Razā*)

Shi'as do not worship the images that are made in Muharram, only Allah almighty is worthy of worship. The purpose of these symbols is to portray the picture of Karbalā' and bring back to our minds the things that happened there, kissing and paying respect to them is actually showing love and respect to Ahlul Bayt just as people kissed the hooves of Imām Razā's horse to demonstrate their love and respect for the Imām.

PART SIX: SOME OTHER ISSUES

Chapter: 36

WAS REVELATION ORIGINALLY INTENDED FOR IMAM ALI?

By

Imām Muhammad. Jawad Chirri[1]

"Do the Shiite Muslims say that the revelation came to Muhammad by mistake, and that it was intended for Imām Ali?" This is a vicious lie widely spread in Egypt, Saudi Arabia, and other Arab countries in order to discredit the followers of the members of the House of the Prophet. This accusation was made during periods of oppression against the Shi'as. The rulers of the periods of the Umayyads and Abbasids used to consider every follower of the Members of the House of the Prophet revolutionary and dangerous. They conspired against these Shi'as and accused them of heresy and disbelief in order to encourage the Muslims to shed their blood and usurp their rights and wealth.

The centuries of oppression passed with all their injustices and terrors. It was expected that during the new period of freedom, the mistake of the past would be corrected. It was hoped that the Muslim scholars would make a serious study in order to see if there is any justification for such terrible accusations. It is very easy to know the truth.

There are hundreds of books written by Shi'a scholars about their beliefs. Had the Sunni scholars read any of these books, they would have found that the Shiite beliefs are in full agreement with the Book of God and the well-known statements of the Prophet. We are living in the era of speed and easy movement. It is easy for Muslim scholars to have conferences, discuss problems, and find solutions. The simplest principle of justice is to follow the commandments of the Qur'an: "*Oh you, who believe, if a transgressor*

---

[1] Reproduced from his book, *The Shiites Under Attack*, (Chapter 2: *Do the Shiite Muslims Say That the Revelation Came to Muhammad by Mistake, and That it was Intended for Ali*). The book was published by the Islamic Center of America, Chicago in 1986.

comes to you with news, try to verify it, lest you inflict damage on people unwittingly; then you may consequently regret your hasty action." (49:6)

The Almighty commanded us to try to find out whether an accusation is true or false, and that we ought not to try people and convict them without questioning them. We do not know of any court in the world in which the judge convicts a person before interviewing him, provided the accused is available and honors the summons. In spite of the ease with which one can find the correct information nowadays, we find that those who accuse and spread hatred among Muslims do not take one single step in order to find the truth which may unite the Muslim world.

While writing these words, I recollect that the Egyptian government during the fifties sent the late Dr. Muhammad Bisar to Washington, D.C., as director of the Islamic Center there. I went to visit him and he received me kindly and informed me of the knowledge he had acquired concerning American Muslims. He initiated a dialogue between us, saying: "Some of the Muslims in this country asked me about the various Islamic sects. I declared to them that all Muslim sects are good except the Shiite Ithanā 'Asharī."

I immediately realized that Dr. Bisar did not know the meaning of the Shi'a Ithanā 'Asharī. Otherwise, he would not have been rude enough to say that to me while I am a Shiite Ithanā 'Asharī. Thus, we had the following dialogue:

Chirri:	What is wrong with the Ithanā 'Asharī?
Bisar:	They believe in things opposed to Islam.
Chirri:	Give us an example of their wrong belief.
Bisar:	They say the revelation came to Muhammad by mistake, and that Imām Ali Ibn Abī Tālib was supposed to receive the revelation.
Chirri:	How did you learn that?
Bisar:	No, I have not.
Chirri:	Then you have convicted millions of Muslims and considered them *kāfir* without asking any of them about this serious accusation. Did the Almighty command you to do that? And did Egypt send you to propagate such a vicious message?

A year after our meeting in Washington, I met Dr. Bisar in Philadelphia at an Islamic conference. He informed me that he re-examined the book of *Al-milal and Al-nihal* by Al-Shehristānī and found that what was attributed to the Shi'as, that the revelation came to Muhammad by mistake, was not the belief of the Ithanā 'Asharī Shi'as school of thought. It was, rather, a sect which existed and disappeared hundreds of years ago. Hearing that from him, I accepted his apology. Yet, I was amazed that it took him a whole year to reread the books and discover the truth.

I spent years studying ahādīth and Islamic history books which were written by Sunni and Ithanā 'Asharī scholars. I never found in any Shiite book a hadīth or historical report indicating that Imām Ali Ibn Abī Tālib was higher than or equal to Muhammad. As a matter of fact, I found only the opposite. The Shi'as consider Imām Ali to be the best man after the Messenger because he was the most obedient to him. One of the ahādīth which the Shi'as pride themselves upon is a hadīth attributed to the Messenger of God. The Prophet said to the tribe of Wolai-ah: "Banī Wolai-ah, you must change your attitude, or I shall send to you a man who is from me to punish you severely." Some of the people who were present asked the Prophet, "Who is the man you are going to send to them?" The Prophet replied: "He is the man who is patching the sole of my shoes." They looked around and found Imām Ali patching the sole of the Prophet's shoes.

It is inconceivable that the Shi'as can be proud of the fact that Ali was the patcher of Prophet Muhammad's shoes and claim that the Imām is higher than or equal to the Prophet. Therefore, I do not find any justification for directing such an accusation at the Shiites who glorify the Prophet the most. The Shi'as say that the highest honor the Imām Ali acquired is that he was chosen by the Prophet to be his brother. When the Prophet commanded every two Muslims to become brothers, he held Imām Ali's hand and said, "This is my brother." Thus, the Messenger of God, the highest Messenger, the Imām of all righteous people, the one who had no equal among the servants of God, made Imām Ali his brother.[2] Certainly the Shi'as are not extremist, and there is no hadīth

---

[2] *Al-Sīrah Al-Nabawiyah,* by Ibn Hushām, part 1, p. 505.

reported by the Shi'as that may justify such an accusation. However, it would not be improper to ask the following question: Are the Sunnis and their scholars free of exaggeration and extremism concerning the position of some prominent companions of the Prophet?

ARE THE SUNNIS CLEAR OF EXAGGERATION?

It would not be out of place to say that the Sunnis are closer to extremism than the Shi'as. We find indications in the books of the Sunni scholars and hadīth recorders that they put Umar in a position higher than that of the Messenger of God. The following are some of the ahādīth:

Al-Hākim Al-Nisabūri in his book (*Al-Mustadrak*, part 3, p. 84) reported that Obay Ibn Ka'b said: "I heard the Messenger of God saying that the first one the Almighty will embrace on the Day of Judgment is Umar. The first one the Lord will shake hands with will be Umar, and the first one the Almighty takes by His hand and admits to paradise is Umar."

Al-Hafiz Muhammad Ibn Majah in his authentic *Sunan* reported that Obay Ibn Ka'b said: "The Messenger of God said that 'the first one God will shake hands with (on the Day of Judgment) will be Umar. The first one God will greet is Umar, and he is the first one Allah takes by His hand and admits to paradise.'"

These ahādīth clearly indicate the Umar will be above all the Prophets including the head of the Prophets, Muhammad. When Umar is to be the first embraced and his hand shaken by the Almighty, all the prophets will be after him. This is a strange and astonishing hadīth. It portrays the Creator of the Heavens and the Earth as a human who embraces people and shakes hands with them.

Al-Hakim also reported that Jābir Ibn Abdullāh said that Abū Bakr said that he heard the Messenger say: "The sun never rose on a man better than Umar." Al-Hakim said "This hadīth is authentic." (*Al-Mustadrak*, part 3, p. 90). If the sun never rose on a man better than Umar, it means that Umar was not less than any of the prophets of God including their highest, Muhammad Ibn Abdullāh. It is reported among the virtues of Umar that the

Messenger of God said: "Whenever Gabriel delayed in his visits to me, I guessed that he was sent to Umar."[3] It is also reported that Umar is the lamp of the people of paradise.[4]

If the Prophet had been concerned whether Gabriel could have visited Umar, Umar would have been equal to the Prophet in position and would have been competitor. Furthermore, how could Umar be the light of the people of paradise while the prophets, including the Messenger of God, are among the people of paradise? This means that the light of Umar is higher than the light of all the prophets. Furthermore, if Umar is the light of the people of paradise, and the width of paradise is the Heaven and the Earth, it means that Umar's light is the light of the universe. Should that be the case, all the prophets would be in need of his light, and that would mean that Umar is above the messengers of God.

In conclusion, I would like to say that I do not mean, through these ahādīth, to accuse our Sunni brothers of placing Umar above the final messenger of God and the rest of the prophets. This is certainly not my intention; but I wanted to say that what the Sunnis attributed to the Shi'as, that Ali is above Muhammad, is an unjustifiable and vicious lie because there is nothing in the Shiite books that indicates this allegation.

The Shi'as consider the spread of such a lie a flagrant aggression against the glory of Islam and the honor of the Shiites. I wanted to bring to the attention of the readers that the Imāmate Shiites are too righteous to accuse their Sunni brothers of placing a man above the Prophet in spite of the fact that there are many ahādīth, which are considered by the Sunni scholars to be authentic, indicating that Umar is higher than the great Messenger and the messengers who were before him.

---

[3] Ibn Abi 'l-Hadīd, vol. 6, part 12, p. 178.
[4] Ibn Hajar, *Al-Sawā'iq Al-Muhriqah*, p. 97.

Chapter: 37

IMĀM HASAN'S TREATY WITH MU'ĀWIYA

By

Dr. S. Manzoor Rizvi[1]

There are two treaties in the early Islamic history which have been a subject of discussion in many circles. One is the Treaty of Hudaibiyah and the other is the Treaty of Imām Hasan with Mu'āwiya. Both treaties were made on identical bases.

The Treaty of Hudaibiyah was made by the Prophet with Mushrikīn-e-Mecca. The credit of undertaking the treaty did not go to the Mushrikīn (polytheist) of Mecca but to the Prophet and the Qur'an termed this as the open victory for the cause of Allah. Likewise, the credit of signing the treaty with Mu'awiya goes to Imām Hasan. It served the cause of Islam. It exposed the hypocrisy of the other party as Mu'āwiya did not carry out any of the provisions of the treaty. We give below the circumstances under which it was made and discuss the details of the treaty.

PHILOSOPHY OF THE TREATY

If the real texts of the Islamic History are viewed with intense scrutiny we will find that it was not Imām Hasan who entered into the treaty, but the treaty was imposed on him by the circumstances. Such were the internal and external circumstances of the Islamic society that the treaty was imposed upon Imām as a necessity and unavoidable must. If anyone other than Imām Hasan had confronted that situation he too would have had no other choice. Now we shall take into account the external and internal conditions of the Islamic society prevalent in those days.

EXTERNAL STATE OF AFFAIRS

We are aware that the empire of the eastern Rome had suffered great many injuries at the hands of Islam. As such it was

---

[1] Excerpted from the title, *Shi'aism Explained* (various chapters), Peermahomed Ebrahim Trust, Karachi, 1972.

-309-

awaiting a chance to hurl a mighty blow on Islam. By the perusal of the Islamic histories, of which one is the *History of Yaqūbī*, it is evident that when Rome was informed of the alignment of troops between Imām Hasan and Mu'āwiya, the potentates of Rome thought that the occasion was affording a best opportunity in order to fulfill their cherished ambition, therefore the insurgence started. Had Imām Hasan protracted the war with Mu'āwiya the enemies of Islam would have given such a sudden blow on the foundation of Islam, that no reparation could have been possible for that impact.

Now arises a question, under those precarious circumstances what a saintly person like Imām Hasan who had been nurtured in the lap of Islam and held Islam dearer than his soul could have done anything else in order to defend a great object than enduring the acridity of the treaty and spiritual torture? The contemporary witness of the sensitivity of the Islamic politics of those days is Yaqūbī who relates: "After accomplishment of the treaty when Mu'āwiya returned to Syria he was reported that the insurgents of Rome were advancing towards him with a band of magnitude. Mu'āwiya at first made a pact according to a resolution, but having strengthened himself started warfare against the Romans and succeeded. Defeated, the Romans agreed to collect the same amounts of money which the Islamic government had been paying to Rome, but Mu'āwiya refused to pay."[2]

The statement of Yaqūbī explains that at the time of alignment of troops by Imām Hasan the Romans were planning to attack the Islamic realm from different fronts, but their designs failed owing to Imām Hasan's policy.

INTERNAL STATE OF AFFAIRS

If one looks into the history of Imām Hasan's life it will be marked that during his revered father, Imām Ali's time he held a position in the foremost line in the battle against enemies. As a matter of fact he preceded others in hoisting the standard of the Battle of Camel and was not afraid.[3] He participated in the Battle of Siffīn as well and occupied a position in the heart of the army

---

[2] *Tārīkh Yaqūbī* vol. II, pp. 206 Published in. Najaf.
[3] *Al Imāmat wa'Siyasat* — vol. 1 pp. 77.

and struggled arduously for the victory of Imām Ali.[4]. He never had any fear and was never afraid of speaking out the truth, so much so that when the treaty was imposed on him he criticized Mu'āwiya and pointed out his weaknesses. After the treaty when Mu'āwiya came to Kūfa he wanted Imām Hasan to ascend the pulpit, perhaps with an intention of insulting him. Imām Hasan ascending the pulpit narrated the services rendered by his family and stated that the rulership of Mu'āwiya was unrighteous and hence perishing. He admonished and terrified those who had acquiesced in the Umayyid government. When Mu'āwiya noticed the adverse outcome of the incident he was highly ashamed.

Now let us examine what actually happened. Why Imām Hasan despite being so highly courageous agreed to enter into a treaty with Mu'āwiya? He was aware that the Kūfites were not truthful and straightforward in their character. Though apparently they had sworn allegiance to him to the effect that if Imām preferred war to him they would fight and if he was inclined to peace they too would follow him. In spite of that they had a clandestine inclination towards Mu'āwiya being allured by his wealth and splendor. He knew that the Kūfites had communicated with Mu'āwiya assuring him their support and that they would even captivate and surrender Imām Hasan to him, if so he willed. He was also aware that one of his military chiefs Ubaidullāh bin Abbās accepting a bribe of ten lakhs dirham from Mu'āwiya had joined him overnight with eight thousand soldiers under him. He was noticing how Mu'āwiya was making false propaganda that Imām Hasan had made a truce with him, and this fraud helped to disintegrate his deluded troops. He knew it well that with a strength, so weak, to fight with Mu'āwiya was not possible, and in view of the protection of Islam and Muslims there was no other alternative left but to come to an understanding. To elucidate this fact we produce here the diction from the text of history.

DICTION FROM HISTORY

Yaqūbī narrates: "After the martyrdom of Imām Ali the people swore allegiance to Imām Hasan. Imām Hasan dispatched an army of twelve thousand soldiers to fight with Mu'āwiya

---

[4] Ibid, p.108.

under the command of Ubaidullāh bin Abbās. The latter was bound to consult with Qais bin Sa'd on executive matters. Ubaidullāh marched, but when Mu'āwiya was informed of the martyrdom of Ali he rushed to Mosal within eighteen days and finally his troops faced those of Imām Hasan.

"Mu'āwiya sent an amount of ten lakhs dirham as bribery to Qais in order either to win him over to his side or to relinquish Imām. Qais being a bold and religious man refused to accept the money. Mu'āwiya sent this very amount to Ubaidullāh bin Abbās and the latter disposed off his faith and religion and changed over the sides to join Mu'āwiya with his eight thousand soldiers. But Qais fought steadfastly, and Mu'āwiya finally sent his spies in the camps of Imām Hasan in order to spread the rumors that Qais had conspired with Mu'āwiya whereas the troops of Qais were told that the Imām has made a truce with Mu'āwiya.

"In this way the troops of Imām were dispersed. Mu'āwiya, famous for fraud and shrewdness sent some known and recognized persons, who were held reliable by the people, to meet with Imām Hasan and who were ordered, on being ushered from the meeting to give out that Imām had negotiated the terms of treaty with Mu'āwiya. The troops of Imām Hasan without enquiring into the facts attacked the tent of the Imām and plundered whatever fell to their hands. Imām Hasan mounting a steed departed. Jarrah bin Sinān, hiding behind a bush, made an assault on Imām and inflicted an immoral gash with his dagger. As a result of this wound Imām was severely weakened and due to sickness was carried to Madā'in. The people forsook him and Mu'āwiya entered Iraq and got control of the situation. The sickness of Imām became intense and availing of that opportunity, when he had no aptitude for war, and his allies having dispersed, the treaty was imposed upon him. Therefore raising himself on the pulpit he eulogized God, blessed the Prophet, and said: 'O folk! God blessed you with guidance through the foremost person from us, and guarded you from the bloodshed through the second person from us. I accomplished a treaty with Mu'āwiya entrusting him the apparent sway.'"[5]

---

[5] Yaqūbī vol. II, p. 204, published in Najaf.

Even Tabarī clarified that Imām entered into treaty at the time when his soldiers had dispersed and left him all alone.[6]

The late Shaikh Mufīd says in *Irshād*: "Imām Hasan's army was composed of diverse groups *i.e.,* the particular followers of him and his father, Khārjites who did not want to support Imām Hasan but were willing to fight with Mu'āwiya; those that were crazy for amassing wealth somehow or other, and such fanatics that only followed the chief of their tribes. This is the reason why the soldiers could not be rigid and very hastily they withdrew from Imām's support, so much so that certain chiefs of some tribes wrote to Mu'āwiya that they were obedient to him and promised to hand over Imām Hasan to him. Mu'āwiya dispatched these letters to Imām Hasan. Qais bin Sa'd who had been appointed deputy to Ubaidullāh bin Abbās informed the Imām that Mu'āwiya had won over Ubaidullāh and for that reason he sanctioned ten lakhs dirham for him of which half of the amount would be paid forthwith and the rest half on his entry into Kufa. Ubaidullāh joined Muawiya's army in the dead of night. Thus the ill-intention and impurity of those persons came to light who had surrounded the Imām. The Imām observed that only small group of faithful Shi'as was with him, hence, in helplessness he entered into a treaty with Mu'āwiya, knowing even that Mu'āwiya had in mind nothing but fraud and that the treaty was only a farce."[7]

It is evident by whatever has been said that the internal circumstances in those days were such that the Imām was compelled to enter into the treaty with Mu'āwiya and had no other alternative; for this reason we say that the treaty was essential for him being imposed upon him and not entered into optionally. The urgency of the treaty was disclosed by Imām to his followers in this way: "I swear by God if the people had pledged for me and supported me the sky would have showered bliss on them and the earth squirted boons, had not Mu'āwiya been avaricious for caliphate. The Prophet of Islam had bidden farewell to Mecca and his tribe seeking refuge in a cavern. Had he been supported he would never have to take recourse to the cave and

---

[6] *Tārīkh Tabarī*, vol. VII p. 2.
[7] *Irshād*, pp. 171-172 briefly.

not forsaken Mecca for good. From the time the Islamic nation followed others and forsook us we had nothing but the treaty left for our destiny.[8]

"By God if I had fought with Mu'āwiya the people would have captivated me and surrendered to him.[9]

"You do not know what I have done. By God whatever I have done was in the best interest of the Shi'as on whom the sun shines and sets. I have accepted this for the sake of the Muslims in order to protect them from the bloodshed."[10]

The real visage of Mu'āwiya is unveiled: Mu'āwiya was the governor of Syria from the time of the second caliph, Umar bin Khattāb. Since Umar respected him, hence he enjoyed an important position there in as much as he was exalted in importance equivalent to Miqdād, Abūzar and Ammār in the eyes of the people. The people failed to visualize his real countenance owing to his practice of fraud and hypocrisy. They actually could not discover his reality as he was. He would subdue anyone with great shrewdness that rose in revolt against him and acquitted self. He used to conceal his intriguing nature and criminal acts by deluding the people and through pretence of love for Islam. He ventured even to the extent of igniting hostility against a pious man like Imām Ali, and contrived to color it in the vengeance for the blood of Usmān.

Evidently, if in these circumstances had Imām Hasan fought with Mu'āwiya and been killed in the battle his blood could have been spilt in vain, and Mu'āwiya, very slyly, could have given it pretence of political war and consequently the real face of Mu'āwiya would have remained in veil. But as a result of the treaty the blood of the Muslims was saved and the risk to Islam was warded off. The real face of Mu'āwiya was exposed to all. This fact is interesting also that the contents of the instrument of treaty were arranged in such a way by Imām Hasan as to be helpful in unveiling the real face of Mu'āwiya's character. A part of the Instrument of treaty was as follows:

---

[8] *Bihār* vol. 44, p. 23
[9] Ibid. p. 21.
[10] Ibid. p. 56.

"Mu'āwiya accepts the responsibility of acting upon the Qur'an and the traditions of the Prophet; would not nominate any successor to himself; Imām Ali and his followers, partisans and friends shall never be molested and no abusive language shall be given vent to for Imām Ali."[11]

But Mu'āwiya did not act upon a single clause. After the accomplishment of the covenant he came to Nakhliya, a place near Kūfa and said in one of his speeches: "By God I did not fight against you that you may pray, fast, go for pilgrimage and pay Zakāt, because these things are observed by you already, but I fought with you only for the sway. I succeeded in my objective and now declare that all the stipulations of the treaty which I entered into with Imām Hasan are trampled under my feet. I shall never fulfill them."

Thus the real face of Mu'āwiya which was so long veiled under the vellum of dissimulation and hypocrisy was exposed. All knew that he had no other object than the sway on Islamic realm with the dishonest tactics, with the show of pomp and splendor and not at all in the interest of Islam and Muslims. When he attainted his selfish ends he forgot the Qur'an, the Prophet's traditions and all the clauses of the covenant of treaty and trampled them under his feet.

---

[11] Ibid. vol.45, p. 64.

Chapter: 38

SHI'A MUSLIMS AND JEWISH TEACHINGS

By

Imām Muhammad Jawad Chirri[1]

The mercenary writers whose goal is to split the Muslims allege that a Yeminite Jew from Sanā, Abdullāh Ibn Sabā (also called Ibn Al-Souda), adopted Islam during the reign of the third Caliph Usmān. They allege that Ibn Sabā, through some doctrines that he spread among Muslims, was a big factor in causing the revolt against Usmān. The following are some of the doctrines attributed to Ibn Sabā.

1. This alleged Jew invented the idea that the Prophet Muhammad would return before the Day of Judgment. He based his allegation on the return of Jesus, saying: "If Jesus is going to come back, Muhammad will also return because he is more important than Jesus." He also quoted the following verse from the Qur'an to support his allegation: *"Certainly the one who revealed the Qur'an to you shall return to you."* These writers say that the Shi'as borrowed from this imaginary Jew the idea that the Prophet would return.

2. Ibn Sabā is the one who propagated the idea that Ali ibn Abū Tālib is the executor and successor of the Messenger of God. He said that there were a thousand prophets before Muhammad, and that each prophet had an executor after him, and that Imām Ali is the executor of the Prophet. Furthermore, Ibn Sabā said that the three caliphs who ruled after the Prophet were usurpers of the Islamic rule.

3. Ibn Sabā is the one who instigated the two prominent companions of Prophet Muhammad, Abū Dhar and Ammār Ibn Yāsir, against Usmān. The mercenary writers also allege that this imaginary Jew met Abū Dhar in Damascus, and that

---

[1] Reproduced from his book, *The Shiites under Attack*, (Chapter 4: *Did the Shiite Muslims Borrow Some Jewish Teachings?*). The book was published by the Muslim Center of America, Chicago in 1986.

he introduced him to the idea of prohibiting treasuring gold and silver. He also said that the revenue from Zakāt and land tax belongs to the Muslims rather than to God.

4. Ibn Sabā persuaded the men who participated in killing Usmān to start the battle of Basra (at night) between Imām Ali's camp and the camp of the three leaders (Ayesheh, Talhah, and Zubeir). He wanted to make each of the two armies accuse the other of starting the battle.

Let us discuss each of these allegations in the order.

THE RETURN OF THE PROPHET

The attribution to Ibn Sabā of the idea that the Prophet would return is ridiculous. It shows the ignorance of the mercenary writers who write such allegations. They misunderstand the history of Islam. Had these mercenaries studied Islamic history carefully, they would have known that the first one who declared the idea of the return of the Messenger of God was Umar Ibn Al-Khattāb.

Muslim historians agree that Umar stood at the Mosque of the Prophet when the Prophet passed away and said: "There are hypocrite men who allege that the Messenger of God has died. Certainly the Messenger of God did not die, but he went to his Lord as Moses, son of Imrān, went to his Lord (for receiving the Heavenly commandments). By God, Muhammad will return as Moses returned, and he shall severe the hands and legs of the men who alleged that the Messenger of Allah has died."[2]

We can not say that Umar took this idea from Abdullah Ibn Sabā or any other person. Ibn Sabā did not even exist at that time, not even in the imagination of Saif Ibn Umar Al-Tamīmī, who invented the entire allegation.

The Shiite school of thought does not consider the Prophet's return a part of Islamic belief. If any Muslim believes in this, it would only be logical to say that the source of this doctrine is the second Caliph's speech on the day the Messenger of God died, rather than Ibn Sabā.

---

[2] Ibn Hushām, *Al-Sīrah, Al-Nabawiyah,* part 2, page 655.

THE DOCTRINE OF ALI'S EXECUTORSHIP

The dividers of Muslims alleged that Ibn Sabā is the one who invented the doctrine of Ali's executorship. Yet history testifies that the Messenger of God himself is the one who declared that Imām Ali would be his executor. Imām Ali reported the following:

"When the Quranic verse: '*And warn your closest relatives*' was revealed, the Messenger of God called me and said: 'Ali, certainly Allah commanded me to warn my closest relatives, and I feel the difficulty of this mission. I know that when I confront them with this warning, I will not like their response.' The Prophet invited the members of his clan to dine with him on a small amount of food and little milk. There were forty of them. After they ate, the Prophet spoke to them: 'Children of Abdul Muttalib, by God, I do not know of any young man from the Arabs who brought to his people better than I brought to you. I have brought to you the goodness of this world and the Hereafter. The Almighty commanded me to invite you to it. Who among you will assist me on this mission and become my brother, executor, and successor?'

"No one accepted the invitation, and I said' Messenger of God, I shall be your assistant.' He held my neck and said to them, 'this is my brother, executor, and successor. Listen to him and obey him.' They laughed, saying to Abū Tālib: 'He (Muhammad) commanded you to listen to your son and to obey him.'"[3]

This hadīth was reported by Ibn Is-Haq, Ibn Abū Hātim, Ibn Mardawahy, and Al-Baihaqī in his book *Al-Dalā'il*. This was also reported by a number of historians including Abū Al-Fidā and Ibn al-Athīr. In addition, Muhammad Hussein Hakel recorded it in his book *Hayāt Muhammad* (first edition). Here we should ask the following question:

Imām Ali reported that the Messenger of God is the one who granted him the office of executorship, brotherhood, and successorship. Saif Ibn Umar reported that the idea of the executorship of Ali had come from a Jew called Abdullah Ibn Sabā. We should ask the members of the Takfīr University (who call everyone who disagrees with them *Kāfir*—unbeliever) the

---

[3] Al-Tabarī, *his history*, part 2, pp., 319-21.

following question: Do you believe Imām Ali's report or Saif Ibn Umar's? Saif was accused by prominent Sunni scholars of weakness, forgery, and heresy. Of course, we should not expect any true Muslim to choose the report of a liar such as Saif Ibn Umar and reject the report of the Imam of the faithful, Imām Ali Ibn Abū Tālib, the brother of the Prophet. The Messenger of God once said to Ali: "Would you not be pleased to be to me like Aaron was to Moses, but there shall be no Prophet after me?"[4]

HADĪTH AL-GHADEER

Do the mercenary writers who endeavor to spread hostility among Muslims forget that while returning from his farewell pilgrimage, and in the presence of over a hundred thousand pilgrims, the Messenger of God declared?

"Do I not have more right over the believers than they have over themselves?"
"They answered: 'Yes, Messenger of God.'
"The Prophet held up the hand of Ali and said:
'Whoever I am his Mawlā (leader), this Ali is his Mawlā.
God, love whoever loves him, and be hostile to whoever is hostile to him.'"

No Muslim would doubt that the Messenger of God is the leader of all Muslims for all generations. The Prophet in his statement granted Ali the same position as his when he said that Ali is the leader of everyone who follows the Prophet. This declaration which was reported by about a hundred companions does not just indicate that Ali is the executor of the Prophet, but also indicates that Ali takes the place of the Messenger in the leadership of all Muslims. However, these mercenaries still allow themselves to say that the belief that Ali was the executor of the Messenger had come through a Jew who declared his Islam during the days of Usmān.

DEFAMING THE BELOVED COMPANIONS

The mercenary workers did not even hesitate to attack the outstanding companions, Abū Dhar and Ammār. They said that

---

[4] Al-Bukhārī in his *Sahīh* reported this through his channel to Sa'd Ibn Abū Waqqās, part 6, p. 3. Muslim also reported this in his *Sahīh*, part 15, p. 176.

Abū Dhar and Ammār met the imaginary Jew Ibn Sabā, were affected by his propaganda, and thus turned against Usmān. They say this while history testifies that Abū Dhar said to Usmān in the presence of Ka'b Al-Ahbar: "Do not be satisfied that people do no harm to others. They should try to assist one another. It could be that the person who pays Zakāt should do more. He should assist his neighbors and Muslim brothers and be generous to his relatives."

Ka'b Al-Ahbar said: "Whoever performs his duty would be free of any other additional charitable spending."

Abū Dhar immediately took his cane, hit Ka'b on the neck injuring him and said: "Son of a Jewish lady, are you trying to teach us our religion?" With such firmness in religion which made Abū Dhar hit and injure Ka'b (who was highly respected by Umar and Usmān) because he tried to give a verdict in the Islamic religion, it is inconceivable that Abū Dhar would learn from the imaginary Ibn Sabā, who never met Usmān or any other caliph before him.

The dividers of Muslims do not hesitate to attack Abū Dhar and Ammār saying that they were affected by Ibn Sabā. However, we should not forget that by their attacking two prominent companions, they actually are attacking the Messenger of God who attested to their purity and righteousness.

Ibn Mājah, in his authentic *Sunan*, reported that the Messenger of God said: "Certainly Allah commanded me to love four persons:" The companions asked the Prophet: "Messenger of God, who are these four persons?" The Prophet said: "Ali is from them (repeating these names three times), Abū Dhar, Salmān, and Al-Miqdād."[5]

Al-Tirmidhī, in his authentic *Sunan*, reported that the Messenger said: "Every prophet was given by God seven righteous companions. I was given fourteen righteous companions." He included in them Ammār and Al-Midād.[6]

Al-Tirmidhī also reported that the Prophet said: "Heaven has not shaded, nor has the earth carried a truer person than Abū Dhar.

---

[5] Part 1, p. 52, Hadīth No. 149.
[6] Part 5, p. 329, Hadīth 3877.

He walks on earth with the immaterialistic attitude of Jesus, son of Mary."[7]

Ibn Mājah, in his authentic *Sunan*, reported that Imām Ali said: "I was sitting in the house of the Prophet and Ammār asked to see him. The Prophet said 'Welcome the good and the purified.'"

Ibn Mājah also reported that Ayeshah reported that the Messenger of God said: "Whenever Ammār is given two alternatives, he always chooses the most righteous of the two."

Al-Tirmidhī, in his authentic *Sunan*, reported that the Messenger of God witnessed Ammār and his two parents tortured in Mecca. The Prophet said to them: "Members of Yāsir's family, be patient. Your destination is paradise."[8] Thus, Ammār and his parents were the first people to be declared by the Prophet to be dwellers of Paradise.

Here we should say: When a Muslim knows that the Prophet has commended these two important companions so highly, and if he is a believer in the truthfulness of Muhammad, he doesn't allow himself to insult these two companions. Such an insult discredits the Prophet.

We find that the hostility of Saif Ibn Umar Al-Tamīmī, who lived during the second century after the Prophet, and the hostility of his students towards the Shi'as motivated them to spread cheap propaganda. Saif knew that attributing the revolt against Usmān to the work of Ibn Sabā contradicted known historical facts which show that the two companions, Abū Dhar and Ammār, were opposed to Usmān's ever coming to power. Because Saif knew of their opposition to Usmān, he tried to smear their reputations by adding the names of the two prominent companions to the list of students of the imaginary Jew.

If Ibn Sabā ever existed he, according to the tale of Saif Ibn Umar, had declared his Islam after Uthmān came to power. Abū Dhar and Ammār Ibn Yāsir, on the other hand, had been opposed to Usmān's caliphate before he came to power. The two companions were followers of Imām Ali. They were firm believers

---

[7] Part 5, p. 334, Hadīth 3889.
[8] Part 5, p. 233.

that he was appointed by the Prophet to be his successor. Since this was their belief before Ibn Sabā's existence, Saif's story about their being influenced by Ibn Sabā is unfounded and untrue.

Thus, in order to clear the third caliph from all the accusations pertaining to his ill-management of the Islamic treasury, Saif accused the revolters of being students of Ibn Sabā. He then completed his story by adding the two companions to the class of Ibn Sabā's students, intentionally overlooking the fact that the two companions belong to the first successful class of the school of Prophet Muhammad. They were among the important companions who were honored by the Prophet. In the end, Saif was led by his untrue story to reject the testimony of the Prophet. By this, Saif had disproved his whole tale.

WHO IS SAIF IBN UMAR?

The authors of the books that deal with the reporters of a Hadīth inform us that Saif was a well-known liar. These authors are: Ibn Mu'īn (died in 233 A. H); Abū Hatam (died in 277 A. H); Al-Nisā'ī (died in 303 A H); Abū Dāwūd (died in 216 A. H); Ibn Habbān; Al-Darqutni (died in 385 A. H); Al-Hakim Al-Nisabūrī (died in 405 A. H); Ibn Abd Al-Barr (died in 462 A. H); and Ibn Hajar (died in 850 A. H). Al-Suyūtī (died in 900 A.H.) said after conveying a Hadīth: "Many reporters of this Hadīth are weak and the weakest among them is Saif."[9]

I should mention that Al-Askārī had a very distinguished achievement. He proved beyond any doubt, in his book *Abdullāh Ibn Sabā,* that Ibn Sabā never existed, and that he was invented by Saif Ibn Umar al-Tameemi.

---

[9] Sayid Murthada Al-Askārī, Abdullah Ibn Saba, pp. 27-28.

Chapter: 39

DU'Ā: ITS RELIABILITY

BY

Allama Sayyid Saeed Akhtar Rizvi

A person wrote: "I am perplexed with a problem that I don't know what I shall do. I recite the Du'ās in the Ithena-Asheri Mosque, and one of the Du'ās which is usually recited is: *Ilāhī Azumalbalā' wa Barihal Khafā'*. So long I have been reciting this Du'ā without any doubt; but recently a certain old man told me that it is *shirk* to recite this Du'ā. He showed me verses from the Qur'an proving his claim.

"For a certain period I ceased to recite this Du'ā. Then my father insisted that I should continue to recite it. When that man heard me reciting this Du'ā again, he asked me why I had resumed it and I replied him that my father told me to continue reciting it.

"Then that man quoted the following Qur'anic verse and said that in this case I should not follow my father: *"And if they (the parents) contend with thee that thou should associate with me (Allah) what thee hast no knowledge of, (then thou) obey them not...."* (31:15) Now whom should I follow, my father or that man? To support his claim that man said that there is not any tradition from the Aimma which says that we can ask them besides Allah."

ANSWER

In short, *Shirk*, is of two kinds; (1) *Shirk* in belief, and (2) *Shirk* in actions. *Shirk* in belief means believing that there is more than one God. We know that your belief is free from that type of *Shirk*. One example of *Shirk* in action, in Islamic Sharī'ah, is doing Sajdah to other than Allah. But this entirely depends upon the order of Allah, and here we cannot use our own judgment. For example, let us look at the above-mentioned example: Allah ordered the angels to do Sajdah before Adam; and when Satan disobeyed, he was not honored as true *Muwahhid* (monotheist), but was branded as a *Mal'ūn*, because he disobeyed Allah. Likewise,

Prophet Yaqūb and his eleven sons did Sajdah to Prophet Yusuf; and they were not called *Mushrik*. But the same thing which was allowed for angels and Prophet Yaqūb is now absolutely forbidden in Islam, and if one does it now, he will be called a *Mushrik*. So, the *Shirk* in action can not be comprehended or adjudged by us. It rests on the order of Allah.

Let us look at another example. There were hundreds of idols in Ka'bah, and the Arabs worshipped them and kissed them and what not. And also in the walls of the same Ka'bah was the Black Stone, also honored and kissed by the Arabs. The Prophet destroyed all the idols; but did nothing against the Black Stone; rather, he made it an object of reverence and kissed it.

Now, the Christian writers allege that the Black Stone is a legacy of paganistic rites. But we know that kissing it and respecting it is not *Shirk* because it is done by the order of the Prophet. Non-Muslims may not understand the difference between kissing an idol and kissing the Black Stone; but for the Muslims the difference is clear.

The trouble is that many people rely upon their own judgment in deciding whether a certain action is Shirk or not. The result is that Sunnis, for example, think that doing Sajdah on a *Muhr* is *Shirk*; making Tāziyah; kissing the Zarīh of the Prophet in Medina is *Shirk*.

They do not understand that so far as our actions are concerned, they have to be governed by the commands of Allah, the Prophet, and the Masūmīn.

After this short explanation, let me tell you that the above Du'ā has been recorded by Sheikh Mufīd through his chain of narrators from Imām Sāhib-ul-Asr. Sheikh Mufīd died in 423 A.H. Then Sheikh Tabarsī (who wrote *Tafsīr Majma'ul-Bayān* and died in 548 A.H.) narrated another incident concerning the same Du'ā. The incident is as follows:-

Abdul Hasan Muhammad bin Ahmad bin Abil-Laith (who was a well-known pious man) was in danger of his life and had fled to the graves of our 7th and 9th Imāms and hidden there. Then Imām Sāhib-ul-Asr came to him and taught him this Du'ā and by reciting it, he was spared his life and the danger passed away. When the Imām was teaching him this Du'ā and came to the words, *Yā Mawlāi Yā Sāhib Uz Zamān,* he pointed to his own chest.

The Du'ā printed in *Mafātīh ul-Jinān* (pps. 115-116) is narrated from Sheikh Kafa'mī (who died in 895 A.H.). There are a few differences in the three narrations, but they are immaterial.

I remember some one had written to me from Zanzibar that this Du'ā is narrated by an unknown person. In view of above-mentioned details it is obvious that the narrator was unknown to only those who do not know.

It is not correct to say that there is no tradition to show that we can ask from Masūmīn. There are some traditions, one of which is quoted here from *Bihār-ul-Anwār.*

Imām Ja'far Sādiq told his companion, Mufazzal bin Umar: "If you have any *Hajat* (need) towards Allah and are unable to fulfill it then pray two Rak'at Namāz; and after Namāz say Takbīr three times; then recite Tasbīh of Bibi Fātima, then go into Sajda and say 100 times, (O! My Lady, O! Fatimah, help me), then put your right cheek on earth and say likewise 100 times, then put your left cheek on earth and recite it likewise 100 times, then go into Sajdah again and say likewise 110 times; then mention your need, and Allah will fulfill it." He is the same Mufazzal who had written the booklet of *Tawhīd-e-Muffazil* from dictation of the same Imām. If seeking any help from anyone other than Allah is *Shirk,* then no prophet and no Imām could be called *Muwahhid.* There are scores of examples even in the Qur'an where prophets sought others' help. Prophet Isa said: "Who are my helpers in the cause of Allah?" The Prophet sought help of the Muslims of Medina and they are called Ansār (Helpers) in the Qur'an, Also, we know that Imām Husyen several times asked the army of Yazīd to help him (*Istighāthah*). Was it, God forbid, bad to seek the help of those unbelievers? Our Imāms had to contend with various types of *Fitnahs* in their days. There were some persons who thought that the Imāms were *Khāliq* and *Rāziq;* others said that they were the *Rabb* (god). While refuting such falsehoods, our Imāms had to emphasize their total dependence on Allah in all matters. On the other hand, there were a great many people who did not know how high the position of the Prophet and his progeny before Allah was. When talking to such persons, (if the circumstances allowed and there was no danger to them from such statements) the Imāms described their exalted position.

For example, Sheikh Karajiki (died 449 A.H.) has narrated that once Imām Abū Hanifah (founder of the Hanafī school of law) took his food with Imām Ja'far Sādiq; at the end of the meal, Imām Ja'far Sādiq said: "All thanks are due to Allah, the Lord of the universe; O Allah! It is from Thee and from Thy Rasūl." Abū Hanīfa said: "O Abū Abdullāh! You ascribed a partner to Allah?" Imām Ja'far Sādiq said: *"Woe to thee! Verily Allah says in His Book: 'And they did not become (your) enemy, but just because Allah and His Apostle had made them rich from His bounty.'"*(9:74) And He says in another place: *"If only they had been content with what Allah and His Apostle gave them, and had said, 'Sufficient unto us is Allah; Allah and His Messenger will soon give us of His bounty.'"* (9:59)

Abū Hanīfa said: "By Allah, it is as though I had never before read or heard these two Āyāt from the Book of Allah."

Imām said: "No; surely you had read them and heard them. But Allah has revealed about you and your like and He said: *"Or are their hearts locked up by them."*(47:24) And also He has said: *"By no means! But on their hearts is the stain of (ill) which they do."* (83:14)

Your 'old man' should not try to refute this hadith by saying that this episode, perhaps, is not authentic; because, even if we totally reject this episode, there is no way to reject the argument given in this hadīth because that argument is based upon Qur'an and Qur'an cannot be rejected.

Chapter: 40

FACTS AND FALLACIES

1. ENEMIES OF ISLAM — BANŪ UMAYYAH

Banū Umayyah under the leadership of Abū Sufyān had been the worst enemy of Islam. Abū Sufyān had fought battles against Islam and the Prophet for 18 years. After the conquest of Mecca, Abū Sufyān along with other members of Banū Umayyah changed the policy of open confrontation with Islam by joining its ranks without any change in the hatred against Islam. The Qur'an called them the "cursed tree." (Suyūtī, *Tafsīr-e-Durre Manthur*, vol. iv, p. 191.)

During the lifetime of the Prophet, Banū Umayyah were outcast from Medina but after his death they infiltrated into the city. Soon after the death of the Prophet and the installation of Abū Bakr as the first Caliph, Abū Sufyān started spreading his tentacles of treachery. Abū Sufyān, finding Ali deprived of his right to the Caliphate, offered his help to Imām Ali to clinch it back from the sitting Caliph. Imām Ali flatly rejected his offer and asked, "Since when he became so sympathetic to Islam?" Then he went to Abū Bakr on the advice of Umar. Abū Bakr presented him the governorship of Syria. As Abū Sufyān was old and blind so the offer of governorship was passed to his son, Yazīd.

After the death of Yazīd the other son of Abū Sufyān, Mu'āwiya became the governor of Syria (*Ibid*, p., 371). During the Caliphate of Umar, Mu'āwiya remained the Governor of Syria.

Banū Umayyah's presence in the corridor of power became more visible when Usmān, a member of their clan was made the third Caliph. Abū Sufyān once advised Usmān, "Now once you have got the ruling power, play it like a ball and keep it in your family and as for Hell and Heaven who knows about it." (Al Istī'āb, *Tharikhe Abul Fada*, vol. iv, pp. 87-88.)

Usmān showered favors on those people of his clan who were not found desirable by the Prophet. Marwān, the son in law of an uncle of Usmān and who was once exiled from Medina on the orders of the Prophet was brought back and was made Usmān's chief Secretary with unlimited power. He was allowed to keep the total Khums collected in Africa and was given the landed property of Fadak, once seized from Fātima az-Zehrā. (*Kanzul Ummāl*, vol. vi p. 90 and Fatahul Bārī, *Sharhe Sahīh Bukhārī*, vol. 3, p. 141.)

Abdullāh ibn Sārah, who was among those who were ordered to be killed by the Prophet on the day Mecca was surrendered, was made Governor of Egypt by Usmān. (Al-Istī'āb, p.393, *Tafsīre-Durre Manthūr*, vol. iii) Walīd bin Aqba who was a known drunkard and a man of bad character and was called a Fāsiq in the Qur'an (Al-'Isāba, vol. iii, p.40) was made the Governor of Kūfā by Usmān. In short, any one who was related to Banū Umayyah secured the high ranking position in the government. Not only they filled their pocket but played havoc with the sanctity of Islamic rules and made a fun of them. Within 25 years after the death of the Prophet Islam was almost defaced and deformed. The brutal monopoly of Banū Umaayah infuriated the masses so much so that they stormed into Medina, besieged the house of the Caliph which culminated in the murder of Usmān

By the time Imām Ali and Imām Hasan were made the Caliph Muslims were spoiled beyond repairs. Their way of justice and equality were unbearable to the people and they could not take the Islamic values anymore. So revolt after revolt was set against Imām Ali and he succumbed to the fatal attack in the Mosque. The treacherous political maneuvering by Mu'āwiya against Imām Hasan ultimately succeeded and he seized the great office of the Caliph of the great umma.

MU'AWIYA

Mu'āwiya was the son of Abū Sufyān and Hinda who remained the bitterest enemy of Islam and of the Prophet since the inception of Islam till their death.

Let us have a close look at Mu'āwiya and his administration which solely directed it efforts to obliterate the members of the house of the Prophet and their followers in order to corrupt and damage the true spirit of Islam for his ulterior motives of founding the Umayyah dynasty of rulers. He took advantage of the situation created by the first three Caliphs that anything presented in the guise of religion was accepted by umma as if it were from God.

Mu'āwiya opened the coffers of state treasury for persuasion and cessation of opposition. When reward would not work murder of people with different opinion, imprisonment of people with doubtful loyalties, burning their houses and killing their relatives became daily affairs of the state. (*Tharikh–e- Khulafa*, p. 129, *Book of Al-Hadas, Spirit of Islam* by Amir Ali, p.245) Imām Hasan was poisoned and the treaty Mu'āwiya signed with him was openly trampled under his feet at Basra. Hujr Ibne Adi was given protection in the name of Allah and then brutally killed. Mālik bin Ashtar was poisoned. Muhammad bin Abū Bakr (son of the first Caliph) was burned to death. The son of Khālid bin Walīd was poisoned. Umaru bin Humuq Qazar who was a respected companion of the Prophet was killed.

Mu'āwiya once told his confident Mūghīra that he did not like name of the Prophet being repeated five times a day in prayers. He also tried to change some of the religious rules and prayers. He stopped saying Bismillāh before starting the prayer and before starting each action. He started reading the Friday prayer sermon while sitting. When going for fighting with Imām Ali he ordered people to say Friday prayer on Wednesday. During Hajj he performed Sa'ī (running between the two mounts) on a horse between Safā and Marwa without any good reason. Above all, he probably was the first person who started folding hands together instead of leaving them open during prayers. He instigated the War of Jamal under the garb of "Revenge of Blood of Usmān" against a legitimate sitting Caliph Imām Ali in which thousands of Qāris, Huffaz and Sahābas were killed. He fought a war, the Battle of Siffīn with Imām Ali and launched a psychological war of cursing Imām Ali from 70,000 pulpits. Now if Shi'as could be dubbed as Kāfir just because they curse the Sahāba, with the same analogy Mu'āwiya could also be called a Kāfir because of cursing and fighting a legitimate sitting Caliph.

Let me add an incidents narrated by Sheikh Muhammad Usled Abdho of the Alazhar University. He says that during one of his trips to Europe he met an historian in Berlin, Germany who told him: "It is incumbent upon Europeans to make golden statues of Mu'āwiya and erected them in all the main cities to glorify him as he helped Europeans not only for their existence but also for their growth. If Mu'āwiya had not fought Imām Ali and manipulated the place for him to be the ruler, Islam would have swayed all over the Europe and the land would not have been ours."

Mu'āwiya was the first to revive the charging of interest and tried to justify it religiously. He openly drank wine and he used to enjoy music and dance. In nutshell, he was able to influence the thinking of the Muslims to change the tide of Islamic teaching away from the truth and righteousness. Last one worst thing which Mu'āwiya did was to appoint his debauch son, Yazīd to be his successor against all Islamic norms.

YAZĪD

Yazīd's grandmother was the famous Arab lady, Hinda who among the women was no less an enthusiastic enemy of Islam than her husband, Abū Sufyān. She was present at the battlefield of Uhud and after Hamza, uncle of the Prophet was killed she opened his abdomen and tried to chew his liver to satiate her enmity towards Islam. Yazīd's mother was Maysūn, a Christian Bedouin who preferred to live in desert even after her marriage with Mu'āwiya. Thus, Yazīd's childhood was spent in desert and this is reflected in his uncivilized behavior, inhuman, wild, and profoundly rude manners. He could not be controlled even by his father.

Yazīd did not have the slightest idea what Islam is and what it stands for. He was never taught Islam and never learned. His belief is reflected in one of his couplet:

"Banū Hāshim (the Prophet and his relatives) played a game to obtain a kingdom. There never came angel (to the Prophet) and never came Wahi to him."(*Muhāzirāt*, Imām Raghib Isphahānī)

With this background, Yazīd became the ruler of a vast Islamic empire. Having become a ruler at a young age it was unbelievable and unthinkable for him to accept that one person by the name of Imām Husayn refused to bow down by not accepting allegiance. It was therefore not surprising to note that the first order he sent to the Governor of Medina was to take the oath of allegiance from Imām Husayn and if he did not agree his head should be severed and sent to Yazīd. Since it was not to be according to Yazīd's wishes Imām Husayn, his family and friends were killed in the desert of Karbala and his children and ladies were arrested and brought to Damascus for insult, torture and imprisonment. On this occasion Yazīd said in his open court: "I wish my ancestors were alive to see the revenge I took from Banū Hashim. My ancestors would have expressed their gratitude and would have said,' May your hands, O Yazīd never paralyzed.' I have taken revenge of my forefathers who were killed by the Prophet's army at the Battle of Badr. I have tormented the family of the Prophet. I would not call myself the son of Khandaf, if I had not done this." (*Tārīkh-e-Kāmil*, Ibne Asīr, vol. 7, p.160, and *Tārīkh-e-Khamīs*, vol. 2, p.184.)

Some of the actions taken by Yazīd are sufficient enough to make him infidel. These are: (1) He tried in the lifetime of his father to marry Ayeshah, the wife of the Prophet against the clear injunction of the Qur'an which made the wives of the Prophet mothers of Muslim. (*Madāraj an-Nabuwwah*, Muhaddis Dehlawī) He was, however, stopped by his father. (2) Yazīd sent a heavy force under Muslim bin Aqaba to Medina. The force almost grounded Medina, killed thousands of people including 300 Qarīs, hundreds of Huffāz-e-Qur'an, and thousands of Sahāba and Tabe'īn. (Sibte Ibne Jauzī and Tabarī.) The girls of Medina were raped. The Prophet's Mosque was closed and dogs and horses were kept there. This incidence is known in the history as the Tragedy of Harrah. (3) In the third year of his reign Yazīd attacked Mecca. The Harm of Ka'bah was attacked and part of it was destroyed. The attack was stopped only when Yazīd suddenly died. (Sibte Ibn Jauzī and Tabarī). (4) Yazīd was a poet and his poetry was in praise of love and wine or against the Islam. He just loved wine, music, and girls. (Ibne Asīr in *Kāmil at-Tārīkh*, vol. 3, p. 181, and Tabarī, vol.4, p. 358) In one of his poems, Yazīd said: "Your God has not said that Hell is for those who drank wine but for those who pray." (*Zibhe Azīm*, Aulad Haider Fauq. p.561.) (*Courtesy: Dr. S. Manzoor Rizvi*)

2. ALLEGIANCE TO YAZID

A questioner wrote: "It seems that Amr bin Sa'd was more sympathetic in that he wanted to prevent bloodshed (than Yazīd or Shimr). This can be seen from the following letter to Ibne Ziyād:-

'Allah has extinguished the fire of mischief. He has resolved the difference and created unity. He has set right the community's cause. Husayn held out a promise to accept any of the three alternatives. Therein lies your as well as the community's welfare. This letter was written after Imām Husayn had offered three alternatives to the latter: (1) Let him go back to the place he had come from; (2) Let him have his case decided by Yazīd himself; and (3) He may be allowed to go to a border place.'

"It seems that when Ibne Ziyād received the above letter, he accepted the proposal. But it was Shimr bin Zil Jaushan who opposed it and hence the latter went to Karbala.

"Please confirm if the above incident is authentic. If not, give me an authentic account with source of reference."

ANSWER

For reply, let me quote Tabarī himself: "Hanī bin Thubayt Hadhramī (one of the commanders of ibn-e-Ziyād's army in Karbalā') says that (Imām) Husayn sent a message to Umar bin Sa'd to meet him at night between the two camps… Umar bin Sa'd came out with about 20 people and (Imām) Husayn came out with the equal number. When they met, (Imām) Husayn told his companions to stay at a distance and Umar bin Sa'd ordered his group likewise. (Hanī says) Therefore, we stood so far from them that we could not hear their voices or their words. They talked a long time and then they went back to their camps with their companions. Then people started talking among themselves, on what those two people might have talked, but all was just guess work on the people's part; they suggested that Imām Husayn had told Umar bin Sa'd, 'Let us go together to Yazīd. (Hanī goes on saying) People started talking like this and they spread such rumors without anybody ever hearing anything like this or knowing what was said.'"

After one more narrative, Tabarī has narrated the words of Aqba bin Sam'ān--he was a freed slave of Bibi Rabāb; and was secretary of Imām Husayn; he was present in Karbalā', fought bravely, was seriously wounded; but he survived and was taken prisoner and one of the original sources of the narratives of the events of Karbalā'-- quotes him as saying:-

"I accompanied Imām Husayn, went with him from Medina to Mecca, and from Mecca to Iraq. And I was never far from him till he was martyred. And he did not talk with anybody a single word, (neither in Medina nor in Mecca; neither in the way, nor in Iraq nor in the army) up to the day of his martyrdom. By God, he never even suggested to the enemies any such thing which they are now propagating like the thing which they suppose that he said that he would put his hand in the hand of Yazīd or that he was ready that they should let him go to any border of the kingdom of Islam. But he only said, 'Leave me, so that I go away in this wide world, till we see what turn the situation takes.'"

After copying all these narratives, Tabarī copies the letter from bin-Sa'd to Ibn-e-Ziyād which you have mentioned in your question. We know by the emphatic declaration of Aqba bin Sam'ān that Imām never suggested any such thing. And the whole nature of the battle of Karbalā' shows that there never was any proposal of accepting the authority or order of Yazīd.

The same Tabarī narrates in the same *Tārīkh* that, on the day of 'Āshūrā', Imām Husayn gave a lecture before the army of Yazīd exhorting them not to indulge in blood-shed and not to kill the only grandson of the Prophet. At the end of that Khutba, he said, "O! People, if you do not like me then let me return to the place of my safety." Then Qais bin Ash'ath said to Imām Husayn: "Why not submit to the order of your cousins (i.e. Yazīd and Banī Umayya), because they will not show you what you like (they will not treat you except in a way which you will like) and no evil will reach you from them." Imām Husayn said: "You are the brother of your brother (Muhammad bin Ash'ath, the killer of Hazrat Muslim bin Aqīl). No by God, I will not put my hand (into theirs) like honor-less person, nor will I accept (them) as do the slaves.' *0 Servants of Allah, I seek refuge in my Lord and your Lord that you do not stone me.'* (Qur'an 44:20) *'I seek protection of my Lord and your Lord from every arrogant who believes not in the Day of Reckoning.'"* (Qur'an 40:271) Are these words those of a person who just two days ago had himself offered to submit to the order of Yazīd? Remember what Aqba said and see how his statement is proved to be correct from all reliable evidence.

In view of such overwhelming evidence, one may only assume

that Umar bin Sa'd wrote all those alternatives (without any basis, of course) just to please Ibn-e-Ziyād, perhaps in the hope that once Ibn-e-Ziyād postponed the battle and talk started, better results might follow. It is a mirror of the honesty of your writer that while he copies the letter of Umar bin Sa'd, he does not think it necessary to quote the rebuttal of Aqba or even Hani bin Thubayt. A more charitable explanation may be that the poor fellow has never seen *Tārīkh* of Tabarī, and has used the name of Tabarī to impress his readers.

I am not interested in the mental luxury of deciding whether Umar bin Sa'd was more sympathetic or not. All we care, and all that matters, is the fact that he was the commander of the army of Yazīd in Karbalā'; and that when Allah gave him a chance to save himself from Jahannam, he refused to grasp the opportunity and plunged into the Fire of Hell. That opportunity was given to him when Ibn-e-Ziyād wrote to him that if he was not ready to immediately wage the battle against Imām Husayn, he should hand over the command to Shimr. He did not. Instead, he sent the first arrow towards the camp of Imām Husayn, asking people to be his witness before Yazīd that his was the first arrow sent towards Imām Husayn. (**Courtesy: Allama Sayyid Saeed Akhtar Rizvi**)

3. REVENGE FOR THE MURDER OF USMĀN

The starting and ending of the movement for the revenge of the murder of the third Caliph, Usmān (Khoon-e-Usmān) is another significant matter in the early history of Islam. What are the reasons for starting the movement and how it culminated is another proof of animosity against Imām Ali which of course resulted in further widening the differences between Shi'as and Sunnis. We are giving below the facts of this movement, leaving it to readers to arrive at their own conclusions.

The third Caliph made major administrative mistakes by appointing his coteries to important administrative posts. He was asked by the people to rescind some of his orders for the appointment of the administrators in certain areas. When no action was taken by Usmān on the peoples' protests they marched to the capital, Medina and surrounded the Caliph's house. The surrounding of the house continued for 40 days and finally Usmān was killed evenhandedly. Imām Ali was then made the Caliph on the insistence of the people. The way the event happened it gives rise to a number of questions. These are:

1. In the Islamic capital, Medina where thousand of Muslims including many Sahāba were living it looked that no one stood up to come to the help of Usmān and no one came forward to intervene or meditate to settle the issues. Was it intentional or preplanned? Or everyone gave up to let it happened whatever happened.

2 No sooner did Imām Ali take the rein of the Caliphate the question of the revenge of Usmān was raised by Ayeshah and Mu'āwiya. No one even hinted at names of those responsible for killing Usmān. The Battle of Jamal was fought against Imām Ali on this basis in which at least 10,000 people were killed.

3. Based on the same demand i.e. revenge of the blood of Usmān the Battle of Siffin was fought by Mu'āwiya, governor of a province against the legitimate Caliph of Islam, Imām Ali in which some 40,000 to 70,000 Muslims were killed.

4. Mu'āwiya became the Caliph after Imām Ali and reined over the entire kingdom up to 60 A.H. Ayeshah lived up to 58 A.H. During these 20 years, Mu'āwiya was the most powerful king and Ayeshah was the most powerful political personality in the country. During this period none ever uttered the demand for the revenge of the blood of Usman. Neither any effort was made to search for the murderers of Usmān nor was any person arrested or punished.

5. Islamic history does not offer any such example of persistent effort of undermining the important role of Imām Ali. The movement for the revenge of Usmān was perhaps initiated as a plot of revolt against Imām Ali. (**Courtesy: Dr. S. Manzoor Rizvi**)

4. UNCLE OF THE MUSLIMĪN — MU'ĀWIYA

In various books of the Sunni writers Mu'āwiya has been called *Khal-e-Momineen* (Uncle of Muslimīn) as he was the brother of one of the wives of the Prophet, Umme Habība. As the wives of the Prophet were privileged to be addressed as "Mother of the Muslim" some one came up with the bright idea of calling Mu'āwiya as the Uncle of the Muslims just because he happened to be the brother of the Prophet's wife. This principle should be equally applicable to brothers of other wives also. This is not so.

Ayeshah had a brother too and his name was Mohammad ibne Abū Bakr. He was also a famous personality of Islam and more than that he was the brother of much famous and respected wife, Ayeshah. No one ever called him Khal-e-Mominīn on that basis. What a contradiction?

The reason for this contradiction can be attributed again to the enmity for Imām Ali. Mohammad ibne Abū Bakr was very close to Imām Ali and was like his son and being in that position he was denied that status. Further giving the title of Khal-e-Mominīn was a futile effort to enhance the status of Mu'āwiya in the eyes of the Muslim vis-à-vis Imām Ali. *(Courtesy: Dr. S. Manzoor Rizvi)*

5. MARRIAGE OF UMME KULTHŪM

This is another persistent fuss that is brought about by people to elevate the greatness of Umar ibn Khattāb. It is said that Umar ibn Khattāb, the second Caliph, wanted to have matrimonial ties with the family of Imām Ali as a sign of great honor to him, so he married one of his daughters by the name of Umme-Kulthūm, aged 5 to 6 years in or around 17 A.H.

First, marrying in a well-known and respected family does not necessarily bring good name: Āsiya, a believer was married to Pharaoh which did not bring any fame to Pharaoh. The wives of Prophet Noah and Prophet Loot could not be saved from the Hell despite being prophet's wives.

Secondly, the daughter of Umar, Hafsa was already married to the Prophet of Islam. What better credentials one could get than this provided one can enjoy and maintain it. In Islam personal piety and good action are the sole criterion of grace in the eyes of Allah.

The fact about the marriage of Umme-Kulthūm alleged to be the daughter of Imām Ali is a total fabrication. However, Umar did marry a girl by the same name who was aged 5 or 6 in 17 A.H., who was associated with Imām Ali. He did not marry the real daughter of Imām Ali who was also named Umme Kulthūm and was born in 6 A.H., and was 11 to 12 years old in 17 A.H., the year when the marriage of Umar took place. Imām Ali had married one of the widows of Abū Bakr by the name of Asma binte Amīs who brought with her a daughter borne out of her previous wedlock with Abū Bakr. Her name happened to be the same and she was born in 11 or 12 Hijra year. In Hijra year 17, Umar requested Ayeshah for her hand. Imām Ali was reluctant to agree to this proposal but Ayeshah agreed, and this Umme-Kulthūm was married to Umar at the age of 5 or 6. Since she was under the guardianship of Imām Ali she was called Umme-Kulthūm binte Imām Ali.[1]

Incidentally many of the wives of Caliph Umar were named Umme-Kulthūm. These were: Umme-Kulthūm Jamīla daughter of Asim binte Sabil; Umme-Kulthūm daughter of Jardal (real name Malīka); Umme-Kulthūm daughter of Aqba son of Ibne Moet; Umme-Kulthūm daughter of Rahils; and Umme-Kulthūm daughter of Asma, daughter of Amīs and daughter of Abū Bakr. *(Courtesy: Dr. S. Manzoor Rizvi)*

---

[1] For reference please see the following sources: Allama Husan Dayarbakari, *Tārīkhe Khamīs*, vol.2, pp 21, printed by Matbatul Amara Al-Uthmānia, Egypt; Allama Athīr, *Tārīkhe Kāmil*, vol. 3, p. 21, printed in Egypt; and Allama Ibne Abdul Bārī, *Isti'āb Fi Mare'fatul Azhar*, vol., 2, p 795, printed in Hyderabad in Deccan, India.

Anti-Shi'a Leaflet Distributed at the New York Muharram Procession

ANTI-SHI'A LEAFLET PUBLISHED FROM HOUSTON, TAXES

conceal the truth when you know (what it is) (H.Q.* 2:42).

Shia scholars say that when Caliph Ali (R*) 1) supported other Caliphs and praised them in Shia book 'Nahjul Balagha', 2) said that the Holy Prophet had forbidden Muta, and 3) kept his copy of Holy Quran in hiding, he was merely practicing Kithman and Taqiya. **When Ali (R*) became Caliph and was in authority, he neither reversed any of those statements, nor did he produce a copy of Holy Quran he supposedly had collected.**

References:
1. Al Hukumat Al Islamis, Imam Ayatullah Khomeini, Al Maktaba Al Islamia Al Kubra, Tehran, Iran, 1981.
2. Commentary of Sharah Nahjul Balagha by Ibne Hadeed, Darul Kutb Mustufa Al Babi, Cairo, Egypt
3. Fasal Al Khitab, Mirza Noori, Iran 1320 A.H.
4. Forooh Al Kafi, M. Kulaini, Darul Kutb Islamia, Tehran, Iran, 1374 AH.
5. Haq Al Yakin, M. B. Majlisi, Maktaba Nawal Kishore, Lucknow, India.
6. Hayat Al Qoloob, Ibid.
7. Islam, Ghulam Sarwar, 1987.
8. Minhaj Al Kiramah, J. Hasan, Maktaba Darul A'roobia, Cairo, Egypt, 1962 AD.
9. Sahih Al Bukhari, Imam Bukhari.
10. Sahih Muslim, Imam Muslim
11. Shia Sunni Perspective on Islam, A. Salameh.
12. Shiite Islam, S. Tabatabai, St. Univ. Press, N.Y.
13. The difference, Saeed Ismaeel, Carbondale, Il.
14. The Holy Quran- Translation by Abdullah Yusuf Ali, Tahrike Tarsile Quran inc, 1988.
15. Usool Al Kafi, M. Kulaini, Darul Kutb Islamia, Tehran, Iran, 1374 AH
* H. Q.- Holy Quran
  P- Peace and blessing of Allah be upon him / them
  R - May Allah be pleased with him / them

Compiled by A. S. Alam, MD. - Edited 1995.

For more information, contact: **INTERFAITH DIALOGUE**, P.O. Box 591033, Houston, Texas 77259-1033. Telephone: (713)- 482-5757

Read all the unique publications of Interfaith Dialogue
Permission is granted to reproduce or to translate this publication without change. Quotations from the Scriptures must be taken from authentic translations.

Share the information with others. Please make copies and distribute.

SHIA

FAITH

&

ISLAM

INTERFAITH DIALOGUE
PUBLICATION NO.
21

1995

TURKISH FATWA ALLOWING MUSLIM TO PRAY THREE TIMES A DAY

Religion

Turkey: Fatwa allows Muslims to pray just three times a day

Ankara, 10 Oct. (AKI) - Turkish Muslims will be allowed to pray only three times a day from Wednesday instead of the usual five without fear of committing a sin.

A member of the Scientific Council of Istanbul University, Muhammad Nour Dughan, has issued a controversial fatwa or religious edict cutting Islamic prayer requirements from five to three times a day.

The move has provoked widespread debate as well as opposition from orthodox imams or Muslim clerics.

Sharia law allows for the possibility of praying three times a day in case of sickness or travel.

The fatwa extends this option allowing Muslims to pray three times a day, especially when they are heavily committed with work or personal issues.

The Turkish debate echoes a similar one that has already taken place in Egypt where the fatwa has also drawn support. Jamal al-Banna, brother of the founder of the Muslim Brotherhood, Hasan al-Banna, endorsed the Turkish move.

"Merging prayers has become a modern necessity," he told the al-Arabiya website. In most cases, people do not always perform the five prayers on time due to the pressures of modern life."

Al-Banna is often criticized for his modern interpretation of Islamic rules. He said the Prophet Mohammad himself had given followers this option that could be applied when prayers cannot be carried out in a given time.

A member of Egypt's Supreme Council for Islamic Affairs, Sheikh Youssef al-Badri, rejected the argument saying it was unacceptable to merge prayers unless it was due to travel, illness, rain or pilgrimage.

For original news item please log on to:
http://www.adnkronos.com/AKI/English/Religion/?id=1.0.140
9142549

LIST OF BOOKS
PUBLISHED BY PYAME AMAN (MESSAGE OF PEACE INC.)
*PO Box 390 * Bloomfield NJ 07003 * RizviHM@aol.com*

1. Salaat – 5th Edition	$3.00
2. In Search of Truth	$3.00
3. Guide Book of Qur'an	$3.00
4. Imamat & Khilafat	$3.00
5. Storybook for Children	$3.00
6. Bible's Preview of Muhammad	$2.00
7. Elements of Islamic Studies	$5.00
8. The Early History of Islam	$10.00
9. Hajj	$3.00
10. The Justice of God	$3.00
11. Urdu Primer	$3.00
12. Facts on the Qur'an -- Respect for Parents	$3.00
13. Wahabis' Fitna Exposed	$3.00
14. Shi'as are the Ahle Sunnat	$10.00
15. Then I was Guided	$7.00
16. Imam Ali – Man of All Era	$5.00
17. The Straight Path	$5.00
18. The Secret Martyrdom	$10.00
19. Textbook of Shi'a Islam *(Available through Amazon.com. BN. com. and local bookstores)*	
Paperback	$13.00
Hard Cover	$23.00
20. Kashkaule New Jersey (Urdu)	$15.00
21. Izhare Haaq (Urdu)	$10.00
22. Zare Khalis (Urdu Poetry)	$5.00
23. Sea of Tranquility	$10.00
24. Muharram	$5.00
25. Humphrey's Diary	$5.00

Under Print

26. Book of Ziyaraat Vol I
27. Book of Ziyaraat Vol II
29. The Pearl of Wisdom
30. Early History of Islam for Children

Shipping and handling: $.50 (per book, up to 10 books).
No shipping and handling charges for more than 10 books

ABOUT
PYAME AMAN (MESSAGE OF PEACE INC.)

MUSLIM FOUNDATION INC. (MFI) was founded and implemented in 1980 in the residential basement of Dr. S. Manzoor Rizvi. It consisted of two main branches with several sub-committees. One branch is known as MFI itself which is mainly a socio-economic and religious organization for the overall betterment and benefit of the community. It is well established and successful, and recognized as a healthy organization in New Jersey. MFI is now based in Somerset, New Jersey where it is working on a multi-complex project including the construction of *Masjide Ali* which will soon be completed.

The other branch, **Message of Peace Inc.** or **Pyame Aman** is working as a publication house of Islamic literature and as a center for dissemination of the true and accurate message of Islam. It organizes educational seminars and brings out publications on various vital topics. It published its first national magazine in the USA from 1982 to 1992 that actually reached many parts of the world.

Till date, **Pyame Aman** has published over 30 books on a variety of important subjects of concern to both children and adults. The selection of topics, carefully chosen, is based on the current needs of the community especially of youths.

Both **Muslim Foundation, Inc.** and **Message of Peace, Inc.** are today a household name not only in New Jersey but in North America.